"A refreshing take on an old story, one that has too often emphasized settler colonial tropes at the expense of Indigenous experiences. . . . *Picturing Indians* is an important and impressive contribution to a growing body of historical literature that asks us 'to look at the movies as a site of work as well as art.' . . . More importantly, [Black] demands that we reckon with the physical presence of Native people in the movie industry, where they exercised their own judgment and made their own meanings for the work they performed within the constraints of the studio system." —ANDREW FISHER, *American Historical Review*

"Necessary reading for anyone interested in studying Native American visual representation." —STEVE PELLETIER, *American Indian Culture and Research Journal*

"Meticulously researched, this engrossing volume fills a deep void in both film studies and Native American history." —KARLA STRAND, *Ms. Magazine*

"A significant contribution to the growing Indigenous studies scholarship in the area of film and media studies. . . . Black crafts a richly detailed historical narrative from studio archives to reveal invisible Native labor and distorted studio fantasies regarding Native 'authenticity.' . . . Scholars of film studies, film history, American Indian studies, and American history will find this book a useful addition to their libraries and classroom." —ANGELICA LAWSON, *Western Historical Quarterly*

"Fresh and original. The first monograph of its kind to focus exclusively on the mode of production of films, particularly Western narrative films, with special attention to labor history, its insights are derived from meticulous and thorough archival research. . . . [Black's] is the first [film analysis] to plumb the depths of the studio system's creation of stereotypical Indian imagery as well as its attempts to produce 'authentic' Indian characters. . . . *Picturing Indians* represents a critical contribution to the field of Native American representations in film with its study of labor history and analysis." —MICHELLE RAHEJA, *Film Quarterly*

PICTURING INDIANS

PICTURING INDIANS

Native Americans in Film, 1941–1960

Liza Black

UNIVERSITY OF NEBRASKA PRESS   LINCOLN

The University of Nebraska Press is part of a land-
grant institution with campuses and programs on the
past, present, and future homelands of the Pawnee,
Ponca, Otoe-Missouria, Omaha, Dakota, Lakota, Kaw,
Cheyenne, and Arapaho Peoples, as well as those of the
relocated Ho-Chunk, Sac and Fox, and Iowa Peoples.

Publication of this volume was assisted by a grant
from the Indiana University History Department.

First Nebraska paperback printing: 2022

Library of Congress Cataloging-in-Publication Data
Names: Black, Liza, author.
Title: Picturing indians: Native Americans
in film, 1941–1960 / Liza Black.
Description: Lincoln: University of Nebraska Press,
2020. | Includes bibliographical references and index.
Identifiers: LCCN 2020006544
ISBN 9780803296800 (hardback)
ISBN 9781496232649 (paperback)
ISBN 9781496223753 (epub)
ISBN 9781496223760 (mobi)
ISBN 9781496223777 (pdf)
Subjects: LCSH: Indians in motion pictures. | Motion
pictures—United States—History—20th century.
Classification: LCC PN1995.9.I48 B53 2020 |
DDC 791.43/652997—dc23
LC record available at https://lccn.loc.gov/2020006544

Set in Garamond Premier by Laura Buis.
Designed by N. Putens.

For Riley, Clare, and Olivia

I'd like to see more and more feature films, lots of feature films because that's what people want. People don't want experimental cinema! They don't! I'll just keep plugging along doing what I do, but people want feature films.

   —Dana Claxton, in *Transference, Tradition, Technology*

When they will not give a doit to relieve a lame beggar, they will lay out ten to see a dead Indian.

   —Trinculo, in Shakespeare's *The Tempest*

CONTENTS

ILLUSTRATIONS

PREFACE

There are no two sides to the history of the United States and its relationship to people who have lived here for thousands of years. There are no two sides to that story. You have no right to displace people, to steal their resources, and steal their lives. . . . What America has done is criminal. And they're still doing it.
—Elizabeth Cook-Lynn

Genesis

This book about the hyperreality of filmic Indians is deeply rooted in my Cherokee citizenship. Living with my grandparents in Arkansas for a year and spending many weekends with our extended family in Oklahoma fundamentally changed my view of the world as I came to understand what it meant to be Cherokee. My aunt's devotion to our tribal nation and the Cherokee people inspired me deeply as a girl. Attending Cherokee dances, visiting the Cherokee Nation Museum and headquarters, watching the Trail of Tears play, and walking through the Cherokee Heritage Center made an indelible mark upon me and led me to this project. Not only did I witness the Cherokee representation of Cherokee Nation, but I did it surrounded by Cherokee relatives, including an aunt who has lived in Tahlequah, Oklahoma, and worked for the nation her entire adult life. She knew the Cherokee performers. They all chatted with her during these performances, which for me gave a double meaning to our visits. I saw the performance itself, but I also saw the performers as Cherokees who were friends with my aunt, who went off script in private. That, I believe, is why I see both the person and the representation in the films studied here and made me want to know everything possible about the Indigenous people who worked in the films of the 1940s and 1950s.

As a citizen of Cherokee Nation, I feel drawn to topics relating to my tribe and wrote my senior thesis on landownership patterns, gender, and Cherokee Nation in our ancestral lands and Indian Territory. As a graduate student at the University of Washington, I intended to expand my thesis to cover the precontact era through the present in shifting patterns of landownership among Cherokee people, documenting the transitions from Cherokee-centered ownership to English domination and finally the U.S. version of settler colonialism imposed through allotment. Yet growing up primarily in Southern California also made me fascinated with the superficiality of Los Angeles, movies, and popular culture. My cultural studies courses in graduate school gave me insight into the complex veneer of pop culture, while my dedication to American Indian and Cherokee history only grew.

What came to intrigue me was the overlap between representations of Native people in popular culture and non-Native understandings of Native people. This is what I endeavored to explore. But the connection between the dispossession of Cherokee Nation and all Indigenous people and the powerful ways in which Native people understand that history was and is always clear. Further, my involvement in the Native community as an undergrad at UC Santa Cruz and then as a graduate student at the University of Washington gave me many opportunities to reflect on what brought us together and what divided us. I grounded my identity as a Native person solely on my tribal identity as a citizen of Cherokee Nation. What I found, though, is that living far from my nation and presenting as white created a dissonance for some, especially for non-Indians. For Native people, tribal citizenship in many ways marks a valid tribal identity. However, for Native people, tribal enrollment serves as only one of many ways of establishing a legitimate tribal identity with other Native people. Yet non-Natives remain blissfully unaware of enrollment and other means Native people use to understand each other as tribal members. Non-Natives often expect a look based in certain skin colors, hair colors, hair length, and hair style. That look comes from movies.

Northern Exposure was a popular 1990s television show featuring a lead played by a Native woman and often Native people in the background. Another source of inspiration was my Navajo friend's appearance on the show; he worked for several weeks as an extra, happily earning twice the wages he earned on campus at the University of Washington. Watching the show to see him completely changed how I viewed *Northern Exposure* and any representation of Native people. Sitting with friends from the Native student group at the University of Washington, looking for our friend to appear on the screen, changed my viewing from one of understanding characters and narrative to looking for our friend, evaluating how he looked on television, and teasing him about how differently he moved on camera. The moment was more akin to looking at family photos than the intended viewing created by writers toward character development and narrative tensions. This seemed to be an alternative reading of the official script and also perhaps a backstage view of the front stage, all of which I was more aware of because of my cultural studies graduate work.[1]

Living in the Pacific Northwest during graduate school connected me in a particular way to *Northern Exposure*, as I and others in the area felt geographically connected to the show's location of Alaska. But the character Marilyn Whirlwind, played by Elaine Miles (Cayuse and Nez Perce), made the show very popular with the larger Native community in the United States. They embraced and enjoyed the show because of her portrayal of a Tlingit woman, especially because her character was full of dignity, strength, and humor.

Purpose

As a citizen of Cherokee Nation who presents as white, I very much wanted to think through the Indian look and its disconnect from tribal identities. Documenting racism and racist imagery was far less interesting to me than thinking about how these images were being negotiated among American Indians. My thinking was that tribal identities survive to the extent that Native people reject images deployed by settler colonialism in favor of their specific, grounded, tribal identities. I wanted to show that the dispossession of tribal nations generated an identity by outsiders through popular culture that erased tribal history and sovereignty. In that sense Native Americans in film seemed to be the perfect project to demonstrate these links, confluences, and synergies. When I found evidence of Indian workers, in the racist films of the 1940s and 1950s, the link became clear to me between the need for high-paying, easy work and the social and cultural capital held by Native people.

Limitation

The book is limited to the 1940s and 1950s, although I reference other periods, as well as the films and actors of those times, to provide a larger context. The silent film and early sound era preceding this book's period served up several Native directors, actors, and Native-controlled scripts and productions. The period following this book likewise features what some consider positive portrayals of Native people and an explosion of Native-controlled films, television programming, and the arts in general. To that extent, my purpose is to expose the extremely racist images and stories generated in the period from World War II until 1960. I seek to document the high point of racism and what would have seemed to be a hopeless moment for Native people in film. This book goes to the most disempowered moment in the history of Native people in film and stays there.

Scope

The book covers all films made about Native people or including Native characters between 1941 and 1960. The book accounts for changes in representations and the variety of representations, but most important is that it articulates the presence of Native people in the films. Relying on archival sources and oral histories, the book places Native people at the center of my analysis, both as fictional characters and as workers in the film industry. The book also makes explicit the pay structure and the physical creation of the Indian look on the film sets of the 1940s and 1950s. The book does not go into great detail about non-Native directors, producers, or actors, nor does it primarily seek to detail the origins of racist images; rather, I wanted to see the Native people who were present, in spite of their lack of influence, power, or strength.

My hope in this project is to uncover the racist aesthetics permeating images of Indians that stem from the midcentury period and to point to the power held by Native people in their tribal histories and identities. Midcentury films represent a low point in representations of American Indians, and federal policy toward tribes in the same period was also at its nadir. However, after this period we see a resurgence of Native strength, vitality, and recovery based in tribal and intertribal movements. This study is about my belief that Indian politics has to be centered in tribal politics and rooting Indian identity in the tribal nation. Indian identity is intimately tied to several centuries' worth of exploitative, derogatory, and inverted images of Indians meant to justify the settler colonial project of Native dispossession. The path to decolonization, indigenization, and stronger sovereignty is the renewal of tribal law, tribal land, and tribally controlled representations. In this book I use many words to describe what non-Natives collectively refer to as Native Americans. This might be distressing to a non-Native reader, especially when I use "American Indian" or just "Indian." I will use the tribal affiliation when I can, as this is the most respectful way to speak of a Native person's identity. For me, to highlight the tribal identity is to support tribal sovereignty. For myself and many others, whether to use "Native American" or "American Indian" is not the central question. There are pressing matters at hand, and I am far more interested in drawing our attention toward the critical issues facing Native America, so the choice between "Native American" and "American Indian" is not key.

ACKNOWLEDGMENTS

My favorite things in life as a kid were school and my teachers. And my two favorite people as a girl and teen were Kanchana Somaratne and Monica Cummins, whom I must thank for so very much.

Professor Ola Washington, I thank you for your mesmerizing lectures. At UC Santa Cruz, where students shopped for classes, I encountered Martha Hodes. That first day of school changed my life and my major. Martha became my faculty mentor through the Faculty Mentorship Program, run by Rosie Cabrera, and she allowed me to be her research and teaching assistant even as an undergraduate. Her trust and guidance built the foundation of my professional life. Lisbeth Haas guided me through my senior thesis on Cherokee women, and I will always be thankful to her for giving me that opportunity to write about my tribal nation. Thank you, Beth, for everything. The path-breaking Rosie brought me into her community with Riyad, Kenneth, Jean, and so many others, and she rendered academia transparent and showed me how to thrive within it. We wrote our statements of purpose, finished our theses, and went on to graduate school together with her leadership. Rosie, thank you so very much for believing in me and all of us. Many thanks go to the man who was my rock and best friend, Paul, for moving three times with me, reading everything I wrote, and giving me unconditional love when I was an undergrad and grad. Thank you for reading my work back then and the emotional support I needed.

I chose to attend the University of Washington to work with Richard White. I benefited from Richard's integrity, laser focus, and work ethic. He also championed my decision to change my dissertation from Cherokee land theft to American Indians in movies. Thank you, Richard, for trusting my intellectual instinct and believing I could do what had not been done, seeing me through the dissertation process, and supporting my career ever since. Susan Glenn, Shirley Yee, Tsianina Lomawaima, and Laurie Sears served on my master's and doctoral committees, and I thank them for their robust readings of my work, which, I hope, made me a better thinker. Thank you also to my stellar classmates at UW, including Ned Blackhawk, Michael Witgen, Coll Thrush, Linda Nash, Matthew Klingle, and Joseph Taylor. Most of all I pay respect to the amazing Native community of Seattle. We put together a stellar powwow as students. Our campus powwow committee was tight, hardworking, and just fun. Aaron Bird Bear, Victor Begay, Lewis Yellowrobe, and so many others were such a grounding part of my life. Augustine McCaffery and Marvin Oliver gave us so much love, and I treasure the support they gave us so generously. I am so very proud of how UW continues to thrive as a Native hub.

The Ford Foundation gave me the funds necessary to thrive in graduate school. With their assistance, I passed my master's and doctoral exams and wrote my dissertation. The film archives in Los Angeles became my second home, and I am indebted to the Ford Foundation for my being able to truly delve into the resources. UCLA became my second home as well. Steve Aron brought me into the UCLA graduate student fold, where he hosted graduate student research meetings in western American history. Thank you so much, Steve, for making me a part of the UCLA grad community. I want to thank the film archivists for bringing every single box for every single movie with an Indian character between the years of 1941 and 1960 to me in the reading rooms. Thank you for assuaging my need to be thorough and letting me stay there until I had read every paper in those boxes. Thank you, especially, to Ned Comstock at the USC Cinematic

Arts Library, where he runs a small yet somehow massive operation and graciously assisted me for months. The library of the Academy of Motion Picture Arts and Sciences is a huge place with security guards, and the staff is in constant rotation. Many people there served my requests for boxes, and I thank them all.

The Institute for the Humanities at Cornell University and specifically Dominic LaCapra, Eric Cheyfitz, and Robert Warrior were instrumental in transitioning my work from being a dissertation to a book. They asked me about my book weekly and ultimately gave me clarity and powerful insights. Harvey Young served the critical function of both friend and colleague. Thanks for all the ice cream, movies, and insights into performance studies, Harvey.

The University of Michigan, both the Department of History and Department of American Culture, provided me with an intellectual home as a new faculty member. Phil Deloria, Tiya Miles, Joe Gone, Alan Wald, Betty Bell, Jonathan Friedman, Sara Blair, Scott Kurashige, Emily Lawsin, Jane Burbank, Fred Cooper, Michele Mitchell, Maria Montoya, John Carson, Jay Cook, Matthew Countryman, Kali Israel, Alexandra Stern, and Catherine Benamou made me a part of a powerful and dynamic intellectual community that, though now dispersed, continues to thrive. Maria brought me into her home, took me shopping, introduced me to expensive skin care, and gave critical insights into the history of the American West. Phil Deloria, whose first book I encountered and was transformed by as a graduate student, became my colleague at UM. Phil gave my writing the critical read it needed at a critical moment. He was unflinching in his focus and vision at UM. I have profound respect for his scholarship, and I am proud to say how pivotal it has been in shaping my own.

At UCLA and UCSB, where I taught when I returned to academia after taking a very long family leave, I have many people to thank: Mishuana Goeman, Shannon Speed, Jessica Cattelino, Joy Holland, Pamela Grieman, Herbert Marcuse, Erika Rappaport, Ann Plane, James F. Brooks, Beth DePalma Digeser, Paige Digeser, Hanni Jalil Paier, Abby Dowling-Baker, Beth Sandoval, Angie Chikowero, Rana Razek, Stephanie Batiste, Candace Waid, Rose Hayden-Smith, Sarah Watkins, and Chris Nofziger. Gabriella

Flores, Gabriel Reyes, and Gabriel Mendoza (Ñuù Sàjvĭ): much love and thanks. You took a chance on a single mom and believed in my future. A big thank you to you all.

Indiana University has welcomed me with open arms. Big thanks to Wendy Gamber, Judith Allen, Peter Guardino, April Sievert, Brian Gilley, Ryan Comfort, Nicky Belle, Cindy Wu, Sylvia Martinez, Alberto Varon, Carmen Henne-Ochoa, John Nieto Phillips, Michael McGeer, Ana Stahlman, Amrita Chakrabarti Myers, Ed Linenthal, John Goode, Deborah A. Lemon, Marissa Moorman, Michelle Moyd, Ramla Farzad, Judy Rodriguez, Jason Jackson, and Kate Eddens. Equally important is the incredible staff at Indiana who support my research in the most concrete of ways: Nicholas Roberts, Mary Medley, Nancy Ashley, Deana Hutchins, and Alexia Bock. Thank you especially to Nancy for all of our inside jokes about *The Office* and all the scans. Priceless.

Matt Bokovoy has graciously shepherded this book through its many stages as my editor and made the book far better as a result. Thank you, Matt, for believing I could resurrect my book manuscript. Michelle Raheja kindly peer-reviewed the manuscript with a discerning eye and made immensely helpful recommendations. I also thank the anonymous peer reviewer who reviewed along with Michelle. Thanks also to Kathleen McDermott for the editing we did together through the peer review process, as well as the reports from the anonymous peer reviewers she obtained. Big thanks to Myla Vicente Carpio, who came to UW to join a panel we created on Native women, and then she insisted I come to the annual Ethnohistory conference where she introduced me to Amy Lonetree. There were very few Native women pursuing PhDs in history at the time, and I am especially grateful for Amy's support and friendship.

I also want to thank Gloria Bell, David Cornsilk, Josh Reid, Dian Million, Janette Doss Sinclair, DJ Bird Bear, David Treuer, Boyd Cothran, Alyssa Mt. Pleasant, Kent Blansett, Jennifer Denetdale, Andy Fisher, Nicholas Rosenthal, Katherine Osburn, Darby Munroe, and Debbi Kinaka.

Thank you to my mother, for the gift of life. To my grandparents, for believing in me and teaching me what it means to be Cherokee. They took me in as a kid when things were tough, and they made me the person I am today. I will always be grateful to them for giving of themselves so generously to me in their old age. I miss them every day and try to embody the values they imparted. To my aunties, for showing me how to be the very best woman. Thank you to Cherokee Nation for a much-needed scholarship that deepened my desire to make our nation proud. Everything I do is bound up with being Cherokee, and that scholarship still means the world to me. My three beautiful daughters bring me a boundless joy and infinite love. My girls, Riley, Clare, and Olivia: I will always love you, cherish you, and be here for you. I am so grateful for you and everything about you, and I want to especially thank Clare, who believes we will be able to buy a beach house because of *Picturing Indians*. We can hope, Clare!

PICTURING INDIANS

Introduction

From the initial moments of American exploration and conquest, through statehood, and into the stages of territorial formation, violence organized the region's nascent economies, settlements, and polities. Violence and American nationhood, in short, progressed hand in hand. From the use of the U.S. Army to combat and confine Indian peoples, to the state sanctioned theft of Indian lands and resources, violence both predated and became intrinsic to American expansion. Violence enabled the rapid accumulation of new resources, territories, and subject peoples. . . . Violence and American nationhood, in short, progressed hand in hand.
—Ned Blackhawk, *Violence over the Land*

Labor, Representation, and Film

Hollywood mocked the historic and continued violence toward Native people. As Chickasaw scholar Jodi Byrd notes, her tribe, and mine as well, lost their lands twice: the tribal lands of the Southeast and those in Oklahoma, through allotment.[1] In historic movies, Natives watch themselves losing in a way that never ends. For non-Natives the experience unfolds differently. Today hipster bars catering to non-Native millennials run old films in the background with no sound or captions, providing a vintage experience of the United States. Westerns allow older generations to enjoy the defeat of Native America thanks to cable TV channels TBS and TCM. I rolled my eyes and fast-forwarded through the extended scenes of violence between settlers and Natives, yet that filmic violence reifies white supremacy and Indigenous erasure. Despite the employment of Native people in these films, the films celebrate the defeat of Native America and present white settlers as both innocent and brave. "Genocide" is the term historians of Native America have begun to use, yet Hollywood's depictions of the moments that indicate genocide come across as childhood games of make-believe and always from the viewpoint of the settlers. Thus, my project, as a critique of 1940s and 1950s films about American Indians, asks you to see these westerns in terms of what they implied about Indian people and what they meant for the Indian people who worked in them. The starting point of this book is the deeply problematic nature of these films; it in no way celebrates the directors, producers, writers, or actors who engaged in representing the West as a place of white bravery and triumph.

This is a book about tribal sovereignty, even though the period covered encompasses the years tribal sovereignty was at its weakest. In fact, movies of the twentieth century supported the erosion of tribal sovereignty. As Anishinaabe film critic Jesse Wente has argued, these films reduced tribes to a single Indian and are mired in accuracies. That is insulting in and of itself, but in this colonialist move, these productions robbed Indians of their tribal identities on the national stage of film.[2] Further, in the 1940s and 1950s there were no academic programs to recruit and train Native filmmakers. The artistic forms of sovereignty written about by literary and cultural studies scholars emerged well after the time period I address in *Picturing Indians*. This book is not situated in the conversations of today's filmmakers, and the organization of the book reflects my approach, meant to be circular in a particular way: it begins with the films as texts but then unpacks each of their modes of production, leaving them disaggregated. This strategy serves to sift and sort the racist components of the films and leave them in that constitutive state. The epilogue brings these pieces back together in hopes of considering film texts, keeping their racist modes of production in mind.

The films I study were written, produced, and directed by non-Native people. Today's Native filmmakers have inspired a tremendous academic response. Their films are fundamental to my courses and to social settings in which my friends and I view them for personal enjoyment. But the Native-controlled films of the late twentieth century and beyond and the analyses of them do not directly address my topic, which is films, largely westerns, that include Indian characters and the Native people who worked in those deeply problematic films.

My reasoning for this format is to point out that Hollywood is still making racist films that have a very wide reach. These films remain the lens through which non-Native people understand Natives. Sadly, most non-Natives know of Johnny Depp's role as Tonto in 2013 or Leonardo DiCaprio's on-screen interactions with Indians in *The Revenant* (Twentieth Century Fox, 2015), but they have no awareness of films such as *Dawnland* (Upstander Films, 2018) or *Kanehsatake* (National Film Board of Canada, 1993), whereas many Native people do. In spite of Native filmmakers and those who write about them, Hollywood continues to produce films for non-Natives based on what non-Natives are willing to pay to see. Even then, production of Hollywood films with Native characters is rare relative to the number of films featuring members of other nonwhite groups. When Hollywood does occasionally put out a movie with Native characters, the result is rarely satisfying for Native people, yet non-Natives will dole out cash to see these films with Indian characters and happily engage in conversation about the films. Hollywood's reach is quantifiably larger and contributes significantly to discourse about Native Americans and their representations. Hollywood has marched on in spite of increasing Indigenous sovereignty in the twenty-first century, spewing out narratives that are laughable and painful for American Indians, while Indian-written, produced, and directed films circulate in niche academic and Indigenous markets.

This realization brings us back to the sustained focus of this book: Hollywood and the employment, presence, and survival of Native people. Hollywood talent scouts sought out Native people to appear in films produced during and after World War II. Native people worked in these deeply racist films, and they continue to work in such productions today. My wish is to highlight the work Native people did in these insulting movies to make a very clear statement: Native people have always been here and always will be in spite of the American nation-state and Hollywood. Mohawk leader Richard Oakes made many powerful statements, recorded by historian Kent Blansett (Cherokee, Creek, Choctaw, Shawnee, and Potawatomi descent), and spoke to Indian presence when he uttered: "Indians are permanent."[3] Claiming Indigenous space in the United States flies in the face of settler colonialism and the doctrine of discovery. To that end, I wish to demonstrate the presence of Native people who worked in the films of the 1940s and 1950s. Their presence should make a difference in how we see them as people and how we view the films in which they worked.

Non-Indians seem to believe they understand Native Americans and certainly believe they could identify a Native American with a quick glance. However, most non-Natives understand absolutely nothing about American Indians, tribal nations, and especially tribal sovereignty. Yet movies and other cultural artifacts have made them believe they do. Movies have provided the knowledge and lexicon for non-Indian misunderstandings of Indians. To a limited degree, this book addresses how images of Native Americans in movies have influenced non-Native beliefs about Native Americans, but this is actually the backdrop of the book. In the foreground are the people themselves, especially Indians, who purposefully entered and inhabited these filmic images not only to earn a living but also to challenge the rampant misrepresentations. For non-Indians, this participation could result in a high degree of economic success. For American Indians, the economic benefits they earned from their film work were far more limited, and they were acutely aware of this irony. This book is about American Indian labor and addresses Native Americans as employees in the film industry that sought to delimit and control their representations. This is not a book particularly about representation nor is it based in cultural studies. To a limited but critical extent, the book considers Native self-representation, as some scholars have done in Native art and film studies. For example, Kiara Vigil looks at Native negotiation with self-representation in the political realm, while Linda McNenly takes a fresh look at the Wild West shows, arguing that Native people engaged these representations, both disrupting and negotiating imagery of Native people.[4]

This book is about work. Here I draw on the scholarship around American Indian labor, much of which was inspired by Richard White and his argument for American Indian "purposeful modernization" as a survival strategy used by Native people. Historian David Beck has made a huge shift in the literature on world's fairs in recognizing that Indigenous people were there, negotiating pay, travel, and the nature of their labor, for the 1893 world's fair in Chicago in particular. Beck contextualizes the fairs in an arc of Native history rather than one of representation. He sees Native people seeking a place in the cash economy of the late nineteenth and early twentieth centuries, much as their ancestors had conducted trade with outsiders but also in the face of tremendous forces meant to deny them financial gain and to promote public disdain for any cultural action deemed inauthentic by outsiders.[5] This attention to the work being done at the world's fairs began in 2005 with historian Paige Raibmon calling the participation of Kwakwaka'wakw in the 1893 World's Columbian Exposition in Chicago an "example of modern wage labor and political protest." As economic opportunities receded in the nineteenth century, Native people used the economic work produced by the cultural binary of authenticity/inauthenticity to gain income and resources. Raibmon centers her argument on uses of authenticity, employing work as one lens with which to do so and ultimately answering questions about how aboriginal people fashion identities they see as authentic in an Indigenous context.[6]

Round Valley Reservation citizen William J. Bauer also uses labor as a category of analysis to explain how the people on his reservation attained power and survived in spite of harsh conditions. They sustained community through various forms of work, especially picking hops. Labor empowered his community; highlighting this aspect of their survival gives Bauer the ability to contextualize the brutality they faced and overcame, such as Indian vagrancy laws and the laws allowing whites to brutalize them for leaving the reservation. Anishinaabe historian Brenda J. Child takes a similar approach in *Holding Our World Together*, her study of the work done by Anishinaabe women to sustain their community and survive in the face of the United States' efforts to displace, remove, and ultimately destroy their communities. She writes, "At each stage, women marshaled much of the economy, and their roles and traditions were critical in sustaining Ojibwe communities."[7] Child followed this book with another, one that explicitly addresses labor in the reservation period, *My Grandfather's Knocking Sticks*. She situates her work in the "new Indian history" and answers the call to be attentive to "power, ideology, and the state" by looking at labor, unemployment, and economic strategies to assure survival, as well as negotiation with the federal agent to gain access to resources.[8] Child was inspired by Raibmon and Brian Hosmer, who completed a comparative study in 1999. Their conclusions are similar to Child's. Hosmer notes that "as Indian peoples gravitated toward the market, some attempted to reshape its operations so as to be less destructive to cultural values on the one hand and productive of political and economic independence on the other." This sustained attention to American Indian labor also owes its insights to ethnohistory, as it engages in the historian's use of narrative and analytical theory to answer this question: "can so-called traditional societies make significant adjustments in one sphere of cultural life . . . while still maintaining a discrete identity?"[9]

Perhaps most distinctively, looking at labor narrows our view to the Native people who worked in the film industry, especially those who never spoke. The "vanishing Indian" trope comes into play when we ignore the fact that Native extras worked in the movies of the 1940s and 1950s. They were there, and that should matter at least as much as the discursive battle going on over filmic representations of Indians. Much film criticism looks only at the text of the film itself, offering a rich analysis of what takes place in the film. Through film archives, however, I repeatedly found material indicating the labor of Native people in movies. My sources, then, are the film materials saved, sorted, and preserved in climate-controlled archives at various centers, all of which are listed in the bibliography. These primarily consist of photographs, payroll records, wardrobe and makeup records, press releases, scripts, and correspondence. Some oral histories with Native people who worked on these sets are included as well. This book is devoted to the archival materials and oral histories, not to theoretical claims, debates, or conversations. I have included extensive material on makeup and wigs, mostly because I found so much of it in the archives but also because my intention was to disassemble the "Movie Indian" in a unique way that broke it apart. Visualizing a box of noses, wigs, or brown paint seemed to capture perfectly the Movie Indian being stripped down to its components. My hope is that filmmakers can at least make films without the clichéd trappings of Indian identity.

Deeply inspiring and hilarious, Hopi filmmaker Victor Masayesva's *Imagining Indians* (Independent TV Service, 1993) challenges not only the film industry but the entire barrage of images of Indians created by non-Indians. Native people and history have been mocked in film, and Masayesva ably uses comedy to mock the racism of non-Indians in their contradictory "love" for Indian spirituality alongside their attachment to narratives of white victories over Indians. Ironically, he uses film to challenge film by using motion picture footage, interviews with Native men who worked in movies, movie posters, and a fictional scene between a racist white dentist and a Native woman who is the dental patient. Like Masayesva, the Indian woman takes over the narrative at the end of the film, grabs the dentist's drill, and applies the tip to the camera lens. Once we can no longer see through the lens, she throws the camera over, and we only hear an Indigenous language without subtitles. My response to this documentary was to write a work of history taking up these challenges in fleshing out Hollywood's fictionalized worlds with the real world of Native people who worked in the constrained environments of the film industry to earn cash.[10]

Cree filmmaker Niles Diamond took up this same theme and challenge in his documentary *Reel Injun* (Rezolution Pictures, 2009), which gives the entire spectrum of historic filmic representations of Native people interspersed with biting and poignant commentary from Native activists and actors, including John Trudell, Sacheen Littlefeather, Jesse Wente, Russell Means, Adam Beach, and many others. The story he tells is one of renaissance and resurgence, with Native workers in the film industry newly empowered to create films that not only "talk back" to Hollywood but also speak to other Native people through Native ways of understanding and worldviews. *Atanarjuat* (National Film Board of Canada, 2001) clearly takes the lead in the celebration of this seismic shift. *Reel Injun* is less ironic and artistic an intervention when compared with *Imagining Indians*, and it carefully separates superb Native acting from Native roles in terrible films, such as Graham Greene's in *Dances with Wolves* (Orion, 1990). Like Masayesva, Diamond's documentary lends its method and direction to my book, in which I seek to connect the dots between racist films to tell a coherent, critical story of Native labor in the film industry.

Some moments in this book are meant to be funny, inspired by *Imagining Indians*, and one of those has to do with the aesthetic of the Indian nose. The film industry may have desired to re-create Native culture for non-Native consumption, but the industry also tapped into Indian caricatures, especially the aesthetic aspect of those caricatures. On midcentury film sets the Indian look was produced through physical objects such as rubber noses, and the origins of this aesthetic go back to the Buffalo nickel. First produced in 1913, the Buffalo nickel has on its obverse side a noble and stoic Indian male silhouette created by the non-Indian artist James Fraser. Iron Tail (Oglala Lakota) and Chief John Big Tree (Seneca) posed for Fraser after being chosen for their particular countenances, especially their noses. These two Indigenous men met the simple physical expectations of white cultural producers and consumers. Iron Tail and Big Tree's amalgamated image on the Buffalo nickel highlights the simplistic relationship between expectations of Indians and representations of Indians. In meeting Fraser's physical expectations of an Indian look, Iron Tail and Big Tree embodied an expected Indian look. Iron Tail in particular offered the anticipated look of the Indian face, but it was his nose that Fraser wanted to capture in silhouette. Iron Tail's nose became the prototype of the ample, extended, noble, and "Roman" American Indian nose. This focus on the nose that began with the Buffalo nickel in the early twentieth century continued into the period under study here: the 1940s and 1950s.

Although Iron Tail's nose set the standard for the male Indian nose in the early twentieth century, by the middle of the twentieth century producers were avoiding casting Indians when scripts called for actors to play lead Indian characters. Instead, non-Indian actors got the calls for

1. Rock Hudson wearing prosthetic nose for his role as Young Bull in *Winchester '73* (Universal, 1950). Courtesy of Universal Studios Licensing LLC.

significant roles—those with character names, close-ups, and numerous lines of dialogue. But to look sufficiently Indian, these non-Indian actors required all manner of makeup, hair, and prosthetics to get the signature Iron Tail aquiline nose and the overall Indian look. Boris Karloff, who appeared as an Indian in *Tap Roots* (Universal, 1948), wore a nosepiece that seemed to capture the ideal Indian nose with particular power. Two years later Rock Hudson wore the same nose in *Winchester '73* (Universal, 1950). After a few more years in storage, the same evocative piece of rubber appeared on Dennis Weaver's face in *Column South* (Universal, 1953). If this nose was particularly adventurous, it was hardly the only one in the business. Cameron Mitchell wore an extra piece of rubber on his nose in *Pony Soldier* (Twentieth Century Fox, 1952), and Antonio Moreno's nose was augmented when he was called upon to play Chief Dark Cloud in *Saskatchewan* (Universal, 1954). On the set of that film Universal spent $250 on a supply of fake noses for just one actor.

2. Profile of supine Rock Hudson highlighting prosthetic nose in *Winchester '73* (Universal, 1950). Courtesy of Universal Studios Licensing LLC.

Why augment the noses of white actors playing Indians? The answer to that question is multilayered and takes us into the business of film, the cultural imperatives of audiences and producers, the pushback of Indians working in Hollywood, and the ways these elements came together in the films of the 1940s and 1950s. *Picturing Indians* intends to be a book about Indians playing Indians based on archival evidence, but it also touches on the tortuous relationship of Indians, film, and the U.S. desire for a particular type of history, one in which Americans stand as innocent victims of Native Americans. In this book my ultimate aim is to approach the most racist period of filmmaking that involves American Indian characters and story lines and put Indians at the center of this analysis, not as images but as employees of film studios. Looking at Indian characters, especially the Indian extras who appeared in the background, the Indian actors with speaking parts, and the little-known films of this period that worked against the conventions of the western genre, puts Native Americans and Native

American studies in a centralizing role. My interest for this book was primarily how Native people approached the studios as a place of work where representations were churned out without Native influence. To do so, I also considered the role non-Natives and the studios played, but my fundamental focus is on Native people themselves.

Picturing Indians unpacks the many representations of Native people in film, taking stock of the multiple layers of representations of tribal people living in the United States. When representing particular tribes, these films explode with a virtual avalanche of characters, images, and histories about tribal nations, many of which are incorrect. But the book is not a correction to the lies, nor is it fundamentally theoretical. My work is based on extensive archival research informed by some of the questions in cultural studies, but it does not use theoretical language. The book relies on a large number of film texts, some 300 films, of which I viewed about 250. This total included all movies made between the years 1941 and 1960 in which any Indian characters appeared. In addition to watching the films, I used studio archives when the documents included formal and informal stills, production budgets, press releases, and contemporary news and magazine articles. Through biographies and tribal histories, I provide connections between Indian actors and the tribes represented on the screen. In making these kinds of links, I also relied on governmental records from the National Archives as well as from their regional branches. For the chapters on labor, I relied heavily on studio labor-history monographs and oral histories of film workers.

Although film is an artistic enterprise, it is fundamentally different from other visual arts and from literature. A piece of visual art can generally be understood through the lens of one particular artist, whereas film functions as a corporate project with dozens of employees. A whole series of hands touched the movies discussed here: those of novelists, then screenwriters, a second wave of studio-employed screenwriters, then directors, actors, wardrobe departments, makeup artists, and studio heads. The proliferation of influences continued once filming began within the temporary community that emerged on the sets. The method used here goes beyond linking societal beliefs and cultural norms of this particular historical moment with the films under question. Due to the work of historians, film experts, and literary critics, we know a great deal about how societal values and norms are expressed through Indian characters and in films about Indians. This mode of analysis has provided us with a rich and nuanced understanding of film narrative and history and proves that history undoubtedly influences film narrative.

Putting history and film together tells only part of the story. *Picturing Indians* prioritizes the many people who produced movies and the community contexts in which they worked. Looking closely at the details of the production process undoubtedly shows how Hollywood thought about race and representation in spite of the narratives in their films. When scripts took physical form on sets with actors' and extras' performances, the Indian extras sometimes mocked the script, the costumes, the wigs, and the makeup. Joking among themselves may not have changed the films, but it was on set that producers and directors occasionally confronted the inaccuracies of their narratives because of their interactions with Natives. For this reason, I emphasize the many people involved in the production process and how their experiences on set existed on a parallel and oppositional track relative to the stories in the films. Actors and extras had to live together for weeks at a time, living in a reality separate from but connected to the film narrative.

Embedded in this book is the constant tension between white representations of Indians, their erasure of Native presence, and the reality of Native survival. Historian Robert Berkhofer coined the term "white man's Indian" to create a shorthand for non-Indian depictions of Native people used for non-Indian purposes and needs. We can see how this so-called white man's Indian infuses films' Indian characters, which are situated solely in the past and in constant conflict with whites. Since contact, Europeans and European Americans have created images of Indians over which Indians seem to have had no influence or control, let alone authorship. Ho-Chunk historian Amy Lonetree writes of the essential nature of the context of survival in any study of Native people. She proclaims that Americans are "stubbornly unaware" of the holocaust and survival of Native America. For me, representation in its many formats—film, historical studies, museums, tourism, art, and so on—is the reason non-Native Americans remain blind to this reality. It falls, then, upon Native scholars and scholars of Native America to contextualize their work with that historical framework in mind. For this study, that means reminding readers that non-Native control over imagery was never total and that Indians worked in many of these films. This book rides on the tension stemming from Indians involved in the representation industry of the 1940s and 1950s. How have Native Americans participated in the creation of films in the twentieth century? How does the involvement and presence of Indians in these films change the filmic content and their historical context?[11]

Picturing Indians begins with an analysis of film narrative and follows the production process from hiring to filming as a means of documenting and analyzing the mechanisms of social production. In doing so, I look closely at the economics of filmmaking. I seek the perspective of Indian actors and extras but also ask: How does the Indian look break down into its component parts? How do images of Indians play out in texts about Indians? How do images of Indians frame expectations of Indians? And how do films tell stories about settler colonialism in such a way that whites are victims and Indians are aggressors? To answer these questions, I set up a series of structures to help explain a particular materialization of ideology, specifically, how filmic images of Indians came to be in mid-twentieth-century America. The structures that frame *Picturing Indians* include work, bodies, and texts, and they tell us a great deal about how the production of images of Indians became tied intimately and ironically to already existing images of Indians, but also to Indians themselves.

Chapter 1 considers the films as texts, analyzing the foundational white narcissism in the films under study. Unlike the chapters that follow, chapter 1 emphasizes the ways whites spoke to themselves about themselves through Indian characters while simultaneously projecting guilt onto Native people and claiming white victimhood and innocence. In this sense chapter 1 is about the whites who made the films and the ideologies they engaged for production. Chapter 2 looks at white and Indian actors as laborers in the movie industry, paying close attention to the influence of actors' unions over pay, hiring, and work conditions. Likewise, chapter 3 considers the work of making movies but from the vantage point of extras, a labor force often unprotected by the umbrella of unions. Whereas actors playing Indians were often non-Indian, many extras portraying Indian characters were Indigenous people looking for temporary, high-paying local employment. Chapters 4 and 5 form a pair in that both unpack the physical creations of Movie Indians with makeup, buckskins, beads, fake braids, and prosthetic noses. Chapter 4 looks only at non-Indians whereas chapter 5 measures the creation of Movie Indians from Indian extras and actors.

Chapter 6 stands alone and takes stock of studios' attempts to capture and represent historical and cultural authenticity in reference to particular tribes. As did anthropologists and tourists of the late nineteenth and early twentieth centuries, the filmmakers in their search for the authentic created more problems than they solved. Studios hired language experts and conducted historical research, yet often their results and recommendations were set aside and simply left on the floor of the editing room. Hollywood churned out movie after movie telling a story of Indian aggression and violence and white victimhood. Yet the search for a meaningful story based on history and cultural traditions should be understood, appreciated, and unpacked for its successes and failures, and especially for its employment of Native people.

Like the earlier scholarly works *Reservation Reelism* and *Native Recognition*, *Picturing Indians* confounds our understanding of the movies of the 1940s and 1950s as they relate to Indian tribes, people, extras, and actors. Scholars have made clear the racism embedded in these films. Taken together, the lack of historical accuracy, the metanarrative of interminable conflict between Indians and whites, and non-Indians dressing up to play Indians leaves no doubt that these films embody racism in its purest form. But the racism of these films runs even deeper. The people behind the scenes of these films could have created historically accurate films with Indigenous actors and extras. They knew how to find Indians actors and extras, and they could have chosen to listen to their stories, their wishes, and their languages. On set, Indians and whites at times befriended, admired, and photographed each other in a manner that could have made its way into the movies. The studios manufactured some of these interactions for their own ends, but the salient point here is that the studios chose racist imagery through a process of methodical deliberation, not ignorance or a lack of options. Studios sold their racist films by the dozens, but this book shows the routes not taken and the efforts of Native people to earn much-needed cash within the constraints of the studio system. This book does not do visual or camera analysis, analyze the differences between studios or their budgets, or analyze singing cowboy films or Will Rogers. My methodology was to consider any movie with an Indian character as part of my range, to seek archival materials (including oral histories) on those films, and to let the archive lead the analysis. Only one chapter contains textual analysis, and for it I chose films that are rarely discussed in the literature. I also chose to separate Indians and non-Indians into different chapters to emphasize that they function differently as signs, symbols, and realities both on and off the screen. For these reasons, the material on skin, makeup, wigs, and noses repeats accordingly.

Intellectual Intersections: Surveying the Field

For my purposes, images of Indians are grounded in history, going back to the first contact Native people endured with Columbus and his ilk. Representations of Native people by non-Natives are bound inextricably to Natives' elimination and genocide by the settler states they have been forced to survive in and against. Native people cultivated their survival economically through trade and diplomacy, all in the context of removal, diminishment of their sovereignty by the federal government, and the destruction of Indigenous families through governmental policies of separation. Filmic images of Indians have many origins, one of which is the western novel of the nineteenth and twentieth centuries. English professor Christine Bold follows in the footsteps of Henry Nash Smith in documenting writers from James Fenimore Cooper to Louis L'Amour. For Bold, this literature has almost nothing to do with Indian characters or Indian people.[12] Moving into the twentieth century, we see the image of the Indian splashed in all sorts of locations: museums, photography, tourism, and art.[13] Other origins include world's fairs of the late nineteenth and early twentieth centuries. Although year-round amusement parks and other entertainment forms largely replaced the world's fair, those earlier spectacles performed the critical work of connecting local regions to national narratives. Matthew F. Bokovoy demonstrates how San Diego did just this in generating a "Spanish heritage" with roots deep in nationalism and destiny rather than racism and exclusion.[14]

When film became a means of representing Native people in the late nineteenth century, they were among film's first subjects. Thomas Edison recorded *Hopi Snake Dance* for the Chicago world's fair in 1893, as well as *Sioux Ghost Dance* and *Buffalo Dance* in 1894. He later offered *Indian Day School* in 1898, followed by Buffalo Bill's *Indian Wars Refought* (1914), a controversial movie that simply disappeared. Buffalo Bill, using Native actors, wanted to contextualize the massacre at Wounded Knee with the historical events leading up to the massacre. D. W. Griffith continued this content by turning his attention to representing the historical conflicts between whites and American Indians, as did many other silent-movie directors. In retrospect, film historians see the silent film period as a positive one for Native people, pointing to the handful of Native actors and directors of the era, as well as the supposedly sympathetic portrayal of Native issues. They connect this sympathy to the carryover of nineteenth-century melodrama into silent films, in their emphasis on family, marriage, and the home. Silent films emphasized Native suffering caused by "white immorality," but they were also used as a means of condemning the North's destruction of the South in the Civil War and the white South's defeat of African Americans following Reconstruction.[15] Others see depictions of Native people in silents and the careers of James Young Deer (aka Nanticoke) and Red Wing of the Ho-Chunk Nation of Nebraska, who created dozens of films as a response to public demand from audiences both white and Indian.[16] However, film professor Alison Griffiths has made a substantially different connection in three book monographs—*Wondrous Difference, Shivers down Your Spine,* and *Carceral Fantasies*—repeatedly calling our attention to early cinema's hidden gaze in ethnography and scientific museums to represent difference and, perhaps most important, to the fact that these representations circulated in popular culture. Griffiths consistently challenges us to see how early cinema was intimately bound together with ethnography and museum visualities. Cinema's connection to anthropology had largely ended by the 1930s, but its origins are deeply rooted in ethnographic representations of the "Other."[17]

Although the very first films depicted Native people in an ethnographic fashion to document Native culture and employed Native people for those depictions, whites playing Indians began very early, including D. W. Griffith's 1912 film *The Massacre* (General Film Company). What Seneca film scholar Michelle Raheja labels "redfacing" began just after the invention of filmmaking and continued well into the twentieth century. What did change is the early filmic sympathy for Native pain, which mostly vanished. It never really vanished, however, because it was never truly present. The silent era is less sympathetic to Indigenous pain and suffering than scholars have led us to believe. Griffith's *The Massacre*, for instance, does visualize the death and destruction of Native people, but far more screen time is devoted to white pain, white families, white love, and white innocence. The film in fact ends on these notes, the message clearly being that white safety and love are possible for the price of Native death and erasure. This arrangement began in the silent period, even though its outlying films contradict this centralizing theme, and it continued with the westerns of the 1940s and 1950s, among which we can still find outliers that condemn white violence against Indians.

Midcentury films shifted away from its earlier cultural connections as well. Significantly, early film representations tie in with other art forms, such as the Buffalo nickel and late nineteenth-century anthropology, but they also inherited the cultural repertoire of the Wild West shows. In 1883 William "Buffalo Bill" Cody created his Wild West show as a mix of circus, ethnographic display, Native American community, and shameless self-promotion. The show became an acceptable place for Native performers to earn high wages while glorifying a Native past, speaking their tribal languages, and living with other American Indians. Although dozens of American Indians took advantage of this economic and cultural opportunity, others looked down on the shows as shallow, inaccurate, and demeaning. This analysis comes from L. G. Moses, who acknowledges the imagery of Native people in the shows as being fundamentally violent and describes the non-Indian reformers simultaneously advocating for an image of Native people as embracing non-Native culture, which they called civilization. Moses chose to acknowledge these non-Native debates about images but yielded the floor to the Native men, women, and children who worked in the shows, thus allowing their voices to enter into the conversation. As a historian, he is aware of the imagery and its power, but he wants to bring our attention to the Native workers in the show rather than the show itself. He believes they should not be "reviled" or seen as victims of exploitation. The present book certainly draws inspiration from such an approach.[18]

Chauncey Yellow Robe, a Lakota from the Rosebud Indian Reservation who graduated from Carlisle Indian School in 1895, condemned the shows by using the same language as non-Indian reformers but from his Lakota perspective. On a very practical level he was concerned about the high wages being used by the performers to purchase alcohol in an almost unlimited supply from whites involved with the show. He likened the Buffalo Bill performances to Columbus parading Indians in front of the king and queen of Spain in 1493. Yellow Robe desired assimilation and equality for Native people and saw Indian participation in popular culture as undermining necessary forward strides. From his viewpoint, the shows equated Indian culture with savagery, and he rejected them as fundamentally false and also regressive. When Indians were not being depicted as savage, Yellow Robe was offended by the representation of Indian cultures as being lesser or lower than the cultures of the United States or Europe. Not only did he condemn Cody's show, he also rejected his films. *The Indian Wars Refought* (1914), Buffalo Bill's filmic depiction of the massacre at Wounded Knee, attracted Yellow Robe's scorn, as he felt it completely failed to capture the viciousness of America's soldiers toward the unarmed Lakota victims and the genocidal nature of the massacre. In spite or perhaps because of his misgivings toward Buffalo Bill's show, Yellow Robe later entered the film industry, establishing a thriving career for himself. He starred in *The Silent Enemy* (Paramount, 1930), which had an all-Native cast, and consulted on many other films.[19]

The origins of filmic representations of Native people thus has roots in

Wild West shows, ethnographic displays, nineteenth-century melodrama, and artistic representations such as the Buffalo nickel. How to analyze and assess those images later became a question of disciplinarity. L. G. Moses, for instance, approached the topic using historical methodology. Although this book uses historical methodology for a topic considered in the realm of Native American studies or even cultural studies, I would like to consider where these paths cross and diverge. Native American history and Native American studies exist as separate fields, with the latter heavily influenced by literary scholars.

Guided by the work of Michel Foucault, Stephen Greenblatt single-handedly ushered in New Historicism, which replaced New Criticism in literary studies. He revisited the well-trodden ground of the historical writings of Europeans in the Americas, but he wrote about them with historical contextualization, seeing them as representations bound up with capitalism, mimesis, and the social relations of production. His work was seen as a huge divergence from the formal analysis that had preceded his scholarship and generated the rewriting of encounters between Europeans and the Indigenous people of the Americas. However, both New Historicism and New Criticism continued to marginalize Indigenous people in their analysis. Another huge influence on literary criticism in the 1990s was Mary Louise Pratt's *Imperial Eyes* (1992). This path-breaking study of travel literature written by Europeans about Africa and South America profoundly challenged the study of literature, history, and anthropology. She found that travel books generated great influence on readers and had spread an exciting message of European "expansion." She used the idea of an imperial center and colonial periphery as a way to explain why Europe had an "obsessive need" to represent this relationship. In addition to their center/ periphery concept, Pratt used the term "contact zone" to talk methodically about the "social spaces where disparate cultures meet, clash, and grapple with each other, often in highly asymmetrical relations of domination and subordination." She adds the idea of transculturation as a phenomenon that exists in the contact zone: this explains how the "subordinated or marginal groups select and invent from materials transmitted to them by a dominant or metropolitan culture." "Autoethnography" is Pratt's term for writing done by marginalized people with the assistance, authority, and permission of the powerful. Last, Pratt uses the term "seeing-man" for the bourgeois European "whose imperial eyes passively look out and possess."[20]

Books like Tonawanda scholar Mishuana Goeman's *Mark My Words* (2013), looking at Native women writers and their critiques of settler colonialism through the tropes of space, land, and cartography, would be key and representative of Native American studies in their detailing of Native perspectives through literature. Goeman finds tremendous import in women writers' use of language to create possibilities for Native people that result in an entirely new vision of the world. Goeman in many ways is responding to Robert Warrior's *Tribal Secrets* (1994) and Gerald Vizenor's many books, including *Fugitive Poses* (1998) and *Manifest Manners* (1999). Both scholars have had a major impact on Native literary studies that in turn became the foundation of Native American studies as a field. Scholars such as Jace Weaver, Craig Womack, Jodi Byrd, and many others responded to Warrior, Pratt, and other figures in constructing criticism that gave primacy to Native voices. They placed Native writing in a continuum, reclaiming forms of speech as literature and situating their writing in a framework that has existed since time immemorial. The list of literary studies on Native uses of language to intervene and challenge the colonialist project of the United States is too massive to discuss at any depth here, but suffice it to say they are foundational to the field of Native American studies.[21]

Scholarship around indigeneity emerges from cultural studies, literary criticism, anthropology, and postcolonial studies, as well as multiculturalism and transnationalism. Ella Shohat and Robert Stam have made major contributions to all of these fields. One collection in particular lays out the intellectual genealogies of these fields and suggests we use all of them to productive ends. For Shohat and Stam the point is "to inculcate the habit of thinking multiculturally and transnationally and contrapuntally, of deploying multiple historical and cultural knowledges, of envisioning the media in relation to mutually co-implicated communities."[22] Perhaps the most important scholar of indigeneity in Native studies is Chickasaw professor Jodi A. Byrd, who comes from a postcolonial studies background. Her book *The Transit of Empire* stands alone in its insistence on an unparalleled notion of indigeneity. She begins with disarmingly simple claims: "colonization matters"; the U.S. empire began with the birth of the United States and its appropriation of Native America; the originary is possible; Indigenous people must be "central to any theorizations of the conditions of postcoloniality." Most pointedly, Byrd suggests that the U.S. deployment of colonialism and imperialism "coerces struggles for social justice for queers, racial minorities, and immigrants into complicity with settler colonialism." Perhaps most brilliantly, Byrd teases out and differentiates racism, racialization, and colonization. She makes the point that this coercion secures white dominance, to be sure, but these conflations also disempower Indigenous people in very particular ways: "American Indian national assertions of sovereignty, self-determination, and land rights disappear into U.S. territoriality as indigenous identity becomes a racial identity and citizens of colonized indigenous nations become internal ethnic minorities within the colonizing nation-state." Byrd claims space for Indigenous people to declare and maintain sovereignty and demands of allies a reckoning with their position on occupied Indigenous lands.[23]

James Clifford also stands at the fore in theorizing indigeneity. In the 2013 book *Returns* he seeks a means to conceptualize indigeneity, sidestepping binaries to reflect the current reality of a "systemic crisis." In considering four case studies from the vantage point of retirement, Clifford concludes that Indigenous survival and identity are now inevitable and begs the question of how to frame indigeneity in modernity.[24] Clifford's scholarship is centered in cultural studies, a space in which questions of indigeneity and performance have drawn significant attention. In that vein the 2014 edited collection *Performing Indigeneity* uses performance and performativity as a theoretical measure against indigeneity, repeatedly questioning the authenticity of Indigenous performativity, seemingly assuming that authenticity is something real. Their intention is to undermine essentialist identity performances in hopes of confirming cultural sovereignty, but their articles all treat Indigenous performance enacted for non-Indigenous audiences. This gives the reader the sense that there is no performed Indigeneity outside of the purview of non-Indigenous people. The clearest essay is that by Ngāti

Pūkenga scholar Brendan Hokowhitu on the cultural appropriation of the Māori haka, forcing Māori not to practice the haka, then taking it up on the non-Māori nationalist stage of New Zealand.[25]

Literary studies and cultural studies often overlap in Native American studies. One node in the burgeoning field of Native cultural studies began with Dakota historian Philip J. Deloria's book *Playing Indian* (1998), which attended to the historic appropriation of Native culture in the United States. This far-reaching and profound work inspired many studies. This subsequent scholarship addressed cultural imperialism and genocide and took aim in particular at whites who appropriated Native religion and art. Many scholars also asked how Native people's self-representation and art were constrained and influenced by white audiences.[26] This narrow scholarship that labeled American Indians negatively for modifying their culture to make a living was short-lived. Most studies around appropriation took a hard look at the historical archive to piece together the relationship between Native people, appropriation, sovereignty, and identity. For instance, Yupik scholar Shari Huhndorf, in *Going Native* (2001), begins with a deep analysis of the film *Dances with Wolves* to support her book's overall argument: the conquest of Native America continued beyond the military conquest through the representation and appropriation of Native culture, and this narrative is the foundation of the United States' historical identity, often reinforced even by those seeking to critique the United States. The literature, media attention, and even podcasts on Native appropriation continue, and this thread now parallels a growing interest in Native self-representation. Deloria went in this direction with his second book, *Indians in Unexpected Places*, and the *American Indian Culture and Research Journal* devoted a special issue to Native self-representation in art.[27] Deloria's arc continued with the 2019 book *Becoming Mary Sully*, which tells the story of his great-aunt's art and life but questions the contours and boundaries of Native Americans, art, and modernism, making bold claims along the way. In contrasting Sully to her American Indian contemporaries, Deloria points to their art as both supported and constrained by the institutions that brought them into the art world, as they always portrayed Indians of the past in ways palatable to white audiences. Sully, in contrast, created truly innovative pencil drawings without support of any kind other than that offered by her sister. As a Dakota woman, Sully was able to "produce works that are complexly Native but also expansive in subject matter and unorthodox in conception."[28] But to be sure, the interest in non-Native uses and abuses of images of Indians continues, and such scholarship often uses appropriation as a way to explain films like *Broken Arrow* (Twentieth Century Fox, 1950), which tells a story that generates white sympathy for Indians only when Indians act like whites. Literary scholar Dean Rader calls this "absorption" and argues that it is caused by the subaltern "aligning" with the hegemonic.[29]

In the turn to contextualizing screen images with off-screen material, many scholars have brought sovereignty into their analysis. Some studies lend an appreciative and a prescriptive tone, such as Randolph Lewis's careful and lyrical treatments of Alanis Obomsawin and Arlene Bowman, two Native women who are filmmakers. Lewis points out that the majority of Native-made films in the late twentieth and early twenty-first centuries are documentaries. Despite that genre being the dominant choice in Native-produced media, Lewis highlights the difficulties prospective audiences have in locating and viewing them. Only university libraries tend to own these films, and theater runs for documentaries are short-lived and rare. Nonetheless Lewis sees documentary as holding the possibility for sovereignty (in supporting tribal rights and legal advancements) and reciprocity (in offering tribes something in return for their filmic images).[30]

Nicolas Rosenthal and Comanche scholar Dustin Tahmahkera analyze nonfilmic visual media. Rosenthal examines American Indian painters of the New Deal era, concluding that this was a "critical period in the development in American Indian art, especially painting." In other words, Native people have long been engaged in the question of what constitutes Indian art and who has the authority to decide.[31] Tahmahkera also seeks an analysis grounded in what lies beyond the visual text. In *Tribal Television* he seeks to highlight the multiple meanings encoded in sitcom representations of Native people, thus contributing to analyses of "indigeneity and indigenous-settler encounters" in "indigenous cultural studies." Tahmahkera embraces the term "decolonization" in his analysis of sitcoms: "decolonized viewing means to open up indigenous critiques through sitcom reception and sitcom production." He uses a dialectic between the "recognizably Native" and the "recognizably Indian," seeing the latter as laboring to "critically resist and creatively circumvent the Indian."[32]

In historical framing Tahmahkera focuses on the 1960s, arguing in particular for a shift away from physical to discursive violence and erasure of Native people. He also sees a direct response to land claims in sitcoms with stories of cooperation and ending with settlers meeting their own needs while Natives do not. Ultimately, *Tribal Television* finds that the power of decolonization resides in Native actors and writers who challenge and transform televisual representations of Indigenous people. In a later work Tahmahkera tightens the connections between films as texts, their production, and their reception by Comanches but goes further in using performativity, hybridity, borderlands, "visual jurisdiction," and other keywords to argue that film "accelerated" representations of Comanches with tremendous ambivalence.[33]

Tahmahkera's work sits in Indigenous media studies, a field influenced tremendously by transnational connections, especially with Australia and New Zealand. This scholarship relies on the notion of not just Fourth Cinema, or that made by Indigenous people, but also the Fourth Eye and Fourth World, which encompass Indigenous perspectives, experiences, and subversions, clearly articulated by Ella Shohat, Robert Stam, Brendan Hokowhitu, and Vijay Devadas. Not surprisingly, the field is divided among those who commit their analysis to Indigenous people, those who look at settler-Indigenous relations, and those who, like film professor Peter Limbrick, look at settler cinemas as fundamentally transnational. Limbrick, as an example, sees his work following the lines of Pratt's *Imperial Eyes*, with its primary focus on travel and transnationalism rather than on Indigenous people.[34]

My book falls outside the parameters of Fourth Cinema, Fourth Eye, and transnational settler cinemas but nonetheless advocates for Indigenous-produced film and scholarship.[35] Fourth Cinema may sound triumphant and celebratory, but English and film professor Corinn Columpar refuses to equate Fourth Cinema with Indigenous cinema as a way of guarding against essentialism. She also refuses, unlike many scholars of Native American film, to invoke the idea of sovereignty around cinema. She instead defines Fourth Cinema this way: "they produce Aboriginality as a sign within their discursive economy—but they do so by a plurality of means and to a variety of ends." For Columpar, it would be erroneous to think of Fourth Cinema as a counterresponse to the colonizing traditions of film, as she sees remnants of those same traditions in Indigenous film.[36]

Film Studies

Although Native literary studies generated literary criticism in response to the beautiful work of Native writers such as N. Scott Momaday, Leslie Marmon Silko, and Joy Harjo, film studies scholars began their heavy lifting in the 1990s in response to the banal and insulting films *Dances with Wolves* (Orion, 1990) and *Pocahontas* (Disney, 1995). The earliest scholarship served as a gathering of data, with filmographies and analyses around the noble and ignoble "savage," an example being the work of English professor Michael Hilger published in 1995. Hilger later brought out a revised version, with 453 pages of filmography and textual analysis, arranged sequentially.[37] Some of this scholarship addressed all forms of representation of Native people, such as S. Elizabeth Bird's edited collection *Dressing in Feathers* (1996), in which she pointed out the need for deep contextualization of Native people rather than overarching claims.[38]

In his coedited work on Native people in film, Peter C. Rollins offered the first collection of essays moving sequentially and systematically through key films representing Indians. This collection, *Hollywood's Indian* (1998), begins with bothersome language by Rollins. In reference to one of the Native contributors, Rollins referred to the author's "people" and "community" without offering their tribal affiliation. Instead of reflecting on the violence perpetrated by the people and military of the United States, Rollins simply states, "Hollywood's limited notion of 'action' often requires a set of jaws to be punched . . . those jaws often belonged to stereotyped bands of whoopin' and hollerin' Hollywood Indians." Astonishingly, Rollins even sees John Ford's work as making a "serious effort to transcend Hollywood imagery—indeed, to condemn the tragic heritage of America's racial stereotypes." He makes his viewpoint and identity clear when he claims that "our pioneers saw the West as empty," the word *our* being the key problem.[39] The collection makes an important contribution, and some professors probably use chapters for movies they teach, but it is problematic that even the editor held some regressive views of Native people. One of the contributors to the volume, Ted Jojola (Isleta Pueblo), wrote a hilarious piece on the history of Native images in film, beginning with a celebration of Will Sampson's powerful and ground-breaking role in *One Flew over the Cuckoo's Nest* (United Artists, 1975). Jojola writes, "In that simple and fleeting scene, a new generation of hope and anticipation was heralded among Native American moviegoers. Long the downtrodden victims of escapist shoot-'em and bang-'em-up Westerns, Native Americans were ready for a new cinematic treatment—one that was real and contemporary."[40]

Later scholars began earnestly unpacking the racism of non-Indians playing Indians, as well as the racist and denigrating filmic images of Natives. Anthropologist Ann Fienup-Riordan wrote *Freeze Frame* (2003), her response to a talk by Donna Haraway that failed to mention the Indigenous people of Alaska in a list of "points of extraordinary density." Fienup-Riordan ties her analysis directly to Edward Said's *Orientalism*, describing how a belief that U.S. culture was superior to that of the Indigenous people of Alaska coexisted with whites believing that there was something in Native Alaskan culture that was noble and worthy of appropriation for films.[41] Cherokee and Choctaw scholar Jacquelyn Kilpatrick's *Celluloid Indians* (1999) stands as an excellent example of just this type of work, serving as a foundation that allows us to make claims about racism toward Native people in casting and film narrative. Although Kilpatrick focuses almost exclusively on non-Native filmmakers, film studies' primary interest lies in today's Native filmmakers. English professor Gretchen M. Bataille devoted her entire career to the intersections of Native history, representation, and literature. The distortion of Native representation went back to first contact and always celebrated non-Indians' defeat of Native America, reflecting the values and perspective of the dominant culture, creating strained relations, and dismissing Native history and culture as not being worthy of inclusion in official histories of the Americas. Bataille edited three volumes of essays and bibliographies on American Indians in film, holding deep concern for the effects of negative imagery on Native people, critiquing problematic films, and asking the film industry to do better in this area.[42]

English professor Armando José Prats was the first to write a poststructural analysis of westerns, arguing that this genre uses Native characters to meditate on and represent social change in non-Native America. Prats has argued that the western both erases and requires the presence of Indian characters to explain and visualize non-Native issues.[43] Angela Aleiss's book *Making the White Man's Indian* (2005) draws on Robert Berkhofer's *White Man's Indian*, insisting that filmic Indians tell us about whites, not Indians. Aleiss goes further than both Berkhofer and Kilpatrick in mapping an arc wherein these images morph over the twentieth century, transitioning into the "white man's Indian" during World War II. After the war, filmic Natives could be treated equally only if they gave up their Indian identity. Aleiss, like most others, does not address the Native labor performed in these films.

Faye Ginsburg provides tremendous support to the effort to bring Native voices into media. In addition to her writing, she has trained Native students in documentary filmmaking, and dozens of them have gone on to work in the field. Her thinking began with the Native people of Australia as she wondered if media engagement would damage Aboriginal culture even more and whether Native people can represent themselves—clearly a response to Gayatri Chakravorty Spivak's "Can the Subaltern Speak?" In that work, Ginsburg answered no to the destruction of Native culture and yes to Natives being quite capable of self-representation.[44] In a piece published more than a decade later, Ginsburg writes of Indigenous media creating "screen memories" that recuperate their collective stories, as in *Atanarjuat*, since they are unknown to the dominant culture and "in danger of being forgotten within local worlds as well."[45] Just a few years later Native scholar and filmmaker Beverly R. Singer (Santa Clara Pueblo: Tewa and Diné) contributed to the literature with *Wiping the War Paint Off the Lens* (2001), which connects Native oral tradition with filmmaking and highlights Native filmmakers, including herself, from the 1970s to the present. Singer truly believes oral tradition and storytelling are the only ways to fully understand Native film, and she wishes for a world in which

Native art is known, celebrated, and circulated. Singer looks especially at Native self-representation through film and briefly treats earlier, racist depictions of Native people.

Edward Buscombe, the non-Indian specialist in westerns, issued the small-format monograph *"Injuns!"* in 2006, making the case that many critiques have already been written about historical and tribal inaccuracies in historic films. He then makes the modest claim that whites effectively constructed filmic Indians for their own purposes. Critical media and cultural studies scholar Denise K. Cummings edited two volumes on contemporary Native art: *Visualities* (2011) and *Visualities 2* (2019). Cummings's aim in 2011 was to highlight the "hybridity" of the visual means used by Native artists "as a primary means of mediating identity," meaning individual and tribal identities, which she borrows from Steven Leuthold's work in the late 1990s.[46] Many of the essays in Cummings's collection challenge the stereotypes put out by Hollywood, which she calls First Cinema, demonstrating how Native artists have challenged those stereotypes through various strategies and that Native artists have been issuing these challenges far longer than previously recognized.[47]

The boundaries between literary studies, film studies, and cultural studies blur in the literature on Native film. Literary scholar Dean Rader exists in the disciplinary space of English departments but continuously uses an Indigenous studies framework to engage a variety of artistic media, including film. In the tome *Engaged Resistance* (2011), he includes two chapters on four Indigenous films: *Naturally Native* (Red Horse Native Productions, 1998), *Skins* (First Look Pictures, 2002), *Smoke Signals* (Miramax, 1998), and *The Business of Fancydancing* (Outrider Pictures, 2002)—all films well outside the time period of my study. Rader calls the idea of "engaged resistance" a "fundamentally indigenous form of aesthetic discourse that engaged both Native and American cultural contexts as a mode of resistance against the ubiquitous colonial tendencies of assimilation and erasure."[48] Film studies scholars LeAnne Howe (Choctaw), Denise K. Cummings, and Harvey Markowitz created a deeply creative and thoughtful collection of essays on thirty-six films representing Native people in *Seeing Red* (2013). For them, representations of Native people bear the marks of both violence and nobility—binaries harking back to the time of first contact between Indigenous people and Columbus. In Howe's contributions to that collection, she reflects on her indignation that Natives are perceived as a vanished people in *The Unforgiven* (United Artists, 1960) and details her frustration at the immense reach of *Smoke Signals*, which gave non-Natives the message that Indians are victims.[49] On an even more direct and personal note, Ponca scholar Eric L. Buffalohead connects the racism he endured as a child and young man to internalized anger, but he eventually gained a deeper understanding that "Hollywood and other media sources in popular culture have created a situation in terms of Indian imagery where fantasy has replaced reality." Buffalohead and M. Elise Marubbio, who together edited *Native Americans on Film*, cite the U.S. educational system as operating in tandem with Hollywood to ignore Indigenous people.[50]

Marubbio, who has a photography and literary studies background, is the only scholar to have written a monograph on the representations of Native women in film, and she argues that these representations fall into three categories: dangerous, innocent, and primordial. The Native female body has been used to represent the conquest of Native America, primarily through the women's deaths or other filmic departures.[51] History professor Hilary Hallett provides an incredible corollary to Marubbio's treatment of Native women in film with her study of white women in Hollywood by interweaving the stories of early twentieth-century urbanization, the development of Los Angeles, the transition to films with audio, and their impact. Although she rarely refers to these women as white, Hallett expertly shows these interconnections, ultimately highlighting the tremendous possibility Los Angeles and the film industry held for white women. The advent of "talkies" catered to white women's interests as well, and the film industry itself had many white women employees. Hallett shows us that Hollywood's early history was deeply influenced by white women, hinting at just how much ground they lost over the course of the twentieth century.[52]

"Sovereignty" has become a keyword in Native American studies, including film studies. In 1995 Tuscarora art historian Jolene Rickard addressed sovereignty and Native art, perhaps the first use of the term "sovereignty" in an art criticism setting. She writes that "sovereignty is the border that shifts indigenous experience from a victimized stance to a strategic one. The recognition of this puts brains in our heads, and muscle on our bones."[53] Sovereignty continues to be invoked, contested, and reformulated in the field, often by adding an adjective to create an art-based idea of sovereignty. With the turn to cultural studies and its attendant language, scholars unearthed significant moments of Native participation in cinema and used theoretical language to explicate Native and non-Native engagement with film. Anthropologist Kristin Dowell uses sovereignty as the framework to describe and advocate for Indigenous cinema specific to the west coast of Canada. Dowell exclusively covers current film work by Indigenous artists, arguing that First Nations media constitute "an act of self-determination" and represent "cultural autonomy" that supports and derives from sovereignty.[54] Like Dowell, Lee Schweninger promotes "visual sovereignty" as the means for understanding current Native filmmakers and invokes Gerald Vizenor's notions of "imagic moments" as stories "offered" by Indigenous peoples and "postindians" as a replacement for the simulations of Indians in films made by First Cinema.[55]

Film scholar Michelle Raheja (Seneca) significantly extends the analysis of sovereignty in film with *Reservation Reelism* (2010). Rather than separating whites dressed as Indians and Indians dressed as Indians into two distinct phenomena, Raheja considers both Indians and non-Indians playing Indians to be a single phenomenon she calls "redfacing," a simple yet complex term that harks back to blackfacing, a cultural form that featured white and African American actors. Raheja's analysis thus presents a kaleidoscope of angles, removing victimhood and other binaries from the conversation. As she puts it, "The ideological and cultural work that redfacing enacts, however, complicates any easy reading of Hollywood Indians." In other words, Native people could and did use redfacing to reject the vanishing Indian stereotype; rather than reinforcing Native stereotypes, Native people used them for their own ends. When speaking of actors who fraudulently claimed an Indigenous identity, Raheja argues in a subsequent work that they reinforced the most racist aspects of the stereotypes to pass. But when Native workers in the film industry engage film, they are invoking "visual sovereignty" as a category of analysis that builds on political sovereignty.

Visual sovereignty exists in the space of the "virtual reservation," creating space for the possibility of decolonization on Native terms. From Raheja's perspective, Native people have been engaging in visual sovereignty "from the beginning of time to the present." This is what makes their artistic maneuvers critical and in need of documentation and analysis.[56]

Much like Raheja, Joanna Hearne's *Native Recognition* (2012) provides a language that deeply contextualizes filmic representations of Native people, striving to connect film with history and especially the role of the family in these representations. Moreover, Hearne highlights contemporary American Indian filmmakers and their efforts at recuperating and perhaps appropriating imagery meant to erase Indigenous people. Through meticulous research, Hearne demonstrates that Native artists in the late twentieth century used racist films and photographs to highlight the presence of Indigenous people therein, as well as to reassert space for those working in the film industry of the past and the present. For Hearne, these problematic films serve a useful purpose for Native artists in that they intervene and engage powerful racist images from the past. Historic films fail to inspire and should not be replicated, she would argue. When whites are performing in roles depicting Native people, Hearne claims that "audiences see a complete expansion of whiteness and white masquerade into the film's symbolic landscape." But the work of Native filmmakers engages and subverts images saturated with negative or erased images of Indians. For Hearne and Raheja, the field of representation in general, and cinema in particular, has done great harm to Native people in its settler colonial gaze, but they also see great hope and promise in cinema as a site of Native intervention and reconfiguration. My book does not engage in the language of Native cultural studies but does seek to answer the same questions they raise, and it does so by using historical methodology.[57]

The critical studies and literary criticism of westerns sit quite separately from Native film studies. These works really began with Henry Nash Smith's *The Virgin Land* (1950) and continue with Richard Slotkin's *Gunfighter Nation* (1992), *Regeneration through Violence* (1973), and *The Fatal Environment* (1985). Scholars spawned dozens if not hundreds of books and articles looking at the myth of the frontier. In 2013 the Pulitzer Prize–winning author Glenn Frankel landed himself on the *New York Times* best-seller list with a 415-page book on *The Searchers*, director John Ford's deeply racist film. Like some of the literature on westerns and the frontier, Frankel marginalizes Native people in his analysis.[58]

Redface and blackface would be an obvious point of comparison. With regard to the history of African American cinema, the questions and answers differ markedly from those in Native film studies. Despite some overlap in discussions of redface and blackface, the historical questions in the study of African American cinema are about the impact of forces such as industrialization, the formation of black urban communities, and expressions of black identity and freedom in films as texts. Likewise, historians of the black cinema discuss early twentieth-century movie houses for black patrons—something that has never existed in Native communities or for Native people. Even though some Native people became urbanized in the twentieth century, there are still no Native theaters. Thus, the literature reflects this historical reality, which focuses predominantly on imagery.[59]

Historian Cara Caddoo sees class conflict embedded in debates about representations of African Americans. Sociologist Maryann Erigha sees those debates as being rooted in Jim Crow segregation and occurring between those African Americans in the film industry who are for or against blackness. In other words, Erigha sees Jim Crow continuing in the attitudes of African American filmmakers. But it is worthwhile to remember that *Birth of a Nation*, a film that used white actors in black makeup, defined African Americans as rapists. Perhaps as a response to *Birth of a Nation*, African Americans formed their own independent companies, used black actors, and distributed their films in African American communities. During the ensuing sound period, African American actors gained employment in the studios but worked in stereotyped roles. In the 1940s and 1950s, largely due to the influence of African American directors such as Oscar Micheaux and Spencer Williams, the focus was on creating positive images of African Americans and the community.[60] With a similar history, Latinx and Chicanx people have been represented largely by outsiders through a series of stereotypes. For women, the types have been limited to the maid, the hot señorita, and the spitfire. For men, it has been a lazy Mexican, Latin lover, violent criminal, "greaser," and bandits of the Mexican Revolution. The last, especially and explicitly, was used to justify settler colonialism and the defeat of Mexico and appropriation of much of its land in 1848. Even with the Latinx and Chicanx actors today entering the world of Hollywood, filmmakers continue to push these actors into caricatures, even when they push back.[61] In the silent period Asian Americans had their own directors and actors, such as Joseph Sunn Jue, Marion Wong, Anna May Wong, and Sessue Hayakawa. But when sound was introduced, both "yellowface" and stereotyped roles became the norm. Yellowface roles became iconic for a number of actors, including Paul Muni, Yul Brynner, Mickey Rooney, and Peter Sellers. Unlike Native Americans, the Asian American community had filmmakers like Esther Eng, who created Chinese-language films and introduced icon Bruce Lee. By 1961 an all-Asian cast had been hired to work in *Flower Drum Song* (Universal, 1961), which received considerable recognition and important awards. Although this is not a competition for which ethnic group has received the worst or best treatment in Hollywood, especially as Native Americans are tribally based and not members of ethnic groups, American Indians have suffered similarly in the film industry but have yet to obtain in cinema what other nonwhite peoples achieved decades ago.[62]

At its core, this book engages the history of Native people, with a particular focus on film in a particular moment in time. In that sense, my concerns are much larger than film and are really about questions of strategies of economic survival. All over the Americas, Native people have managed to survive, and this book documents a particular aspect and moment of that survival in the midcentury film industry. *Picturing Indians* will tell you exactly how much Native people made doing this work and what they wore, and it suggests we think about the financial possibilities and cultural limitations of generating images for pay.

1

"Just Like a Snake You'll Be Crawling in Your Own Shit"

American Indians and White Narcissism

> The key ideologies describing Indian people—inevitable disappearance, primitive purity, and savage violence, to name only a few—have brought exactly this kind of uneven advantage to the social, political, economic, and legal relations lived out between Indians and non-Indian Americans.
>
> —Philip J. Deloria, *Indians in Unexpected Places*

Prior to the move toward cultural studies, the literature on American Indians in movies and, more generally, representations of Indians throughout popular culture aimed to expose the many untruths and distortions put forth by these images. By focusing on the inaccuracies and the negative aspects of the Indian characters, these studies implicitly rendered Indians victims, both on the screen and off. More recent studies move outside this analysis by looking at films made by American Indians, films other than westerns, and films made outside the United States. This work demonstrates the attempt to erase Native people and Native self-representation through representations, and it highlights the ultimate failure of that attempt due to Native survival. Moreover, these studies place twentieth-century American Indian history and struggles for sovereignty alongside representations of Indians to show the relationship between the two and the ways Native people have used the image industry to their own ends. In this chapter I argue that films with Native characters place whites and white consciousness at the center of the narrative and that they construct and see Indians from the perspective of the white characters. The journey of white characters westward across the U.S. empire reinforces the settler colonial version of U.S. history: brave white settlers innocently moved into Native lands in spite of the unmerited violence of Native people and thus gave birth to the United States through their martyrdom and victories over Native Americans.[1]

The larger argument of this book places great emphasis on the American Indian people who worked in these films, yet some literature implies that, in essence, Indians had nothing to do with the movies under study here. Failing to document Indian presence in film implicitly endorses the myth of the vanishing Indian, thereby implying that Indian people did not survive settler colonialism. Recognizing Indian involvement in films decolonizes film studies and challenges the unexpectedness of their presence in twentieth-century films. Scholars use history to establish the veracity of images of Indians and to establish a deeper understanding of historical relations between Indians and non-Indians. Some film critiques follow an entirely valid trajectory: Apaches wore these kinds of headbands, not those; the Lakotas had these kinds of tipis, not those; this is what happened at the Battle of the Little Bighorn, not that. In this sense history serves as a litmus test for the evaluation of images of Indians as either positive or negative. But even the most ridiculous images need to be understood and evaluated in a deeper historical context. The embedded nature of settler colonialism figures as a key aspect in virtually every movie with Indian characters. Additionally, understanding Indian presence in these films changes their simplistic victimization to one in which Native people are negotiating representation in a settler colonial context.

Yet films from the 1940s and 1950s tend to be treated as though they are not about Native Americans at all. Film scholars find buried in these films all sorts of meanings that have nothing to do with Native people or settler colonialism. For instance, the 1950s saw a return to the home for many Americans, literally and figuratively. Americans embraced a newfound domesticity through their suburban homes and cars. These social changes were reflected back to Americans on television programs such as *The Donna Reed Show*, *Leave It to Beaver*, and *Ozzie and Harriet*. In the midst of the return to the home that the 1950s represented, Paramount created *The Far Horizons*, a film on the Lewis and Clark expedition into the stolen lands of Native people in the Midwest and Pacific coast regions. Paramount cast Donna Reed, a 1950s paragon of white femininity, to play Sacajawea in the film.[2] The dispossession of Native people and their lands, exploiting Sacajawea as a negotiator with tribes, and selling the land of Native people to whites all serve as the necessary ingredients to justify and create the white home in *The Far Horizons*. Much as real estate developers pushed into land outside urban areas to create suburbia in the 1950s, so too did Hollywood re-create the U.S. empire through the lens of Lewis and Clark claiming the West.

The film highlights a romantic relationship between Clark and Sacajawea, whereas historical accounts emphasize the role of the nation-state in the expedition and Sacajawea's encounter with the team. When Lewis and Clark were living with the Mandan Nation, they met Sacajawea, who was perhaps sixteen. She had been kidnapped by Hidatsas at the age of ten and traded to Dakotas, who sold or traded her to Toussaint Charbonneau, a French Canadian trader. She spoke Lakota and Shoshoni proficiently and knew some French and English as well. She joined Lewis and Clark for reasons of her own and acted as a mediator upon meeting members of other tribes.

In Paramount's filmic version of the expedition, Sacajawea and Captain Clark become involved romantically, and their relationship ends sadly and abruptly when Clark returns to the East. The plot emphasizes Clark's innocence in the genocidal context in which his invasion of Native lands took place. The film also features a mythical farewell letter from Sacajawea to Clark that articulates their happy memories, again with not even an oblique reference to settler colonialism:

> There is much we both can do for our people. Many things we have learned from each other we can teach to them: patience, kindness and the wisdom to know the truth. You would not have let me say these things to you, but in your heart you will know they are true. You will

be sad, as I am sad, and you will think of me as I will think of you many times in the years to come, when you see a river of whitewater dancing in the sun, or clouds hanging high above the mountains. But soon the memories will grow dim as memories should, and there will be others to take their place. May they be happy ones for you, my love, as happy as those we shared together all the days of your life.

In that sense her letter justifies, supports, and applauds the dispossession of Native people. This is a Sacajawea cut entirely from a colonial gaze that needs American Indians to cooperate with their conquest.

This letter and the whole of *The Far Horizons* created a false history in which Sacajawea was the strongest ally and supporter of Lewis and Clark's project of taking the West from Native people to generate conditions suitable for settler colonialism. The letter suggests that the reason for their intimacy was their emotional and psychological maturity and connection, which she sees as the foundation for the future cultural exchange between whites and Native Americans. Yet Sacajawea was in fact the partner/slave of Charbonneau and never had a romantic relationship with either Clark or Lewis. The film creates an inaccurate historical landscape based firmly on one pillar of settler colonialism: that the colonized desire all that the colonizers bring and all of their intentions.[3] Sacajawea's letter also fits into a long tradition of farewell speeches from Indians to whites as part of the vanishing Indian tradition. Just as Sacajawea wanted Clark to remember her with fondness, her focus is solely on the past, not the present or the future. This filmic Sacajawea fits into the avalanche of representations of Indians uttering their final farewells as they pass into obscurity, after being overtaken by white settlers.

The vanishing Indian, filled with melancholy, resignation, and disappearance, obscures from view the violence and horror of U.S. history. Through romance, *The Far Horizons* and similar films tell us that American Indians consented to the hostile takeover of Indian lands while pretending that dispossession never occurred.[4] Sacajawea poses as timelessly wise, tragically so, and out of sync with the present. She remains rooted in a distant past, free from oppressors and victims. Sacajawea's letter bears important similarities to Chief Joseph's famous speech, much of which was written by a white man but attributed to the Nez Perce leader. Both demonstrate an American need to see Indians as wise, cooperative with colonialism, and providing a clear demarcation between their present lives and the genocidal past that is never directly articulated. Her moment of surrender, given through her goodbye, erases the conflict that necessitated that surrender. Her use of poetic speech also confirms the belief that Indians are fundamentally different from whites. Their unique character creates a cultural and social divide, and Sacajawea's language naturalizes separation and conquest.

From the vanishing Indian of the nineteenth century, we move into the termination of tribes in the twentieth century. When Native people did not vanish in the nineteenth century, the federal government funded and imposed forced assimilation on Native survivors. Through boarding schools and allotment, families were torn apart, tribal languages and cultures were decimated, and tribes lost the majority of their tribal holdings. After President Franklin Roosevelt's New Deal put an end to the practice of allotment, some tribes successfully generated income through business endeavors, and many men served in the military. These Native accomplishments gave Congress the excuse to terminate tribes altogether. The congressional destruction of tribal sovereignty is the historical backdrop for the films of the 1940s and 1950s that include Indian characters.

Historical Context: Termination and Urbanization

Film historians view the 1950s as a time of great change in representations of race, and much of that attention turns to African Americans, Asian Americans, and Mexican Americans to make this argument. With Hitler and the Holocaust as a backdrop, Americans needed to see themselves as distinct from Nazism and slowly began to accept nonwhites as Americans. When African Americans demanded the end of segregation in public transportation, the civil rights movement began, eventually leading to some progress in the treatment of African Americans. Social relations between whites and ethnic minorities were clearly in flux in the 1940s and 1950s, yet the direction was ill defined and marked by inconsistencies and violence.

Ultimately, postwar changes in racial relations were uneven, having been both progressive and regressive. After World War II some ethnic minorities were able to vote or serve in an integrated military, but racism continued unaltered through direct violence, housing discrimination, police brutality, and de facto segregation.[5]

The wrenching attempt to create ethnic harmony in the postwar United States resulted in a series of legal decisions that changed the country. U.S. courts attempted to legislate racial harmony through racial integration of public schools and the military. Although some whites came to accept integration, many upheld racial segregation regardless of the widespread social changes surrounding them. Minority entrance to private schools was precluded with high tuition and the social networking required for gaining entrance to private universities, thus preserving segregation in those venues. School districting, one of the most controversial political issues of the late twentieth century, was yet another way of upholding segregation. This meant that less substantial tax bases in minority neighborhoods would be unable to support the sophisticated equipment and highly qualified teachers that schools in white neighborhoods could afford. Americans upheld social segregation in the workplace by hiring minorities but not promoting them, laying them off first, or promoting an elite few to create an appearance of racial integration. Ironically, what resulted from integration was an entire series of civil rights movements that continue into the present, now challenging police brutality and the prison-industrial complex.[6]

The conventional wisdom suggests that changes in race relations between African Americans and whites created a parallel shift in images of African Americans in the 1940s and 1950s. War and postwar films reflected, at first timidly and tentatively, the new logic of antiracism. On a material level a handful of African American actors were held up as examples of the new acceptance of African Americans in Hollywood, and the stories they told invoked interracial friendship to indicate life in the United States had changed fundamentally. These moves toward equality failed to satisfy in that their politics and artistic merit ran shallow, even though the films were set in the North and West, thus disrupting the South's monopoly on representations of African Americans. Despite these integrationist impulses in the film industry, the market determined the product. Whites continued to produce images of African Americans that in some ways diverged significantly from the blackface tradition, but African Americans began creating images of themselves, generating products that differed tremendously even from these improved images. Whites owned the studios and wrote the films, and their films were seen by both black and white audiences, but films produced by African Americans were viewed almost exclusively by African Americans.[7] This dichotomy meant that African American actors faced a choice: either work for studios in regressive roles or work in a largely underpaid yet black-controlled format.[8]

The drama of integration played out perhaps most forcefully in education. African Americans entered all-white schools with the sound of white racists in the background shouting and jeering, while African Americans viewed school integration as a tremendous step forward in the plan to enter fully into U.S. society. The integrationist impulse at the heart of the civil rights movement may have been part of the reason the government embarked on an effort to terminate tribal life. But from within the timeline of American Indian history, termination seems to function as part of a larger effort to force assimilation upon Indigenous people and further dispossess tribes of their tribal lands. When policymakers applied the logic of integration to American Indians, with American Indians being forced to assimilate, move away from their reservation homes, and work for low wages in physically demanding jobs that were often debilitating, many tribes rejected this logic altogether and viewed it as an assault on their sovereignty. From this perspective, termination is particular to Native Americans and has little to do with the civil rights movement.

When American historians talk about race in the mid-twentieth century, the story centers on African Americans and the narrative around ethnic minorities, usually ignoring Native Americans altogether. But when we look at the history of American Indians in the mid-twentieth century, the story looks strikingly different in film and in federal policy. Film scholars Steve Neale and Joanna Hearne were the first to proclaim this difference and to strategically connect westerns of the midcentury with federal termination policy. Both scholars firmly rejected the idea of Native characters serving as an allegory for other ethnic groups or political issues, and they pointed to direct links between American Indian historical moments and particular moments in films.[9]

In the 1930s, as President Roosevelt laid out the New Deal for the United States, he also introduced an Indian New Deal. The president appointed John Collier as head of the Bureau of Indian Affairs (BIA). Collier instituted a program that closed down the few remaining boarding schools, which had aimed to wipe out American Indian culture and identity, and set out to reverse the federal government's forced assimilation goals of the late nineteenth and early twentieth centuries. His stated goal was the affirmation and reinvigoration of traditional, tribal cultures.

The crowning achievement of the Indian New Deal, at least as Collier saw it, was the Indian Reorganization Act (IRA). The IRA was meant to provide economic and spiritual rehabilitation to Indian communities. Congress passed the IRA in 1934 for all tribes, but the law had to be voted upon by each tribe within one year. Tribal approval was met by a majority vote rather than consensus, and absentee votes counted as affirmative votes. The IRA was an open admission that the assimilationist policy of allotment and the division and privatization of reservation lands had wreaked havoc on tribes. The IRA called for several specific changes, including self-governance, development of reservation resources, training of tribal members for jobs formerly held by non-Indian BIA employees, establishment of scholarship funds for Indian students, and the consolidation of allotted lands. When a tribe accepted the IRA, members also took responsibility for establishing rules for governance and writing a tribal constitution, all of which had to be approved by the secretary of the interior. Many tribal members were deeply concerned about the control held by the federal government over tribes through the IRA, and many tribes (78 in total), including the Diné, Haudenosaunee (other than the Wisconsin Oneida), and Crow Nations therefore rejected the IRA, and others (a total of 174) barely passed the act. The IRA thus failed to achieve many of its goals. Nevertheless, the Indian New Deal produced some dramatic changes in government policy. Tribes who accepted the act regained several million acres of lands that had been lost under the allotment program and moved forward in the areas of education, cultural preservation, and control of their own affairs. As commissioner of Indian affairs, Collier displayed sympathy for Indian culture and recognized the importance of tribal self-determination.

The IRA had been designed to respond to failures in federal tribal policies. Although the legislation was intended to support tribal communities and cultures, Congress instead moved toward tribal termination after the Indian New Deal. Ironically, this shift resulted in part from the tremendous enlistment rates of American Indians in World War II (about twenty-five thousand total). Upon their return, many of these men moved to cities, usually near their reservations, and sought the best wage work they could obtain. They took advantage of employment policies that gave preference to veterans, much like their non-Indian peers did. The federal government interpreted this shift as a clear sign that tribes no longer needed their unique relationship with the federal government. For Congress, termination and urbanization became the next logical step in a plan of what they called total assimilation. For many Natives, this was another move to prevent tribes from functioning autonomously. In this way, termination and urbanization policies bear striking similarities to earlier federal policies based on forced assimilation such as boarding schools and the federal government's history of creating tribal policies without tribal input, control, or influence, such as allotment.

The 1948 election of Harry Truman to the presidency marked the beginning of termination and relocation. At the end of the war, tribes existed in a state of wardship, which members of Congress found too similar to dependency and therefore un-American. During Truman's presidency, the federal government severed its trust relationship with many tribes at the suggestion and direction of Dillon Myer in his role at the BIA, where he landed after serving as head of the War Relocation Authority, which oversaw the internment of Japanese Americans during World War II. Together, Truman and Myer expunged the BIA of all pro-Collier staff and completely revamped the organization. With the election of Dwight Eisenhower to the presidency in 1952, the federal government continued these policies and pursued what they called equality through the elimination of tribal nations as sovereign entities in a dependent relationship with the federal government. For American Indians, what the federal government viewed as integration eliminated legal rights of tribes and thereby severely compromised the very foundations of tribal sovereignty.

In the minds of legislators, federal services to tribes went against postwar ideals of U.S. self-sufficiency. The IRA held a provision for the creation of an Indian Claims Commission, but it had been voted down because of the cost. During the termination era, Congress did establish the Indian Claims Commission (1946–78) to settle all Indian land claims. At the same time, the Hoover Task Force Commission (1948) recommended that tribes become self-sufficient; the goal was for the federal government to terminate all federal services to tribes. A series of bills facilitated termination and assimilation policies, immediately for some tribes and later for others.[10]

In 1953 the House passed H.R. 108, which terminated the Menominee Nation and prepared others for termination. Congress justified this move by arguing that the resolution logically extended the rights of citizenship. That same year Public Law 280 shifted federal trust status to state jurisdiction. The result was that Indian dependency on federal aid decreased, while dependency on state aid increased. In this shift of oversight to state governments, Indian needs went unfulfilled due to insufficient state funds. The federal government erected yet another block to self-determination by setting up relocation offices offering vocational assistance and training that proved largely ineffective.[11]

Legislators considered their plan to be applicable to all tribes. In addition to overriding tribal votes rejecting the legislation, Congress also disregarded cultural, social, and historical differences among tribes. Federal bureaucrats adopted the pious tone of American exceptionalism without considering the internal dynamics and plights of Native America. In applying the logic behind social integration and assimilation for nonwhite groups, Congress had put into motion a plan that could destroy tribal sovereignty, dispossess tribes of their lands, and erode American Indian cultures. As the BIA moved young tribal members into non-Indian communities, the federal government hoped they would no longer identify as American Indian. Legislators hoped the capitalist impulse would replace cultural retention and identity as Indigenous people. Postwar members of Congress hoped that by eliminating tribal governments, American Indians would no longer be American Indians. This version of social integration, termination, and relocation devastated tribal sovereignty and even tribal existence in some cases.[12]

Non-Native Americans lived in ignorance of these changes in federal Indian policy, but they all watched movies. At the movies non-Native Americans saw themselves on the screen. The narrative arcs encouraged them to idolize movie stars, and the greatly improved close-up of the mid-twentieth century allowed viewers to identify even more completely with white protagonists.[13] For some U.S. moviegoers of the 1940s and 1950s, movies were the only place where they saw Indians.

Many historians have addressed the twentieth-century seismic shift of American Indians being relocated from reservations to cities. In 1940 only 5 percent of the total American Indian population lived in cities. By 1950 the number had risen to 20 percent. In 1940 almost half of all Indian males were farmers or farm managers. By 1946 this percentage had been reduced to about 25 percent.[14] By 1960 almost nine thousand American Indians were living in Los Angeles. Although more Indians lived in U.S. cities than ever before, compared to the white population their numbers were small. Those who lived in Los Angeles after the war could afford only the least expensive areas: East Los Angeles, Bell and Bell Gardens, or downtown. In these neighborhoods American Indians lived in communities of poor whites, Mexican Americans, Asian Americans, and African Americans. Because of gentrification, beginning in the 1960s, the American Indian population shot upward outside Los Angeles proper, in cities such as Cerritos, La Mirada, Rolling Hills, City of Industry, and San Marino. Housing remained less expensive in those areas, which made it possible for American Indians to remain in the Los Angeles area. Thus, by the 1970s many Native people were living in and around Los Angeles. Historians such as Nicolas Rosenthal have emphasized both change and continuity for Native people, because many kept their connections to tribal communities. Additionally, Native migration to cities paralleled the immigrant experience but differed substantially in that Native people belong to sovereign nations and thus maintain a legal relationship with the federal government.[15]

Regardless of Indians' increasing urbanization and incorporation into wage economies in the postwar period, from the beginning of the motion picture industry Indians stood at the fore, representing an important part of an American national identity. Thomas Edison was one of the first to create on-screen images of Indians, in films such as *Daniel Boone* (1907), *Pioneer Days* (1907), and *Pocahontas: A Child of the Forest* (1908). D. W. Griffith did much the same with films like *The Call of the Wild* (1908), *The Red Girl* (1908), *The Redman and the Child* (1908), *Comata, the Sioux* (1909), *The Indian Runner's Romance* (1909), *The Mended Lute* (1909), and *The Red Man's View* (1909).[16]

These earliest films visualized nineteenth-century nostalgia for an imagined time that was simple, authentic, and less materialistic. In the American imaginary, nostalgia for a simpler and more authentic past looked to American Indians for assistance in this search. This nostalgia, fraught with ideas about honest emotion, emerged in the late nineteenth century, when Americans collectively imagined a past that existed prior to industrialism and its attendant changes in work, religion, gender, and society. Despite their own direct and indirect involvement in the dispossession and displacement of Native people, non-Natives "remained fascinated by what they regarded as savagism."[17] In fact, they inhabited the contradiction of being fearful of and guilty about Indians, both of which took up residence in their nostalgic recollections of American Indians, especially in film.

Drawing on this tradition of using Indians for their own purposes, mid-century film producers created a false past in which brawn, might, and strength defined relationships among white and American Indian men and posited an idyllic future, free of racial tensions due to Indian consent to their own defeat by whites.[18] Filmic battles between white and Indian men tell the story from the vantage point of the white male protagonist, who conquers Natives through strength and wit.[19] Hollywood used Indians to deny their role in settler colonialism and their fears of Indian retribution through violence.[20]

These films employed visual and verbal cues from the frontier metaphor and its attendant sets of bifurcated and oppositional relationships: wilderness and civilization, the individual and the community, and good and evil.[21] Layered onto these tropes was the persistent motif that Indians derive their meaning solely from their relations with whites. Scholarship on the postwar United States likewise pays undue attention to white heroes and their metaphorical relationship to Cold War policies.[22] Numerous scholars see movies' narrative paradigms as stemming directly from the midcentury political climate of the United States.[23] For these scholars, Indians and other Native people exist in the movies only as metaphors to explain white dilemmas. In other words, the films say nothing about Indians per se.[24] Others see the use of Indians in film, in the 1950s especially, as a cleverly hidden mechanism for discussing civil rights.[25] Even today graduate students writing on Native filmic representations are encouraged to see Indian characters and themes as telling us only about non-Native people in the United States.[26] Yet, as more Native American scholars enter the field of American Indian studies, this path has been replaced by thorough documentation of Native work in the film industry and theories around the relationship between sovereignty and representation.

The work of Joanna Hearne ably demonstrates Native presence in cinema and Native ways of seeing film. For Hearne, film criticism that claims Indians serve as allegories for other historical phenomena "extends popular beliefs that Indian images are public property, and overlooks the Western's manipulation and misrepresentations of specific Native histories, legal rights and relationships to homelands."[27] This is not to deny that American Indian characters act as metaphors for American dilemmas such as foreign policy, the course of American civilization, and relations between African Americans and whites. But to treat Indians only as metaphors is to accept the tenets of nostalgia and narcissism: that Indians are not interesting per se; they are interesting only insofar as they represent something that explains non-Indians to themselves. Film companies meant to transform Indian actors and extras into caricatures of themselves, yet Indians forced filmmakers to encounter them as human beings who were playing roles and earning an income. This book considers the work of Indian actors and extras as a particular means of undermining the erasure of Native people in film.[28]

Films from the post–World War II era reflect more than the Cold War. The challenge for historians is to connect the postwar era with larger issues of the twentieth century and to understand how contemporary non-Native

Americans saw their culture as fundamentally different from that of earlier decades.[29] This study emphasizes movies from different genres whereas other scholarly works focus solely on westerns.[30] Westerns are not the only genre in which Indian characters appear, but in western films Indians enter at the height of narrative tension between internally divided groups of whites. The films sometimes vilify Indians; at other times Indians become highly prized friends of whites.[31] Perhaps most important, in the deluge of studies of westerns there is a lack of attention to comedies that deal with Indian characters; these comedic films tell stories very different from those of classic westerns. Those who wrote comedies seemed to know that representations of Indians reveled in the ridiculous.[32] This chapter looks at four types of films. In my treatment of westerns, I pay close attention to two types: one in which white love triangles are resolved by violence between Indians and whites, and one in which interracial friendship operates as a central theme. This chapter also looks at comedies that serve as satires on what I call the Movie Indian. The final category comprises dramas portraying modern Indians. Studies of westerns and of Indians in movies often focus on a handful of famous films, neglecting the many films made in the postwar era. Using this small number of films as evidence, they cite racist and inaccurate images of Indians. This book weighs the consequences of many films, not just the usual suspects like *The Searchers* or *Broken Arrow*.[33]

Love Triangles: *Valley of the Sun*

Most older Americans probably consider themselves extremely familiar with westerns, despite having viewed only a small number of them. Although the ideas Americans have about westerns are numerous, these notions tend to be repetitive, unchanging, lacking in depth, anecdotally driven, and based on only a few well-known films. For those who actually saw these films in theaters as children and now consider themselves progressive and antiracist, Indians in movies present them with a serious dilemma. They love these films because of what they evoke about their childhood and the American nation, yet they feel guilty for enjoying them. They know these films made mistakes when it came to representing Indians, yet they love them.

Throughout most of the twentieth century westerns remained the primary vehicle for portraying Indians, but they rarely highlighted Native women as key figures. An exception might be the variations on the story of Pocahontas, which were ubiquitous prior to the 1940s and 1950s, as well as representations of white men partnering with Native women. When the Native woman dies, the man can return to a white partner, as pointed out by many scholars, including Philip Deloria, Andrew Brodie Smith, M. Elise Marubbio, and Joanna Hearne.[34] In earlier films and novels the plot devices used in westerns relied on gendered stereotypes of whites and Indians.[35] When westerns of the 1940s and 1950s are reduced to their basic plots, the genre can be seen as a vehicle for a particular nationalism rooted in relationships between white characters. The basic narrative paradigms used in westerns were love triangles and interracial friendships. The two were distinct but not exclusive. Love triangles involving Indian characters are repeatedly interwoven with interracial friendships between white and Indian men. Most often, two white men traveling west just after the Civil War vie for the love of a white woman. The white woman remains unsure of her choice until they encounter hostile Indians, whom the white men fight, demonstrating their bravery and courage. After the white men defeat Natives, the white woman chooses her mate. Thus, Indian characters acted as the glue that held postwar heterosexuality together. In the classic love triangle, violent Indians serve little purpose except as a device for conflict resolution. In other triangles, a Native man who supports white endeavors provides resolution. There are love triangles resolved through white violence or death and even love triangles with Indian cupids. Much more rarely, films center on two Indian men vying for the love of an Indian woman, examples being *The Deerslayer* (1943), *Taza, Son of Cochise* (1954), *Apache* (1954), *Chief Crazy Horse* (1955), and *Apache Warrior* (1957).

When Americans remember films of the 1940s and 1950s, they think of small groups of white men killing huge numbers of Indians, often to protect white women. Yet many westerns also ride on the tension between ethical and unethical whites. Unethical whites usually desire economic control over a town or reservation, and they use underhanded means to gain that control. Ethical whites befriend everyone equally and maintain honesty in their relationships. Ethical whites often wear leather clothing, but unscrupulous whites appear in suits and sometimes even operate illegal black markets as Indian agents. This love triangle repeats itself many times in films such as *The Omaha Trail* (MGM, 1942), *War Arrow* (Universal, 1953), *The Searchers* (Warner Bros., 1956), and *The Unforgiven* (United Artists, 1960). By looking closely at one of these films, *Valley of the Sun* (RKO, 1942), we can unpack the function of Indians in these particular narratives.

In *Valley of the Sun*, Johnny, Jim, and Christine, all of whom are white, constitute the love triangle. Johnny functions as the white character who is friendly with the Apaches, speaks Apache, and is quite close with the Apache leader, Cochise. Jim, Christine's fiancé, is the corrupt Indian agent who steals rations from the Apache Nation. Christine owns and runs a restaurant and is happily anticipating her wedding day with Jim. But on her wedding day the trio is captured by Apaches because of their anger at Jim for withholding rations. Johnny ably negotiates with the Apaches through his friendship with Cochise, but Geronimo, Cochise's opponent, stands against both Johnny and Cochise in wanting to kill Jim and start a war. Johnny and Geronimo perform what are supposed to be traditional competitions to determine a path for the Apache Nation to follow with Jim and the federal government. Johnny easily beats Geronimo in each challenge, thoroughly humiliating Geronimo in front of the entire Apache Nation.[36] By dividing Apache leaders between peaceful and warlike, the film engages a historic plot device going back to the colonial period. Historically, this configuration allowed white male characters to see themselves as heroes pitted against American Indian warmongers fueled by hate. Johnny also engages in these challenges with Geronimo to demonstrate just how useless Jim's tactics of negotiations are in the Apache cultural context. When the trio returns safely to town, Geronimo leads the Apache Nation in an attack. While under siege, Johnny once again forges peace by releasing Cochise from jail. Cochise stops the Apache attack, except Geronimo defies Cochise. Once again Johnny steps forward and beats Geronimo physically. Geronimo skulks away, humiliated once more in front of a crowd of Apache warriors. Once Jim is exposed for his duplicity and greed, peace is restored between settlers and Apaches, and Christine marries Johnny.[37]

Although in these films white men learn Indian ways, especially ways of manliness, the white men repeatedly beat Indian men at Indian masculinity in competition and war. These tests expose the white male characters for who we are supposed to believe truly are: white men with Indian traits and abilities. They demonstrate they are better at being Indian men than Indian men are.[38] In *Valley of the Sun*, Jim struggles to be the hero of a film that begins with a crowd of white men suggesting that all Apaches be killed to make way for "us Americans," but Christine's love turn to rejection when she learns of his theft and lies while witnessing Johnny's strength and determination to protect the Apache Nation. Chris discovers her true feelings in the crucible of white and Apache conflict.

Valley of the Sun is set in the nineteenth century and tries to mimic that era's gender norms, but they line up more accurately with the 1940s. In the love triangles white women's romantic and marriage choices parallel the goals of postwar U.S. society. During World War II white women's sexuality was linked repeatedly to international danger and the need for domestic peace. White American women were encouraged to tie their femininity to the nation's well-being. Further, postwar white men and women felt encouraged to marry and to do so at an early age.[39] In films, the white male characters perform acts appropriated from supposed Indian culture to impress white women with their strength and diplomatic ability to deal with Indians. In the movies, while white women functioned as inferiors, white men commanded dominance and superiority over both Indians and white women. White men acted as a bulwark against the outside forces of warlike Indians as well as corrupt white men. They display their brutal power by fighting Indians and their cultural power through negotiations with Indians during which they easily speak Indian languages and perform Native customs. For the sake of their own protection, these white men are shown to understand Indian culture while killing Indians and keeping white deaths to a minimum.[40] The foundation of their romances with white women illuminates the larger phenomenon of war and postwar white heterosexuality: white women choose men based on their strength and ability to perpetuate violence against others in the movies. Heterosexuality needed violence—even if only an imagined version of an actual past—to create comparisons between men and to give women the information needed to make marriage choices.[41]

In *Valley of the Sun* Indians are constructed as a subordinate force that is easily subdued, restrained, and mastered. Like Christine, the audience learns of the dynamics within tribes through their interactions with whites. Cochise favors peace and allies himself with Johnny, while Geronimo remains at war with white Americans. In the movies, Indians almost never speak to each other. When they do speak to each other, the topic is always whites. What movies like *Valley of the Sun* say, then, is that Indians matter in how they relate to whites, not for what they are, in and of themselves.[42] In this movie and others Apaches exist to bring the white couple together. Can a film that is meant to tell us about whites tell us anything about American Indians? RKO hired Pueblo men and women as background extras for *Valley*. The literal and actual presence of American Indians on the set of *Valley* means the Indian characters we see in the film cannot be reduced to simple metaphor.

Filmmakers could have chosen another group to act as the catalyst for white love, but they chose Indian characters and hired Indian extras.[43] Besides enabling emerging white relationships, Indian characters could also threaten existing romantic relationships and cement emergent ones simply by being present as a potential source of violence. Indians enter the scene and literally threaten a white couple's wedding in *Canyon Passage* (Universal, 1946). On very rare occasions white death was the method used to end a love triangle, as in *The Last Hunt* (MGM, 1956). Sometimes individual Indians who were sympathetic to whites died as part of the resolution of the love triangle. This trope was used in *Seminole* (Universal, 1953) and *Unconquered* (Paramount, 1947). Indian characters also acted as cupids in love triangles. The films that employed this trope were often comedies or satires. For instance, *The Dude Goes West* (Allied Artists, 1948), *Sitting Bull* (United Artists, 1954), and *Annie Get Your Gun* (MGM, 1950) use Indian chiefs to bring white couples together.

The narcissism of the white characters fuels the narratives in love triangles. Non-Indians needed an easily defeated enemy to undergird romance. The narrative paradigms of love triangles proved very flexible because they could contain numerous variations. The ensemble of romance, violence, and narcissism can be found throughout American popular culture and goes back to the nineteenth century, when companionate marriage emerged as an ideal. Because white women's families no longer chose their husbands, white men had to find ways to prove themselves worthy to those they pursued. For white women, their freedom to choose a husband rested on his ability to not only provide but also protect through violence.

White characters possess and inhabit Indian identity by dressing as Indians to fool both Indians and whites. They mime Indians in dress, language, worldview, and especially interracial friendship. Through what Michelle Raheja calls "redfacing," white men bond with Indian men as friends through their imitation of Indians. Interracial friendships present us with a filmic reality in which whites and Indians are fundamentally similar within Indian culture and Indian identity is easily replicated and imitated by whites. Yet the films teach us nonetheless about the seeming intransigence of a belief in race in that whites remain separate from Indians politically and socially and continue to live with, identify with, and relate to Indians as superior conquerors, regardless of their "redfacing."

Interracial Friendship: *Hudson's Bay*

Films like *Pinky* (Twentieth Century Fox, 1947) made headlines for breaking down the walls of racial segregation between whites and African Americans. But films about Indians and whites generated the same kind of antiracist logic in the same time period. For movies with Native characters, writers often relied on a simple theme: a white man and an Indian man who were childhood friends reencounter each other as adults in the middle of a major dispute between Indians and whites. The old friends rekindle their interracial friendship, drawing on the innocence of childhood, which they later see as naïve in the context of adult realities. Examples of this come from *Arrowhead* (Paramount, 1953) and *Seminole* (1953).[44] In these friendship films, morals define people, not ethnicity, tribe, nation, or race. Moral and peaceful whites have more in common with like-minded Indians than they do with immoral whites.[45]

These films also emphasized multiethnic patriotism and military service, often through friendship.[46] Those who had been formerly excluded from

American life were suddenly included because all Americans were needed to win the war.[47] After the war, when the production of westerns increased tremendously, so too did the interracial friendship theme.[48] Filmmakers began earnestly and eagerly seeking out Indians in hopes of creating authentic images that television producers were unable to create. Just as lawmakers sought total assimilation for Indians, so too did filmmakers create Indians who were meant to seem not so different from whites. The story of Cochise, the Apache leader who fought against settler colonialism for more than a decade, was created repeatedly on the screen in the 1940s and 1950s, with Cochise depicted as a Native who could be admired by whites.[49] For white characters the boundaries separating whites from each other have to do with the law: those working within the law and those working outside the law when it came to tribes. White male characters changed tremendously during and after World War II: ethical white men sympathized with Indians, spoke Indian languages, had Indian friends, and grew up with Indians. Unethical white men took advantage of Indians, hated Indians, and killed Indians. Conversely, Indians who were fighting against the American empire were cast as unethical and doomed to failure.

Among those presented as Indians willing to be subservient to whites, behaviors like cooperation, friendship, and peace with nearby whites are dominant. These filmic Indians submit to settler colonialism and refrain from violence. They hold values similar to those of the settler colonists in the films. Both seek to protect the people they lead in the most ethical ways possible. Both stand against those who act unethically, regardless of their ethnicity. Unethical Indians are represented as irrational, angry, and interested in division rather than unity. Some Indians may gain American acceptance, but only at the cost of pushing all other Indians into a space where any and all violence against them is necessary, and the reasons behind the violence remain unexplored and muted.[50]

The vast majority of filmic interracial friendships are between men. Between the years of 1941 and 1960, only one example of a white male/ Indian female friendship exists, and there are no depictions of Indian female/ Indian female friendships. The white male/Indian male friendship theme can be found in films such as *Hudson's Bay* (Twentieth Century Fox, 1941),

They Died with Their Boots On (Warner Brothers, 1941), *Valley of the Sun* (RKO, 1942), *The Lawless Plainsmen* (Columbia, 1942), *Romance of the West* (PRC, 1946), *Black Gold* (Allied Artists, 1947), *The Last Round-Up* (Columbia, 1947), *The Cowboy and the Indians* (Columbia, 1949), *Indian Agent* (RKO, 1948), *She Wore a Yellow Ribbon* (RKO, 1949), *Broken Arrow* (Twentieth Century Fox, 1950), *The Battle at Apache Pass* (Universal, 1952), *Saskatchewan* (Universal, 1954), and *The Lone Ranger* (Warner Bros., 1956).

Hudson's Bay goes back to the seventeenth-century world of the international fur trade to demonstrate the power of friendship between a Frenchman, an Englishman, and an Indian man. Over the course of the film, friendship and loyalty are tested and the friendship between the Indian and the Frenchman remains intact. Playing the main Native character, Orimha, was Victor Daniels, known professionally as Chief Thundercloud, who claimed an American Indian identity and was accepted by Hollywood as an American Indian.[51] Daniels's part, although significant, is dwarfed in screen time by the European characters. The somewhat true story centers on the life of Pierre Esprit Radisson (1636–1710). The actual Radisson indirectly founded the Hudson's Bay Company, which shifted allegiances repeatedly over his lifetime. The movie Pierre does much the same, but he never wavers in his concern for and loyalty to his Algonquin friend, Orimha. As the movie opens, Pierre and his friend Gooseberry have been imprisoned by the New York governor, and it is in prison where they meet Edward, a convict who is a former English lord. Edward needs money to make a life for his fiancée, and Pierre strikes a bargain with Edward whereby they will travel to Hudson's Bay to enter the fur trade. After their escape, the men travel to Montréal, where they meet up with Orimha, the Algonquin man who had adopted Edward years earlier because of the bravery he demonstrated while being tortured by Haudenosaunee.

Acting on the strength and vitality of his friendship with Pierre, Orimha quickly befriends Edward because any friend of Pierre is a friend of Orimha. Upon acquiring a vast supply of furs, the men set out to sell their goods, but the New York governor steals their merchandise in lieu of payment on their fines and taxes, and the men are again imprisoned. When the entourage arrives in Albany, French agents arrest them. Orimha and other

Algonquins provide for Pierre and Edward's escape and take back the furs. Outraged, Pierre and Edward travel to England, where they implore the king to claim Hudson Bay for England. The king agrees, but Pierre disagrees vehemently with the English over the method of negotiating with Algonquins and other Indian nations. Pierre wishes to treat them with respect, always keeping in mind the goal of peace. But the English want only to acquire wealth, regardless of the social and political cost to Indian empires. Together Pierre and Edward claim Hudson Bay for England, where they establish the Hudson's Bay Company.

Earlier in the film, Orimha proves his loyalty to Pierre, and during the second voyage to Hudson Bay, Pierre demonstrates his loyalty to Orimha in return. Edward's future brother-in-law, Gerald, joins the men but hates life in New France. He refuses to join Edward during their trapping expedition and instead remains at Fort Charles during the winter. While there, he deliberately disobeys Pierre's prohibition against selling liquor to Indians. The Algonquins kill the neighboring Hurons to acquire enough furs to satisfy their demand for liquor. Gerald kills an Indian man who demands more liquor, and Orimha demands Gerald's life in return for peace. Pierre shoots Gerald himself to continue his friendship with Orimha. After their return to England, Pierre is arrested but quickly released after he convinces the king of England that if he is kept in prison, Orimha and the other Indians will begin trading exclusively with the French. Again, due to English greed, Pierre's desires are fulfilled.

Throughout the film Pierre is portrayed as a man straddling two cultures, French and Indian. Perhaps the screenwriters generated this viewpoint from their historical reading. Some historians of the French fur trade would agree with this particular aspect of *Hudson's Bay*. The French, in both the film and in history, being neither English nor American, presented a unique way of negotiating with Indian empires. Pierre, much like the French engaged in the fur trade, ably mediates with Indians and non-Indians alike, relying on his friendship with Orimha in particular, as well as his understanding of Indigenous people (having been raised by Algonquins) to attain as much as he can in both cultures. Perhaps more important, Indians in *Hudson's Bay* represent a world in which their loyalty is absolute and based on their preference for the French as trading partners. Orimha never wavers in his devotion to Pierre, Pierre's economic goals, and Pierre's partnerships. Orimha kills other Indians on behalf of Pierre, demonstrating time and again the idea that friendship can override loyalty to one's tribe or other Indians. This representation of the fur trade places the story on the terrain of individual choices and pushes the conversation away from settler colonialism, exploitation, and genocide and toward individual and private decisions of individuals whose national identity became irrelevant through intercultural friendship.

In the world of film, Indians and whites benefited from their relationships with each other. Filmic friendships articulate and embody the post–World War II triumph over scientific racism and the moves toward social integration. In emphasizing the interracial aspect of these friendships, filmmakers exaggerated racial difference by employing the stereotyped language, dress, and behavior of Indian characters. In emphasizing the differences between Indians and whites, the filmmakers pushed nationality and ethnicity to the fore while establishing character arcs based on loyalty and friendship.

Perhaps filmmakers faced a near impossibility in their hopes of representing equality. Creating equality alongside difference remained a challenge in American society and in film. World War II's effects were many, and one of them included a recognition that the United States was steeped in inequality in spite of fighting against fascism abroad. Americans slowly moved away from segregation after World War II, mainly in the military and public education. Yet these changes were stopped short by racial canons that conflated skin color with race, race with social standing, white skin with superiority, and dark skin with inferiority and submission. On film, interracial friendship became a way of portraying racial harmony and interracial friendship at a time when many white Americans rejected close contact with nonwhites.

Comedies: Ride 'Em Cowboy

Despite being overlooked by film critics and historians, several films of the 1940s and 1950s opted to problematize stereotypes of American Indians. These films held up racial tropes for ridicule and satire. In comedies, artifice is purposefully exaggerated and satirized. These comedies are also an entirely new phenomenon. In the war and postwar periods comedy became a means of commenting not only on the superficiality of Indian identity when based on phenotype and dress but also about white fears of Indians and Indian culture. Comedies explored a certain self-consciousness about representation itself. The vast majority of films representing Indians in the 1940s and 1950s use formulas involving white heroes, love triangles, and interracial friendship. However, a small but important number of comedies appeared, including *Ride 'Em Cowboy* (Universal, 1942), *Girl Crazy* (MGM, 1943), *The Paleface* (Paramount, 1948), *Annie Get Your Gun* (MGM, 1950), *The Senator Was Indiscreet* (Universal, 1947), *Bowery Buckaroos* (Monogram, 1947), *Ma and Pa Kettle* (Universal, 1949), and *The Sheriff of Fractured Jaw* (Twentieth Century Fox, 1958). A few of these films were well known, and they influence our understandings of Indians in film.[52]

On a cultural level these comedies converse with westerns. The Indians in comedies are portrayed as modern characters, satirizing Indian stereotypes. The Abbott and Costello film *Ride 'Em Cowboy* perfectly demonstrates this sort of play. The name of the lead Indian character, Jake Rainwater, in and of itself embodies the idea that Native people only have surnames related to nature. With a satirical name as his starting point, Rainwater takes up work selling Indian trinkets at a train station. He embodies several Native stereotypes.[53]

Rainwater meets Duke (Abbott) and Willoughby (Costello) at the Gower Gulch depot, where he has a small tourist shop.[54] When tourists arrive, Rainwater covers his dress shirt and pants with buckskin clothing, hides his book and reading glasses, and covers his short hair with a long, black, braided wig. In doing so, Rainwater exposes his dissemblance and divided identity, a dissemblance meant to be hidden from whites. He strategically replaces his daily look with a façade of Indian identity. He knows he cannot be seen with short hair, glasses, and non-Indian clothing if he wants to earn a living selling Indian culture. Rainwater embraces his participation in the tourist industry immediately, and this scene sets the tone for his movement back and forth from modern Indian to Indian caricature. This early scene pokes fun at the limited representations of Indians and at the ways Indians knowingly use those representations for their own ends.[55] This scene also shows the Indian perspective on the intercultural exchanges taking place at tourist destinations: Indians must don an expected, stereotypical, false identity to earn cash from tourists. When Willoughby arrives at Rainwater's store, he casually shoots an arrow he finds on display in the store, which happens to pierce the tipi of Rainwater's daughter, Moonbeam. Based on a fabricated yet ancient tradition, Rainwater insists that because the arrow landed in her tipi, Duke must marry her. Duke feels no attraction to her, only repulsion based on her appearance. He spends the rest of the film trying to escape from Rainwater and Moonbeam.[56]

Indians stalk Willoughby in reality and in his imagination as he dodges Rainwater and Moonbeam. In response to Willoughby's hysteria over Rainwater, the ranch workers fool him by placing an exact replica of Rainwater on his bed. Just as Rainwater copies an imagined Indian, so too does the effigy mimic Rainwater's Indian look.[57] Willoughby becomes hysterical when he sees the effigy but talks himself into believing the effigy is fake and not a threat. As he recovers outside, the actual Rainwater replaces the fake Rainwater with himself, which further heightens the sense of fakery and copying. Willoughby reenters, believing Rainwater is the effigy. Willoughby air punches Rainwater, and Rainwater does not flinch. Willoughby turns his back to Rainwater to hang his hat while he looks at himself in the mirror, and Rainwater throws a knife, impaling the hat on the wall. They stare at one another in the mirror, Willoughby's back to Rainwater. Willoughby touches the image of Rainwater in the mirror, trying to discover whether the image is real, yet he does not reach out to the object itself. When Duke accosts Rainwater, Rainwater does not reply in any way, thus allowing Willoughby to regain his calm.

With a sense of bravado, Willoughby tests Rainwater again, and Rainwater replies in kind. When Willoughby squirts water in Rainwater's face, Rainwater spits it back. Rainwater slips his knife from his right hand to his left hand and back again. Willoughby asks Rainwater if he moved, fully expecting no reply, but Rainwater answers with a lie: "No." As Willoughby looks at Rainwater's image in the mirror, Rainwater throws a knife, which lands near Willoughby. While Willoughby runs out to get

Duke, Rainwater puts the fake Indian back on the bed and races out of the cabin. Duke treats Willoughby as though he is paranoid when he proves the effigy is fake.

This sequence highlights the disconnect between actual Indians and the simulacra provided by films. But even as it pays homage to the simulacra, *Ride 'Em Cowboy* embodies Indian survivance in Rainwater's disruption of the simulacrum of himself. The Indian effigy affects Willoughby more powerfully than the real Rainwater, just as Hollywood's representations of Indians are more real to Americans than are actual Indians. The real Rainwater appropriates the artificiality of the effigy just as Native people have used representations of themselves for their own ends as workers in the performance industry. Rainwater's method works in opposing directions: he uses silence to mimic the effigy, consenting to being replaced with a simulation, but he also speaks and acts against the effigy, challenging the very idea that he can be silenced and erased. Rainwater's speech and affect underscore American Indian survivance and strategies for thriving in the American empire.[58]

Rainwater and Moonbeam haunt Willoughby by day, but during the night Indian people in general stalk his mind. In the dream sequence, *Ride 'Em Cowboy* suggests that what non-Indians believe about Indians retains more power than actual Indians.[59] The sequence begins when Willoughby enters Ha Ha Sanitarium, a name that perhaps is an allusion to Minnehaha, a character in the famous poem "The Song of Hiawatha" (1855) but also a reference to laughter. Willoughby seeks medical help because of insomnia caused by his paranoia about Indians. Yet the hospital staff are all Indians. Some pretend to be white but are in fact Indian. The doctor who appears to be white becomes an Indian when his two black braids fall out from under his medical cap and a single feather pops up. The nurses also are revealed to be Indian, and when Willoughby finally falls asleep, he has several dreams, all involving Indians: Moonbeam waters him as if he were a bed of roses; a swami, possibly referencing another type of Indian, reads his palm by painting it red; Custer loses to Sitting Bull and falls dead at the feet of Willoughby. When Willoughby awakes, Duke tries to prove to him that he is safe from Indian threats. But when Willoughby opens the closet door, he sees Rainwater standing inside, slowly raising his arms straight out from his torso as though he were a ghost, again highlighting Indian survivance even if limited to a closet. Rainwater disrupts Willoughby's fantasy but in fact reinforces it, as Willoughby cannot distinguish between actual Indians and imagined Indians. This configuration mimics the larger filmic reality of non-Indian beliefs about Indians in that films often transposed their beliefs about Indians onto actual Indians, attempting to eliminate Indian people from that constitutional loop. The power of this lies in its demonstration that non-Indian beliefs about Indians come from movies, not from Indians. Just as Indigenous artists today challenge this imagery, so too did Rainwater inhabit and push back against the very representation of himself as constructed by Willoughby.

Still later in the film Rainwater is on horseback as he chases Duke and Willoughby as they try to escape by car. Rainwater loses sight of the duo temporarily, but he sneaks up behind Willoughby and stands silently. The chase begins once more and ends with Rainwater being fooled into believing that Willoughby has accepted his fate with Moonbeam when, in fact, Willoughby's male sidekick is dressed as Moonbeam.[60] Again, the power of the image of the Indian is inescapable, all-consuming, and entirely resistant to change. Yet Rainwater himself is an actual Indian who, even as he inhabits a representation of himself, refuses to forfeit the struggle to define himself and challenge Willoughby's assumptions about him and all Indian people.

Ride 'Em Cowboy works as the inverse of the classic western. In comedy, repressed fears surface. Indians represent a haunting presence to whites in this film in particular. But the film also presents that classic sense of male bravado and superiority toward Indians. The sense of haunting continues throughout the rest of the film, with Indians appearing everywhere, even in Willoughby's dreams. He feels their presence when he is working at the ranch and even when he performs in the rodeo parade. Instead of portraying Indian violence, *Ride 'Em Cowboy* depicts the fear of Indian violence and the projection of a violent nature onto Indians. Because of his imposing, terrifying, and violent nature, as imagined by Willoughby, Rainwater's character bears striking similarities to the violent nature of the Indian characters of the westerns.

Ride 'Em Cowboy speaks to another odd fear: that of violating an unknown cultural taboo, or making a cultural mistake that results in serious consequences. For testing a bow and arrow in a store, Willoughby is forced to marry a woman. This aspect of the film underscores the sense that Rainwater operates according to values that are esoteric and random. *Ride 'Em Cowboy* presents forced marriage as a timeless Indian tradition. This sets up several competing tensions: one between Willoughby and Rainwater in Rainwater's insistence that a white man, Willoughby, marry his Indian sister, Moonbeam; and one resulting from division within Rainwater, who is a twentieth-century Indian man with glasses, Oxford shirt, and reading material and who also wishes to unite an Indian woman and a white man in marriage due to a fabricated custom.

The film sets out to resolve tensions by highlighting and exaggerating them, thereby rendering them comedic. Buried in comedies lie serious messages and important insights that other films consciously explore and often fail to deliver. *Ride 'Em Cowboy* ridicules whites' projections of Indians and also shows the convoluted inner world of the brave white man: madness, paranoia, projection, and neurosis.[61] *Ride 'Em Cowboy* ably exploits the vast comedic value lying untapped in images of American Indians, especially those taken up by Indians themselves. Comedies with Indian characters situate the narrative firmly on stereotypes, thereby suggesting their overwhelming influence and power. They highlight, distort, magnify, and satirize the customary behaviors of Indian characters. Perhaps this stereotyping normalizes behaviors and looks, but such films undoubtedly force the viewer to confront this stereotyping rather than expect it. These comedies do not necessarily change the material world, but they render concrete the normalized visions of Native people. Unlike the film dramas of the 1940s and 1950s, they do not pretend to move beyond the world of race, racism, and cultural misunderstanding. These films instead revel in the kaleidoscopic nature of representation and create the possibility of something new and different.

Intending to be funny, these comedies are in fact quite serious. Not only do they satirize representations of Indians, they ultimately question the entire American fantasy of Indians. Although comedies recognize difference, they also ask us to question the depth of those differences. In these movies white characters openly fear Indians, not just as a physical threat but a mental one. The comedies place white characters in tremendous tension with their imagined Indian through Indian characters who challenge and ridicule the fantasy through speech, dress, and bodily performance. Comedies succeeded where liberal critiques of race failed. In attempting to go beyond race, liberal critiques reified race by subscribing to base notions of racial difference, whereas comedies admitted to racism and used it to explore entirely new narrative paradigms.

Modern Indians: *Black Gold*

Few midcentury films with Indian characters were set in the twentieth century. The vast majority of films from the 1940s and 1950s represented nineteenth-century Indians. However, a handful of important films explore the dilemmas faced by twentieth-century American Indians in changing economies, gender roles, and ethnic identities. These films include *Black Gold* (Allied Artists, 1947), *Tulsa* (Eagle-Lion–Wanger, 1949), *Jim Thorpe, All American* (Warner Bros., 1951), *Battle Cry* (Warner Bros., 1955), and *To Hell and Back* (Universal, 1955).

The film *Black Gold* portrays a modern Indian couple struggling with their economic future, their adopted son's education, their own differing levels of education, and racism. They work as farmers and later in horseracing and oil drilling. Although the film depicts Indian-white conflict, the conflict functions as a backdrop to the real story of the relationship between a husband and wife and the personal, interior battles of a twentieth-century Indian man. This makes *Black Gold* fundamentally different from other films of the 1940s and 1950s that had Indian characters. The film is steeped in twentieth-century dilemmas and the foil of a simpler, self-sufficient, Indian life. The couple in *Black Gold*, Charley Eagle and his wife, Sarah Eagle, are portrayed as opposite but kindred spirits. As Charley puts it in his broken English, Sarah is "educated, taught in reservation school. Charley just plain Indian, know only to hunt, fish, ride horse." Sarah wishes Charley would stay home with her at all times, but Charley can live indoors only part time: "Old ways speak to me. I have to go then. Walls get too close. Must have stars, night wind."

The couple adopts Davey, a Chinese orphan. Although Sarah believes Davey should attend public school, Charley prefers to teach Davey hunting skills and tell him stories about his Indian parents and grandparents. Charley loves horses, and when he gains $1 million for selling his land, he buys the best horse he can find. When the new owners begin drilling for oil, he feels tremendous guilt for betraying the land and his ancestors. The story seems to draw on the history of the Osage Nation, but *Black Gold* never mentions it or any other tribal nation. Charley lives in mental anguish over his former land being drilled, thinking aloud, "They dig up holes. Put up derricks. Make land ugly. Land Charley love all his life." This realization begins Charley's descent into despair. When the oil derrick strikes oil, he is maimed by a flying piece of wood, which makes him wonder whether he is receiving divine retribution for selling his land.[62] Still later, he suffers a heart attack at the racetrack, again suggesting that Charley has transgressed his Indian upbringing and received punishment for having done so.

These moments heighten Charley's inner tensions. Having betrayed his tribal values, Charley's inner conflict expresses itself in his downcast demeanor. His clothing indicates his place in the twentieth century (jeans and flannels and sometimes suits), yet his inner self is obviously at odds with his appearance: uneducated, unassuming, naïve, and suspicious of whites. When he and Sarah host an elegant party, Charley wears a tuxedo, yet he refuses an invitation to meet the state senator. Upon seeing the maid, however, he talks easily with her and remains in a conversation with her away from the party. When a couple at the party announce their engagement, Charley stands away from the crowd, partially concealed by a curtain. After these episodes, Charley leaves their home, and Sarah and Davey find him asleep in front of a small fire. On his deathbed he asks Davey to win the Kentucky Derby and to stand proudly beside Sarah when accepting the cup, "proud like Indian." He then kisses Sarah and dies.

Unlike most films representing Native Americans, *Black Gold* brings Indians to the forefront and whites stand in the background. The nineteenth century is virtually absent. Yet the film becomes predictable in its narrative closure of the vanishing and tragic Indian. *Black Gold* falls into line with the many films in which Indian men die, physically separate themselves from whites, or are brought into white society through submission to white dominance. In *Black Gold*, Charley maintains balance and lacks tension when he lives apart from white society and values whereas other Indian characters live in a state of perpetual violence with whites. In the film's opening sequences Charley is comfortable with his self-sufficient farm, his ability to live outdoors for indefinite periods of time, and his hunting abilities. He views these activities as inherently Indian and perhaps inherently male. These activities constitute Charley's personal essence, his truest self.

Charley moves from this comfortable position into an identity rife with division and difficulties. Because of his desire for a racehorse, he sells the land he loves. The racehorse becomes the means by which Charley succeeds in white society, yet that success precipitates his downfall as an Indian. His heart attack occurs at the racetrack. When he realizes death is near, he grasps at what is left of his tribal identity and dies outdoors near the warmth of a fire. Because the film ends with Charley's death rather than a renewal and a return to his life prior to selling his land, the film suggests that Indian men are fundamentally opposed to modernity and even capitalism. The values and ways of living that once sustained Charley prove entirely ineffective once he has been exposed to wealth, parties, and racetracks. Where Rainwater's character fundamentally challenges white fantasies of Indians, Charley reinforces the notion in his fundamental opposition to modern life, culture, and economics, all because he is an Indian man. In terms of Charley's physical appearance, he wears his hair short and his apparel consists of a long-sleeved shirt and jeans. His face is constantly sweaty, and he appears nervous. He avoids eye contact with whites and comes across as bashful and awkward. His confidence returns only when he hunts, speaks to another dark-skinned person, or spends time with his wife and son. Whereas Charley lacks comfort, Sarah appears at ease. Her demeanor remains the same regardless of context. In other words, Sarah and Charley represent the polar opposites of assimilated and unassimilated.

Settler colonialism denies the existence and survival of twentieth-century American Indians. From a sense of guilt, non-Indians have recognized their ancestors' duplicity in manipulating American Indians, yet screenwriters often relegated that duplicity to the nineteenth century. These films apologize for wrongs involving peaceful Indians and serve as memorials to nostalgia and narcissism, but they do not apologize to violent or angry Indians and never for actions taken in U.S. history. We see this same phenomenon when racism toward Indians flares in land conflicts between whites and Indians today, usually in reaction to Native people asserting their treaty rights.

Just as the character of Charley in *Black Gold* is portrayed as being fundamentally opposed to modern life, Indians in most films are relegated to distant and remote tribal lands or reservations in the nineteenth century and rarely do they appear in the modern world in films. In the mid-twentieth century Congress alone seemed aware of the existence of Indians outside of the movies, as it marked tribes for termination. In its view, any existing tribe no longer needed its sovereign relationship with the U.S. government. Just like in the movies, Congress viewed twentieth-century tribes as oxymoronic.

Conclusion

Many scholarly studies have described the ubiquitous stereotyping, universalizing, and demonizing of Indians in films. Although this negative aspect of filmmaking is undeniable, the comedies, dramas, and friendship films serve as foils to our understanding of representations of Indians in postwar movies. These less well known films manifest considerable variety, a complexity that begs to be understood. In the production process filmmakers certainly created Indian characters who looked and spoke similarly, but the narratives themselves demonstrated a tremendous diversity. Interracial friendships coexisted with racist, dehumanizing images of Indians, perhaps serving as an alternative for filmgoers. The comedies and modern-day dramas presented a direct challenge to classic westerns in which Indians merely acted as a physical threat.

Indians exist in an overall film narrative that says conflicts with Indians must be placed in the past. Filmmakers did not create these narrative constraints, because they go all the way back to the first moments of contact in North America between the English and Native people, on the northeastern coast in particular. In a sense these constraints prevent contemporary artists from creating films about twentieth-century Indians.[63] But Indians survived settler colonialism and continue to live and thrive today. Indians carry out their lives in all sorts of ways, but most midcentury movies fail to represent those realities.[64] Today the constraints have been subverted to some extent because of the intervention of Indian artists and those sympathetic to their insights. All artists depicting Indians work within this national conversation about Indians, describing, speaking back, upturning, satirizing, and parodying but also engaging with those constraints and past representations.

A turn to history takes us deeper into these dilemmas rather than out of them. The ways in which professional historians frame conflicts between Indians and whites often run parallel to Hollywood's scripts. Written history represents the past as much as filmed history does. How historians and filmmakers frame the past matters. Historians' adjectives and verb choices perform the same work as filmmakers' use of silence, monologues, speech, and dress.[65]

Twentieth-century Americans remained fascinated with nineteenth-century Indians.[66] Moreover, postwar whites followed a long tradition in using Indians to understand themselves. In searching for an identity that made sense in the war and postwar milieu, they turned to Indians to tell themselves they were smarter than Indians, yet sympathetic toward them, and that they hated Indians, yet needed and admired them. Indians provided whites an opportunity to create cultural and ideological artifacts and to capture and replicate them in a history and identity of their own. But some films went beyond this. Crudely and haltingly, they began to examine what it meant to be Indian in twentieth-century America. More successfully, they examined, satirized, and ridiculed white fears, guilt, and even the artificiality of the white-created Indian.

To consider the films alone is insufficient for an analysis of Indians in movies. The films' narratives ultimately are only a small part of the picture, even though I chose to begin the book with narrative analysis. The literature on films including Indian characters emphasizes the metaphorical aspects, but even the Indian characters who simply rode horses, shot arrows, and exited effectively propelled the narrative forward. Their actions and their presence added essential elements to the films, and studios sought Indians to play Indians in their movies. In the following chapters I explore film production, considering actors' and extras' labor on the film sets where these films were produced. Although many scholars have critiqued the over-abundance of whites playing Indians in the movies, I found a tremendous diversity of actors and extras, including Indians who lived in Los Angeles and on reservations throughout the West, not just in the United States but in Canada and Mexico as well. Just as Indian characters could be used to achieve certain effects in the films' narratives, Indian actors and extras were actively recruited and hired for the films of the 1940s and 1950s. Having Indians play Indians meant something to filmmakers, and they traveled far and wide to find them, employ them, and capture their images on film, albeit well behind the white men who stood in the foreground.

2

"Indians Agree to Perform and Act as Directed"

Urban Indian (and Non-Indian) Actors

It concerns me, however, when we fail to provide the context that makes our survival one of the greatest untold stories. Americans—and most of the world—seem somehow stubbornly unaware of what Indigenous peoples on this continent actually faced. Telling the full story of the Native American holocaust proves a testament not to Native victimhood but to Native skill, adaptability, courage, tenacity, and countless other qualities . . . that made our survival a reality against all odds.
—Amy Lonetree, *Decolonizing Museums*

Movies offer us an imaginary world, one that for a moment is complete in itself. Films are produced in social settings, however, and moviegoers devour details about the private lives of actors. When American Indians were a part of that backdrop of fan interest in the 1940s and 1950s, Americans displayed an equal hunger, expecting Indians to give them an imaginary alternative to the postwar milieu of capitalism and consumerism.[1] Yet films are more than imaginary worlds. People who work in movies do so for money. The public is less interested in this aspect of film production, but this chapter looks closely at the labor of those in the films.[2] Movies tell stories that have nothing to do with the people in them or how those films were produced. Movies constitute an artificial reality, and all filmic framing excludes the many hands involved in its creation. Hollywood never publicized information about those who cooked and cleaned or moved heavy equipment. Cinema's glamour stems from its seeming disconnection from the mundane. Films did not emerge fully formed from the minds of writers. Men and women worked on film sets to create the images writers imagined. Despite the ways labor and film intertwine with each other, audiences tend to separate the two. Cinema seeks to conceal "the very techniques used to achieve it and the de-realization of the economic transaction."[3] Yet pulling the curtain back allows us to explore the question of who worked in these films and under what conditions. We can also trace the career trajectories of several Indian and non-Indian actors. Both Indians and non-Indians worked for the studios that produced the films, both Indians and non-Indians viewed them, but the highest levels of economic success remained the terrain of non-Indians.[4]

Studio heads and employees saw actors, both Indian and non-Indian, and reservation Indians as entirely distinct, separate groups. Studios paid actors according to union agreements and individual contracts, and the actors were relatively well paid. From the studio perspective, Indians were people living on reservations who did not possess the skills or experience of actors; they worked strictly as extras. Thus, studios considered the very idea of Indians acting as contradictory. Filmmakers thought reservation Indians were Indian by virtue of their physicality and their proximity to a reservation. They did not need to act Indian: they had to *be* Indian.[5] A midcentury Indian, for them, laid claim to a powerful physicality that exuded Indian identity. But perhaps more important, these reservation Indians could also evoke the mythic nineteenth-century past for the studios. Reservation Indians with a certain look could provide a shortcut to Indian presence, a powerful visual cue that these were not just Indians on the screen but also Indians with a direct connection to the past.

Indian actors did of course work in Hollywood, and they certainly acted. In fact, Indian actors worked tirelessly to present themselves as *actors*. Some trained in drama schools. They worked in all sorts of entertainment venues. They struggled to be paid on the same scales as other trained actors and to publicize their availability for film work. But filmmakers categorized Indian actors in fundamentally different ways than they did reservation Indians. Hollywood tended to value the Indian identity of Indian actors over their identity as actors. These boundaries between urban Indian actors and reservation Indians were largely artificial, and because of that artificiality, Indian actors tirelessly strove to promote their talent. Sadly, their acting talent was often wasted in one-dimensional Indian roles.

In this chapter I look at the labor of the Indian actors who played Indians, especially those actors who lived in Southern California, most of whom were Screen Actors Guild (SAG) members. These explorations highlight the labor of American Indians in war and postwar film production by considering union categories and hierarchies. Finally, this chapter shows how the filmic construct of Native people shifted labor relations toward hiring unskilled, nonunion workers. Indian men are overrepresented in these films, which meant very few Indian women were hired for film work in the 1940s and 1950s. Although actors have always earned more than extras, when Native people entered this hierarchy, the effects became blurred, as Indians tended to be lumped together because of their identity as Indians. As Native people were usually pushed into Native roles, often with one-dimensional and limited character development, their exposure, pay, and economic security remained low. By contrast, white actors, male and female, benefited from expanded economic opportunities and were hired to play characters of any race or ethnicity.[6] For Indian actors of the 1940s and 1950s, only a handful reached the middle range in the acting hierarchy, and most eked out a living with sporadic acting at the lower levels.[7]

Early Indian Actors

Native American actors functioned as part of the war and postwar American capitalist economy. However, because Indians acquired little power in the new industrial economy, they had little or no control over the images created in movies, some of which had a cartoon-like quality. The involvement of Native people in the popular culture industry stretches back at least to the Wild West shows and into the 1910s and 1920s.[8] In 1926 several Native people working in the movie industry formed the War Paint Club to protect

Indians from being exploited by the film industry. They promoted hiring Indians for Indian parts by serving as a registry and employment agency for actors.[9] By 1935 this group had expanded and re-created itself as the Indian Actors Association. Eight men acted as officers and directors, and nineteen women formed the Ladies' Auxiliary Indian Actors Association. The group comprised Indians from a wide range of tribes, and many used Indian names (not translated into English).[10] The members considered themselves actors and Indians, and they actively promoted their talents.

Thomas Ince, one of the first producers and founders of the studio system, created Inceville in the Santa Monica Mountains in the 1920s. One of the actors who worked for Ince, Ann Little, recalled the many Lakotas from South Dakota who lived in the hills and had previously worked in the Wild West shows. Little came fairly close to ridiculing their labor in claiming that they worked to save up what she called "trinkets" to take home to their families. But read another way, her comments acknowledge how little these workers earned.[11] Other actors from the early twentieth century include the Penobscot entertainer Molly Spotted Elk. She worked as a performer in all sorts of venues, including several films, in the 1930s and 1940s. She starred in *The Silent Enemy* (1929), *Ramona* (1936), *Lost Horizon* (1937), and *Last of the Mohicans* (1936). Her sister, Apid Elk (Winnifred Nelson), had a minor role in *The Silent Enemy* and several Hollywood movies of the 1940s.[12] Cherokee performer Will Rogers starred in sixty-eight films, most of which were in the silent period and several of which were directed by John Ford. Rogers identified as Cherokee and American Indian and made regular visits to Oklahoma, but he also made derogatory comments about Indians, especially Osages, and never reached out to other American Indian actors in Los Angeles. His on-screen roles were not identifiably American Indian, and he has been left out of the scholarship on Natives in film. As Amy Ware has written of Rogers's film career, "simply because Rogers did not perform Indianness on screen does not mean he wasn't working as an Indian in the film industry."[13]

Indian actors in the postwar period worked in the larger historical context of organized labor in the film industry. In the very early years of filmmaking, however, Hollywood laborers worked outside of any organized system.

Organized labor made its first move in 1926, signing its first contract, the Studio Basic Agreement of 1926. The establishment of the Academy of Motion Picture Arts and Sciences in 1927 quickly followed the agreement. The organization had five branches of specialization. It was not a union, but its powers ran deep, as it was in the control of a hand-picked and powerful few. Until the 1930s only craft workers in the film industry were truly organized, and even then organizers and workers fought constantly over categorization; where carpentry ended and set decoration began became difficult to pinpoint.[14] After the craft workers, the exhibition workers followed suit with their own union.[15] Studios turned to non-Indians to play Indians more resolutely in the mid-twentieth century, and those non-Indians were not just white—or at least the studios made it a point to highlight their various ethnic backgrounds: German, English, French, Irish, Jewish, African, Mexican, Albanian, Lithuanian, and Russian. Despite their increased hiring of non-Indians, studios continued to employ Indians to play Indians. They hired the small group of Indian actors who lived in the Southern California area and paid them Screen Actors Guild rates, but they also traveled to reservations to hire Indians there to work as extras.[16]

By the 1940s and 1950s actors were jockeying for position with the legal protection of SAG. They scrambled to gain entry into SAG, which would not only increase their chances of getting hired but also raise their hourly wage. In 1947 the actors would be paid according to the following scales:

Day players: $55 a day
Freelance and multiple picture players: $175 a week
Stock and contract players under age thirty: $120 a week
Those over thirty: at least $160 a week
Beginners in their first six months: $60 a week
Beginners after their first six months: $75 a week[17]

These union pay scales did not apply to stars. Their rates were laid out separately in a clause attached to the guild's contract. Essentially, the stars and their agents negotiated flat sums, which went far beyond what they would have made in the above categories. The guild was far less concerned with wages than they were with working conditions, however. The incredible disparity in pay received by stars and other actors mirrored life on film sets, where all workers received food and sleeping accommodations, but conditions varied widely. Eight years later, when the guild negotiated a new basic agreement, minimum wages remained unchanged. The guild focused even more on issues such as meals and rest periods, work hours, overtime, makeup, hairdressing, wardrobe, Sunday work, work on holidays, fittings, interviews, auditions, screen tests and wardrobe tests, night work, publicity interviews, publicity stills, script lines (extras were explicitly prevented from speaking written script lines, although they could speak lines created on the set), and conversion to weekly bases.

These rules applied to all Indian actors who were also SAG members. And all Indian actors would have to become SAG members or remain at the level of extras. Once they had SAG membership, they had no choice but to work within these structures of hierarchy and pay. In other words, Indian actors in no way existed outside of the system because of their status as Indians. They figured into the system like everyone else in the film industry. In some specific ways, Indian actors were treated neither better nor worse than anyone else scrambling for the top in Hollywood.[18]

Los Angeles Indians

The midcentury hiring of Indian actors peaked in the early 1950s, the time when most films with Indian characters were made. A handful of Indian men, including Jay Silverheels (Mohawk), William Malcolm Hazlett, aka Chief Many Treaties (Blackfeet), and Daniel Simmons, aka Chief Yowlachie (Yakama), were SAG members.[19] Most of these men only played Indians, and they made a lifelong career of it. The studios also hired Indians who lived in Southern California but who worked primarily in nonfilm industries. This group included men who, like Jim Thorpe, worked in all sorts of capacities and played bit parts as both Indian and non-Indian characters (more often non-Indian). Other Indian actors, or actors who may or may not have been but were accepted as Indian, such as Pat Hogan and Charles Stevens, played non-Indians on occasion.

The labor hierarchy and the racial hierarchy of the United States worked together in Hollywood to keep Indians out of the highest echelons of the acting industry. The lead actor in a film received the highest pay, sometimes more than the director received. Not a single Indian actor received a lead role in the 1940s and 1950s. Indian actors reached only the middle level of the bit part hierarchy, which could include roles with character names, speaking lines, and screen credits, but these parts were at an even lower level than those of supporting characters. As a result, their hires are not as well documented as are those of the leads and supporting characters.[20] The more established Indian male actors may have used the services of talent agents, but most simply became known to the film community for their ability to play Indians.[21] Archival records demonstrate that lesser-known Indian men sought work in movies and did so by appealing directly to the studios. Warner Bros. hired Joseph Vance Chorre, aka Suni Warcloud (whose mother was the Luiseño actress Gertrude Warcloud), only days before his scenes were filmed for *Jim Thorpe, All American* (1951). A producer saw Warcloud in *Counterpunch*, contacted him, hired him, and never even did a test. Monte Blue, who lied about being Cherokee or Osage through his father, simply wrote Jack Warner when he was interested in being hired in the production of *They Died with Their Boots On* (1941). Bud Leith, who claimed to be Native American, also wrote Jack Warner directly asking for a part in *They Died*.[22]

By the end of the twentieth century the Indian male actor most remembered by Americans, Indian and non-Indian, was Jay Silverheels, whose birth name was Harold Preston Smith. Silverheels is among a very small group of Native actors whose identity was undoubtedly legitimate. Some actors who identified as Native and were accepted as such have discrepancies in their background, resulting in scholars being unsure how to classify them. But Silverheels's family lines are definitively Mohawk.[23] He worked against the hiring of white actors for Indian roles in the 1960s by forming the Indian Actors' Workshop.[24] In the 1940s and 1950s he had pursued similar goals on an individual level. Silverheels's fame dwarfed the presence of other Indian actors of the time. Although several other Indian men worked in Hollywood in the 1940s and 1950s, one studio publicist claimed that without Silverheels, Hollywood would be left "without an Indian."[25] This statement exaggerated the predicament, and the publicist surely knew this. But the comment speaks to Silverheels standing at the pinnacle of the profession. His unique position, then, provided him with many opportunities, albeit in the framework of normalized representations of Indians. Silverheels also functioned as a token for all American Indian actors and seems to be used in that publicity statement in that sense as well. Studios may have hired Silverheels as a means to justify ignoring other Indian actors and continuing to place non-Indians in prominent roles.

This same anonymous publicist claimed that the need for Indian actors increased with the introduction of Technicolor. No longer could the studios use blue-eyed actors, at least not until the introduction of dark contact lenses.[26] But despite the publicist's claim, the increase in the use of Indian actors correlated with the increase of films including Indian characters in the 1950s, not necessarily with the introduction of Technicolor. Native people were consistently being hired for bit parts well before the introduction of Technicolor, and this simply continued after the introduction of Technicolor. Studios in no way shifted their employment patterns with Indian male actors, but they did hire reservation Indian extras on location far more frequently in the 1950s, but not because of Technicolor. Indian extras were seen en masse from a distance, and their eye color would not have been detectable. For lead actors, however, light eyes may have posed a challenge for a time, but dark contact lenses had been introduced and were in use by 1950 for lead actors playing Indians.

Although Hollywood continued to hire whites to play Indians, Hollywood executives also feared the public's rejection of their strategy. The Universal publicist was speaking indirectly to a fear in the filmmaking community about whites' representations of American Indians. The fear that film audiences might detect non-Indians playing Indians speaks to a larger concern: that what is meant to seem real is obviously fake. Filmmakers worked their way out of this artificiality by employing Indians for parts other than the lead. Sometimes employing Indians provided the necessary Indian look the studios sought; other times, Indians failed in the eyes of the studios. In either case, the desire for authenticity and the move away from artificiality motivated these hires. At least some Hollywood circles were aware of the Indians in town who were ready to play Indians. A Universal

Studios publicist dubbed the Los Angeles community of Indian actors the "apartment house Indians." The writer informed the larger American community that these potential employees were actors, Indians, and city dwellers. The writer saw them as Indian but also saw them imitating Indians for the camera, with their nonwhite identity making them a more valuable commodity. He used racist language steeped in the idea that Indians are violent, whites are innocent victims, and Indians—not whites—possess power in Hollywood. This imagined landscape that reverses actual historical processes shows up in movies as well as historical treatments of Native people. It comes as no surprise, then, to see Hollywood publicists borrowing this language of Indians scalping and overpowering whites:

> [Apartment house Indians] are a hybrid mixture of stunt men, part time extra players and bit players who have made a specialty of impersonating Redskins. . . . The Apartment House Indians have come in handy lately around the studio back lots where a renaissance of Injun fighting has set the use of the real McCoy at a premium.
>
> Casting directors say that there are only between fifty and seventy-five genuine Indian extra players around town. Whichever studio gets first call on them for a cinematic scalping party usually corners the entire market.
>
> Of the six bona-fide red men being used in "Column South," four are Navajos and two are Sioux. They've been working in Indian epics around twenty years apiece, and none of them will ever see the lighter side of fifty again.
>
> And to let you in on a little trade secret all of them are apartment house dwellers themselves.[27]

Johnny Rennick, a casting director, claimed the "apartment house Indians" had dwindled by the 1950s to the point that he could locate only eighteen Indians for a casting call for *The Stand at Apache River* (Universal, 1953). Rennick thought that far more Indian actors had lived in Los Angeles in the 1930s but that they had moved away when there was less of a demand. As a result, he relied on Indians, mostly Diné, from Arizona and Utah.[28]

These "apartment house Indians" were often born on or near reservations and later moved to Los Angeles. Some were athletes, while others had performed in rodeos and Wild West shows. After moving to Hollywood, they usually changed their names to line up with American expectations of American Indians and worked as actors for many years. Because most Indian actors never achieved the same level of fame as white actors playing Indians, their biographical information is not widely known. For instance, Chief Yowlachie was born Daniel Simmons in 1891 on the Yakama reservation. He attended the Cushman trade school and trained as a concert and operatic singer before entering the acting profession.[29] Chief John Big Tree was born in about 1855 and died in 1967. His birth name was Isaac Johnny John, and he posed for the 1912 Indian head five-cent piece. Big Tree was Seneca and is buried at the Onondaga reservation in New York.[30] Shooting Star was a Lakota born Louis Heminger on a South Dakota reservation, and he attended Pipestone Indian School.[31] Chief Many Treaties of the Blackfeet Nation played only Indian characters. His birth name was William Hazlitt. Many Treaties was a member of the Screen Extras Guild board of directors. After graduating from the Carlisle Indian Industrial School in 1895, he worked in rodeos, then as a film actor. In later years Eddie Little Sky, a Lakota actor, worked in some films but mostly television.

John War Eagle also maintained a career as an Indian actor. He was born in 1905 on one of the South Dakota reservations. He attended a government primary school, then attended Rapid City High School. In 1942 he relocated to Denver. A year later he moved to Los Angeles to work in a defense plant. In 1945 he began seeking work in the film industry. His first part was in *Canyon Passage* (Universal, 1946). His other roles included Nahilzay in *Broken Arrow* (Twentieth Century Fox, 1950), the Shoshone chief Lone Eagle in *A Ticket to Tomahawk* (Twentieth Century Fox, 1950), and the role of Red Cloud in *Tomahawk* (Universal, 1951).[32] In 1950 he was living in Alhambra, California, with his twenty-one-year-old daughter. War Eagle read, wrote, and spoke Lakota. The Potawatomi and Oneida actor Pat Hogan played Indian and non-Indian characters. He was born in Oklahoma to Claude Red Elk and Ann McTigue. According to publicity records, he played Indian characters until he was offered fewer and fewer opportunities to work. In reaction, he began bleaching his skin so he could play whites. After only a few years, however, he stopped lightening himself and took Indian roles again.[33] Rodd Redwing jokingly referred to himself as a "double Indian." Working as an actor and technical advisor, he claimed to be a member of the Chickasaw Nation and a South Asian Indian. He was an expert in firearms, fencing, knife throwing, whip fighting, rifle shooting, and military tactics and drills. Redwing taught famous white actors such as Richard Widmark and Burt Lancaster how to shoot weapons in a realistic manner. He appeared in nearly all of Cecil B. DeMille's films and in some films played whites.[34]

All of these men's lives provide fascinating details that speak to the complicated interplay between identity, nation, race, and representation, but perhaps none does so more than Iron Eyes Cody. Cody began his career of steady employment as an "Indian" actor and technical advisor beginning in the 1930s, but he achieved national fame with his appearance in an antipollution commercial in the 1970s in which he shed a very visible tear over the environmental destruction of the planet. This was the moment when Americans became familiar with Cody and the Native perspective on the environment. The public believed he was crying distinctly Indian tears for the environment, but there was no public discussion of his tribal status until after his death. It was then that film scholar Angela Aleiss revealed his real ethnicity, which resulted in a flurry of publications exposing Cody as an Italian American with no American Indian ancestry. These claims were based on family interviews, birth records, and census records. According to his half sister, May Abshire, Cody's mother was Francesca Salpietra of Sicily and his father was Antonio DeCorti, an Italian immigrant to New Orleans. Cody's mother arrived in New Orleans in 1902. His parents worked in the sugarcane fields of Louisiana. Cody was born Oscar DeCorti on April 3, 1904, in Kaplan, Louisiana, and christened Espera at Holy Rosary Catholic Church. His parents established a small grocery store in Gueydan, Louisiana. His father ran into trouble with the local mafia and escaped alone to Texas, while his mother remarried and moved to Orange, Texas. Cody's father died in 1924 at the age of forty-five. Upon his father's death, Cody and his brothers relocated to California, where they changed their name from DeCorti to Cody. The written record is clear on Cody: he was not American Indian. His sister confirmed this in interviews.

This new perspective on Cody stands in dramatic contrast to an established and previously undisputed biography of Cody: he dedicated his life to Indians and married the daughter of the Seneca anthropologist Arthur C. Parker. Many family members, especially his son, as well as friends dispute the claim that he was Indian or they simply deem such claims irrelevant.[35] During his lifetime, Hollywood accepted Cody as an Indian and trusted him for decades. Likewise, the Los Angeles Indian community accepted and treated Cody as an Indian. Some of these people begged the media to stop exposing his Italian ethnicity. For them Cody's ethnicity, received from his parents, was irrelevant. They saw Cody as Indian because of his dedication to Indians. His acceptance in the Los Angeles Indian community was based not on his actual lineage, because they knew he was Italian. Because Cody embraced another avenue of Indian identity—generosity and connection—so too did some Native people of Los Angeles accept and cover his lie. He immersed himself in the Indigenous community of Los Angeles by attending cultural events and being part of the support network. Cody donated thousands of dollars to Native causes and personally helped Indians obtain jobs and medical care. He also covered travel expenses for local American Indians. This dedication and support served as both a cover and a personal identity for Cody, and the Indian community shielded him from exposure, perhaps because of his dedication to them. His ambiguous identity speaks volumes about the tensions among Indians over questions of identity. For non-Indians Cody represents the artificiality of race and ethnicity. For others Cody serves as a focal point for articulating new definitions of Indian identity and community, based on commitment, friendship, and generosity to the Indian community. Cody himself never admitted to his lie, even when Angela Aleiss interviewed him, nor does his son, who appears in the *Reel Injun* documentary and defends his father as being a Native American.[36]

One way out of these confluences, tensions, and confusions is to think through and employ sovereignty. Tribes are nations, not ethnic groups. Tribes, not individuals, not even individual tribal members, hold absolute power in determining who is and who is not a member. What matters here is whether the tribes in which these men claim to be members in fact claim these men as members. What about descendants who were removed from their families, adopted, and have no legal proof of their ancestry? Some of those descendants claim their tribal identities but struggle with their lack of information, connection, and knowledge. That is altogether different than Cody and others who outright lie about their Native identity or repeat family stories without doing any research. Many, perhaps most, Native people today identify as Native in spite of not being enrolled, and the question of Native identity remains a difficult one.

The public has latched onto Cody's ethnic fraud, whereas others have equally questionable backgrounds and claims to an Indian identity. For instance, Chief Thundercloud claimed to be Cherokee and Muscogee, was accepted as Cherokee and Muscogee, but was probably neither. He was named Victor Daniels at birth. He and the studios that employed him always claimed Thundercloud was born in Muskogee, Oklahoma, but he was born in Arizona and was most likely Mexican American. Daniels's father was Jesus Daniel, born in May 1860 and who spent his life working as a day laborer, while his mother was Tomasa or Tomaca, born in April 1880 in Mexico. Thundercloud worked as an Indian actor frequently. In fact, he was the first Tonto in *The Lone Ranger* (1938), a role later played by Silverheels. Although Daniels uttered broken English countless times for pay, he also made some efforts to challenge this racism and may have brought Indian actors together to make their presence felt in Hollywood and increase the hires of Indian actors for Indian parts. Much like Cody, he hid his fraud behind altruism in the Native community.[37]

Ethnic fraud may have been common in Hollywood. Widely accepted by Hollywood as a descendant of Geronimo, Charles Stevens worked as an Indian actor and built a career that spanned decades. He was in fact Mexican American, yet he claimed and the studios publicized the story that his mother was the daughter of Geronimo, the famous Apache leader. In truth, a stepmother whom he never knew was Apache but not the daughter of Geronimo. Stevens's father, George Stevens, was white and founded the town of Solomonsville, Arizona. His first wife, Francesca, was a White Mountain Apache woman whose father was Escetecela. But Charles was born of his father's second marriage, to Eloisa Michalana, a Mexican American woman who may have had Native ancestry from a Mexican tribe but was not Apache. She bore Alberto and Carlos (who later changed his name to Charles), used his father's first wife's Apache identity to claim his own Apache identity, and changed her ancestral line from Escetecela to Geronimo. Stevens's relationship with Geronimo fueled his reputation and film career, yet Stevens knowingly falsified his identity as an American Indian for personal gain. Stevens knew his mother was Mexican American.[38] His half siblings were Apache without a doubt. Historian Angie Debo identifies Carlos's father as the Indian agent at San Carlos who was "married to a White Mountain Apache woman."[39] Carlos took advantage of his father's first wife's Indian identity and his half siblings' Indian identities to create his niche as an American Indian in the highly competitive bit-actor market.

Stevens built a solid and steady film career on his fake Apache identity. He claimed to have worked in Wild West shows and rodeos, which supposedly inspired him to relocate to Hollywood to begin acting. His first film job was *Birth of a Nation* (Griffith Corp., 1915). Over the years he appeared primarily in Douglas Fairbanks films, such as *The Lamb* (Triangle, 1915), *The Mystery of the Leaping Fish* (Triangle, 1916), *Robin Hood* (United Artists, 1922), *The Gaucho* (United Artists, 1927), and *The Iron Mask* (United Artists, 1929). Other films in which he appeared (but Douglas Fairbanks did not) include *M'Liss* (Paramount, 1918), *The Vanishing American* (Paramount, 1925), *Mantrap* (Paramount, 1926), and *King of Kings* (Pathé, 1927). Fairbanks and Stevens were close friends, and Carlos named his son after Douglas. He played an Alaska Native in *Call of the Wild* (United Artists, 1935), "Injun Joe" in *Tom Sawyer* (Paramount, 1930), and the grandfather of Ira Hayes (played by Tony Curtis) in *The Outsider* (Universal, 1961).[40] Carlos also supplemented his acting career with work as a stunt performer.

The identities of other Los Angeles Indians fell into more than one ethnic category. Unlike those who lied about their ancestry, these other men descended from multiple heritages and played characters of many ethnicities. Noble Johnson considered himself an African American, Anglo, and Native American. On his 1936 application for a Social Security card, he wrote "Indian" in the space marked "Other." Yet he elaborated, "Am neither white, Black, nor Red, but have blood mixture of the three races, to what extent of each is undetermined." He founded the Lincoln Motion Picture Company, which produced movies by, for, and about African Americans. In the early 1940s he was reportedly using the name Mark Noble and passing as white. Johnson played characters of many ethnicities, including a Native chief in *King Kong* (Radio Pictures, 1933). He played Indians in *Eagle's Nest* (Lubin, 1915), *Badlands of Dakota* (Universal, 1941), *Hurry, Charlie, Hurry* (RKO, 1941), *Ten Gentlemen from West Point* (Twentieth Century Fox, 1942), *She Wore a Yellow Ribbon* (RKO, 1950), and *North of the Great Divide* (Republic, 1950). Film professor Jane Gaines identifies Johnson as an African American actor and the founder of the Lincoln Motion Picture Company.[41]

Producers hired non-Indian actors to perform as characters of any ethnicity, whereas Indian actors were mostly limited to playing Indians. Studios claimed they preferred Indian actors to play Indian characters, but they certainly hired non-Indians more often for this task. Those who successfully lied about their American Indian identity gained preference over other non-Indians but also could be chosen over Indian actors who were in fact Indian. Small Indian roles were filled by Indian and non-Indian actors, sometimes in the same film. In *Unconquered* (Paramount, 1947) Indians and non-Indians filled the bit parts.[42] However, in *The Prairie* (Screen Guild, 1947), only Indian actors filled Indian bit parts. Absolutely no films, however, feature Indian actors in Indian leads; for instance, Cochise (in *Broken Arrow*), Sitting Bull (in *Sitting Bull*), Yellow Hand (in *Buffalo Bill*), and Massai (in *Apache*) were played by non-Indian men.

When studios chose individuals for parts involving close-ups and dialogue, they insisted on hiring *actors*, who were very often non-Indian. Only actors, Indian and non-Indian, were chosen for bit parts. An MGM employee put it rather succinctly in describing the studio's experience with hiring for the lead Indian part in *Ambush* (MGM, 1950): "A Hollywood actor was used because the role demanded acting experience."[43] This simplistic, didactic statement is loaded with racialized and racist definitions. When comparing Indian actors to reservation Indians, Hollywood emphasized their identities as actors. Yet when Native actors were compared to white actors, suddenly Indian actors were just Indian, not actors. A handful of

Indian men lived in Hollywood, worked on film sets, took acting courses, and sought work as actors. Indian actors challenged the bifurcated world of Indians and actors every time they arrived for an audition. They were both Indians and actors. But, as the statement above makes so clear, those in power in Hollywood refused to see Indian employees as anything other than what they knew of Indians from the movies, which reified the idea that they were not actors. In that sense, casting directors were creating and controlling the images of Indians based on their understandings of past films. For casting directors, actors lived in Los Angeles, were trained, and were white. According to filmmakers and their larger cultural world, Indians were not actors. When given the opportunity, reservation Indians and Indian actors challenged and reversed this assumption.

Hollywood Hierarchy: Indian Actors and the Glass Ceiling

Paradoxically, the films in which Indian characters were named in the credits and spoke lines nearly always had non-Indians cast in those roles, and yet those films often questioned the racial hierarchy of whites conquering Native people. These films questioned or blurred the historical relationship between whites and Indians: whites become the innocent victims of Indian violence. Through unprovoked attacks and whites who befriend Indians, these films emphasize whites attempting to create harmony and cooperation. In the end the films reinforce racial boundaries and stereotypes, especially through their depictions of whites. The employment of famous non-Indian actors as Indian leads heightened the sense of white innocence in movies about Indians. This explains the casting of Jeff Chandler in *Broken Arrow* (Twentieth Century Fox, 1950), Rock Hudson in *Taza, Son of Cochise* (Universal, 1954), Burt Lancaster in *Apache* (United Artists, 1954), and Victor Mature in *Chief Crazy Horse* (Universal, 1955).[44] The impulse to cross over racial lines (as in blackface) can even be found in the racially liberal films of the 1940s that centered on African Americans and whites, such as *Pinky* and *Body and Soul*. Even as racial "cross-dressing" disrupts racial supremacy and logic, it also recuperates it. In the films centered on American Indians, the characters played by Indian actors and extras reinforced racial boundaries between Indians and whites. Likewise, American Indian actors questioned their exclusion from lead roles, but Hollywood failed to listen to them or publicize their views. White writers created scripts that questioned racial boundaries, and white actors playing Indian characters transgressed those boundaries.

When whites played Indians, their acting was effectively a sort of ventriloquism. Indians appeared to be speaking; Indians appeared to be standing in front of the camera; Indians appeared to be moving in three-dimensional space, but in fact these are whites playing Indians, and non-Indians wrote all of their lines. Indians were both there and not there when whites played Indian characters. What Michelle Raheja calls "redfacing" subverts the idea that race is an immutable category in that non-Indians were easily crossing those racial boundaries on the screen, yet they were doing so temporarily and the crossing only went in one direction. More important, the characters themselves took on a permanency in the racial divide between whites and Indians. Non-Indians held a near monopoly on Indian leads in the 1940s and 1950s, and the roles themselves remained rigid.[45] Many films looked to bridge racial boundaries by depicting interracial friendship, yet non-Indian actors were doing the acting, never actors such as Jay Silverheels or Daniel Simmons (aka Chief Yowlachie). Studios were absolutely unwilling to put an Indian actor in a lead Indian role, and crossing racial boundaries was only acceptable if famous white actors were questioning those boundaries through the characters they played.

Because of their ethnic identities, non-Indian actors found themselves in an ideal position. Not only could they play non-Indians, they could play Indians as well. Indian roles served as only one role among many they could play. Many of these men and women eventually moved away from westerns entirely, putting their Hollywood B-list status behind them to achieve A-list "star" status, economic power, cultural capital, and fame. At the seventieth Academy Awards ceremony, in 1998, Shelley Winters, Charlton Heston, and Jack Palance appeared for a tribute to past Oscar recipients. None were Indian actors, but all had appeared in movies that used Indian characters to portray white male strength and to cement romantic and sexual bonds between white men and white women. In the 1940s and 1950s Indians who played Indians remained at the level of bit parts, with only a few achieving even a modicum of fame, but non-Indians who played Indians often became famous and wealthy.[46] Taking Indian roles provided much-needed work for white actors just beginning their careers. Once non-Indian actors demonstrated their acting abilities, they left the world of Indian roles and other nonwhite ethnicities to embrace their original career goals: white roles that generated popularity, fame, and economic security.

Portraying Indians opened the space for white male sexuality to flourish as well, at least for non-Indian actors. At the movies American men and women watched tall, strong men making decisions, encountering danger, and negotiating with other men, all of them with exposed chests covered with copper skin. Jeff Chandler embodied this phenomenon, especially in the role of Cochise—bare chested, noble, and romantic. White American women eroticized Chandler and embraced him as a potential mate, though he lived in West Hollywood and lived openly as a gay man within the gay community. In publicizing *Broken Arrow*, Universal suggested to American women what they would soon discover in the film: that in the role of Cochise, Chandler was "suddenly revealed as a very sexy hunk of masculine beefcake" and that the actor himself was certain that being stripped to the waist would lead to immense sales at the box office. Not only strong copper chests but also bald heads sexualized white actors in much the same way. When Hugh O'Brian shaved his head for a Mohawk role in *Drums across the River* (Universal, 1954), the well-established sex symbol became even more popular with American women. His shaved head invoked an ethnic sexuality centered outside the white, masculine, sexual identity.[47]

As white actors stripped down to expose their muscles, Indian actors experienced a complete desexualization. They were barred from acquiring a heightened sexuality through playing Indian characters. Although Indian men also sometimes stripped down to the waist, this exposure was read as threatening rather than sexualizing. Whereas many Indian characters played by white actors fell in love with white women on screen, Indian actors playing Indians were denied these on-screen romantic liaisons with white women and thus remained less popular and never achieved stardom. Indian women who worked in Indian roles, although few, played roles based exclusively on the image of being overworked, exhausted, and nearly mute. Beulah Archuletta, one of the only dark-skinned women who acted on more than one occasion in this period, played Look in *The Searchers*. Archuletta did not attend the premiere parties for *The Searchers*, nor did fashionable postwar designers send her evening gowns, furs, or jewelry.[48] In general, playing Native characters meant career stagnation for Native actors.

Indian actors, not necessarily Indian roles, performed a masculinity devoid of sexuality. In policing the parameters of fame and allure to include only white men and white women, Hollywood controlled Indians' cultural capital and kept it in the hands of whites. Indian roles were in fact open and full of variety in some ways. For films, writers can create characters of any kind, yet casting directors who hired Indian actors gave them nonsexual roles. Film historians pay great heed to the effect of film on society and society's effect on film, yet ultimately it was casting directors and screenwriters who segregated Indian characters in violent roles and cast Indian actors for roles far different from those for white actors. Casting directors and screenwriters made decisions that resulted in the cultural formations we see on film. Here we can see exactly how particular Indian male and female actors were locked out of particularly powerful nodes of power, not because film made it so but because the film industry made film follow the industry's preferred course.

Although Indian actors were paid according to scales established by SAG, Indian actors' racial and ethnic identities took precedence over their acting abilities. As a result, Indian actors were denied the cultural sexual allure and professional mobility only stardom could bring. For Indian actors, their Indian identity informed not only their film roles but a racialization that remained with them regardless of their training, personal attributes, and employment. Indian actors accepted and were offered Indian roles, yet none of them achieved the star status of their non-Indian competitors.[49] Jay Silverheels may have achieved popularity, but he did not receive the economic rewards of true Hollywood stardom.[50] Studios wanted the public to think otherwise when they sent out a press release announcing that his pay was $850 ($141 for a six-day week) and he drove a black Jaguar. The studio wanted the public to believe he was successful and materialistic in the same ways as white actors. Silverheels may have been no different in his aspirations, but in spite of his achievements he remained distinct and lesser in that he never earned the kind of money stars did nor did he own a home in Los Angeles.[51]

Studio publicity machines exaggerated the acting skills of white actors in nonwhite roles yet equated Indian actors' roles with the Indian actors themselves, as though they were not performing but simply being themselves in front of cameras. Indian actors could not revel in the wealthy Hollywood lifestyle, and in fact most never even owned their own homes. Whether or not they were in front of the camera, their Indian identity limited their employment opportunities. Yet white actors could cross racial boundaries, playing whites, Indians, and members of various other ethnic groups. In other words, Indian performers' pay was protected through union contracts, but their American Indian identities limited their overall earning ability and prevented them from acquiring the truly high-paying jobs.

Not only did the films produced by Hollywood reflect the social hierarchies they lived in, but so did Hollywood's unions. SAG determined its guidelines and regulations using categories established by the film industry. Instead of challenging the status quo, SAG regulated inequalities already in place. Leads (always white) were paid far more than bits (Indian and white), and bits were paid far more than extras (Indian and white). Although this structure prevented each level from being undercut by those willing to work for less, it also meant that the logic of settler colonialism kept Native actors working at the lowest pay levels designated by unions associated with the film industry.

In the category of leads, non-Indian actors such as Rock Hudson, Anthony Quinn, Victor Mature, and Jeff Chandler reaped huge sums of money for their work. Jeff Chandler was paid $8,000 for *The Battle at Apache Pass* (Universal, 1952), $1,000 for his cameo appearance in *Taza, Son of Cochise* (Universal, 1954), and $30,000 for playing the lead in *Foxfire* (Universal, 1955).[52] Even Indian bits were repeatedly filled by non-Indian actors such as Perry Lopez, Rudolph Acosta, Charles Stevens, and Nick Thompson. Chief Yowlachie, Chief Many Treaties, Chief Thundercloud, Jay Silverheels, and Rodd Redwing also worked as Native bit actors. Like the bits, the extras who played Indians were Indian and non-Indian. These kinds of pay differences meant Indian actors and white actors who played Indians lived very different lives in Los Angeles, including where they could afford to live. While Rock Hudson owned two mansions in the high-dollar real estate sector of the foothills around the San Fernando Valley, Chief Yowlachie rented a granny flat behind someone else's home in East LA. Jeff Chandler lived in West Hollywood, not as upscale as Rock Hudson's homeplaces but much more affluent than the very working-class neighborhood of Jay Silverheels near Western and Melrose. Moreover, Chandler owned his home, while Silverheels rented. Barbara Rush lived in the wealthy area surrounding the University of California, Los Angeles, and Jimmy Stewart, who played a white man who loved an Indian woman, owned a home in Beverly Hills. Los Angeles's neighborhoods varied tremendously in cost and ethnic composition. As a heterogeneous landscape, the inner city of Los Angeles and industrialized areas were the least expensive choices. Beverly Hills, the beaches, and the foothills were the most expensive and admired areas of Los Angeles. From west to east, Hollywood marked the transitional zone to working-class neighborhoods, and Western Avenue marked the limit of largely white neighborhoods.

From 1941 to 1960 studios hired Indian actors every year, with only one exception. That year was 1945, when only three movies included Indian characters. This limited production was probably caused by the striking craft workers. Low-budget films were canceled or postponed while features went largely unaffected.[53] A small group of Indian actors received offers of work repeatedly, and their pay remained consistent. Jay Silverheels earned $400 a week for *Broken Arrow* (Twentieth Century Fox, 1950), $850 a week for *The Battle at Apache Pass* (Universal, 1952), $850 a week for *Saskatchewan* (Universal, 1954), and $1,750 a week for *Walk the Proud Land* (Universal, 1956). In some of these films he earned more than non-Indian actors. Victor Millan played Santos in *Walk the Proud Land* and earned $750 a week. The non-Indian men who played "drunken Indians" in the film were paid on day-player agreements, $100 a day, for a total of $500.[54] Non-Indian rates were similar to those of Indian actors. In *War Arrow* (Universal, 1953), Susan Ball earned $500 a week, Henry Brandon earned $750 a week, and Dennis Weaver earned $350 a week.[55] Actors' pay was extremely uneven despite unionization. Actors preferred to negotiate their pay individually for a flat rate per film, not on a weekly basis. If paying actors on a weekly or daily basis, filmmakers had an incentive to use those actors less to reduce their production costs.

Because actors, Indian and non-Indian, were members of SAG, studios paid them according to union scales.[56] Bit players were paid at steady rates in the 1940s and 1950s. In 1948 Paramount paid non-Indian actors more than the Indian actors in *The Paleface* (Paramount, 1948), but this was not always, or even often, the case.[57] The same year that Chief Yowlachie made $500 a week for *A Ticket to Tomahawk* (Twentieth Century Fox, 1950), the non-Indian actor Charles Soldani earned only $200 a week for *Broken Arrow*. For *Saskatchewan* (Universal, 1954), Jay Silverheels earned slightly more than one non-Indian actor and slightly less than another non-Indian actor.[58] White women who played Indian women earned approximately the same as the other non-Indian and Indian actors who played Indians. Susan Cabot earned $250 a week to play Monahseetah in *Tomahawk* (Universal, 1951), and the Indian actor John War Eagle earned $200 a week for playing Red Cloud.[59] Their on-screen time and number of lines were often low because of being confined to bit parts, which meant equal pay but unequal offers of work.

Whereas studios saw Indian actors as primarily Indian, reservation Indians were thought of only as Indians. Filmmakers equated reservation Indians with authenticity and a nineteenth-century past, but some reservation Indians used their performance abilities to surprise Hollywood and blur the boundary between Indian and actor. In the 1940s and 1950s several reservation Indian men were hired as extras but negotiated for speaking lines once on set, which was allowed by SAG and was in the best interest of the studios, as it was cheaper than hiring actors. These men made the transition with ease, using the system for economic gain. These moments highlight the ambiguous position of men who were temporarily both Indians and actors. In their production of *Colorado Territory* (1949), Warner Bros. brought Grey Eyes, a Diné man, back to the California studio to finish production. While playing Zuni, Grey Eyes had his wife, Irene Stewart, interpret for him, as he was not fluent in English.[60] George Looks Twice

(Pine Ridge Lakota) was an extra chosen to perform a death scene in *Tomahawk* (Universal, 1951). He surprised the crew when he performed the death perfectly with only one take, thereby saving the company on production costs.[61] Similarly, producer Aaron Rosenberg discovered Ralph Buckle, then a twenty-two-year-old Diné, who had been appearing at the Tucson Little Theater. Rosenberg cast Buckle in *Winchester '73* (Universal, 1950) and planned to send him to Hollywood for a screen test.[62] After interviewing several Indians, director Raoul Walsh found the right "Buffalo nickel" nose on the Cree farmer Jonas Applegarth, who had been an extra in *Saskatchewan* (Universal, 1954) and *Drum Beat* (Warner Bros., 1954). Walsh chose him for the part of the Diné private, Shining Lighttower, in *Battle Cry* (Warner Bros., 1955).[63] On his way to the studio, Applegarth was denied entry at a Calgary hotel in Canada. However, when he arrived in Hollywood he was treated as an actor and taken in a studio limousine to the Knickerbocker Hotel in Los Angeles, near Hollywood and Vine.[64]

In their effort to maintain the boundary between actors and Indians, Warner Bros. portrayed Applegarth as being fundamentally Indian in spite of his stay in Hollywood. Up until working for Warner Bros., he had lived in a farmhouse or tent, traveled by horse or buggy, and attended about two movies per year. His parents died when he was quite young, and he was adopted by Sam Buffalo. He was a Catholic, had two daughters, Rachel and Bernice, and was married to Helen Applegarth. After his time in Hollywood, Applegarth tried to change his legal name to Jonas Wild Horse, a request his tribe denied. According to the studio, he too saw his Hollywood work as a brief foray; he worked as a farmer for the rest of his life.[65] His brief treatment as an actor and the attendant social segregation turned out to be temporary and never became a long-term economic option.

Conclusion

In the category of bit parts, Indians were usually paid the same but sometimes more than non-Indians. Some Indian actors built their careers on acting and obtained steady employment for years. Actors made more than extras regardless of race or ethnicity, but which actors rose to the level of leads had everything to do with race. Indian actors were never allowed into the uppermost category of leads. This remained strictly the domain of white actors. For some non-Indian actors, playing Indians provided the springboard that launched the rest of their careers. This was never the experience of Indian actors. The best they could accomplish was consistency in hires at the level of bit parts. What was more common for Indian actors was a life in Southern California and an involvement in nonfilm trades, supplemented by acting work. This would be evidenced by Jim Thorpe, who worked in all sorts of working-class trades. These men may have preferred a lifestyle in which they could avoid working five days a week, eight hours a day. Acting supplemented by day labor in construction or in other entertainment venues throughout Los Angeles meant Native people could build their work commitments around their community and family obligations.

The complicated categories that made up the Hollywood acting hierarchy do not allow for simple theories of dominance and victimization. American Indian labor in war and postwar movies can best be described as opportunistic, for both the studios and the Indians who worked for them. Indian actors consented to their film work, but by the same token these men and women lived in a world of narrow economic choices. Along with the popular equation of Indians with a nineteenth-century past full of Indian violence and white innocence and supremacy, Indian actors had to contend with the twentieth-century reality of social segregation and economic exclusion from material success. Unlike their white contemporaries, war and postwar urban Indians lived outside the new reality of suburban life and steady economic success. The training they received through relocation programs was geared toward low-paying and physically demanding work. This made acting that much more attractive: it paid more, held more prestige, and did not require a long-term commitment by forcing them to forgo cultural activities and commitments. Finally, acting used the capital held by postwar urban Indians: their Indian identity and sometimes their Indian appearance. They may not have held economic capital, but they held something the studios wanted dearly: their identity as Native people.[66]

3

"Not Desired by You for Photographing"

The Labor of American Indian (and Non-Indian) Extras

Sometimes all you can do is sell what you've got. Your face. Your breasts. Your Otherness. Your frailty. Your story. Or the story people with money want to hear.
—Deborah Miranda, *Bad Indians: A Tribal Memoir*

Indians began performing for Europeans almost from the moment of contact, when Columbus captured Natives and brought them before King Ferdinand and Queen Isabella of Spain for entertainment. Historians see Indians entering the performance arena in significant numbers in the late nineteenth century, beginning with Buffalo Bill's Wild West shows. In fact, all of the Indians in Buffalo Bill's Wild West were actual Indians. He never costumed non-Indians to play Indians.[1] Scholars such as historian L. G. Moses have proven that Indians have worked in the film industry as producers, directors, extras, bits, and leads from its inception. This is not to say that their reach, power, and influence were equal to that of non-Indians, but taking the full picture into account reveals a much higher degree of Indian engagement in the entertainment industry than the general public might assume, with the 1940s and 1950s actually representing a low point in the hiring of Natives for movie work. American Indians were nearly always shut out of lead roles, even if their on-screen appearances were numerous, and important work continues to be done on the historic moments of Native engagement with filmmaking throughout the twentieth century. The gap, however, in documenting Native participation lies in the 1940s and 1950s, a period that saw the production of incredibly racist films.[2]

Directors, producers, and agents courted Native people for film work throughout the twentieth century. Although the Indians they sought were clearly their contemporaries, the studios identified Indians with the nineteenth century. Hollywood created and exaggerated an image of the Indian rooted in a precolonial past and used racist language to undermine the existence of contemporary Indians. As the studios expected Indians to be situated in their version of the past, they also exploited them as cheap, temporary labor with no benefits or physical protections. By the mid-twentieth century Congress had terminated many tribes and thousands of tribal members were moving to cities through the relocation program managed by the Bureau of Indian Affairs (BIA). A handful of urban Indians made their way into the entertainment circuit, including movies, while those who remained on reservations took film work whenever a film crew came to shoot on location at their particular reservation. Film work meant trading their look and identity for cash without the physical demands of factory, mining, or other types of manual labor. In the 1940s and 1950s reservation Indians throughout the United States were suffering from the highest rates of poverty in the country, a fact the studios did not publicize. Only once did the studios acknowledge the hunger observed on the Navajo reservation, when they documented Diné asking to take home some jerky that was about to be thrown away.[3] For the most part, studios' publicity departments wanted the American public to take note of their efforts to hire Indians but consistently faulted them for being modern.

Studios preferred reservation Indians and claimed they were more easily managed on film sets than Angelenos. They believed Navajos were well suited to movie work, because the people listened well and followed instructions perfectly, even when provided through interpreters.[4] One director appreciated how they controlled their facial expressions during filming. He was surprised that being in front of the camera did not bring out any extraverted tendency to get noticed. He found Diné extras to be quiet, unlike Hollywood extras, and the sets were thus less noisy. From his perspective, this made the work environment simpler, with no time wasted quieting the set.[5] His assistant director claimed the Diné stayed close to the crew and began working as soon as they were summoned. The Diné extras never complained about the work and conducted themselves in a way that made filming seamless.[6] This particular piece of publicity refrained from pretending these Diné extras were somehow in the present but locked in the past. The press releases issued from the filming location actually recognized the extras' unique contribution to the film and readily acknowledged their social assets in the filmmaking process.

When studios set out to film at reservations in the Southwest, their publicists often tapped into the mythology surrounding the region. The studios juxtaposed the landscape and people with the rest of the United States and suggested Indians were fundamentally different. One publicity director described the Diné town of Kayenta as being lost in the nineteenth century:

And now they are coming in ... Indians right out of the storybooks, in covered wagons, on ponies, with their little clans and tribesmen, hundreds and hundreds of them. The whole unbelievable scene is a throw-back to 1865, for there are no telephones here, no daily newspapers, no radios, mail comes but twice a week.

Time has been turned back here in Monument Valley and the cast and company of "My Darling Clementine" are seeing scenes that were familiar to Kit Carson when he came up Canyon De Chelly in 1864, but faded from view sixty and seventy years ago.[7]

The year 1864 was a time of defeat for the Diné, who endured forced relocation to a place four hundred miles from Canyon de Chelly, which Kit Carson attacked to force them out. The verbal portrait painted by the studio publicist erases this violence and instead creates a premodern wonderland by emphasizing what Kit Carson saw: a pastoral scene of happy, peaceful Diné clans rather than what the Diné people saw: destruction of food supplies, separation of families, violence, and death. When the publicist talked about the scene fading from view, he suggested that the Diné people, or at least the nineteenth-century romantic version, had disappeared. His assumption, despite the presence and employment of Diné people for the film, equates them with the past. Yet there they are, walking right before his eyes and ours, as he reports their presence, yet erases them by placing them in a distant past lacking the mention of genocidal violence.

Hollywood's version of American Indian history engages a set of questions not asked by historians. Hollywood concerned itself with grand tales of white heroism and Indian defeat in the nineteenth century, whereas historians seek to understand sovereignty, cultural change, tribal formation, and tribal law.[8] As often as the Diné people and others would show themselves to be modern, those involved in hiring them would, like studio publicist Harry Brand, deny it or repress it through humor. The Diné people, especially by this time, had been soldiers, worked for the Civilian Conservation Corps, and suffered through the government's livestock reduction programs. What Hollywood's film professionals knew to be true—that Indians were both modern and Indian—they nonetheless steadfastly denied. But they constantly reminded audiences of the Indians' presence in films to promote the authenticity of their productions.

Native people at times solicited studios to use their reservations for location filming as a means of bringing in some cash. In 1941 the Crow Agency created a committee composed of Robert Yellowtail, William Bends, Mark Real Bird, and Harry Whiteman.[9] Together they drafted an agreement for renting tipis, filming ceremonies, and hiring Crows for film work. Robert Yellowtail was the reservation superintendent from 1934 to 1945 and tribal chair beginning in 1952. His dealings with Twentieth Century Fox were most likely part of his intense desire for Crow economic self-sufficiency. While superintendent, Yellowtail exhibited this desire through various projects, including new reservoirs and roads, logging, and renewed participation in the Crow Fair. Whiteman was a boarding school graduate from Black Lodge and was in favor of grazing leases.[10] Yellowtail and Whiteman were on one side of a political divide on the Crow reservation. Through these two powerful Crow men, Twentieth Century Fox hired Crows as extras, rented their tipis, and purchased photographs of them during their Sun Dance.[11] Several years later Paramount hired hundreds of Crows for *Warpath* (1951), through the assistance of Yellowtail once again. He is officially thanked, along with the Bureau of Indian Affairs, at the film's end. Years later in the Southwest, Warner Bros. turned to an Indian reservation superintendent to gain help in securing reservation Indians for labor. Studio officials contacted Lester Oliver, chair of the Apache Tribal Council, and he served as intermediary. Oliver orchestrated the hiring of two hundred White Mountain (called White River by the studio) Apaches, who played Modocs in *Drum Beat* (Warner Bros., 1954). The Apache extras traveled by bus to the set location in the Coconino National Forest in northern Arizona.[12]

Under the leadership of Robert Yellowtail, the Crow Nation sold use of their reservation for filming and photographs of their Sun Dance to Twentieth Century Fox studios for their film *Buffalo Bill*. But the values and goals of the Crows did not completely overlap with those of the studio. The studio desired a precolonial Crow Nation just as they did with the Diné. Twentieth Century Fox wrote this into their contract with the Crows, legally precluding modern elements from the Sun Dance ceremonies.[13] In response, the Crow Nation agreed to "keep out of camera range, modern tents, automobiles, or any modern equipment, persons, people or other objects not desired by you for photographing."[14] Within these constraints, Fox photographed the Crows' Sun Dance and annual buffalo hunt. Despite the agreement to shield the camera from contemporary technologies, those adaptations crept in nonetheless. By preference and medical necessity, some Sun Dancers wore prescription glasses and sunglasses. In a similar vein, Crow children wore street clothes at the Sun Dance. A World War II veteran in uniform participated in the dance itself as well as the work needed to prepare for the dance. Glasses, street clothes, and U.S. military uniforms presented no conflict for Crows. For them, their use of contemporary products and military participation did not take away from, pollute, or undermine the Sun Dance. But, in the eyes of the studio, any acceptance of the modern by Crows made them less Crow and their Sun Dance less authentic and valuable.

Despite the Crow Agency's guarantee that no elements of the modern would disrupt Twentieth Century Fox's attempt to create a nineteenth-century illusion, the Crows demonstrated themselves to be the able contemporaries of the industry by negotiating a legal contract with a major film studio. Also guaranteed in the Crow Agency's contract was the studio's right to use the medicine lodge after the ceremony was complete. In the end the studio exercised this portion of the contract to produce its own version of the Sun Dance after the actual Crow Sun Dance, and the two are quite different: there are no sunglasses or prescription glasses, no street clothes, and no military uniforms visible in the studio's version.[15] Twentieth Century Fox used images of buffalo herds and the buffalo killed by the Crows in the film, and there the essence of the Sun Dance is missing, as the Crows refused to re-create those particular elements. The only Indian gathering in the final version is a long shot of about one hundred Indian men dancing around a bonfire, then riding away to attack the army. There is no arbor or main pole. The ample research and documentation of the Sun Dance and medicine lodge never even made it into the film.

This dissonance between who Indians were and who the studios expected them to be repeated itself on many film sets. Through the production process, Indians showed Hollywood that they lived and breathed in the twentieth century, but Indians were seen as useful only to the extent that they measured up to Hollywood's definition of what it meant to be Indian. This left Hollywood with easy justifications for not hiring tribal people. In the late 1940s United Artists began production on *Mrs. Mike* (1949) and planned to represent the Dane-zaa Nation of Canada. They expressed their desire to use members of the Dane-zaa Nation, but they fabricated an easy lie and reported the tribe's disappearance. The studio turned instead to the Indian actors of Los Angeles to fill the roles.[16] This was pure fantasy on the part of United Artists, because in 1949 a thriving Dane-zaa community lived in the Peace River region of western Canada.[17] Just as confounding, director George Sherman claimed in 1954 that he could find no Kiowas, so he hired stunt performers, actors of several ethnicities, and some Apaches instead.[18] Here, the notion of the vanishing Indian functioned more as an ideological projection than a misbelief. Were it simply a misbelief, then it would have been replaced by a revised belief after interacting with Natives. In spite of facts to the contrary, producers, directors, and others from Hollywood held on to the notion that Indian people had disappeared. Even when they acknowledged the existence of Indian people and subsequently hired them, their fundamental adherence to the myth of the vanishing Indian remained intact.

Because of this ideological projection of the vanishing Indian, any aspect of a twentieth-century Indian that fell outside that projection was potentially ridiculed. For example, Universal Studios staff compiled a press release that contains details of questionable veracity and that mocked English-speaking Hualapais after it was discovered that the Indian extras were educated speakers of English. On the Oatman, Arizona, set of *Foxfire* (Universal, 1955), the studio hired several members of the Hualapai Nation. The men may very well have spoken English, but the studio's publicity release claimed they were all college educated: five University of New Mexico graduates and four UCLA graduates. They also claimed three had attended Carlisle, a claim that seems very reasonable. Entirely preposterous is their suggestion that two of the men held medical degrees. The studio did not name the men, but Dr. Frank Clarke was, to my knowledge, the only Hualapai medical doctor in the country in the 1950s.[19] That the Hualapai men spoke English does not seem surprising, but the idea that so many were college graduates is a simple fabrication. The studio most likely encountered a few English speakers and experienced surprise and discomfort with that discovery. Perhaps one or two of those English speakers had attended college or held university degrees. The studio then exaggerated the story a bit to emphasize the disconnect between the non-Native image of Indians and actual Indians.[20] But this notion also closely parallels the dispossession of Native people. Native people are not disproportionately college educated, yet here that reality is reversed, not to praise Native Americans but to suggest disappointment. Not only were the Hualapai given no power over their filmic representations, but the studios also precluded their ability to fashion their own images for public relations surrounding the film. For the Hualapais, the loss of their Native language was caused by dislocation, violence, and forced assimilation through boarding schools. That painful past and reality have resulted in most Natives speaking only English, and this outcome is a deep wound in Native America that can function as a barrier to achieving a closer connection to Native culture. For the studio to ridicule the men for being fluent English speakers is the height of contradiction and hypocrisy because it failed to acknowledge that genocide and forced assimilation were the causes.

The studios drafted many press releases telling essentially the same far-fetched, racism-steeped story. The studio's publicity managers fabricated a story in which the non-Indian actor Noah Beery Jr. spoke both Diné and Apache whereas the Diné and Apache men on set did not speak their own language. The press release claimed Beery translated Apache and Diné on the set of *War Arrow* (Universal, 1953) but that the men failed to respond as they did not speak their Native languages. The release even claimed several of the men were college graduates. Beery relayed that he had "never felt so silly in [his] whole life."[21] The loss of Native language literacy among Indians on the set was duly framed in an ironic tone by the publicity department and related to high levels of college education among members of the two tribes. This pure invention upended the truth: Apaches and Diné by this time had been forcefully torn from their families to attend boarding schools, where they were taught English and violently forced to stop speaking their Native languages. The loss of Native languages is the direct result of genocide, a point the studios easily could have made had they listened to the Native people on set. Instead, these Native survivors looking for short-term work were ridiculed by press agents and blamed for not meeting white expectations that they should be exactly who their ancestors were. In fact, if this episode played out the way the studio claims it did, the Natives on the set may have felt sorrow at not being able to understand the Native languages being spoken.

The long history of Indians as performers and film extras was part of the modernity that studios sought to deny. Indians were workers living in the twentieth century, and studios sought these obviously modern Indians for movie work through modern channels such as the BIA. Yet they desired the employment of reservation Indians not just for authenticity but also to exploit their appearances for the lowest financial investment possible. Hiring reservation Indians meant avoiding the high cost of union pay scales. The recruitment of reservation Indians was sometimes spontaneous, but it was just as often handled in advance through reservation superintendents who oversaw the hires, assured their legality, and dealt with correspondence. For *Buffalo Bill* (1944), Twentieth Century Fox ran negotiations with superintendent James Stewart in hiring Diné, and Paramount used Robert Yellowtail in hiring Crows for *Warpath* (1951). Whereas the hires of men who lived in Southern California were largely casual and spontaneous (although still legal under Screen Actors Guild [SAG] guidelines and scales), the hires of reservation Indians required planning, foresight, and a rudimentary knowledge of the workings of the BIA.

The Navajo Nation

Diné received more work as film extras than any other tribal members in the 1940s and 1950s. They and other reservation Indians who appeared in movies were not professional actors and worked as extras anywhere from one day to two weeks. It was extremely temporary work that took place most often in June and July in the western portions of the Diné reservation. Perhaps the western area of the reservation was slightly drier than the eastern and had the desert look studios sought. Those living on the reservation practiced sedentary agriculture and raised stock, perhaps more so in the western regions. In fact, in Canyon de Chelly and Canyon del Muerto, Diné relied on agriculture alone because of the configuration of the landscape. Most Diné who worked on film sets came from the western region of the reservation, although some traveled great distances from the eastern areas to earn cash. A complete listing of Diné extras from one film shows the breakdown of their areas of residency: fifty-four from Cameron, thirty from Tonolea, four from Flagstaff, four from Cedar Ridge, two from Tuba City, two from The Gap, two from Pinon, one from Black Mountain, one from Copper Mine Trading Post, and one from Kayenta.[22]

Did Diné resist the western genre and its inaccurate, disembodied, and disempowered portrayals of their people in Hollywood westerns? Indians and non-Indians alike tell stories of Diné in the background of John Ford's films speaking Navajo and conveying private messages this way. Those who are sympathetic to the Indian perspective imagine that Diné were critiquing the fundamentals of settler colonialism or ridiculing white actors and their low pay. Even non-Indian writers such as Tony Hillerman like to re-create the possibilities of Indian resistance. In his 1993 novel *The Sacred Clowns*, laughter ripples through the all-Diné audience at a drive-in showing of John

Ford's *Cheyenne Autumn*. Indigenous artists such as James Luna likewise use the western genre as a focal point for critique and reinterpretation. These myths and artistic interventions function as the salve for the onslaught of racist images of Indians issuing from the western genre.

Cree filmmaker Niles Diamond set out to document the treatment of American Indians in film and found that Diné did indeed resist their representations through private humor, at least in the 1960s. In his documentary *Reel Injun* (2009), Diamond brings a copy of the film *A Distant Trumpet* (Warner Bros., 1964) to the home of Effie and James Etna, a Diné couple. They were teenage sweethearts when they worked as extras in the film but had never viewed it until Diamond brought it to their home. As we watch them watching the film for the first time, together with their son and *Reel Injun*'s film crew, they laugh repeatedly as they see themselves on the screen and comment to each other in Diné about the images they see. Diamond devotes screen time to one scene in the film in particular, one that features James speaking extensively in Diné to the army officer who threatens the Chiricahua leader (played by James) and all Chiricahuas with violent and swift deaths if they do not submit to the U.S. military. Their son listens to his father's on-screen speech and translates: "You will be like a snake crawling in your own shit." The officer responds as though he understands Chiricahua but speaks in English. He defends himself as though the leader has called him a fool and claims not to be a fool. The Etnas' son again translates his father's lines: "Obviously you can't do anything to me." Again the officer demands his surrender. James repeats himself, condemning the officer to a bleak future: "Just like a snake you'll be crawling in your own shit." This moment in *Reel Injun* stands at the apex of American Indian resistance to the western genre and the powerlessness Native people had over these images in the midcentury period. Not only did James Etna as the fictive Chiricahua leader push back against the abject submission demanded under threat of violence—the kind of racist imagery and dialogue deployed in thousands of westerns—but in observing and translating this filmic moment as a Diné family, the Etnas enter a larger sense of intertribal resistance. They enter their own representation with the Native documentary filmmaker who created the necessary setup for this layered moment of meaning, translation, resistance, connection, and family. The original moment in *A Distant Trumpet* is reconfigured by the Native documentary filmmaker and extras to become something entirely new and their own.

In hopes of re-creating such a moment, I asked a Diné speaker to watch films in which Navajos had appeared and to decipher whether they spoke Diné and how it translated into English. Yvonne Curley (Diné) found that of the films in which Diné appeared, most of the Diné never actually spoke Diné. In the films in which Diné did speak Diné, they never uttered a word of resistance or even annoyance. In *Fort Apache* she found no Diné with speaking parts. In *The Searchers* one Diné had a line: "There's someone coming." In *Rio Bravo* John Wayne says hello in Diné and the Diné respond with hello, also in Diné. The Diné then sing the beginning of a war song, but the rest of the song, according to Curley, is gibberish. Later in the film one of the Diné says, "The officer said stop singing. They're trying to sleep. Put that fire out. The enemies can see us when that fire's on. You're giving away our position." Still later the Diné sing the beginning of a "preparation" song, then do some more singing of made-up words. Even though Diné play Indians in *Buffalo Bill, Bugles in the Afternoon, Western Union, War Arrow, Sergeant Rutledge,* and *My Darling Clementine*, Curley heard no Diné spoken in any of these films. Curley's work demonstrates that Diné controlled their use of the Diné language by choosing to use Diné only when the lines were meaningless and neutral. When asked to speak lines they disliked, they chose to speak made-up words, a choice that slipped right past the non-Diné filmmakers. For songs that may have had a spiritual nature to them, the Diné extras also chose to sing gibberish, perhaps to protect the songs and their language, as well as to adhere to prohibitions about their use. In this way Diné controlled the use of their language, and this countering measure, even though undetected by non-Diné speakers, influenced relations among Diné on set.

Native extras also pushed back against detribalization and simple inaccuracy in films through jokes about other tribes. Diné extra Joe Quivero worked in Ford's *Sergeant Rutledge* (Warner Bros., 1960) and was quite aware of the fact he was playing an Apache. When he fell off his horse, per Ford's direction, he declared, "This could never have happened if I'd been playing a Navajo."[23] Quivero makes the simple claim that any Diné would be a skilled rider and would never get shot on a running horse. His assertion also claims tribal awareness and carefully challenges the studio to think about tribal differences, even from a pro-Diné perspective. Quivero took the money for falling off horses, but he also wanted to expose the studio to his self-image.[24] He spoke back to the erasure of tribal differences, tribal histories, and the inaccuracies engendered by one tribe playing members of another tribe. Part of maintaining tribal differences for tribal members lies in jokes and humor about one tribe being better than another. Although Quivero uttered this comment within earshot of non-Natives, Diné must have heard him as well. Quivero's distinction told the non-Natives that hiring Diné to play Apaches made no sense, and it told Diné that he was Diné, not an Apache. The studio then used this humor to its advantage to publicize their film and the fact that they hired actual tribal members.

When questioned by an interviewer about his resistance to the inaccuracies in movies, one Diné extra had very little to say. Billy Yellow (Diné) worked for John Ford on several films, including *Rio Grande* (Republic, 1950), and deftly used movie work for his own purposes. Yellow and his daughter, Evelyn Nelson, explained that he was not at all interested in or concerned about the issue of American Indian representations in film. With continued queries, Yellow reluctantly explained that sometimes extras were told which tribe they were playing, but not always. From Yellow's perspective, they had no control over their representations in films. They were told what to wear, where to stand, and how to ride, and they simply followed instructions. Nelson only recollected that she stayed with her grandmother when her mother and father were working on movie sets. At the time of his interview, Yellow was eighty-seven years old, lived in a hogan in Monument Valley, spoke no English, and had never viewed the films in which he appeared. Nelson had seen a few, but she offered no opinion on them when asked.[25] Likewise, of the seventy-five Diné men hired for *Smoke Signal* (Universal, 1955), fifteen never saw the film. These extras perhaps did not have the means to see it, which could have required extensive travel in addition to movie tickets, and perhaps they chose to ignore the film because it was simply work performed and not worth viewing. In comparison to the earlier examples, Yellow's and Nelson's comments support the idea that movie work was a survival strategy that allowed Diné to earn cash while avoiding the full burden of entering into and engaging in the disempowered, vanishing Indian of the western genre.

Although studios, unions, and the BIA appear to have shaken hands over the Diné extras, the Diné film workers made their presence felt and their demands heard, showing themselves to be part of a vital, modern, and articulate nation with clear boundaries and goals. When Fox producers sought the employment of Diné in 1946 for *My Darling Clementine* (Twentieth Century Fox), the superintendents and the Diné pushed their requirements forward explicitly by actively participating in the employment negotiations.[26] When studio officials presented their terms, they assumed the Diné would simply consent, but the Diné demanded more than just daily wages. Film work required a considerable sacrifice for them to be on the set each day, so they steadfastly sought compensation for that additional effort that would be unknown to the studio. They demanded additional fees for their travel to the shoot, care of their cattle, and still shots of the extras. The Diné knew the studio would prefer the Diné to absorb these costs, but they sought payment anyway. The Diné rejected the plan to pay them as little as possible in exchange for any and all use of their representations. They pushed assiduously to obtain control over and compensation for their images, to receive funds for the care of their animals, and to secure additional pay for photographs of their children. The studio reported these demands in demeaning tones, creating a sense that the Diné were pushing beyond the norms of negotiations with Indian extras:

> How about bales of hay? How about water? Who will feed our cattle, our herds of sheep and goats when we bring them in? The Diné talked to the 20th Century Fox interpreters and business agents for days and days and nights and nights. Will those who bring their cattle from afar get more than those who bring in their cattle from nearby? Finally all plans were completed; the pow-wows were over. Far away in the mountains Diné tribesmen had their local pow-wows, delegated their own appointees to take . . . the cattle to John Ford's location, 187 miles from a railroad in famous Monument Valley Pass.[27]

The Diné saw the necessary arrangements as encompassing far more than hourly wages, something the studio had assumed the Diné would not challenge. But this tale, albeit voiced by the studio's representatives, tells us something that goes beyond the many layers of what Diné saw as their responsibilities and possibilities for earning extra cash. The story speaks to the tension between twentieth-century Diné and the fantasy Indian. The studio bosses and even the BIA representatives foresaw all pertinent labor issues as involving the set price for their daily wages, whereas the Diné perspective encompassed a whole series of questions only Diné themselves or those who saw the world from their perspective could have anticipated. And from their perspective, the care of their children and animals had to be arranged, planned, and paid for by the studio if images of them were to be represented in any way in the film. Navajos also sought to avoid the painful history of being photographed without consent or payment. This speaks to a history of exploitation by non-Indians who have photographed and filmed Native people without permission and used those images to earn cash with virtually no wages, royalties, or residuals to the Native subjects. Diné as tourists' subjects are well aware of not getting paid for photographs, as Elsie Begay voices twice in the documentary film *The Return of Navajo Boy* (2000), when she sees dozens of postcards for sale with Diné on the front.

Where individual Indians held little power in labor negotiations, the actors' and extras' guilds held great power, at least on the broadest level. Because of labor agreements, studios were legally obliged to receive approval from the Screen Actors Guild, and later from the Screen Extras Guild (SEG) as well, for permits to hire nonmembers when filming on location. Fox received permits when hiring Indians in Utah in 1941 for *Western Union* (Twentieth Century Fox).[28] In 1952 Warner Bros. requested permission from SEG only when it wanted Diné men to do stunts for *Bugles in the Afternoon*; there were no SEG permission requests for Diné extras in general.[29] Whereas the guilds held power in Hollywood, on reservations the BIA superintendents maintained control over the hiring of Indian extras. Hiring reservation Indians differed markedly from hiring actors or extras in Los Angeles. In 1943 for the film *Buffalo Bill* Twentieth Century Fox began their search for Diné extras with the Chicago BIA office, which put the studio in touch with Diné superintendent James Stewart. The Chicago BIA sternly recommended that the studio treat the Diné with "respect and to be meticulous" in their agreements with the Diné Tribal Council and with the superintendent. Further, the studio was informed of the existence of "many sacred, religious objects scattered in various places on the reservation." Jason Joy, Twentieth Century Fox director of public relations, suggested that the studio determine the location of the sacred objects and places so as to avoid any ill feelings.[30] In this particular exchange the tribe and their representatives held the power and the studio was willing to submit to their authority and demands.

The BIA hoped for complete control over the process and made many requests of the studio. The studio initially agreed to this power imbalance but quickly shifted its thinking to one in which the studio paid the Diné as little as possible to do anything the studio desired. In the end the Diné relinquished all rights to the Twentieth Century Fox product, which was one of the studio's goals. Because the recruitment records for *Buffalo Bill* are plentiful, they provide a glimpse into how the studio hoped to recruit and negotiate with the Diné. George Dixon, an employee in Twentieth Century Fox's legal department, hoped to retain the "right to select only those types and persons as we see fit to use," meaning the studio retained the right to discriminate against Diné based on height, weight, age, gender, and so forth.[31] He wanted all employed Diné to have Social Security numbers for tax purposes as well as federal identification, which meant that many Diné would not be hired because their lack of the studio's preferred form of identification would have made payroll more complicated.

Coming from a world of images, Twentieth Century Fox planned to obtain the "exclusive right to use and utilize all pictures we take." The photos, used for publicity, would create value for the studio but not for the Diné subjects, who would not receive compensation. On the same note Dixon made it clear that if, once on the set, studio personnel decided to take photos in different settings, the legal department had to be sure the contract only paid Navajos who were actually photographed, not anyone with them, and that they would only be paid for days they were being photographed, probably meaning they would not be paid for travel days.[32] For

Diné already on set and being paid as extras, they could be photographed with or without their knowledge, would receive no extra pay and no copies of the photos, and would have no control over how the photos would be circulated. Unlike the Diné appearing in *My Darling Clementine*, this group of workers lost all control over the reproduction of their own images.

Twentieth Century Fox wanted the ease and efficiency of dealing with extras through a union but without having to pay union wages. In the effort to avoid paying the higher union wages, Fox wanted to deal with Diné in the aggregate, not as individuals. They wanted dealings mediated by the BIA and by agents appointed by Diné. In effect, this mirrors the federal government's historic insistence on negotiating with tribal leaders rather than entire tribes. As Dixon described in an additional outline of the studio's legal assertions, "Indians to appoint committee with whom we can deal representing all Indians." The studio wanted a unified Diné position in negotiations with the studio. They would hear only the single voice of unified representation in one selected Diné.[33] These labor negotiations demonstrate a win for the studios in that they continued a tradition of giving Native people as little as possible in exchange for use of their land and labor. But the studio contracts also served as a win for Native people in that they were incorporated into the union structure of wage protection and physical safety in the workplace, and tribes used leaders to negotiate for more pay and control.

Somewhat reflective of the desire for a unified Diné position represented by one negotiator, Dixon wanted the Diné to look uniformly "Indian" for *Buffalo Bill*. He required that all Diné agree to a particular yet very generic appearance. His first requirement was that "we need 600 good male riders and horses, all in full war path regalia, breech clout etc, long hair or wigs, able to ride bareback." In addition, the Diné were all to wear a "wardrobe as selected by us or ours if we furnish it." They were also to decorate their horses and themselves in "war paint," but they were obliged to follow the studio's explicit and detailed instructions. Only the studio could make decisions about the nature of the imitation: "Indians agree to perform and act as directed in war dances, rides, rituals, ceremonies, etc."[34] The studio prevented any influence by the Diné and even the possibility of the Diné expressing their concerns, discontent, or other suggestions. The studio intended to hire six hundred Diné but cut that number to two hundred because of "the restrictions on gasoline and tires" due to World War II.[35] Twentieth Century Fox may have been unwilling to hire more than two hundred Diné because so many of them did not conform to what Fox said Indians look like, and many Diné may have been unwilling to work in a controlled and uncooperative environment. Diné superintendent Stewart was made aware of this change and immediately informed his supervisors in Chicago of the change of plans and included a copy of the agreement in his letter.[36]

For the Diné, a film crew's arrival on the reservation was a significant event because it offered the opportunity to earn money, but it also meant more tourism, exploitation, and a deeply unfair and unequal trade of access to Diné land, bodies, and images in exchange for the smallest fraction of the exploiter's profits. The studios that spent massive amounts of money to bring supplies, workers, cameras, and food to Arizona repeatedly spun this asymmetrical relationship to portray themselves as generous, thoughtful, friendly, and accepting of Diné. They used that supposed generosity to elide the power differential and the simple math that they were indeed paying very little to access the Diné reservation and use images of Diné in their film. For instance, the studio claimed that when Diné learned that a film crew was arriving, many Diné began strategizing immediately about obtaining this work and planning the care of their homes, families, and animals so they could travel to the set. Rather than suggesting an embrace of the studio and their representations, this more likely hints at the poverty some Navajos lived with or feared and their strong desire to earn a living.

When the studio supposedly spoke for the Diné, they were actually drawing on the words of a white couple who squatted on Diné land until the state sold them the title to a parcel of land they had no authority to sell. Harry and Leone Goulding are the ones responsible for extending the exploitation of the Diné Nation that began with the military and extended through movies, tourism/trade, and mining. The truth of this extraction of resources sometimes burst through the couple's stories, like when they admitted Diné were desperate for cash, which is what made them eager to make arrangements to work in films. Their words suggest spectacle and amusement at witnessing these "great lengths," but the truth is Diné brought livestock numbering in the thousands to the set, which was fifty miles from their homes.[37] Leone Goulding also hinted at Diné hunger when she spoke of the Diné extras' eagerness for the studio's catered lunches. The studio promoted the experiences to override and silence Diné voices, but nonetheless the Diné voice is there and speaking to the struggle to eat, live, and thrive on a reservation where all forms of resource exploitation, extraction, and destruction were normative and profound. In his book *Making Settler Cinemas* (2010), Peter Limbrick ably explores the link between the Gouldings as settler colonials in a settler-colonial context and the structural inequality on the Diné reservation. They squatted on the reservation, refusing to leave. They had resources Diné needed. Through those resources they obtained wealth because of Diné poverty, as did studios such as Argosy and Universal, lead actors such as John Wayne and Henry Fonda, and directors such as John Ford.

The documentary *The Return of Navajo Boy* shows how the film industry's exploitation of the Navajo Nation tied in with other means of exploitation such as traders, tourism, and mining. Many studios filmed on the Navajo reservation, but John Ford is the director who filmed there repeatedly. The film documents the role of the Gouldings in drawing Navajo families into dependent relations through trade but also tourism. They brought tourists to the Cly family daily, and the film suggests this was done without that activity being properly negotiated with the Cly family. The mother, grandmother, and one of the boys in the family began suffering from lung cancer due to uranium mining on Navajo land. Even as they suffered, the Cly family was being filmed by a documentarian. When the Cly mother had her sixth child who had not yet been named, John Wayne, who was there for a film shoot, suggested his own name for the child, and the Cly family accepted. When that boy turned two, his mother died from lung cancer. His grandparents, Happy and Willy Cly, were caring for the children, but white missionaries took John Cly, adopted him out to a white couple, and promised to return him when he was six years old. John Wayne, the actor, knew of this injustice and did nothing to help the Cly family. Perhaps worst of all, the documentary shows how American companies gutted the earth to mine uranium on the Diné reservation during the Cold War in yet another phase of settler colonialism or perhaps imperialism that was accepted by the nation because of poverty. When the Cold War was over, these mines were abandoned without proper procedures, after having been operated without safety protocols. In addition to experiencing poverty as a result of being colonized, Diné people also suffer aggressive cancers as a result of their continued subjugation and exposure to U.S. militarism.[38]

Beyond Navajo Land

The Diné reservation was just one center of production; studios filmed westerns all over the country and even in Canada. Sometimes they filmed in the Southwest but used Apaches or Pueblos instead of Diné. On one fascinating occasion they brought reservation Lakotas to Hollywood. In 1940 Warner Bros. actively recruited several Lakota men from Standing Rock Reservation for their re-creation of the Battle of the Little Bighorn in *They Died with Their Boots On* (1941).[39] The process of hiring the men began with a note from a Warner Bros. production manager, T. C. Wright, to Russel Trost, a casting agent, in July. His request made clear his need for young Lakota men: "15 Sioux Indians here from the reservation for our picture. . . . These are to be used in the foreground and are the real Sioux Indians and are young men around 21. Naturally, we will use a lot of Indians, but we want just these for our foreground work. Kindly see if we can secure a waiver from the Guild to use these indians [*sic*]."[40] Sixteen Standing Rock men signed an agreement with the studio.[41] Perhaps because the work did not require a permanent or long-term stay, these Lakotas agreed to travel to Hollywood.

Problems arose between the Lakota men and the crew almost immediately, and as a result three men were sent back to their hotel for the rest of the day.[42] Only a week later, when a studio bus was sent to fetch the men for that day's filming, five of them were unable to be found because they had not returned to their hotel the night before. Although one studio executive recommended all the men be fired and given tickets back to Standing Rock, the studio arranged for a fake adoption ceremony as part of their public relations package for the film.[43] As part of this stunt, the studio sent Flying Cloud, Fast Horse, Village Center, Holy Bear, and Grey Eagle an invitation for them to adopt director Raoul Walsh and told them Walsh would "become Thunder Hawk, a blood brother in the Sioux Nation."[44] As this telegram that coerced them to adopt non-Lakotas was on its way to their hotel, the Standing Rock men were lodging a variety of complaints with SAG regarding their treatment. One studio executive warned, "No doubt we will hear about them."[45] The studio did in fact hear about their complaints, and at least one Lakota man announced his decision to leave Los Angeles and return to Standing Rock immediately without full pay. After some cajoling from the studio and other Lakotas, he changed his mind and continued on with the other men for the duration of the work agreement, after voicing his concerns to SAG and the studio.[46]

The conflict between the studio and the Standing Rock men quickly escalated. Twenty-seven-year-old Alvin Elknation and Joseph Fasthorse Jr., thirty-three, were injured by a driver while they were walking in LA. Their injury attracted the attention of the Los Angeles Police Department and landed them in the hospital.[47] Elknation and Fasthorse received treatment at the downtown Los Angeles emergency room. Then Warner Bros. moved them to Cedars of Lebanon Hospital and placed them under the care of the studio's doctor.[48] Although Warner Bros. had contractually assumed responsibility for the Lakotas while they were away from Standing Rock, the well-resourced studio balked at paying their medical bills. Frank Mattison, a producer at Warner Bros., received the bills and immediately suggested that the legal department attempt to force Louis G. Murray, the man who had struck the Lakotas with his vehicle, to pay the bills and thus relieve Warner Bros. of the financial responsibility.[49] When the men arrived on the set for makeup and filming, they instead announced they would return to their reservation immediately. They blamed this change in plans on a fight among themselves, but they were told they would need the studio's permission to leave.[50] They were essentially in Hollywood as unfree men, unable to leave, unable to control their representations, and being used as puppets to create a façade of interracial cooperation.[51]

The story of these sixteen Standing Rock Lakota men demonstrates the studios' intense desire to secure Native people, especially those living on reservations. They wanted them to lend their films authenticity and to acquiesce to such elements as the script, wardrobe choices, and their treatment on the set in addition to their appearance in the film. Yet the Lakota men chose to acquiesce only to the wages and the free trip to California, while at the same time endeavoring to disengage from the studio's attempts to gain further submission from them. The studio offered cash and free travel to Los Angeles, but they sought complete control over the men: their look in the film, their lines in the script, and their behavior outside the film set. Forcing them to pretend to adopt the director served as the ultimate irony. Native adoption of outsiders is a choice made by Native people themselves, not those they adopt. Here the studio used this well-known cultural action of Native people for an entirely manufactured adoption, overriding the men's self-representation and personal autonomy. They had come to Hollywood of their own accord, but the studio showed no flexibility in being willing to listen to the men, assist them, or even pay their medical expenses. The studio wanted an aura of authenticity from these sixteen men, even as it attempted to turn them into empty props and steal their freedom to leave Los Angeles. The studio benefited from the public and artificial moments of interracial friendship amid a private background of white men wrestling for control of the Standing Rock men. More recently, Comanche social activist LaDonna Harris "captured" and adopted actor Johnny Depp in anticipation of his role as a Comanche in *The Lone Ranger* (2013) as a conscious reversal of past studio relations with tribes. Comanche film studies scholar Dustin Tahmahkera argues that this was Harris's way of using Comanche kin relations to garner power from Depp and the Walt Disney Company, not in relation to herself but to the Comanche Nation. This adoption was reported much like the adoptions manufactured by Hollywood, but in this case it was Harris who held the reins.[52]

Unlike the Diné, who nearly always appeared in films shot on their reservation and with their extended family present, the Lakota men from Standing Rock had to leave their reservation to work for Warner Bros. They were away from home and their families and located in the densely populated urban area of Los Angeles. Historically, steady and well-paid employment often requires leaving the reservation, living away from family, and being forced to cast aside family connections, ceremonies, and regular visits home. The Lakota story demonstrates how Indian employment looks when viewed from the perspective of those whose film work required them to leave the reservation rather than work temporarily within its confines. Whereas the Diné negotiated as a nation to receive greater compensation from the studios, the sixteen Lakotas were a small group of young men with no clear leader or means of securing their needs from the power structure of Warner Bros.

Warner Bros. decided that their investment in bringing Indians to Hollywood had yielded a disastrous return. Because the sixteen men were Indians, the studio refused to concern itself with their common, human problems. The Lakota men were offended by the studio employees' lack of respect for them, even when the Lakotas demanded it. Although Warner Bros. had assumed general responsibility for the men, they attempted to shirk that responsibility the moment it would cost them money. No other group of reservation Indians left the reservation to work in Hollywood during the 1940s and 1950s, and the story of these Lakota men demonstrates the reasons Native people may have avoided such arrangements.

Studios often turned to non-Indian technical advisors such as David Miller because they proved useful to the studios for casting Indians. Miller, a non-Indian painter who spent summers in South Dakota, became an important figure in several productions, including *Tomahawk* (Universal, 1951), *The Savage* (Paramount, 1952), and *The Last Hunt* (MGM, 1956). He was known for his ability to communicate with Lakotas, and he ably negotiated dozens of Indian hires for these films. Miller's career was devoted to the study of American Indians. He wrote a book entitled *Custer's Fall* that offered a story of the Battle of the Little Bighorn from an Indian perspective. He had interviewed many Indian survivors of the battle, including Lakotas as well as Indians supporting the U.S. Army in their attack on the peaceful encampment of Lakotas and Cheyennes.

In 1951 Miller organized all aspects of hiring Lakota extras for *Tomahawk* using a culturally consistent and perhaps appropriate method for doing so.[53] He visited Lakotas, chatted with them and let them determine the pace and duration of their meeting. He brought gifts when he asked them to work on the film. Ninety-four Lakota men made agreements to work on *Tomahawk* through these visits with Miller. On the set the men allowed Miller to complete their time cards and keep track of their pay and withholding. Some of the Lakota men appearing in *Tomahawk* also worked on *The Savage* and *The Last Hunt*: Ben American Horse, James Red Cloud, John Sitting Bull, Joseph High Eagle, Dewey Beard, and Andrew Knife.[54] Another of the Lakota men on the *Tomahawk* set, Benjamin Kills Enemy, had played an Indian character years earlier, in *The Overland Limited* (Gotham Pictures, 1925).

As Lakotas received Miller in their homes and listened to his proposition, they heard nothing about the content of *Tomahawk*, which was Red Cloud's War. When the Lakotas discovered it was a film about Red Cloud, six of the men left the set immediately and refused to work in the film. They did mention that they would have appeared in a movie about Crazy Horse.[55] Clearly, these Lakota men were concerned about film content. Whereas Crazy Horse never signed a treaty or allowed his picture to be taken, Red Cloud signed the 1868 Treaty of Fort Laramie, voluntarily moved to the reservation, and converted to Catholicism. From the Lakota men's perspective, Crazy Horse had led the tribe in a way that avoided compromise and stood against settler colonialism in a clear, bold manner. Red Cloud on the other hand had compromised repeatedly and cooperated with the federal government in hopes of securing peace. Those two men, in these Lakota men's eyes, existed at opposite ends of the spectrum of Lakota leadership. For them, Crazy Horse may have been worthy of emulation and even imitation, but Red Cloud did not deserve the honor of a biographical film and they had no interest in promoting widespread knowledge of Red Cloud over Crazy Horse. In this sense the Lakota extras resisted the definitive power of the film studios. Likewise, the Standing Rock Sioux, through their chairperson David Blackhoop, made their objections loud and clear when Twentieth Century Fox filmed Sitting Bull in Mexico and hired Mexicans to play Lakotas. The studio claimed they tried to hire locally but could not reach a mutually agreeable price. Standing Rock repeatedly went to the studio and the media to complain that their tribal members had not been hired for the film.[56]

Indian extras repeatedly voiced their opinions on sets about how studios were representing Native American history. Diné extras showed their preferences for the version of history in which Indians win over whites. They were especially happy when they beat the cavalry on the set. On one occasion they kept shooting arrows and rubber bullets even after the director yelled, "Cut!"[57] In this limited sense Natives exposed their desire for winning in the battle between Indians and whites for land, as well as their enjoyment of beating the U.S. military when reenacting settler colonial violence.

Whereas the studio could have easily held a casting call for a large number of men with certain physical characteristics in Los Angeles and had the jobs filled in a day, they instead paid David Miller a per diem to visit Lakotas on site in North Dakota to secure their employment for *The Savage* (Paramount, 1951). These extras were to have very little screen time and almost no lines. Yet their physical appearance, personal histories, and connection to a Lakota past made their presence a valuable one that the studio was willing to pay cash to exploit. While organizing the hires for *The Savage*, Miller again went from home to home, asking Lakota men to join the cast. The actor Van Heflin accompanied Miller on a visit to Andrew Knife and claimed that the other visits were identical. Miller always brought gifts of cigarettes, loose tobacco, chocolate, and gum when requesting participation in film work. Miller joked and laughed with the men as well. Knife listened to Miller's description of the movie and the production process. He accepted the gifts but rejected the work offer after hearing about the responsibilities and pay. Miller left, but Knife's wife followed him as he left. Outside their home, she accepted the job on her husband's behalf. Miller gave her a few candy bars, instructions on when and where Knife would need to arrive on set, and the deal was closed. Van Heflin claimed it took Miller three days to sign up the ninety-four Lakotas who played Indians in *The Savage*.[58]

Indian men occasionally served a critical role for the studios in locating and hiring American Indian men for work in movies. Not only did they provide a valuable service to the studios, but their lives highlight historical changes for American Indians in the twentieth century. Men acculturated either by force or by choice often created a bridge to tribal members, as they were willing to communicate and negotiate with non-Indians. When Universal shot *Pillars of the Sky* (1956) in La Grande, Oregon, the studio hired Gilbert Conner, a Nez Perce man from the Umatilla reservation, to recruit Indian extras from an Oregon reservation.[59] Conner's life spanned a historical terrain of religious conversion, military service, and government work. He was born in Lapwai, Idaho, to Edward and Sarah Conner. His maternal grandfather was Olokut, Chief Joseph's brother, and Conner's father was a Presbyterian minister.[60] Conner was an educated Christian man who served in the military and married a Nez Perce and Umatilla woman, Elsie Spokane; together they had ten children. From 1903 to 1904, he was a student at the San Francisco Seminary, and in 1908 he was ordained a Presbyterian minister. In 1911 he left the Presbyterian denomination and became a Methodist minister in Lapwai. Conner died in Pendleton, Oregon, in 1967.[61] He also worked as a mail carrier and interpreter at the Umatilla reservation.

Conner recruited and hired seventy-five Native men to appear in *Pillars*, but only a handful of those men ultimately appeared in the movie. Studio publicity documents claim only a few men arrived on the set at the appointed time because the majority overslept after a late-night stick game at the Pendleton Round-Up. Conner himself appeared in the film as Chief Elijah, and Manuel Squakin (Okanagan) appeared as a background extra. Although the studio blamed their no-show on a lack of sleep, the men may have just as easily disliked the script, costumes, narrative, or control by the studio over all aspects of their representation.[62] Like Conner, Donald Deer Nose (Crow), who worked as an extra in *Warpath* (Paramount, 1951), recruited other Crow men for *The Big Sky* (RKO, 1952). He was paid about $33 a day for forty-two days of work, including his time convincing other Crows to sign up for employment as well as his on-camera appearances.[63] For the early 1950s on a reservation, this was significant pay. But his pay was significantly higher for recruiting Indians than for playing an Indian. These Indian men who worked as recruiters for the film's producers earned a great deal of money that they probably enjoyed using for long-awaited purchases and gifts to family and friends.

Universal Studios created a press release claiming that several Indian men had formed a casting company in Tucson, but this was most likely a publicity stunt fabricated by the studio. The group was said to be headed by two Diné men—Charlie White Fish and Grey Eyes Judels—who quickly signed up three hundred Indians for movie work with Universal Studios. Universal Studios mocked the Diné talent agency for using a telephone instead of smoke signals to communicate with their Indian extras. This sort of talent agency would have made the production of Universal's movie far easier, yet the studio ridiculed such efforts at becoming part of the film industry in the customary manner of using an office, calling talent, and booking gigs for extras. As this was a press release, the entire episode may have also been entirely fabricated.[64] In still other cases, Indians simply recruited themselves and arrived at set locations to ask for work. Paramount hired Navajos, Lakotas, and Apaches for *The Last Outpost* (Paramount, 1951), shot in Tucson, because the men arrived on the set with Indian-style wardrobes in hand:

> The location cameras for his big-scale Technicolor spectacle had barely been set up outside Tucson when a horde of job-seeking Indians swarmed on the scene lugging valises stuffed with tribal beads and feathers.
>
> Thanks to the renewed popularity of Western films, any brave who can ride and draw a bow is fairly certain of finding work in the many outdoor pictures going before the camera. Thus, by car, by bus and by thumb, young Indians travel to the outdoor location centers, places like Phoenix, Flagstaff, and Tucson.[65]

The studio suggested these men arrived in large numbers and implied they did so with great enthusiasm. Time and again Native people sought film work in spite of distance, weather, and outside constraints such as family and animal care. But this eagerness and perseverance came from economic insecurity and determination to ensure their family's survival, in spite of the films and their content. Many Native people never saw the films in which they appeared, as even that was beyond their financial power.

Sixty young Pine Ridge Reservation men showed up on the set of *Tomahawk* (Universal, 1951) hoping to secure the role of Crazy Horse. They discovered where the crew was shooting, arrived at the set, and made it clear they wanted to compete for the prominent part. In the end Crazy Horse was not a character in the film. John War Eagle played the only Indian lead (Red Cloud), so the sixty Pine Ridge men were probably offered parts as extras.[66] A handful of Shoshone and Lakota men (it is unclear whether they were Shoshones, Lakotas, or both) beat their drums outside the Alex Johnson Hotel in Rapid City, South Dakota, until director George Sherman hired them for *Chief Crazy Horse* (Universal, 1955).[67] When an Indian named Bud Leith was living near Chiloquin, Oregon, he wrote a letter through the local Indian superintendent asking Jack Warner for a part in *They Died with Their Boots On* (1941). Leith claimed he had appeared in a few films as an Indian extra, but Warner Bros. failed to make him an offer.[68]

Often studios hired reservation Indians but left no record as to how they located or contacted them, and this aspect of filmmaking seldom makes its way into film criticism. In the Southwest, Diné were hired most frequently, but studios recruited members of other tribes as well. Twentieth Century Fox planned to hire Apaches but switched to Tewas for *Two Flags West* (1950). Darryl Zanuck, head of Twentieth Century Fox at that time, probably had something to do with the change. He felt their studio paid White Mountain Apache extras too much for their work in *Broken Arrow* (1950), shot in Sedona, Arizona.[69] He specifically requested that the *Two Flags* writer streamline the scenes with Indians to cut down on expenses.[70] Warner Bros. hired local Seminole men for *Distant Drums* (1951), though it is unknown how they were recruited. Among them were Sidney Capo, who played Little Cloud; George Deer, who did voiceovers in Creek; and four anonymous Seminole extras who appeared randomly in the background.[71] Two years later Warner Bros. filmed *Hondo* (1953) in Mexico. They recruited Mexicans, Apaches, stunt performers, and 150 Tarahumaras to play Indians.[72] Warner Bros. hired men from several Plains tribes for *The Command* (1953).[73] In 1946 MGM hired two hundred Shoshones and Arapahos in Wyoming for *Bad Bascomb*.[74] In 1950, for *Devil's Doorway*, the same studio hired Indians in Colorado with undisclosed tribal affiliations; James Harper, Samuel Little Bear, and Bertha Cody were among them.[75] One year later MGM hired Lakotas for *Across the Wide Missouri* (1951).[76]

Follow the Money

The hiring of American Indians for film work was rarely a simple process. A variety of intermediaries negotiated their employment. No single person or agency, Indian or non-Indian, held total power in recruiting reservation Indians for film work. Films seem to be about narrative and arc, but money is actually the axis on which movies revolve: movies cost money to produce, audiences pay money to see them, film workers want to earn money, and film investors are looking for profit. As early as the 1920s the lowest workers in the film industry began trying to find ways to protect and increase their earnings. In 1924 a labor study concluded that employment conditions were favorable in the industry but recommended a free central registration point for extras so that they could avoid agent commissions. On December 4, 1925, the Association of Motion Picture Producers created the Central Casting Corporation (CCC) to act as a personnel office for Hollywood extras. With CCC, extras received work assignments over the phone. Previously they had raced from studio to studio all day, standing in what were called "bull pens," often without being hired. The non-negotiable vouchers that forced extras to work in one location, receive a voucher, and travel to another location to cash them were abolished. One year after the Department of Industrial Relations was founded, it established an eight-hour work day and overtime regulations for extras. At that time, however, the department did not oversee wages.[77] The changes the CCC instituted had no effect on reservation Indian extras; the new rules that applied to extras excluded all Indians living on reservations.[78]

The CCC defined an extra as someone who worked primarily as an extra, owned and maintained a wardrobe for extra work, and lived in the greater Los Angeles area. It defined extras in this way to keep wages high but made no effort to prevent nonextras from working as extras. The organization simply did not want them enrolled with CCC because it would officially bring down wage rates.[79] With the Studio Basic Agreement of 1937, the definition of extras remained specific and exclusionary but allowed for permits to those living three hundred miles or more outside Los Angeles.[80] Because of unresolved issues relating to extras, a standing committee was created.[81]

Regardless of the additional layer of management, minimum wages were increased with the 1941 and 1945 agreements, and work conditions (travel time, overtime, hairdressing, makeup time, etc.) improved in both years as well. In 1945 SAG relinquished all control over extra work.[82]

Because they were not incorporated into the guild system of actors and extras in Los Angeles, reservation Indian extras were paid far less than professional extras and stunt performers. On the set the studio could use the clauses in their agreement to hire extras for stunts at lower pay, but the spirit of the agreement was to protect the high wages of stunt performers:

> The Producer agrees that all stunts called for by the script shall be performed by stunt men hired directly and not by extras adjusted on the set, except where a stunt player has been hired to perform the stunt and for any reason is unavailable or unable to properly perform the stunt.
>
> An extra hired as such may perform a non-script stunt, in which case the extra shall be signed off as an extra and employed as a stunt player. The player so adjusted may be closed and signed off as a stunt player and be re-employed in the same photoplay to perform extra work.[83]

Organized labor wanted to keep location extras' pay minimal and keep their own members' pay high.[84] The Indian extras' pay ranged from $3 to $13 a day. Those who made more were doing stunts or playing chiefs. The vast majority made about $6 a day. Indian women and children often made less.

Although underpublicized then and now, reservation Indian labor fueled the production of movies that included Indian characters in the 1940s and 1950s. Without them, studios continued to represent Indians by using non-Indian extras for a pantheon of complicated reasons, but those representations worked in a fundamentally different mode. In symbol, then, Diné and other Indians held the ultimate power and influence over the Indian look. Focusing strictly on Indian characters as symbols in movies makes them seem to be powerless victims of the racist machinery of the studio system, but Indians cannot be identified solely as powerless victims in that the studios wanted them, if they were cheap and accessible, but also because Native people chose to work in these films and to use this work to achieve their own goals, which had little or nothing to do with imagery and everything to do with solving the problem of poverty and creating paths toward survival. In spite of this, Indians were not well placed to manipulate studios. Navajos, for example, were still reeling from the effects of forced livestock reduction and their rejection of the Indian Reorganization Act. The studios used Diné and other Native people for cheap, extremely temporary employment. The Diné used the studios to obtain cash in an economy lacking high-paying wage work. In the 1940s and 1950s many reservations, but by no means all, desperately needed work for tribal members, especially short-term work that did not require a permanent move off the reservation.

Film work in the 1940s and 1950s became part of the Navajo people's own increased reliance on a wage economy. By the 1950s they had shifted from a primarily stock-raising economy to a wage economy, and the hiring of Diné in the 1940s and 1950s fits into the larger pattern of wage employment on their reservation.[85] In the 1940s Diné were being paid about $6 a day for film work, but Twentieth Century Fox employee George Dixon envisioned paying Diné men $5 a day, women $3 a day, and $2 for horses, if fed by the Diné.[86] In the end the men were indeed paid $5 a day and women $3 a day. They also received $1.50 a day for meals and were limited to ten days' work.[87] While shooting *She Wore a Yellow Ribbon* (RKO, 1949), however, Diné extras earned $18 a day, almost twice as much as the Mormon extras doing the same work.[88]

John Ford's contemporaries claimed Ford remunerated the Diné extras quite fairly. In 1939, while making *Stagecoach*, Ford paid the Diné extras the same rate he would have paid Hollywood extras: $3 a day, for a total of $48,000 in wages to Diné. This was the first time he hired Bob Many Mules and the Stanley brothers, Diné men who went on to work for Ford many times in the 1940s and 1950s.[89] Ford also hired Lee Bradley on numerous occasions to interpret for the Diné extras, including those on the set of *Stagecoach* (1939). Bradley was paid far better than the Diné extras, however: $25 a day.[90] By 1946 Diné extras were being paid slightly more. Fox agreed to pay unskilled laborers $6.60 per day and skilled laborers, of any type, $9.50 per day plus one meal for their production of *My Darling Clementine* (Twentieth Century Fox, 1946). There were also provisions for horses, cattle, and water tanks.[91] Fox hired Frank Bradley and Fred

Yazzie to guard the Monument Valley set for $100 a month (about $4 a day).[92] Five years later Ford filmed *The Searchers* (Warner Bros., 1956) and hired Diné extras and day laborers. Bradley interpreted for the Diné once again.[93] Warner Bros. paid a total of $35,000 to the Diné for their labor.[94]

Although Ford established consistency in wage rates when filming on the Diné reservation, other studios' wage rates indicate a high degree of fluctuation. In 1950 Diné worked on several film productions. Universal went on location that year to Sedona, Arizona, to film *Comanche Territory*, and the Diné were probably paid $6.60 a day, although some records show they earned as much as $7 to $16 a day. The Diné working on *Comanche Territory* doubled their pay by working simultaneously on the set of *The Eagle and the Hawk* (Paramount, 1950 [reissued in 1962 as *Spread Eagle*]).[95]

During the 1950s pay for Diné extras increased appreciably. In 1951 Universal hired Diné extras and paid them between $6 and $10 a day, as they did for the non-Indians who played soldiers.[96] In 1952 Warner Bros. paid Diné extras an extremely high rate of $12.50 a day plus $4 for subsistence when they were not working but just on hand.[97] The Diné men who were willing to perform stunts received $55 a day.[98] In 1953 Paramount hired Diné extras for $10 a day plus $3 per day for subsistence. They hired Diné even though the film was shot in Brackettville, Texas.[99] That same year Universal paid Diné extras $16 to $22 a day.[100] In 1954 Universal hired Diné to work in a production filmed in Moab. Two of the Diné, Edna Parrish and Seth Bigman, received special rates of $70 a day. Universal hired other Diné as well, but it is unknown how much they were paid.[101] Diné men working in nearby mines earned only about half the pay Diné men working in movies as extras were earning. A 1955 study shows that Diné miners hired by the Argentine Mining Company earned a total of $1,549.46 per man between July 1953 and June 1954. If they worked five days a week without absences, they earned about $6 a day. On the other hand, those working in the film industry were earning an average of $15 a day that same year.[102]

When looking at wage rates for Indian extras other than the Diné, the picture becomes less clear, with the rates covering a range that makes it impossible to generalize, most likely because the rates were for different types of work. These hires were also scattered across the country and thus their compensation does not lend itself to firm conclusions. In 1941 Warner Bros. paid men from Standing Rock $5 a day.[103] Some eleven years later Paramount hired Shoshones, Arapahos, and Flatheads near Moran, Wyoming, at the rate of $10 a day, while riders earned $12.50 a day.[104] That same year Universal paid Shoshone extras $4 to $10 a day.[105] Paramount paid Utes $10 to $100 a day in 1951. Those earning above $10 a day performed stunts or played chiefs.[106] In 1951 Universal paid Lakota extras between $6 and $10 a day and non-Indian laborers $8 to $11 a day. The pay for Lakotas was lower for women and children, but most of the men received $10 a day.[107]

The wage rates resist generalization because neither government rules nor unions were in the mix. Those who were paid higher wages were simply lucky, they were given a line to speak, or their role was to fall off a horse. When Universal filmed near Banff, Alberta, in 1954, the studio hired two hundred Crees and Lakotas for $7 to $25 a day, with most earning $6 a day.[108] The Cree farmer Jonas Applegarth earned $9.80 a day ($10 extra per fall).[109] They were limited to two to seven days of work. The non-Indians who were hired to play Mounties were paid similarly: $15 a day.[110] In 1956 Universal located its set in Oregon, where it hired several Umatillas from the reservation. The studio also hired National Guard members to play background Indians. All appear to have been paid $7 to $10 a day.[111] In the Southwest film studios hired Indians other than Diné, but there is little evidence of how much such extras were paid for their work. For example, Papov Da (a Tewa) was hired to "direct them [the film crew] away from the hidden shrines" in 1950, but there is no known record of how much he was paid.[112] 1955 Universal employed Hualapai extras at $10 a day. Those who performed stunts earned up to $70 a day.

Studio records do not always contain information about extras' tribal affiliations, which makes it almost impossible to distinguish between tribal members playing members of another tribe and non-Indians playing Indians. Such records only mention "Indians" when referring to the people hired to play Indians, and there is often no indication of the identity of those people playing Indian characters. Nonetheless, these "Indians" were paid slightly higher wages than reservation Indians. In 1947 Paramount paid 150 "Indians" $10.50 to $100 a day; one of them, Iron Eyes Cody served as a technical advisor.[113] One year later the studio hired Indians and paid them between $15.56 and $35 a day.[114] In 1953 they hired unidentified "Indians" at many rates: $12.50 a day, $50 a day, $10 a day plus a $2 a day.[115] In 1950 Universal hired "Indians" from throughout southern Arizona for $10 to $16 a day. Three years later they hired "Indians" for $16 a day, with a few earning up to $45 a day.[116]

The film productions affected not just those hired for the shoot but the Indian communities the crews entered. Besides the wages received by the Indian extras, tribes sometimes received funds and infrastructure in the form of buildings, lumber, and roads.[117] Twentieth Century Fox built an army barracks and left it to the Tewas, who converted it into a youth center offering movies, radio, a library, and table tennis after the filming of *Two Flags West* (1950).[118] While filming *Fort Dobbs* (1958), Warner Bros. constructed an additional thirty-five miles of road in Kanab, Utah, and Fort Kanab was rebuilt at no cost to the city.[119] On the South Dakota set of *Chief Crazy Horse* (1955), Universal bought tipis for background shots, and the Lakotas then purchased them in hopes of using them as roadside tourist attractions.[120] In Twentieth Century Fox's application to film on the Diné reservation for *My Darling Clementine*, the studio agreed to pay the tribe $25 a day for use of the location; the tribe received location pay because filming activity would involve use of water sources and cattle.[121] After completing the filming, the studio requested permission from the Department of the Interior to leave a street set in place for one year in case they again filmed on the reservation. The department granted permission but promised no protection for the set.[122] Later the studio offered the set to the Diné for $5, and the tribe purchased it.[123] Mike Goulding reports that the set was left up for five years, and the Diné Tribal Council rented out the set to other studios before breaking it down to use the lumber.[124]

In 1944 Crows rented out their allotments while Twentieth Century Fox was filming ceremonies related to the Sun Dance being held on the reservation. Elaine Whitebear rented out her allotment for one month for $10. Clifford Takes Horse rented his to the studio for three days and received $5.[125] Fox paid Dan W. Maddox $50 to arrange contracts with the Crows who were photographed during ceremonies related to the Sun Dance held in connection with the studio's production of *Buffalo Bill* (1944).[126] For a fee of $500 the Crow Agency Committee gave Fox the right to photograph the event and its participants, the buffalo herd, and the killing of the buffalo for Fox's production of *Buffalo Bill*. The studio also hired Crows for selected film sequences for $1 to $7.50 a day. Many Crows rented out tipis for $5 a month for four months.[127] Film companies also affected Indian communities by increasing tourism. The presence of film stars Cornel Wilde, Linda Darnell, and Joseph Cotten, for example, drew an unusual number of tourists to San Ildefonso Pueblo in New Mexico. The Tewas were reported to be selling so many goods that they had to request more from other Pueblos in Taos.[128] Reportedly, the local economy of Kanab, Utah, took in an extra $100,000 from tourism during the filming of *Fort Dobbs*.[129]

Although these movie economies on reservations were temporary, they fit into the introduction of wage labor on reservations. Many reservations desperately needed additional sources of income for tribal members. Film studios left cash in the hands of the reservation residents who played Indians, but others prospered from film production as well. Some of those people included the Gouldings. Hotel owners, caterers, and even the electric company made money from Hollywood's brief but highly intense stays in rural and reservation communities. Like western towns of the nineteenth century that had intermittent visits from white men with substantial cash in their pockets and reasons to spend it, these towns and reservations gained support from the presence of film sets and crews. In supporting local businesses, the studios often changed the people and the landscape, but Hollywood's arrival in the rural West did more than leave money behind. Filming in the rural West brought Hollywood to these isolated communities. Many residents did not have televisions. Also, not every town had a movie theater, and not everyone who lived in these communities had transportation to town. As later chapters show, some Indians were well versed in their knowledge of Hollywood, but for those who lacked knowledge, this was a first-hand introduction to the ways of Los Angeles, Hollywood, and image production.

Although their film work was temporary, American Indians adjusted to the movie system and used it for their own purposes. They were modern people using a modern system and medium. Some changed their names. Others used movie props to decorate their cars. For one Oklahoma Muscogee, the memories tell a complicated story about family, small-town life, and the desire to make quick and easy money. Dr. Cecil Meares recalled that his mother compelled him to seek film work as an Indian extra. He attended the casting call at Severs Hotel in Muskogee. Meares indicated a high level of excitement, anticipation, and even wonder at the entrance to the unfamiliar and glamorous world of Hollywood in the familiar and quite unglamorous place that Muskogee represented to him. This moment, when Warner Bros. entered Muskogee, meant a great deal to Meares, then and later on. For him, the film company's arrival "turned out to be the most exciting event in that part of the country since Tyrone Power and others rolled into Neosho in far southwestern Missouri a few years before to film a movie about the western gunfighter and outlaw, Jesse James. Half the people of eastern Oklahoma drove their A-model Fords up there to watch the filming. About the same amount of fervor attached itself to the crowd crowding the streets [when] the Jim Thorpe company arrived."[130]

For Meares, it was familial—specifically, maternal coaxing—that motivated his appearance at the audition. His mother was "thrilled and yelled with delight" when she learned Cecil had made the cut. And unlike the Diné extra Billy Yellow, who had little to say about his work in *Jim Thorpe, All American* (Warner Bros., 1951), Meares used the word "pleasure" to describe how he felt at the time of filming and how he felt looking back. He said he owned a copy of the film, which he stored in a "safe place . . . for private viewing and reminiscing." Meares gained a "certain amount of celebrity status" for his appearance in *Jim Thorpe*, which he found enjoyable. He was paid $50 a day, as he was considered a bit player. Warner Bros. paid $17 to the extras. Meares remembered both wage levels as "unheard of riches to Okie Indians in 1950."[131]

Other Indians categorized movie work as simply work, no less and no more. Louis Andrade, a Luiseño from the La Jolla Nation, worked in movies during summers in high school. He lived in Los Angeles with his parents, sisters, and brother. He and his family never looked for movie work themselves. Instead, another tribal member also living in Los Angeles would call his family when work was available. She, in turn, received notice of work availability from Iron Eyes Cody (and like other Indians, Andrade knew Cody was not Indian). Andrade and his family would travel to the studios together for work as extras, which they were glad to have, but Andrade had no interest in full-time work as an actor. He enjoyed the work, as he was on his summer break, and remembered looking at World War I bomber planes on the studio lot with more excitement than when he met movie stars. In fact, the single movie star he mentioned by name he pointed out was "stuck up." Andrade emphasized repeatedly that his family was glad to have the extra money, especially as this took place during the Depression. When invited to join SAG, his father declined, and the family never worked in movies again. His father worked the rest of his life as a plaster tender, and his son followed in his footsteps. Andrade also created silver jewelry that he and his wife sold at craft shows. In the overall scheme of his life, movies had a small and largely insignificant part, and it had little impact on their identity as Indians. For them, it was simply and only a way to supplement their other sources of income without much physical output.[132]

These films repeatedly featured Indians falling off horses to indicate their defeat, but for Indian extras, falling off horses became a source of income. *Comanche Territory* (Universal, 1950) director George Sherman hired non-Indian stunt riders to fall off their horses for $55 a day. He hired them instead of Diné because the Diné "fell off their horses too gracefully," which did not create the desired image of Indians randomly and violently falling off their horses.[133] In 1954 Diné men started throwing themselves off of their horses when they saw the stunt performers doing so. They learned how to perform the stunt by observing the professionals' methods; they knew they could earn more money by falling and doing it correctly.[134] By the mid-1950s studios had produced many films on or near the Diné reservation, and by then Diné men were well aware of the clear economic benefits of performing stunts for the studios. Diné superficially adapted to the expectations of film studios in all sorts of ways. One Diné created and used a name strictly for the purposes of getting more work as an Indian extra in the movies. His birth name was Francis Phillips, but when looking for film employment, he identified as Milton Happy Nose because the movie companies gave him more work with that name.[135]

In communities seldom sought out by producers, Indians looking for movie work had to accept the studios' work conditions. Director George Sherman was thrilled to work with Crees in 1954 because he thought other Indians (he was probably implying Diné) had become lethargic after appearing in so many films. As this comment appeared in a press release, it could also mean the studio wanted to represent itself as frequently employing Native Americans. But like the Diné, Crees voluntarily flung themselves off their horses after learning about the extra pay ($10 per fall); director Raoul Walsh even had to reshoot scenes because there were too many falling Indians. Similarly, some Indians became aware of their earning power after having contact with film crews and learning the value of their image on film. To make some quick money, Crees demanded $1 per photograph from tourists and from Universal photographers.[136] On the 1951 South Dakota set of *Tomahawk*, Lakotas also charged to have their pictures taken.[137] Even driving could earn an Indian additional pay. Chief Deerfoot, an Apache who had once worked with Tom Mix, was hired by Robert Taylor to chauffeur him around the Gallup, New Mexico, set of *Ambush* (MGM, 1950) and to take care of the horse he brought with him.[138]

All of this should make clear just how motivated Native people were to work in film, as it provided significantly higher wages than their regular work and required little physical exertion. Indians living on reservations worked in movies and for film crews because of their great need for cash in poverty-stricken circumstances. If Billy Yellow is paradigmatic of Diné extras who worked only for the wages and never even saw the films in which they worked, Lee Bradley, the Diné interpreter, represents the other extreme. He claimed to have seen every movie on which he worked. He drove hundreds of miles round-trip to visit a movie theater.

For the most part, reservation Diné and other reservation Indians who worked in movies temporarily were not interested in becoming actors or moving to Hollywood. They simply wanted to earn cash as quickly as possible in between their other household and community commitments. But the examples of star-struck Diné, of Diné taking photos of stars like

William Holden, and of Diné women expressing their preferences for white male leads complicates the picture. One Diné teenager was enamored with Virginia Mayo. Another young Diné man knew the latest Hollywood gossip, supposedly from reading *Variety*.[139] Only one Diné, Grey Eyes, went to Hollywood. His visit was very brief, and he insisted on bringing his immediate family with him.

Although some Navajos were working off the reservation during this period, most Diné preferred not to do so, even temporarily. Movie work appealed to reservation Diné because it provided wages on the reservation. After finishing production on *Comanche Territory* (Universal, 1950), director George Sherman found he needed to retake a scene that was done on the Arizona set using Diné extras. Universal wired Shine Smith, a reservation missionary, asking him to send several Diné to Hollywood by plane, with all expenses paid by the studio. Smith called the studio with their response: they had no interest in working in Hollywood, but they would be happy to work if the scenes could be filmed in Arizona. Universal concluded, "Hollywood holds no lure for the Navajo Indian." Sherman thus painted and wigged non-Indians for the retakes.[140] Reservation Diné had little desire to leave their homes for even temporary work in Hollywood. The vast majority of them had responsibilities for family and livestock that would go unmet if they traveled such a long distance. No amount of money could compensate for the lack of care for their families and homes in their absence. Moreover, being at such a great distance would have prevented them from quickly returning should an emergency have arisen. From the perspective of the studio, a Diné turning down an employment opportunity from Hollywood made no sense. They saw desperate actors every day and projected the actors' eagerness onto the Diné. Universal had presumed that nobody would reject an offer to be flown to Hollywood for work.

Studios audaciously claimed that reservation Indians rejected some film work due to their demands for luxury items, a claim that seems far-fetched at best. According to studio documents, when Diné arrived for the filming of *Drum Beat* (Warner Bros., 1954), they left when they discovered the television reception at the location was horrible.[141] This story suggests that Diné were not desperate for employment and that they may have accepted the roles but expected amenities on set. However, television was still relatively new in 1954, and many of the Diné on the reservation did not have electricity. In that sense, the story seems perhaps designed to ridicule the Diné and erase their poverty. The story ignores the tremendous poverty on the Diné reservation and every other possible reason they left the set. There may have been a setback or mistreatment they were not willing to accept that had nothing to do with television, such as the content of the film. When Native people rejected film work, they may have complained and found no support for their difficulties. George Silver Bow experienced some trouble as an Indian extra in *The Covered Wagon* (1923) that caused him to not work in another film for twenty-five years. The only explanation the studio offered based on his comments was that he found actors to be "crazy." Silver Bow's statement can be read multiple ways, all of which suggest criticism of Hollywood, film, and movie stars.[142]

Conclusion

Actors, regardless of their ethnicity, received more work and more pay than extras. Indian extras earned small sums when compared to actors, but they received cash in newly established wage economies and they did so without having to leave the reservation. Moreover, American Indians stood to gain a great deal by working in films as extras, rather than leaving their reservations to work in mines or factories. American Indians could fit film work around their other responsibilities, and they made more per day on sets than they did in industrial jobs. The drawback of the film work was its sporadic nature and the prohibitions against Native employees influencing content.

Why did American Indians work in these films? What made some of them travel far from home for this work, sometimes bringing and other times leaving family members? Offering their time as extras was a trade in which Indians pretended to be directly from the past and were compelled to hide their modern identities for the day. They auditioned and arrived on sets looking for employment despite the insulting nature of the work because it provided cash they needed. In a historical sense Indians were not doing anything terribly different from what they had done in previous generations. They were working with outsiders in a trade relationship even though the trade was for wages. The studios can thus be seen in a larger context of American Indians negotiating with outsiders over their goods and their physical presence in front of the camera.

Studios could and did make movies with Indian characters without hiring Indians, but they also hired Indians to play Indians throughout the 1940s and 1950s. The studios collected their names and Social Security numbers and made the legal deductions from their pay while making movies that, ironically, denied them their place in the twentieth century. Indian extras consistently tried to receive more pay and better conditions, and they were able to gain advantages at times. They sometimes demonstrated their knowledge of movies and the Hollywood scene, but they were constantly put in stereotyped roles lacking in nuance and character development. Studios meant for their audiences to behold strong white men with vanishing Indians massed together in the background. In addition to the incredible inequality between Indians and whites in general in the 1940s and 1950s, the narrative structures mirrored that inequality, with Indian characters serving as the backdrop and foil. Even Native actors who dedicated their lives to entertainment only rose so far in Hollywood's hierarchy. White actors held an absolute monopoly on film roles. To turn Indians into stars instead of mere extras would require an altogether new relationship with tribal nations and a fundamental change in casting and content.[143]

Although they actively recruited Native people for film work, filmmakers made American Indian roles available to all ethnicities. The person behind the makeup may have been any one of several ethnicities, but the image was the same regardless. Filmmakers held fast to their physical image of Indians, yet they showed deep ambivalence as to whether these parts should be played by Indians or non-Indians. This conundrum led filmmakers into the subject of chapters 4 and 5: reducing Native people to a race denoted by a certain look rather than a wide variety of tribal nations. Race, as a category of analysis, is wholly fictional, yet race does have a reality: a social and political reality with a history. Bodies are the places where this social fiction is told. On bodies being prepared for screen time, race as a social fiction is rendered concrete and material. Race is told as a wholly fictional story with a concrete genealogy, and yet on film sets the creation of a race of Native people required a great number of confounding details. After the complicated process of hiring was complete and production dates were set, actors and extras arrived on the set to be photographed. Before they could step in front of cameras, they were transformed from their actual selves into Indians easily recognizable by audiences. Regardless of who took a seat in the makeup chair, the body was literally made over. To their Indian bodies studio staff added brown makeup, black hair, and buckskins, and this particular combination was largely the same for every film, regardless of tribe or historical period. In chapters 4 and 5 I look closely at the makeup, hair, and wardrobe of the non-Indians and Indians who performed as Indian characters in the 1940s and 1950s. According to the variety of stories told about Indians in the films and the complicated history of labor in the film industry, Hollywood attached pronounced noses, brawny muscles, black wigs with braids, and brown skin to one and all.

"White May Be More Than Skin Deep"

Whites in Redface

Settler colonialism destroys to replace.... On the one hand, settler society required the practical elimination of the natives in order to establish itself on their territory. On the symbolic level, however, settler society subsequently sought to recuperate indigeneity in order to express its difference—and, accordingly, its independence—from the mother country.

—Patrick Wolfe, "Settler Colonialism and the Elimination of the Native"

In the world of films representing history and dramatic clashes and battles, huge numbers of bodies provide the backdrop. Viewers watch a protagonist, but that figure walks and speaks in front of hundreds of American Indians, who also watch the protagonist. Although the viewer's eye is drawn to the Indians in the background, the eye is immediately drawn back to the protagonist. Even when an Indian character interacts in the foreground with the protagonist, the camera demands that our eyes return to the white protagonist. The protagonist's whiteness stands in contradistinction to the Indian's brownness. In this sense filmic bodies are marked racially through skin color as they stand in front of the camera, and this racial distinction was intentionally created and manipulated by the studios' makeup departments.

The physical creation of Indian characters from the bodies of whites is the subject of this chapter.

In films produced with Indian characters between 1941 and 1960, the amassed Indian bodies either do not speak or their speech is extremely limited. Therefore, the representation and presentation of their bodies communicates their presence rather than their speech. Hollywood spent time, money, and a great deal of care constructing Indians from real Indians and non-Indians alike. Someone had to make a decision about which bodily markers denoted Indian identity in the effort to create Indians for the screen. But they also considered the kind of bodies they were looking at as they prepared to paint and bedeck them with wigs and other apparel: were they looking at Indians or non-Indians? In making decisions about the actors' and extras' racial identities, filmmakers often resorted to the same markers they used to create Indians. In breaking down how makeup departments approached the creation of Indian characters, we can historicize Hollywood's images of Indians in a unique way. We can dissect the on-screen images for their implications, but these racial visions were inscribed on the bodies of actual people, both Indian and white. The Natives who were bedecked must be part of the analysis of this problematic imagery; otherwise, we too erase Native people from the history of Hollywood.

Those who played Indians succumbed entirely to the dictates of the studios' Indian stereotypes, and such stereotypes centered on physical appearance. Any midcentury audience would have recognized the look: darkened skin, war paint, and buckskin wardrobes. The Indian look possesses a seemingly universal power. A nineteenth- or even eighteenth-century audience would have recognized these characters as Indians immediately. Where does this look originate? The dark skin came from a belief in the discreteness of racial categories, indicated by skin color. The war paint and buckskin wardrobes were pulled from many images, most of which would have been part of Plains Indians' cultures. Regardless of studio, era, or tribe, most Indian characters were made to look virtually identical.[1] The studios may have inherited this axiom from the nineteenth century, but they solidified it in the minds of non-Native Americans. Twentieth Century Fox stated the idea that no real differences exist between Indian characters in movies: "an Indian is an Indian."[2] Indian characters moved on the screen but rarely spoke. When Indians entered the film's narrative as mute sources of violence, their costumes and makeup spoke through their physical movements. They arrived en masse, a silent, anonymous collective.[3] However, the way this silence works rests on the physical markers of Indian difference. Without the physical markers of difference, these background Indians could have been misperceived as non-Indian. Without speech, their only means of character development was through racial markers and group appearance.[4]

The studios' beliefs about racial identity rested on deep ambivalence and manipulation that were apparent in their publicity materials, both photos and press releases. Even photos meant to appear casual were staged, and press releases often have a farcical quality. These materials do not bear witness to the truth, but they certainly bear testament to the studios' intentions. They point the way to the studios' agendas around race, Indigeneity, and whiteness. And they show a pattern in creating a parallel universe to the movie as text in which non-Indians can play with racial identity while maintaining whiteness. They also reinforce the story from the movies themselves: that Native people are fundamentally different, often violent, or vanishing. The studios made the boundaries of race fixed in that the wigs, noses, and contact lenses they adopted to communicate Indian identity were bounded material items. However, these objects also emphasized the flexibility of race when nonwhite actors were transformed into Indians with relative ease. The studios needed to remind the public that their non-Indian actors were, in fact, not Indian, while maintaining the idea that they looked quite Indian while in costume. Hollywood grounded whiteness by accenting the difference between role-playing and real life. The movie industry depended on stars whose identity as stars was constant even as their roles shifted. By holding onto opposing understandings of race, film studios confronted the inherent paradox in such a position. Additionally, audiences knew who was behind the makeup. There was no getting around the public's awareness of the false front of makeup and wigs when it came to non-Indian actors and extras. Midcentury audiences wanted images of Indians that were believable, and actually knowing who was behind the makeup could, oddly enough, permanently disrupt a viewer's enjoyment of a film with Indians in the background or the fore.

The American public wanted to see an Indian character on the screen, but they also wanted to see the actor, the social being behind the makeup. Studios knew that audiences readily developed affinities for certain actors. They also knew that audiences would reject movies in which an actor and the actor's role were poorly or awkwardly matched. Not only might they reject the film because of the disconnect between the actor and the role, but this mismatch could reduce an actor's fan base permanently. Typecasting limited actors to playing characters of only one race, and playing a character of another ethnicity could be damaging to their careers. But playing an American Indian could also increase popularity and an appreciation for having extended their repertoire. Many white actors who played Indians in the 1940s and 1950s did not have star status, and this perhaps explains their turn toward nonwhite roles. For successful white actors, taking Indian roles was seen as a career killer. This chapter is dedicated to an exploration of white actors taking Indian roles in film.

Makeup

The prevalence of white actors taking Indian roles tramples supposed racial boundaries, but studios and news services used non-Indians dressed up as Indians to send a message to the American public about the intransigence of race.[5] Whereas whites used blackface to reinforce the idea of black criminality and justify their violence and prejudice toward African Americans, studios used redface, a term coined by Michelle Raheja, to amplify the erasure of Native people in the larger U.S. society.[6] In 1949 Warner Bros. hired the blonde-haired, blue-eyed Virginia Mayo, a member of the Daughters of the American Revolution no less, to play an Indian character. Mayo's face and legs were painted brown for her role as Colorado Carson in *Colorado Territory* (1949). The studio claimed she required an inordinate amount of retouching because "her coloring kept wearing off."[7] Warner Bros. sold the dilemma as one that went beyond a physical matter of makeup rubbing off Mayo's body due to faulty makeup or application. Instead, Mayo's whiteness was defined as a transcendent quality.[8]

One contemporary magazine writer equated her whiteness with purity. He found Mayo's skin to be abnormally white. The writer praised Mayo for allowing her white body to be tainted in such a way. He also used Mayo's inability to darken as a cautionary tale to nonwhites on the futility of lightening their skin. Because of the vernacular used by the writer, the nonwhites he refers to are most likely African Americans—yet another instance in which American Indians are written out of a twentieth-century existence:

> They painted Miss Mayo a delicate shade of brown. On the following day, however, when the footage was projected, Miss Mayo's screen image was as white as before she was painted!
>
> Miss Mayo was then darkened three shades. She still projected white. By the time they got her so that she would register on the screen as a light-brown, she was as dark to the naked eye as Topsy, or sumpin!
>
> Nobody at Warner's has been able to explain the phenomenon. The cinematographer thinks Miss Mayo's body must reflect light in some peculiar manner. The make-up experts are trying to get her to pose for a picture in a dark room without any light at all. They insist that her skin must be luminous, or something.
>
> But to many a fugitive from a jar of Dr. Fred Palmer's Skin Whitener, all this is just further, discouraging evidence that *white may be more than skin deep*![9]

This writer conveyed all kinds of cultural messages; for example, when filmmakers painted and dressed non-Indians to become Movie Indians, they relied on the ease of crossing the line from white to Indian with the simple application of makeup. The studios wanted Mayo and other non-Indian actors playing Indians to look believably Indian, but they also chose to define whiteness as something so powerful that it refused to disappear. The magazine writer took the story to an even deeper level by relaying the idea that whiteness was inherently obstinate. In this telling of the story, body painting was used to denote the rigidity of the racial body. Ironically, Mayo's body was painted to create an Indian/brown/red skin, not a black/

African skin. The two phenomena exist in stark difference, yet here the writer circles around redface and treats the episode as if it were blackface, effectively erasing Indians from the equation altogether.

The writer treaded heavily on racial paradigms. In portraying Mayo as deeply white, he reinforced the ideological gap between what made Mayo white and what made Indians Indian. While emphasizing both the ease and difficulty with which makeup artists blurred racial lines, he confined this power to makeup artists alone. The writer even moved in and out of racial voice just as the content of the story moved from white to brown to black to white. The cultural vernacular "sumpin!" directly references a racist version of African American speech, depicting African American vernacular as uneducated.

Like Warner Bros. in the case of Mayo, Universal Studios grounded Susan Cabot's whiteness in the temporary nature of dressing as an Indian. For *The Battle at Apache Pass* (1952), the Universal publicity department planned a magazine article showing how makeup transformed Cabot as well as Jeff Chandler into Indian characters. Because Cabot had acted in nonwhite roles several times by 1952, the studio publicists suggested a layout featuring Cabot in each of her nonwhite roles alongside photos of her in street clothes.[10] Universal planned a similar layout for Anne Bancroft, who played Indian characters in *The Last Hunt* (1956) and *Walk the Proud Land* (1956). Universal wanted not only to emphasize the difference between the actress as a social being and the actress in character and costume but also to display her "being transformed by the makeup department into an Indian."[11] *Parade* magazine liked the idea enough to run a feature, titled "Bronx Indian," on the life of Susan Cabot. The article juxtaposed images of Cabot in street clothes and ethnic costumes, while the text discussed her Bronx upbringing.[12] In relating the stories of Cabot's origins in the Bronx, the studio and magazine drew on the history of ethnic neighborhoods of New York City to let readers know Cabot was white but had a particular ethnic immigrant background. Nonetheless, the text presented Cabot as being essentially white and only temporarily and safely nonwhite, returning quickly to her irrevocable status as a white woman. Similarly, studio photographers juxtaposed photos of Jeffrey Hunter and Debra Paget in street clothes with pictures of them in costume. Hunter wore short hair in the glamorous shots of him with his wife, while Paget's blonde hair is complemented by slim-fitting dresses.[13] The studio photographs created an effect that emphasized the whiteness of the actors, who were only temporarily playing Indians. By posing them in this manner, the studios marked Cabot, Hunter, and Paget as actors who in real life were entirely dissimilar from Indians.

We might assume that only white men wore braided wigs when playing Indians in westerns. As the next chapter will show, however, Indians and non-Indians alike sat in makeup chairs to undergo physical transformations for the big screen. Actors and extras had their skin painted brown and wore buckskin, beads, and braids. The brief sample below of those painted brown is based solely on studio production records.[14]

Stunt performers in *Unconquered* (Paramount, 1947)[15]
Janis Carter in *The Half-Breed* (RKO, 1952)[16]
Helen Westcott and Vera Miles in *The Charge at Feather River* (Warner Bros., 1953)[17]
Jack Palance in *Arrowhead* (Paramount, 1953)[18]
Charles "Chuck" Hayward in *Hondo* (Warner Bros., 1953)[19]
Debra Paget and Jeffrey Hunter in *White Feather* (Twentieth Century Fox, 1955)[20]
Carlos Rivas in *The Deerslayer* (1957)[21]

Surely hundreds of examples exist of non-Indians playing Indians with little detail as to the process of applying makeup to the actors. However, some records do prove that the studios undertook tremendous effort and expense to create a look that communicated Indian identity.

Manufacturers of film makeup changed their products in the twentieth century to create a natural look. In the early twentieth century, technicians painted makeup on actors by hand. Initially, they used greasepaint makeup but later switched to pancake makeup at the urging of directors, because the former created a glare that showed up on the screen.[22] Film professor Lorna Roth suggests that creating a natural-looking skin tone became even more important to cinematographers with the advent of Technicolor, and by the 1940s artists were using Max Factor's Pan-Cake Make-Up, which was thin, translucent, could be applied with a sponge, and took minutes rather than hours to apply compared to the waterproof versions. From the 1940s through the 1990s, however, color film processing eliminated yellow and brown tones, which meant that brown-skinned actors' skin color was distorted and the contrast with white skin in the same frame was especially problematic.[23] When painting massive numbers of bodies brown, technical difficulties could threaten an entire production. A large group of non-Indian women from Kanab, Utah, had their skin covered with body paint for their roles as Indian wives in *Bugles in the Afternoon* (Warner Bros., 1952). Although by 1952 many films had been made using Diné women as extras, the *Bugles* producer claimed to be unable to find any Indian women or children.[24] Once the non-Indian women were hired, makeup artists set to work on them but faced some challenges.[25] Makeup personnel began working with ten gallons of "Indian makeup," but they discovered that the makeup contained too much glycerin, was taking too long to dry, and prevented the "poster-color" from adhering to it. Warner Bros. frantically flew in another ten gallons of makeup with a different chemical balance. When the makeup dilemma was solved, the brushes proved problematic as well; they were too small, and makeup application slowed work on the entire set. Along with the new Indian paint, makeup personnel ordered poster brushes that were much wider and would allow for quicker application.[26]

This episode in Utah cost the studio nearly three times the budgeted makeup costs. In addition to losing money on makeup and brushes, the studio lost money paying the cast and crew during the time they waited for the extras' makeup to be finished. Shooting according to schedule was crucial to producers, because they needed to stay within budget, and to directors as well. Hoping to decrease time spent on makeup application, makeup artists relied more often on sprayers when they needed to apply greasy, dark body makeup quickly and evenly. For instance, despite playing an Indian character with both Native and white ancestry, actor Thomas Gomez had his face and hands sprayed with dark greasepaint for *Pony Soldier* (Twentieth Century Fox, 1952).[27] Makeup artists especially preferred sprayers when painting large numbers of men. The white National Guard members who played Indians in *Pillars of the Sky* stripped off their shirts and walked through the "bronze spray paint production line."[28] Working as an extra always meant a certain level of disrespect, but being spray painted en masse must have felt especially disrespectful. My examples are deliberately repetitive in that these bodily interventions were repetitive, simplistic, and totalizing. Not only do these applications repeat in this chapter, they appear in the next as well to emphasize that Indian and non-Indian extras were treated in the same way and expected to undergo the same physical interventions.

For those playing lead Indian characters, makeup artists had to return to older ways of body painting, using brushes and sponges, because the quality of the application mattered much more for leads than for extras in the background. Besides being an arduous task, quality makeup application could take several hours for one actor, especially for those who would appear in close-ups. This meant that when filming began at either 8:00 or 9:00 a.m., makeup had to be applied at 5:00 or 6:00 a.m., well before the actor was to make a set appearance. The more famous actors who played Indians left accounts of their time in the makeup chair, as they had to be paid for this time. Jennifer Jones, who played a Native woman in *Duel in the Sun* (Selznick, 1946), had to be in the makeup chair by 6:00 a.m. to have her brown makeup applied. Removing the makeup took several hours in the evening as well.[29] The Italian performer Marisa Pavan began her time in the makeup chair at 5:30 in the morning for her role as Toby in *Drum Beat* (Warner Bros., 1954). Makeup artist Norman Pringle covered her face daily with a very dark base makeup and blackened and thickened her eyebrows. While Pavan held her buckskin up, Nora Brone, the woman who browned Mayo's body, covered her legs with the same dark makeup.[30]

No fewer than four actors had to be painted brown each morning on the set of *Taza, Son of Cochise* (Universal, 1954). In one scene Barbara Rush's character, Yellow Moon, is slapped by her father. The director ordered thirteen retakes, and in each one the slap wiped away her dark makeup.[31] The Italian American actor Victor Mature played the title character in *Chief Crazy Horse* (Universal, 1955). His makeup took two to three hours to apply, and he, like the others, had to be in the makeup chair by five or six in the morning.[32] The non-Indian actor Ray Danton, who played the mixed-blood character Little Big Man in *Chief Crazy Horse*, also spent several hours each morning being painted and wigged.[33] In addition to the laboriousness of body painting and the investment in hours spent transforming actors and extras, studios spent a great deal of money on makeup and makeup artists. Universal purchased ten gallons of brown body makeup (at a cost of $140) for the extras in *Pillars of the Sky* and spent $1,080 on labor costs for the makeup artists.[34]

Wigs

Makeup artists also relied on hair to create the Indian look. They often avoided the real hair of non-Indian actors and opted for various types of fake hair in their endeavors to create the Indian look. Every non-Indian playing an Indian in the 1940s and 1950s appears to be wearing synthetic hair. I cover wigs here and in chapter 5 to substantiate the details of the physical processes involved in creating Indian characters and how precisely those same methods were applied to Native people. Rather than guessing who wore fake hair in the movies, I base my claims solely on production records. Jeff Chandler and Susan Cabot wore wigs for their roles in *The Battle at Apache Pass* (Universal, 1952).[35] Helen Westcott and Vera Miles wore braided wigs in *The Charge at Feather River* (Warner Bros., 1953).[36] Larry Pennell donned an Indian wig in *The Far Horizons* (Paramount, 1955). Debra Paget donned an expensive braided wig for *Broken Arrow* (Twentieth Century Fox, 1950) and did so again when she appeared with Jeffrey Hunter in *White Feather* (Twentieth Century Fox, 1955).[37]

The cheapest wigs were inexpensive, stiff, and did not sit well on the head.[38] These simple wigs used on actors playing Indians were made of black synthetic hair woven into two braids with a part down the middle, and a headband held the braids in place. What made these wigs even more unnatural in appearance was their method of attachment: the wigs were held in place with a few bobby pins, often resulting in wigs clearly askew on the head.[39] The five hundred to six hundred non-Indian men hired to play Indians in *They Died with Their Boots On* (1941) wore these quite simple wigs that the Warner Bros. makeup department cleaned nightly.[40]

For the leads, or those in front of the camera for significant lengths of time, studios used hairlace wigs, which were more expensive and much less stiff. By spending more money, the studios allowed makeup artists to go beyond the standard look of two braids and a headband. Although both hairlace and weft wigs existed as options for studios in the 1940s and 1950s, hairlace wigs were never used on extras playing Indians. Hairlace wigs still looked unnatural but less so than the cheapest wigs because they had hairlines. When applied, they were glued to the actors' foreheads. Unlike the hair on the cheapest of wigs that was sewn in a circular motion, with large sections of hair in one stitching, hair on hairlace wigs was woven into the actor's hair with a needle, thus creating a look more similar to real hair, attached to the head at many points. But hairlace wigs, also known as skullcap wigs, had to be placed over the real hair, which had to be painstakingly pulled through the wig cap.[41] This more expensive process of pulling hair through a cap was used on Carlos Rivas for his role as an Indian in *The Deerslayer* (Twentieth Century Fox, 1957) because of his status as an actor and his significant screen time in the film. The makeup artist placed a cap over Rivas's hair to create the appearance of baldness. After gluing the plastic into place, he attached a Mohawk-style wig to the top of his head. These types of caps ended at the edges of the face and had to be blended with dark, thick makeup. The line could be noticeable nonetheless.[42]

The hairlace/cap-style wigs required far more labor for makeup artists than braided wigs held in place with a few bobby pins. The actor's hair had to be smoothed down and covered with the fake hair. The artist would then cover the fake hair with plastic or cloth and pull several strands of hair through the cap with a tool similar to a crochet hook. The actor Cameron Mitchell, of Scottish and German heritage, wore this more expensive type of wig for his role in *Pony Soldier* (Twentieth Century Fox, 1952). Behind-the-scenes photos show this process from beginning to end. The hairstylist wrapped both his hair and the fake hair in cheesecloth, and Mitchell grimaced in pain as the makeup artist pulled the combined hairs through the skullcap.[43] Makeup artists wigged Jack Palance with a skullcap-style black wig for his appearance as an Indian in *Arrowhead* (Paramount, 1953), again because of his status and screen time.[44]

In the mid-1940s, studios and makeup artists incorporated hair falls into their repertoire of synthetic hair options for actors playing lead Indian characters. With falls, hairstylists could create bangs, three braids, loose braids, completely wrapped braids, long, straight, and loose hair, or "Mohawks." With weft and hairlace wigs, hairstylists covered the actual hair of the actor with the synthetic hair of the wig. This alone made the wig look more like a wig and less like the actor's actual hair. But with hair falls, fake long hair was incorporated into shorter, real hair.[45] This made the hair appear much fuller, thicker, longer, and more natural. Using hair falls also eliminated the time-consuming process of pulling hair through holes in caps. Hair falls also meant there was no plastic or cloth to blend into the makeup on the face. When looking at the actor's face, especially the edges, the fake hair would not be detectable when a hair fall was used. When Marisa Pavan was wigged for her role as Toby in *Drum Beat* (Warner Bros., 1954), studio hairstylist Linda Cross attached fake hair to Pavan's hair. She created two braids from the fake hair and Pavan's hair, then wrapped them from their base to the bottom with long ties.[46]

The wigs were considered cheap, but Universal spent almost as much money on wigs as they did on wages for the extras playing Indians in *Pillars of the Sky* (Universal, 1956). The studio bought eighty-five Indian wigs for $30 each (total of $2,550).[47] This investment in braided wigs was made for the National Guard members who played Indians in the film. The admittedly expensive wigs cost about seven times as much as weft wigs. For *Chief Crazy Horse* (Universal, 1955) the studio spent $450 on two wigs for Victor Mature, $300 for Suzan Ball's wig, and $125 for her double's wig.[48] Studios paid top dollar for fake hair when it involved stars or important actors. When compared with the earnings of extras outside Los Angeles of from $2 to $13 a day and the poverty on some of the reservations where these films were made, the comparison illuminates the studios' values.

Actors resisted changing their own hair and negotiated for the use of fake hair paid for by the studios. In fact, they enjoyed a completely different appearance in a film if they could revert to their known look after filming.

This actually prevented typecasting and added to their reputation as actors. Wigs, caps, and falls changed the actor's appearance dramatically but left no signs of change once removed. Dyeing actors' hair left them with a completely changed appearance, one to which their fans might react unfavorably. Non-Indian actors feared being typecast for playing nonwhite roles and changing their bodies such that the change outlasted filming. In the case of Barbara Rush, she used her own hair for her role as Oona in *Taza, Son of Cochise* (Universal, 1954). During Rush's three hours in the makeup chair, the hairstylist spent a great deal of time darkening and braiding her hair. Although both her skin and hair were darkened, doing her hair took the longest. Rush agreed to temporary dyes to avoid the fundamental shift in her look that might diminish her fan base. Each morning hairstylists brushed in temporary dye one section at a time, using a small brush coated with carbon tetrachloride.[49] Although hairstylists used a hair fall for Victor Mature, his own hair was dyed black to mask the hairline. Hair technicians dyed Burt Lancaster's hair black for his role as Jim Thorpe and the decision to use his own hair rather than a wig was presumably because Thorpe did not wear long hair.[50] White actors clearly preferred protecting their hair, just as they preferred white roles. Not only did dyeing their hair increase their chances of fan rejection and being associated with nonwhites, but the dyeing also damaged their hair, as did other treatments, such as pulling it through a cap. In the superficial world of Hollywood, damaged hair was no help to a working actor.

Although white actors steered clear of any permanent changes to their hair, some embraced the changes in hopes of bolstering their off-screen images. Makeup artists could have easily applied a cap and blended its edges with makeup, but they instead shaved Hugh O'Brian's head for his role as a Mohawk in *Drums across the River* (Universal, 1954). The studio most likely made this decision because shaving his head would result in a more natural appearance on screen. According to 1950s American women, O'Brian, a well-established playboy, was decidedly more attractive with his shaved head, or at least the studio's publicity department wanted the world to interpret the shaved head along those lines. Much like Yul Brynner, O'Brian saw his baldness linked positively to an exotic quality and appeal.

But these popular notions often arose from the hard work of publicists schooling the American public on which actors to prefer and why.[51]

Hairstylists rarely attempted to make the real hair of white actors simulate Indian hair. They imagined Indian hair was not only dark and long but also thick. They also imagined that Indian men had no body hair and that most white actors' bodies were covered with hair. Because nearly all male American Indian characters exposed their legs, arms, and chests in the movies, studios made a concerted effort to rid non-Indian men of their body hair when they played Indians. In the movies the many bare chests are always hairless. The job of shaving chests, backs, arms and legs belonged to hairstylists and makeup artists. Even background Indians for *White Feather* (Twentieth Century Fox, 1955) had their chests shaved.[52] For the studios, body hair meant whiteness. The Indian look included dark, thick hair only on the head, not on the body.[53]

Studios and hairstylists went to a great deal of trouble to transform white actors into an image that communicated an Indian look. They spent vast sums of money over the 1940s and 1950s on wigs and on wages for hairstylists. Like makeup, styling Indian wigs could take hours. Because studio staff used temporary dye on Barbara Rush's hair each day, she also had to shampoo her hair each evening to remove the dye, sand, and dirt.[54] These efforts to remake actors and extras according to their image of authentic Indian people demonstrates a strong ideological and financial commitment, in spite of the failure to re-create images worth celebrating.

Dark Eyes

Eye color was an important part of the Indian look for some filmmakers, although others made no effort to conceal blue eyes. The only option for concealing blue or green eyes was to fit actors with dark contact lenses. Although Indians and non-Indians underwent bodily transformations when playing Indians on screen, only non-Indians altered their eye color. According to a press release, Diné were befuddled by the application and removal of contact lenses. Most Americans, including the Diné, were probably unfamiliar with contact lenses at that time, but it was more likely that the studio wanted to depict off-screen Diné as out of step with contemporary American life. Universal claimed Diné extras had named actor Bart Roberts "Man Whose Eyes Come Out," thus offering a joke that mocks Indian naming practices and projects a vanishing Indian trope. The Navajos on set may have been fascinated with watching the actor putting in the contacts, as it is grossly fascinating for many people today, but Universal would not have known definitively what their thoughts were. If the studio gave him this name, it would have been a joke among themselves about how ridiculous it was to watch a man stick his fingers in his eyes to pretend to be an Indian on the set of *Taza, Son of Cochise* (Universal, 1954).[55]

The actor Edgar Barrier used dark contact lenses prior to any prompting by the studio. Before his screen test for the part of Cara Blanca in *The Stand at Apache River* (Universal, 1953), the studio claimed he remembered that Walter Hampden had used brown lenses in *Union Pacific*; several men performed as Indian characters for that film, but Walter Hampden was not among them. The publicists claimed Barrier promptly fitted himself with the lenses, arrived at the audition with seemingly brown eyes, and got the part.[56] Makeup artists made over non-Indian actress Debra Paget to play Sonseeahray in *Broken Arrow* (Twentieth Century Fox, 1950).[57] Perhaps because of the discomfort involved, Paget waited until she was in complete costume and on the set to place the contact lenses in her eyes with the assistance of a crew member.[58] Like Paget, Jeffrey Hunter was a popular choice for Indian roles, and his eyes were covered with dark contact lenses when he played the Native character Joe in *Broken Lance* (Twentieth Century Fox, 1954).[59] Both Paget and Hunter changed their eye color again for their roles as Indians in *White Feather* (Twentieth Century Fox, 1955), and again the studio documented their transformation. Hunter poked fun at himself and his transformation into an "Indian" vis-à-vis his changed eye color. On the *White Feather* set, he placed a sign in his dressing room that read, "Jeff Hunter's Eyeball Clinic," since it was where he and Paget placed the dark brown contact lenses in their eyes.[60] Hunter mimicked brown eyes twice in 1955; he used dark contact lenses again on the Mexico set of *Seven Cities of Gold* (Twentieth Century Fox, 1955) for his role as Matuwir.[61]

The Indian Nose

Because of the Buffalo nickel, studios believed Indians had large noses, and manufacturers provided the material for Hollywood's dreams with rubber attachments. The fake noses used for the creation of Indian characters were literally interchangeable. The nose worn by Boris Karloff in *Tap Roots* (1948) was worn several years later by Rock Hudson in his role as Young Bull in *Winchester '73* (Universal, 1950). Three years later Dennis Weaver wore it for his role as Menguito in *Column South* (Universal, 1953).[62] A makeup artist added a piece of rubber to Cameron Mitchell's actual nose to create the effect of a larger nose for his part as Konah in *Pony Soldier* (Twentieth Century Fox, 1952).[63] On the set of *Saskatchewan* (Universal, 1954) makeup artists applied a rubber nose to Antonio Moreno's real one for his role as Chief Dark Cloud and used an entire set of large rubber noses for the extras. The studio took the nose issue so seriously that it spent $250 on fake noses for one actor.[64] The nose may have received less attention than did hair and skin color, but the attention to this particular body part demonstrates the unique imaginings about Indians in the mid-twentieth century and on the nose in particular as the signifier of an Indian face.

For Indian men the nose communicated Indian identity to audiences quickly and efficiently. The Indian nose comes into play in Thomas King's novel *Green Grass, Running Water* as the American Indian character Portland regains employment as an actor by using a prosthetic nose. His solution to his unemployment creates its own problem in that Portland lives with the nose at all times to support his new image as an Indian with a perfect Indian nose. The nose made it hard for him to breathe and changed the sound of his voice. Portland found it difficult to eat and drink with the nose, and it began to smell like rotten vegetables. Eventually he was no longer offered roles, and his life returned once more to unemployment. In King's view the nose serves as a metaphor for all that is expected of modern Indians and how embracing a false image of oneself empowers one only briefly, as the power is based on an untruth. In meeting the needs of Hollywood, Portland's gains are short-lived. He seems to have no viable choices: either embody the false image of the Indian and suffer as an employed actor or represent yourself as the Indian you are and suffer unemployment. *Green Grass* would concur with redfacing, as Raheja defines it; this practice provides only short-lived success. Adding to the irony, the author of *Green Grass, Running Water* claims a Cherokee identity that he is unable to prove.

Body Type

Bodies, before and after their transformation by makeup artists, wardrobe artists, and hair stylists, were thoroughly analyzed and dissected in production. Makeup artists could create nearly any look the studio desired, but the real bodies of actors could become important parts of the decision-making process in casting. Their skin, their muscles, and their bone structure were carefully evaluated when casting directors chose actors for roles as Indians. High cheekbones and a muscular build in male actors secured employment, at least for Indian leads. Jack Palance, Michael Ansara, and Charles Bronson especially exemplify the brawny look filmmakers preferred for Indian characters. In playing Indian men, white actors displayed their muscles and benefited from the conflation of muscles with American Indians. Whereas white characters stayed within fairly narrow parameters, performing as Indian characters gave white actors the opportunity to show studio bosses and directors their range.[65] Casting records on this phenomenon are scant, but filmmakers evaluated actors' bodies, looking for the best possible way to create the Indian look.

According to Hollywood's logic, reservation Indians could mimic Indians with the most ease. Indian and white actors could do so as well, but the studios never failed to emphasize in their publicity materials the identity of anyone who played an Indian character. Actor Noble Johnson embodied the ability to play a character of any ethnicity. He identified as white, African American, and American Indian, but he passed as white in different phases of his life. One studio made it clear that Johnson's body was the base upon which makeup could be added for him to play virtually anyone. One writer specifically attributed his ability to play multiple ethnicities to his multiethnic background.[66] Although Johnson did not consider himself primarily American Indian, his multiheritage ethnicity became conflated with his ability to play characters of any nonwhite race. The perception of his body as nonwhite, rather than the quality of his acting, made studios perceive him as able to play American Indian, African, and Asian characters. Ethnic costumes and dark makeup were seen as enhancing his identity as a nonwhite man.

With Jeffrey Hunter's high cheekbones and overall youthful look, Darryl Zanuck cast him as the Native character Joe in *Broken Lance* (Twentieth Century Fox, 1954).[67] Warner Bros. chose Burt Lancaster to play Jim Thorpe because of his bodily strength. His family was originally from England, and he never emphasized any affinity for American Indian roles in his biographies or his stills portfolios.[68] Critics and producers connected Lancaster's suitability for the Thorpe role strictly on his body type. For them, the most important factor in choosing Lancaster to play Thorpe was his athletic ability. According to one critic, Lancaster "performs brilliantly all the sports Thorpe was famed for and he also captures the mood and feeling of the man in all his complex structure—the unleashed animal spirits, his sensitivity, stubbornness and defiance."[69] Lancaster's agent wrote Warner Bros. in April 1949 campaigning for his client because he fit the role "both physically and histrionically."[70] Lancaster's body became synonymous with Thorpe, as the studio intentionally downplayed and even ignored Thorpe's Native identity.

Because Warner Bros. sought an athletic body rather than a dark-skinned body or Native American, the studio decided it could choose an actor of almost any ethnicity for the character of Thorpe. They rejected the idea of hiring an American Indian man for the part: "From the standpoint of casting, it should be kept in mind that Jim Thorpe was part Indian, part French, and part Irish. There are no restrictions, therefore, except for Nordic blondes, on how the part must be cast. There are at least six stars who would be well cast in the part. It is not necessary, or desirable, that a specific 'Indian type' be sought. This is true, also, for the most [part], with respect to other characters."[71] *Jim Thorpe, All American* producers wanted to convey his athletic ability through a strong, masculine body, with barely darkened skin. They chose an athletic white-skinned body and darkened it. In creating Thorpe from Lancaster, Hollywood rejected its own creation—the beads, buckskin and braids—in favor of an athletic look and reminded the audience of his Indian identity through dialogue.

Buckskins and Beads

Because buckskins signified Indian presence quickly and efficiently on screen, all Indian costumes, regardless of size, shape, or tribe, involved cheap imitations of buckskins. Buckskin and imitation buckskin was the base on which the rest of the Indian character was created, and wardrobe departments created buckskins in simple and repetitive styles. Although the buckskins have a homogenous look, Hollywood hired wardrobe consultants for costuming those playing Indian characters. Joe De Yong was the "Indian wear" expert on the set of *Unconquered* in 1947. Based on this consultant's expertise, Cecil B. DeMille ordered that Boris Karloff's buckskin be modified so the fringe was running down the front instead of the side, to conform to Seneca practice, which is actually not true.[72] De Yong also incorporated jewelry, feathers, and other paraphernalia into the costumes to replicate what the studio claimed was a Seneca look.

Filmmakers went to extremes in representing Indians, either covering performers' bodies entirely with buckskins or leaving them mostly exposed. In exposing rather than concealing the skin, white actors broadened their range through this sexualizing move. White men playing Indian men wore buckskin breechcloths that allowed them to proudly display their bare chests. In these cases, the chest played the part more than the buckskin or even the actor.[73] In *The Deerslayer* (Twentieth Century Fox, 1957), actor Carlos Rivas wore armbands, several necklaces, a feather in his Mohawk hairstyle (an invention of Hollywood), and a naked chest.[74] The fights between men were used especially to display their muscles and their strength. It also provided an additional opportunity for men playing white characters to take off their shirts. Director Ray Rennahan remembered with great zeal a fight scene between Charlton Heston and Jack Palance (who was playing Toriano) in *Arrowhead* (Paramount, 1953). In fact, it was the only moment he remembered from the movie: "They put on this terrific fight, up on this mountain and they fought all the way down. . . . The first team did the whole fight and they were both tremendously big strong men you know, and they were each showing their strength, it was a terrific fight, and we covered it well."[75]

In playing Indians, white men displayed a corporal sexuality rarely expressed in white male characters.[76] As Indians, they could easily express their sexuality through costume. For women, the costumes were more sexualizing but also objectifying. Just like male actors, female leads playing Indian characters wore expensive and ornate costumes in comparison to those worn by extras playing Indians.[77] In *Buffalo Bill* (Twentieth Century Fox, 1944), Dawn Starlight (Linda Darnell) climbs through the bedroom window of Louisa (Maureen O'Hara), Buffalo Bill's love interest. As Dawn places one leg over the sill and onto the floor, she pauses for several seconds, exposing her leg up to her hip. There are extensive examples of non-Indian women wearing buckskins with extreme splits on both sides of their legs. Extras who were only seen in the background wore complete buckskins covering their bodies, neck to ankle. In publicity stills for *The Charge at Feather River* (Warner Bros., 1953), Vera Miles appeared in the extremely unlikely combination of a short buckskin with fishnet stockings.[78] Jennifer Jones, the star of *Duel in the Sun* (Selznick, 1946), wore off-the-shoulder blouses that were always on the verge of falling off altogether. When she moves in with her adopted family, she is naked and covered only with a blanket. Because of the character's physicality, the sexual nature of the story, and Jones's affair with David Selznick, the public nicknamed the film "Lust in the Dust."[79] Finally, just as some men made a career out of playing nonwhite characters, some women did as well. Susan Kohner played Indians on several occasions and an Italian at least once (*To Hell and Back*, Universal, 1955). When not playing an explicitly ethnic character, Kohner was used as the dark counterpart to lighter women.

Bathing scenes, regardless of an actor's gender, became popular tropes in westerns, but Indian men were never featured in nude scenes in the 1940s and '50s.[80] Women's bodies were objectified as sexual objects through the body's exposure and emotional vulnerability, whereas men's bodies were objectified through displays of their physical strength. Male characters returned to costumes that lacked objectification, whereas Indian female characters returned to costumes that reveled in sexual objectification. Indian female characters were intensely sexualized before, during, and after displays of nudity in bathing scenes. In *White Feather* Debra Paget sleeps in the nude, then sits up in bed with a bearskin loosely covering the front of her body while she speaks with the white hero and heroine. In *The Last Hunt* (MGM, 1956), Paget bathes in the nude, then slowly puts on her short, slim-fitting buckskin while Sandy (Stewart Granger) watches. The Motion Picture Association of America strongly suggested that she wear a bathing suit in this scene, but this was not the end result.[81] The Native character Jolie also bathes nude in *The Last Wagon* (Twentieth Century Fox, 1956), as does the Native female character in *Apache Woman* (American, 1955).[82]

Although white women's costumes were almost universally sexualized, the exceptions lent themselves to maternal and modest costumes. In Katherine DeMille's role as Sarah Eagle in *Black Gold* (Allied Artists, 1947), she wears simple cotton dresses. Dolores del Rio as Neddy Burton, the Kiowa mother in *Flaming Star* (Twentieth Century Fox, 1960), was almost entirely unadorned. She wore simple calico dresses and nightgowns.[83] Likewise Audrey Hepburn's wardrobe consisted of calico blouses and long skirts when she played a mixed-blood Kiowa woman in *The Unforgiven* (United Artists, 1960).

Conclusion

Makeup artists manipulated the appearance of non-Indian actors and extras according to what they imagined Indians looked like in a timeless past. Although scholars often see film and media as the creators of images, in this case filmmakers thought they were simply reproducing something that already existed in the minds of moviegoers. Yet the way the American public believed Indians should look was conditioned at least in part by Hollywood. The origins of these images go back in the most direct sense to films of the early twentieth century, but beyond that these images ride on the Wild West shows of the late nineteenth century. The shows focused exclusively on post–Civil War conflicts between whites and Indians on the Great Plains. To push the question of origins a bit further, we can see the genealogy going back to dime novels, captivity narratives, and Puritan writings on Indians.

The genealogy of images of Indians explains the repetitive and generic nature of Indian characters in film. Although at particular moments some filmmakers chose to represent tribes accurately and authentically, more often filmmakers paid only the most minimal attention to the wardrobe necessities of the specific tribe they were representing, and the makeup was simply dark, often called "Indian makeup." Yet they always strove to make their Indian characters look recognizably Indian. In addition, virtually all preceding representations of Indians rested on the conflict between Indians and whites. The screenplays dove into Indian cultures, striving to create a written record of Indians of the past, but their vantage point was entirely from a settler colonial perspective, and the narratives upheld a constant allusion to profound conflict and differences between whites and Natives, resulting in violent conflict.

In making films that included Indian characters, studios pursued one goal: profits. Studios mainly wanted to produce profitable movies that Americans would leave the comfort of their homes to view in theaters. The other actions of the studio should ultimately be seen through the prism of the desire for profit. For instance, their quest for authentic images of Indians ultimately had more to do with making financially successful films. Likewise, they featured stars in their films, or future movie stars, in hopes of selling more tickets. Studios gambled on the idea that audiences wanted to see stars playing Indians in the foreground, with Indian extras out of focus and in the background. Perhaps audiences would have rejected Native American stars, but the studios never tried. Instead, they remade their white stars into Indians, relying on physical markers of Indians: brown skin, dark eyes, black hair, and big noses. Although the studios and their makeup artists tried to conceal the mimicry involved in white movie stars playing Indians, their simulated Indians read as transparently artificial. Audiences knew that Rock Hudson and Susan Paget were white actors playing American Indians because they were familiar with these famous actors. They knew that their dark hair and darkened skin were artificial. This formulaic version of the past proved consistently profitable in the midcentury United States.

That profitability stemmed at least partly from studios insisting that white actors could play Indians believably and yet still be regarded as white. Studios worked with great intensity to increase the distance between the actors and their roles by drawing attention to the production process. They reminded moviegoers that their favorite actors were indeed white and just "playing Indian," as Phil Deloria coined. Non-Native Americans seemed comfortable with this irony. As long as the false fronts of wigs, contact lenses, and rubber noses did not draw undue attention to themselves, Americans accepted non-Indians playing Indian roles.

Studios and the public enjoyed watching Indian characters on the screen as much as they enjoyed watching movie stars in dramas and films noirs. To create an authentic aura that would potentially appeal to audiences, studios went to reservations throughout the continent to secure the employment of American Indians. Their bodies were treated similarly to non-Indians; they were darkened, put in wigs, and dressed in buckskins. Yet even as the studios chased after Indigenous people to appear in films, they projected disappointment because those people were living in the twentieth century; the studios then proceeded to pile makeup and wigs onto their bodies. Hollywood adhered rigidly to its version of America's past and that written by non-Indian writers and never seemed to consider consulting with tribes before projects were undertaken, training Native people in filmmaking, or writing screenplays greatly influenced by interviews with tribal members. In that sense the filmmakers clung to their own reality rather than the reality of Native America. Their re-creation of an American past in which American Indians are rightly conquered, subdued, and vilified by white Americans also reflects a profound alienation from the Indian people they worked with on sets and toward whom they claimed to feel care, concern, and understanding. The contrived physical markers of Indian identity took on a life of their own on the film sets of the 1940s and 1950s. In applying these markers of the Indian look to American Indians on sets, the studios nourished ironies that only grew deeper and more apparent. In placing Indian wigs on Native employees, the artificial nature of Hollywood's version of Indian people became that much more obvious.

5 "A Bit Thick"

The Transformation of Indians into Movie Indians

The ironic oxymoron—real Hollywood Indian—stands in for a tricksteresque, self-conscious, sometimes-anguished play with language and performance on the part of Native American actors. Native Americans in redface countered the national narrative that Indigenous people had vanished, and they also subverted representations of Indians in colonial discourses through their divergence from stereotype.
—Michelle Raheja, *Reservation Reelism*

In August 1950 a young Muscogee (Creek) man named Cecil Meares auditioned for the movie *Jim Thorpe, All American* (Warner Bros., 1951). The film documented the life of the famous mixed-blood Sac and Fox athlete with unparalleled abilities and a life story full of setbacks and mistreatment. At Meares's audition in his hometown of Muskogee, Oklahoma, he witnessed the complicated racism espoused by the studio and the film's director. Talent scouts had brought local Indians to the set for evaluation, and the director, Michael Curtiz, forcefully rejected Indians he identified as "city and college guys." On their second attempt, the recruiters located the opposite of the "city and college look," yet this too resulted in the director's ire, and again Meares watched this scene unfold.

According to Meares, "The headhunters found and brought to the set the most primitive Indians I'd ever seen—and I grew up in Oklahoma. Old, some of them toothless, short, thin, maybe undernourished, long stringy hair, shapeless clothes, some women in bonnets. Curtiz went ballistic. Raving and ranting, he ran around the set and cameras yelling, 'I wanted Indians who LOOK LIKE INDIANS!' as the Indians looked on in surprise and dismay. After a while, the headhunters, now chastised, understood he wanted photogenic Indians, healthy, with smiles. Next day, a better-looking crowd showed up."[1]

Meares and the recruits were mystified as to what exactly Curtiz thought Indians looked like. But Curtiz, and by extension Hollywood, had over-looked the simple fact that both the "toothless" Indians and the city Indians were all Indians. Curtiz was interested in a particular type of Indian, not in Indian people as they actually were. Urban and college-educated Indians did not appeal to Curtiz, nor did malnourished, rural Oklahoma Indians. Indian poverty ranked nowhere on his list of what should be represented on screen. Reservations, tipis, and wise grandfathers ranked somewhere on that list, but Hollywood had no interest in starving Indians with bad teeth or in upwardly mobile American Indian college students.

The casting agents went from college Indians to impoverished Indians to "healthy" Indians in their search for Hollywood's version of Indians. The director made no effort to hide his disapproval from the Indians waiting for acceptance or rejection. Meares was well into his eighties when he shared this recollection of his experience, and he remembered it distinctly. He must have looked Indian in the way Curtiz imagined he should; otherwise, he would have been rejected. Yet Meares did not criticize Curtiz in recounting the story. In fact, the tone he used was a humorous one, but the humor was bittersweet. After growing up in humble circumstances and struggling to attend college, Meares and the other young Indian men had been condemned for embodying what non-Native Americans defined as successful. Despite his own pride in his accomplishments, Meares knew he had been surrounded his entire life by Indians in dire need and felt personally affronted when they were rejected for being poor and for showing poverty's impact on their bodies. Meares's recollections speak to willful rejection of anything that made the studios acknowledge the impact of settler colonialism on Native people or of history from the perspective of Indigenous people.

Just as Europeans created the term "Indian" to inaccurately name the people of the entire North American continent, the stereotypes associated with "Indian" highlight certain tribes in such a way that they come to typify all tribes and even engender the sense that there are no other tribes. The Hollywood Indian derives its look from national and international imaginings of the American Indian, and that Indian look consists of a particular and simplistic aesthetic centering on hair, skin, and dress. Studios gave white Americans the Indians they expected but in a closed loop of reinforcement in that Hollywood images were at least partially responsible for the American public's images and expectations of Indians. Not only were Indian characters based on inaccurate history, they also blurred into a single, monolithic tribal nation. Although studios sometimes veered in the direction of accurate tribal dress, they nearly always modeled their costumes on the clothing of Plains or southwestern tribes; never did they base films on less well known tribes. Moreover, Indian extras from one tribe played members of other tribes because, in fact, the studios reduced all Native people to the Hollywood Indian, which further reinforced the notion that anyone could play a Native American and that tribal differences are irrelevant.

The lack of grounding in reality allowed Hollywood's version of Native people to remain rigid and static, with very little change in demeanor or character development. With such prescriptive attention to the outward symbols of Indian identity, the Hollywood Indian was more a caricature than a character. In spite of this closed loop between representations and expectations of American Indians, studios simultaneously sought to grasp an authentic American Indian past even as it slipped through their fingers. At times they searched for correct or authentic representations in their films to create realistic Indian characters, and they hired Native people to supply that authenticity. But from their perspective, authenticity could be achieved only with the employment of American Indians, and American Indians differed considerably from who the studios thought they were and should be. The hiring process exposed this loop between expectations of Indians and representations of Indians. Native employees gave low-budget films an authentic quality that was unattainable for high-budget films that hired non-Indians to play Indian roles. For this reason, studios hired Indians throughout the 1940s and 1950s, promoted this fact in their publicity materials, yet painted them a darker shade of brown. Muscogee and Cherokee writer Jacob Floyd writes extensively of the publicity machine in Hollywood as a deliberate and influential arm of film production, release, and distribution. These employees were hired to increase audience size and profits, but looking closely at them tells us about the production of these films and the studios' expectations.[2]

In some instances studios expected to hire Indians who would require no makeup to appear as Indians in front of the camera. The transition from Native person to Indian film character, they hoped, would be a seamless one.[3] But studios and the directors who worked for them often relocated film sets to reservation communities, where they discovered Indians who, from Hollywood's point of view, did not act like Indians, or at least these are the stories they told in their releases. The studios knew of course that these were Native people, but they nevertheless clung rigidly to their expectations against which their Native employees were measured. In this sense their expectations set the standard, and the humans standing before them on the set were sized up accordingly.[4]

Indian extras sometimes reacted with confusion to the costumes and makeup used on set. They were unfamiliar with the process, and this lack of familiarity struck non-Indians as odd. Non-Indians expected reservation Indians to apprehend the film culture because they believed it was grounded in an accurate, historical version of the Native past. Indians of course knew they were real, not the wigs and buckskins used to make Indian characters, and their confusion may have masked a deeper sense of disgust with Hollywood's portrayal of Native people.

Filmmakers continued to seek Indians for Indian parts in movies, even as they persisted in believing that they often lacked fundamental aspects of their definition of Indian identity: long black hair, dark skin, and lean, muscular bodies. Ultimately this proved to be not much of an obstacle; studios would simply superimpose features to create the intended look.

While relying on their Native employees, they viewed Indians as lacking in Indian features, due to the presence of modern elements in their appearance. This absence—what they were not—and presence—what they were, which was undeniably Indian—hung together uneasily. Filmmakers used signs of modernity to document the absence of Indians who look Indian. Short hair and light skin in particular, but also jeans and large bodies, signified modernity and a lack of Indian signifiers.

For the studios, the coexistence of modernity and Indians engendered a social deficit. The value of Indian actors and extras lay precisely in the space of the visual terminology of braids and dark skin. In needing a particular look in hired Indians, Hollywood denied and recognized Indian modernity. Studios went out of their way to work with Indians, which made their twentieth-century existence obvious, but Indians looked and behaved differently from what filmmakers expected, which presented a real threat to their ideas about Indians. Studios needed bodies for the background Indians in their films, but they needed actual Indians to fulfill their self-imposed definition of authenticity. Without being told they were seeing actual Indians behind the façade of filmic Indians, audiences could potentially assume otherwise. Studios put their publicists to work to ensure that the American public would be aware they were seeing Native employees behind the film images. In emphasizing this distinction, publicists drew attention to the very thing they wanted audiences to see through: the façade. To generate a link for film audiences between a particular film and the presence of actual Indians in the film, publicists grabbed anecdotes, and perhaps generated tall tales, to emphasize that the extras were Indian, but they also reminded the public that these Indians were somehow lacking. In a sense, then, hiring Indians solved their problem of a self-imposed authenticity, but Indian presence in a particular film also drew attention to the artificiality of the studio's filmic constructions. Considering Raheja's notion of "redfacing," in which the word is more a verb than a noun, an action based in play and domination, it is entirely possible that my distinction between whites playing Indians and Indians playing Indians breaks down into one phenomenon that is just as appealing to white audiences as are pretenses of authenticity.[5]

Hollywood, and in the larger sense the United States, birthed this dilemma in its insistence on replacing Native people with the movie version of Native people and of America's past. Against the narrow movieland definition of a true Indian, few Indians could actually measure up to Hollywood's standards. Although Hollywood required the physical presence of Native employees on their film sets, they also needed the presence of a series of symbols that created the image of an Indian as much as they needed actual Indians—if not more so. These symbols could be reduced to physical markers, and those physical markers could be easily reproduced by makeup and wardrobe departments and overlaid on the bodies of Indian extras and actors. Nowhere did these two physical realities—actual Indians and the physical elements that signify Indian identity—come together more directly and forcefully than on the bodies of the men and women playing Indians. Looking closely at this collision between Native employees and the filmic Indian allows us to see exactly how Hollywood's version of Indian people coexisted with Indian actors and extras on their bodies.

Navajoland

Hollywood remade Indians and whites alike to fit a filmic stereotype. Although studios went to a great deal of trouble to hire Indians, often those living on reservations, their makeup and wardrobe departments made these actual Indians into Movie Indians. Indians were painted, wigged, and costumed in the same fashion as non-Indians. Diné were by far the Indians hired most often to play Indian characters in the movies in the 1940s and 1950s. They stood as the paragon of the authentic Indian, yet they too had to be painted and bedecked to mirror Hollywood's look, and getting the look right involved considerable planning and execution. The desire for authenticity and the need for their own version of Indians clashed when making films with the Navajo because they and their reservation were seen as authenticating objects. At the same time, Diné were seen as being insufficiently Indian. For example, on the Moab, Utah, set of *Taza, Son of Cochise* (1954), Universal Studios made the decision to paint the Diné extras' faces and bodies because their skin was "not quite dark enough for Technicolor." In fact, that decision was probably made during production, and the paint was budgeted in at that time and brought to set.[6] Navajo men and women also received an application of brown makeup on the sets of *Buffalo Bill* (Twentieth Century Fox, 1944), *The Battle at Apache Pass* (Universal, 1952), and *Bugles in the Afternoon* (Warner Bros., 1952).[7]

Sophistication was unnecessary for correct makeup application to extras. The job had to be done quickly and efficiently. In many cases there was no difference, at least artistically, between the Navajo bodies and the artificial sets.[8] Hollywood sought uniformity, so makeup for Indian characters was identical no matter their tribal group, and makeup could thus be sent from set to set. Makeup artist Gordon Bau sent the leftover makeup compound he created for the Diné in *Only the Valiant* (Warner Bros., 1951) to the makeup artists who were painting the Seminole extras in *Distant Drums* (Warner Bros., 1951).[9] Tribal differences did not matter for filmmakers; color obscured all differences. Makeup artists simply needed to get the color right.

Rubbing the makeup over the skin was time consuming and expensive, but sometimes the studios let Indians do it themselves, as in the cases of *Valley of the Sun* (RKO, 1942) and *Winchester '73* (Universal, 1950).[10] But on most occasions the studios preferred to use their makeup artists, possibly because of union laws, but they also discovered that using sprayers lowered overall makeup costs because they allowed makeup artists to quickly paint multiple extras in assembly-line fashion. Diné were sprayed brown in this fashion to play Comanches in *Comanche Territory* (Universal, 1950).[11] Warner Bros. again sprayed Diné in 1957 for their production of *Fort Dobbs* (Warner Bros., 1958). Because they did not budget for the gas-compressor hose and spray guns, they had to borrow sprayers from the Warner Bros. scenery department. Although the reader saw this same strategy in chapter 4, the emphasis here needs to be that this application was used on all Native actors or extras in spite of the studio having sought them out for being Native and publicizing their Native identities. In repeating the makeup process discussed in chapter 4, my intention is to draw out the similarities in expectations of all employees playing Indian characters on the screen.

Not only was there no difference between the mechanics of painting Indians and non-Indians, as if Indians brought nothing different to the set, but the method itself proved unsuitable to personal dignity. With hand application of makeup using sponges and brushes, Indian men and women would be worked on in an individual fashion. Spraying, on the other hand, introduced an entirely different dynamic by treating the extras as a mass of bodies. An assistant who worked on the crew of *Only the Valiant* (Warner Bros., 1951) described the spray painting in a way that speaks to the awkwardness of standing in line to be painted brown: "Over 200 Indians lined up naked. Each Indian would turn and wash the back of the man next to him."[12] This process was unpleasant at best and insulting at worst. The use of sprayers created a sense that these men were inanimate objects, not individual human beings. The men were wearing essentially their undergarments as well, which added to the insensitivity toward possible preferences around modesty. In addition to the lack of bodily privacy and being part of a mass-production assembly line, these men were painted according to a standard they apparently did not measure up to, even though they themselves were Indian.

Hair length and style signified Indian presence in the midcentury movies as much as brown skin. Black braids, nearly always with a headband, served as the central accessory for Indian characters. Using Frantz Fanon and Homi Bhabha as critical reference points, Barbara Babcock writes of Pueblo women's heads being the key sites of communicating cultural difference, accompanied by the feathered headdress of Native men in advertising in the tourism and travel industry of the Southwest. These critical signifiers functioned distinctively when worn by Indigenous people, and the space of the head operated as a particular site of signifying Indian identity.[13]

Many Diné hired by studios in the 1940s and 1950s wore their hair in the crew cuts popular in midcentury America, so the studios covered them with cheap braided wigs. As before, this information repeats here some material from chapter 4. When the Diné for *Buffalo Bill* (Twentieth Century Fox, 1944) were wigged, a contemporary writer provided the following caption with a photograph of the process: "Authentic Cheyenne hair pieces were imported from Hollywood to adorn the Navahos, who were unscalped by [Twentieth Century Fox stylist] Marie Burge."[14] Obviously, there is nothing Cheyenne about cheap, braided wigs. The writer's irony was heavy handed, but his eye was accurate enough. The hairpieces were neither authentic nor Cheyenne. By claiming the Diné were "unscalped," the writer was suggesting an ironic twist: a white person gives Indians hair whereas in the past whites took the hair of American Indians through scalping. But the writer also suggests that the hairstylist was providing them with hair that was formerly theirs but that they had long since lost.[15] This notion of dispossessing Native culture, then offering Native culture back to Native people, stems from the imagined reversal of victims and oppressors. Whereas non-Indians should recognize the genocide they perpetrated against Native people, the studio presents whites as generously returning Native culture—reduced to long hair—back to Indians.[16]

The juxtaposition of short-haired Navajo men with fake braided hair became the greatest source of irony on film sets for whites. Just as Indian skin was seen as being too light, short hair went against the grain of the Indian look for movies. In 1953, when the Navajo extras hired by Paramount wore short hair, the studio decided to put them in black skullcap wigs for its production of *Arrowhead* (1953).[17] These were slightly more expensive and could create a more natural appearance. That same year, Universal decided the Navajo extras' hair was too short, and they put them in black braided wigs for *Column South*.[18] Once in production for *Fort Dobbs* (1958), Warner Bros. shipped two hundred wigs to Kanab, Utah, when they discovered most of their Navajo extras wore crew cuts.[19] Universal purchased approximately 150 Indian wigs for Navajo extras playing Comanches in *Comanche Territory* (Universal, 1950), because the Diné wore crew cuts.[20] When Indian extras wore their hair long, the studios would allow them to appear without wigs. In 1955 only twenty-five of the seventy-five extras wore their hair short and had to don wigs, whereas the remaining fifty had hair long enough that the studio decided they did not need braided wigs for their appearance in *Smoke Signal* (Universal, 1955).[21]

Studios imagined Indians of the past as lean, expected the same of potential Native employees, and rejected contemporary Natives who were not strong or did not have an athletic build. In 1941, when casting *Western Union* (Twentieth Century Fox, 1941), director Fritz Lang decided to use Diné instead of the historically accurate Paiutes, citing aesthetic reasons.

The studio claimed twentieth-century Paiutes did not match the director's vision of nineteenth-century Paiute bodies: "Although he was in the heart of Paiute country, Director Lang took one look at them and sent to Hollywood for the movie contingent of Indians. The Paiutes were too short and rotund to match the public's conception of the American Indian. Even the Hollywood Indians didn't completely satisfy Director Lang. They had too much avoir dupois which showed when they wore G-strings. So Lang hired a physical culture expert who put the Redskins through such strenuous workouts for a week that they lost an average of 12 pounds each."[22]

This story is obviously at best an exaggeration and at worst a lie. Losing twelve pounds in a week is far-fetched. But most salient here is that this was the publicity department's handiwork, and regardless of studio, publicists created the same binaries in their stories about Native employees. After rejecting the Paiutes because of their bodies, the director nevertheless ordered that the Navajo bodies be altered to fit his vision. Lang thought he knew how Indians should look, and instead of changing his image of Indians, he changed the Diné to fit his image. Although he wanted their bodies slimmed down, he did not seek muscular Indian bodies. Where muscular bodies were required for Indian characters who spoke lines and were seen in close-ups, it was considered unnecessary and perhaps distracting when it came to Indian male extras who were to be seen but to be mute, thereby drawing the eye back to the white male protagonist.[23]

Indian bodies could also be too thin. When *Comanche Territory* (Universal, 1950) director George Sherman saw the Diné his crew had hired, he noticed immediately how thin they were. Although he never commented on the cause of their body size—personal preference or, perhaps, poverty and malnutrition—he insisted the Diné be served excellent food while they waited for filming to begin. In true Hollywood style, Universal Studios brought in their own nutritionist to manage and oversee the menu for the Navajo actors. The extras ate and slept for a week before they were called to work, by which time they had gained some weight. After the week of full-time eating, the director even worried they resembled "beef trust" politicians.[24] Thin Indians disrupted the unreal, imagined, athletic, well-nourished Indian. Although decreasing and increasing Indian body size according to imagined standards meant a confrontation with Indian extras and actors, the imagined standard held enough sway that Indians had to change to fit Hollywood's ideal.

Filmmakers also used clothing to convey the difference between Indian and white characters. Buckskins and their imitation formed the base of the costume angle of the Movie Indian look, which could be complemented with a variety of other objects, including elaborate beading, headdresses, jewelry, and moccasins. The buckskins worn by Indian characters could be as small in coverage as a man's undergarments, which was often the case for films set in the Southwest, or as extensive as long pants, long shirt, and moccasins, a look common in films set on the plains. Although white characters, both men and women, often wore buckskin clothing, their clothes mimicked "white" clothing and never featured any beading. White characters never wore headdresses, feathers, or moccasins.

Indian costumes may have been casually thrown together, but the individual pieces that together created the Indian costumes were carefully organized by the wardrobe departments because each and every item was usually rented, costing the studio money. To create the Indian look for the Diné playing Indians in *Only the Valiant* (Warner Bros., 1951), the studio shipped spears, bows, arrows, and tomahawks to Gallup, New Mexico, with tags reading "Property of the Warner Bros. Studio."[25] The items provided the key signs of Indian identity, but the studio made it clear who owned the Indian props. Studio purchases cost money, and spending money meant the studio and director valued that purchase or rental. The costumes seem silly in retrospect, but they still required time, effort, and money, which means the look was carefully constructed between costuming and the financial department.

In their rush to make movies with Indian characters who functioned as symbols, filmmakers sought to create and profit from them, not to analyze them. Whether or not they consciously drew on these symbols or images, they did not leave much evidence that they had deliberated on them. Publicists could be quite conscious and explicit about the artifice of the Indians on the screen and the supposed reality of Indians off screen. Just as publicists saturated magazines with stories of white actors going from white to Indian and back to white, they did the same with Indians going from Indian to Movie Indian and back to Indian again. This narrative was meant to heighten the sense that Hollywood's version of Native Americans, including their version of life on the film sets, was all there was—that audiences were experiencing a truth grounded in reality. Hollywood thought their created Indians on the screen matched the Indian ideal far more than did the Native American actors and extras portraying them. The publicity departments were often ready to exploit the way Navajo extras disrupted the boundaries that filmmakers had imagined between modern and premodern Indians. When *Universal* purchased forty of the usual cheap black wigs for the Navajo extras playing Indians in *The Battle at Apache Pass* (Universal, 1951), the publicity department planned to use the transformation of the extras into Movie Indians for a magazine spread on the employment of Native people in film production.[26] Had the Indians from the Umatilla reservation arrived as planned on the set of *Pillars of the Sky* (Universal, 1956), Universal would have taken photographs and written news releases on their transformation into Movie Indians. But Universal also hoped to highlight a before-and-after aspect to the story, one in which a man's makeover would be featured in *Life* magazine and would begin with him arriving on the set wearing a business suit and driving a new car, all of which was to be documented via photographs.[27] Phil Deloria in *Indians in Unexpected Places* writes extensively on cars, noting that for non-Indians, "there is something disorienting about Geronimo . . . cruising around in Cadillacs," and "most Native people lacked the material resources that let one acquire an automobile." Without coincidence, the goal of nineteenth-century reformers was to move Native people from "radical difference to unremarkable similarity," while others expected Native people to develop methodically along certain steps and thus going straight to engine-powered cars was not tolerated. Deloria looks at Indians buying, driving, and enjoying cars, placing it in a larger story of Indian mobility and embrace of technology. Here, the plan was concocted by a movie studio, and the Umatilla man was not involved in the planning. Perhaps this is why the stunt failed to materialize: perhaps he spoke back and refused to enter a representational space in which his image being posed with a car was meant to be riddled with mockery around his supposed poverty and savagery.[28]

Studios associated a lack of dark skin color with the introduction of civilization and erosion of Indian culture. Giving the filmmakers the benefit of the doubt, the comments that studio representatives made to that effect can be interpreted as referring to the idea that Indians now spent far more time indoors than they had a century earlier. On the other hand, their comments also hinted at intermarriage with whites. In either case, studios expressed great disappointment about needing to paint Indians brown. They had imagined that Indians would be dark enough that they would not need makeup. On the one hand, Diné lent authenticity to Warner Bros. production of *Only the Valiant*, but Warner Bros. felt the Diné had to be darkened because "civilization had bleached them out," a truly distorting statement.[29]

Yet studios also wanted the inverse to be true: that their Indian employees would bring an authentic Indian identity that would result in higher profits for the studios. At the same time that publicists released stories emphasizing the ways Indians lacked what they considered to be an Indian look, they also released stories to the press about Indians acting the way the American public might think Indians should act. For instance, the Navajo men on the set of *Taza, Son of Cochise* (Universal, 1954) had long, thick hair, but they did not want it brushed by the hairdresser because she was female. When they relented, she had to order pet brushes because her regular brushes would not comb their hair. According to the publicist, the men came to like the pet brushes so well that they brushed each other's hair between takes. Most of this is likely untrue. The men probably did have thick hair, but they very likely wanted to keep the hair that came out into the brush. They probably found the pet brushes made it easier to remove all of the hair and thus keep that hair in their possession. They also very likely refused to have a nonrelative, a stranger, a non-Navajo, and a woman brush their hair for all sorts of reasons. What matters here is that the studio learned something about Diné from these Navajo men but spun a tale quite different in meaning from what they most likely learned.[30]

One year later Navajo men insisted on braiding their own hair for the production of *Smoke Signal* (Universal, 1955), possibly because they did not want a stranger touching their hair, especially a woman. They may have also preferred brushing and braiding each other's hair because of the importance of controlling where the hair left in a brush goes.[31] Although there could have been several reasons the Diné brushed their own hair, the fact that Universal Studios chose to publicize this rather small point tells us that they felt the Diné were making a significant point when they took the brushes away from the hairstylists: Diné were different from whites in meaningful ways.

Today we express discomfort with the idea that Indians appeared in these movies, and we expect to learn that Indians objected strongly, openly, and repeatedly to the costumes, the story lines, and the stereotypes. Indians never took over sets, resorted to violence, or demanded to speak to the director in the 1940s and 1950s. In the few instances in which Indians objected aloud, they shared their thoughts with those closest to them socially—each other—and physically—a makeup artist or wardrobe crew member who happened to be within earshot. Complaining in a formal manner, in writing or directly to producers or directors, would have meant leaving the set and forgoing the cash they would have earned. On the set Indians faced several options: accept the Hollywood stereotypes completely, challenge the stereotypes indirectly and discreetly, or leave the workspace and give up their wages in protest. In most cases Native American extras voiced mild complaints and kept working.

In *Buffalo Bill* (Twentieth Century Fox, 1944), Diné played Cheyennes, while Arizona stood in for the Great Plains. When the makeup experts began applying brown makeup, the Diné voiced their concerns. According to the press releases, the Diné found the makeup to be "a bit thick," and the whole effect suggested the crew were "overdoing" the look. By using the term "thick," the Navajo men were objecting to the density of the makeup application, but their general description referred to Hollywood's caricature of American Indians. "Thick" also referenced the inability and unwillingness of Hollywood to portray Indians as they actually existed in the twentieth century. When the time came for the Navajo men to be dressed as Cheyennes, the film's crew highlighted the inability of the Diné to correctly situate and wear the costumes, the fact that the extras had to be instructed. This inability could very well have been feigned but perhaps was an outward rejection of Hollywood's interpretation of American Indians. According to one writer who picked up the story, the Diné both did and did not complain: they verbalized their feelings that the clothing was too warm to be worn in the middle of an Arizona summer, which suggests that they did complain, even if only indirectly. But the writer also noted their joking and laughing with each other in reference to the "Cheyenne" costumes. Their humor suggests a certain method of resistance that creates a sense of intracommunity relations rather than a resistance seeking to disrupt the studio's power.[32]

Into this mix of complaint and compliance came Chief Thundercloud (Victor Daniels), who lied about being Cherokee to gain work as an Indian actor. He served as the technical advisor on all matters relating to Indians on the set of Buffalo Bill. Thundercloud assisted the Navajo men when they dressed for their film appearances, persuading them to wear the clothing and makeup by convincing them that Cheyennes looked the way they were being portrayed in the film. He reminded the Diné of their relatively high pay and negotiated for excellent horses once they agreed to the brown paint and inaccurate costumes. The horses and their earnings may have had more to do with their decision to cooperate than did the supposed historical accuracy of the Cheyenne costumes.[33] The crew, publicists, and magazine writers found the introduction of Movie Indian culture to Diné to be odd. They focused on the irony of Diné being taught how to inhabit Movie Indian culture: how to properly wear Indian clothing and apply Indian makeup. But the Diné were struck by the irony as well. They may have been laughing among themselves because the clothing was so completely inaccurate, as well as being unsuited to the desert weather. They complained about the makeup and the extra heat the costumes created, but they poked fun at the costumes only with each other. The Navajo men may not have revolted, but they did voice their objection and they certainly found the humor in the situation in which they found themselves: Diné being taught by a fake Cherokee how to look Cheyenne in Arizona.

The Diné may have had to trust Thundercloud and allow themselves to be used by the studio for fast cash, but Utes were fairly close neighbors to the Diné and a tribe they had associated with extensively. Because of that historic relationship, the Diné were well aware of how Utes looked, and thus they voiced their concern when Hollywood relied on the usual Movie Indian look when creating Ute costumes and hairstyles on the set of *Flaming Feather* (Paramount, 1952). The Navajo men hired to play Utes clearly recognized that they did not look like the Utes they were asked to play. According to Paramount, Utes wore their hair up, with bangs. The Diné thought Paramount was wrong, and in response Nat Holt, the film's director, flew in a new set of hairdressers to comply with the request of the Diné to have their hair arranged with no bangs. This last-minute change in hairstyling reportedly pleased the Diné and shows that when a complaint was quite specific, a director would potentially take it seriously.[34] The studio's inability to understand the distinctions made by the Diné may have stemmed from their strict categorization of all Native people as Plains Indians, not even allowing distinctions between northern and southern Plains Indians. Based on that bifurcation, Indian extras were routinely given the long, braided wigs and rarely the shoulder-length wigs.[35]

Beyond Navajoland

Although studios filmed in Arizona using the Diné time and again, they located film sets in other parts of the American West, as well as Canada and even the Southeast on a few occasions. Like the Diné, other Native employees underwent skin darkening and wore dark braided wigs and buckskins. Just as the Diné never played Diné in the movies, Indians from other tribes never portrayed members of their respective tribes. Instead, they usually played Lakotas or Apaches, all with similar looks. When it came to makeup, filmmakers and the studios they worked for walked a contradictory line: seeking Native employees for their film yet deciding— sometimes even beforehand—that the Indians were not dark enough and needed dark makeup to present in the way desired by filmmakers. Studios always equated the need for brown makeup with a deficit. The studios never attributed the need for makeup to a need for an even skin color or a standard color among all the Indian extras. Indian extras had their skin painted brown on several occasions: Cree farmer Jonas Applegarth was painted brown despite his "bronze" phenotype for his role in the World War II film *Battle Cry* (Warner, 1955).[36] Seminole extras had their skin darkened with brown makeup in *Seminole* (Universal, 1953).[37] Likewise, Tewas had their bodies and faces painted brown on the set of *Two Flags West* (Twentieth Century Fox, 1950).[38] Occasionally the studios steered clear of any explanation for hiring and then darkening American Indians, and when they did address this contradiction, they blamed American Indians for needing brown makeup.

In 1948, when Twentieth Century Fox went to Canada to film *Canadian Pacific*, the studio employed Nakodas from the Morley Indian Reserve to play Natives attacking whites in the film. Although Fox crews traveled from Los Angeles to Canada to film tribal members, a Fox press release emphasized what Nakodas were not—dark-skinned and warlike—rather than what they were:

> As with red men generally, the Yiskabees [Nakodas] are no longer versed in the arts of war, and have genuinely forgotten how to apply war paint. So Greenway and his corps of assistants would each day line up the Yiskabee tribesmen and apply a base coat of pancake makeup to such part of their tawny skins as would show, to make certain the Yiskabees would not photograph as pale-faces (or pale-torsoes); and over that a full-color job of warpaint. These markings had the desired effect, both pictorially and psychologically. An Indian in warpaint becomes a fearful [*sic*] customer to behold—and feels it, too—all of which made for utter realism when the painted warriors attacked the railway construction railhead.[39]

For filmmakers, Indian identity resided in skin color, not the person. They believed the makeup application turned the Nakodas into fearsome Indians wearing war paint rather than simple brown foundation makeup. Yet the press release walks a fine line: these were Indians, and yet they were not. The studio could have much more easily hired non-Indian men dressed in brown makeup and covered in "war paint" to attack the train, yet they hired not just Indians but First Nations people from a Canadian reserve.

Although the script of *Broken Arrow* (Twentieth Century Fox, 1950) invoked cultural pluralism and Fox hired White River Apaches to play Apaches, they were painted according to the normalized standards of what Hollywood believed Indians should look like. As had been the case when Fox hired Nakodas, the studio was anxious to hire Apaches, yet when the filmmakers actually saw them, they immediately decided their skin color was too light: "Since *Broken Arrow* has an 1870-setting, when the Indians wore far fewer garments than they now don, another problem grows for the studio in turning the epidermis of the redmen into the proper hue for the Technicolor cameras. Greasepaint by the gallons was daubed on the Native Americans to give their pale skins the outdoor look that tradition demands."[40] In the case of the White River Apaches, Fox blamed the extras' light skin on the shift to indoor living, rather than any inherent lack in the Apaches. But even this contrast remains securely in the pattern of comparing Native people to a standard of the correct color for Indian skin.

This pattern of Hollywood seeing Native employees as failing to meet Hollywood standards of the Native look continued into the 1950s. In Montana, Paramount hired hundreds of Crows to play Lakotas in *Warpath* (1951), but the studio felt they were too light skinned for the camera and promptly painted them a particular shade of brown, while simultaneously lamenting that the Crows were unfamiliar with "war paint." White actor Edmond O'Brien bemoaned their light skin color and attributed it to the erosion of Crow culture.[41] He blamed their light skin on living indoors, "fully clothed and sheltered from the sun." Although his comment praised non-Native culture, he criticized Crows for adopting that same culture and failed to place their adaptation in the context of the American nation stripping Native people of their land, families, and culture. O'Brien evaluated their lighter skin as making them less Crow. Here, being Crow and Native is conflated with living outdoors and having dark skin. O'Brien also reported that some of the Indians were lighter than the non-Indian crew, which the non-Natives found disturbing. The makeup department from Warner Bros. entered these unfair evaluations and used "red-dish pigment," which they sprayed on the faces and bodies of the Crow employees.[42] Oklahoma Indians received the same analysis and treatment. On the set of *Jim Thorpe, All American* (Warner Bros., 1951), the local Indians hired to play Indians were also deemed too light by the studio. Just as studios often identified Indians with the past, they also used signs of Indian modernity to criticize Indians, portraying them as being less than Indian. As Warner Bros. put it, "Modern-day Indians were not as dark-skinned as their fathers and grand-fathers in the 1907 to 1912 era at Carlisle. . . . Because dark makeup had been established on the stars in the preliminary scenes made in Hollywood, a corps of makeup men had to darken faces and hands of the real Indian extras daily so they would not look like palefaces alongside Burt Lancaster, [Steve] Cochran and the other Hollywood players."[43]

Warner Bros. decided to darken Burt Lancaster for his part as Jim Thorpe. The studios decided to darken the much sought-after Native people who were playing Indians as well because the studios deemed them less Native than their ancestors; in the eyes of the studio, these Indian actors were modern, light skinned, and failing at being Indian. In addition, once the decision was made to darken Lancaster, anyone else playing an Indian—even if that person was Native American—had their skin darkened as well. The contrast of dark and light skin meant differences were easily recognizable on the screen, but these contrasts in skin tones seem to have comforted the cast and crew as well, who wanted striking differences between whites and Indians on the set.

Studios often decided beforehand to cover Indian extras and actors in brown makeup prior to filming. Normally they did not discover light-skinned Indians on the set and obtain makeup as a result. They most likely made these decisions regularly in the production and budgeting phase of film development. In one documented case, Universal Studios decided in conferences a year beforehand that they would be using brown makeup, well before they ever saw the Crees and Lakotas they hired. Universal bought "war paint" for $450 and four gallons of body makeup at $12 a gallon to paint the Crees and Lakotas who played Indians in *Saskatchewan* (Universal, 1954).[44] The studio hired professionals to apply the brown makeup, and one of the writers who visited the set, Alyce Canfield, expressed shock that the Crees and Lakotas were unfamiliar with the application of "war paint." If she actually meant war paint, this equates them with a past of war and fails to acknowledge their survival and presence in the twentieth century. If war paint meant brown makeup, they could not be expected to know how to do something they had never done before. When it was convenient, those associated with filmmaking assigned modernity to Indians, especially to explain light skin, but in this case it was also to fault them for their supposed lack of cultural knowledge and connection to the historical past. Canfield also assumed that Hollywood's understanding of war paint was identical to the ways the Cree extras' ancestors had applied war paint. Perhaps the confusion among the Cree actors stemmed from information they knew was inaccurate, false, and simply created out of whole cloth.[45]

Because the midcentury Movie Indian look necessitated two long black braids, Natives with short hair (which meant many midcentury Indian men) were put in wigs of all kinds to create the look studios desired. The sixteen Standing Rock Lakota men whom Warner Bros. had eagerly sought for close-up shots in *They Died with Their Boots On* (Warner Bros., 1941) wore their hair short. These men from North Dakota had to don wigs daily, and each night the wigs had to be cleaned.[46] Likewise, in 1951 Paramount hairstylists placed black braided wigs over the actual hair of the Crow extras on the set of *Warpath*. Most of the Crow men probably wore crew cuts similar to that of Donald Deer Nose, one of the extras whose own hair was covered with a braided wig.[47]

Universal always wigged its Indian extras, regardless of location or tribe. In 1953 Universal hired eighteen Indians living in Los Angeles and seven Indians from Arizona with undisclosed tribal affiliations for *Stand at Apache River*. Perhaps one of them had the type of hair sought by the studio for their roles as Apaches because Universal spent $480 on twenty-four Indian wigs.[48] The studio wigged the Indian extras hired to play Seminoles in *Seminole* (1953), as well as the Shoshones hired for *Chief Crazy Horse* (1955).[49] Just as Universal decided the Crees' skin was too light, it also decided they would need to have their heads adorned with black wigs for *Saskatchewan* (1954).

Just as studios planned to bring brown makeup to sets prior to seeing Native extras, studios also ordered braided wigs in the same way. In preproduction meetings for *Saskatchewan* (1954), well before seeing the Cree extras, Universal executives decided they would need to purchase wigs for them (at the same time, they decided they would need to order makeup as well). Again, this means that had a Cree arrived on the set with long hair, the studio might have covered it with artificial hair nonetheless.[50] They bought one hundred Indian wigs and five Indian hair falls.[51] Most likely the extras received the less expensive wigs and bit players used the falls. Universal also hired hairstylists to place the wigs and create the film Indian look.

In the minds of the filmmakers, Native people of the past were active and competitive, spending hours hunting and warring. Filmmakers, therefore, could not fit large-sized Indian men into their image of Indian men of the past. Filmmakers and studios also knew that hiring Indians and filming on location could edge out competing studios for audience attendance and profits, but they were willing to forgo accuracy in favor of aesthetics. Many filmmakers felt Indians of the past must have been lean, so they looked for Indian extras with this same body type. Employing Palouses for his film would have fit into director George Marshall's historical re-creation effort with *Pillars of the Sky* (Universal, 1956), but he chose Nez Perce extras instead because they looked "perfect." According to Marshall, Nez Perces maintained their health, practiced sports, and looked like "wiry warriors," and their bodies were "lean and muscular." Palouses, on the other hand, "did not look lean and fierce enough for the fray."[52]

Jonas Applegarth, a Cree farmer, sought film employment and underwent close scrutiny focused on body shape and skin color. After his successful exam, he was chosen for a bit part in *Battle Cry* (1955) largely because of his height, weight, and musculature. Warner Bros. pronounced him "definitely photogenic. He possesses good features and a well-muscled body. He weighs slightly over 200 pounds and there isn't an ounce of fat on his frame. His coloring is almost a clear bronze."[53] Although studios did not hesitate to employ the services of makeup artists, hairstylists, and wardrobe consultants to create a façade of Indianness, strong and lean male bodies could not be so easily transformed. Muscle mass on Indian extras could distract from the main white characters. But in *Battle Cry*, a strapping Indian man was portrayed as an individual among the other military protagonists.

Costuming

Costumes occupied a place of importance as much as hair or makeup in creating Indian characters for the screen. White men playing Indians often played lead roles in which they displayed their chests and wore small loincloths and other paraphernalia indicating the presence of an Indian. Indian men seldom obtained lead roles, but when they did, they most often were covered with buckskins. Even in their head shots, Indian actors posed in full buckskins, never with their chests bared. Costumes worn by extras were always a cheap synthetic made to simulate buckskin. When playing Indians of the Southwest, some extras were assigned small loincloths and little else besides moccasins and jewelry. Indians wore short hair and non-Indian clothing only in films depicting World War II as well as in a handful of films that depicted modern Indians. In these cases, the filmmakers nevertheless remained faithful to darkened skin.

Just as filmmakers expected Indians to have extremely dark skin and long black hair, they also expressed shock to find Natives working on film sets wearing modern clothing. Paramount provided buckskins for the Lakotas in *The Savage* (Paramount, 1952) because, the studio noted, by the 1950s the Indians preferred "flannel trousers and sport jackets" for their daily apparel.[54] When Warner Bros. went on location to Muskogee, Oklahoma, for *Jim Thorpe, All American* (1951), they employed "Indian types" as extras. For the scene depicting Thorpe's return to Carlisle after the 1912 Olympics, Warner Bros. hired four hundred Oklahoma Indians: "Many were in their own colorful native costumes, while Warner Bros. furnished costumes to others. Some of the Indians had never before donned so much as a pair of moccasins, much less a feathered headdress. Completely modern, their clothes are those of other Americans."[55]

Because these Indians did not have clothing perceived by film producers as Native, the studio provided costumes. But in providing the modern Native employees with Indian costumes with a look derived from no particular tribe or historical moment, the studio seemed to feel this made the Indians slightly less Indian. Modernity proved to be a veritable litmus test of Indian authenticity. When Indian modernity was recognized by non-Indians on film sets, it was always in a negative context: what Indians did *not* wear, what Indians did *not* know. The implication was that physical symbols alone made Indians Indian. If Indians possessed no Indian symbols and yet the studios held in their warehouses a vast supply of wigs, buckskins, and headdresses, the filmmakers kept wondering what made Indians Indian. They went in circles with their answers, from Native people to filmic Indian symbols back to their Native employees.

Despite the use of makeup to transform Native film workers for the camera, an awareness also emerged that this transformation could be taken too far, potentially so far that the image—which audiences knew was unreal because it was, after all, a movie—became obviously unreal. In a memo on a revised script, Fox's Bill Adler suggested ridding *The Last Wagon* (Twentieth Century Fox, 1956) of extremely painted Indians since "the audience laughs at them." He also pointed out that moderate lines of paint under the eyes of the White River Apache extras would be acceptable, but anything more would not be in line with the Apache appearance of long hair, bandannas, and a lack of face paint.[56] The White River Apaches, in the eyes of the studio, were not Indian enough, but the studio also thought the makeup and wardrobe crew could potentially make the Apaches cross over into the outlandish. Audiences wanted a certain Indian look, but capturing the intended look of a filmic Indian was a target easily missed. When missed, non-Native audiences immediately recognized they were seeing a caricature.[57] Popular perceptions were already set in the American public's mind, thanks in part to Hollywood's depictions. Hollywood, then, put itself in a position where it had to meet standards that were of its own making.

Universal Studios began devising publicity tours featuring American Indians to connect its Native employees with its films in the minds of the non-Native public. It organized tours for the release of several of its movies that featured Indian characters and extras (*Comanche Territory*, *Battle at Apache Pass*, and *Seminole*) and hired American Indians, or actors who claimed a Native identity, to publicize the openings of these films.[58] Studio publicity departments believed American Indians were popular with film goers and used the tours to gain attention and a wider audience. They never employed Indian actors from Southern California for these tours, however; they wanted Indians who were not part of Hollywood and would not be recognized by the American public. The tour material sheds light on negotiations and communications between Native employees and the studios. These men and women traveled throughout the country making appearances on radio and television shows, at county fairs, baseball games, department stores such as Macy's, and amusement parks like Coney Island.

Publicity departments specialized in tie-ins, choreographing visual connections between their film and various products or services.[59] In crafting tours, publicity departments regularly turned to carefully chosen reservation Indians. They preferred men from reservations with famous ancestors. The paradoxes of modernity became clear in the studio's hiring plan: they wanted dark-skinned Native men who were willing to work for very little money, but they also wanted them to have grown up on a reservation, speak English and their Native language, speak well in front of crowds, be well versed in tribal history and customs, and be willing to leave their homes for indefinite periods of time. The studio also sought total control over their Native employees' appearance and actions. This work disempowered Indians on a socioeconomic level in a way that differed measurably from temporary work on movie sets.

One Navajo man and several Comanches and Kiowas from Anadarko, Oklahoma, were part of the campaign to showcase *Comanche Territory* (1950).[60] Wesley Bilagody (Navajo) worked for Universal in this capacity, but the names of the Comanches and Kiowas were undisclosed.[61] The bulk of their tour took place in New York City: Macy's decorated its window displays in American Indian themes and created an entire line of Native American–inspired children's clothing. The store utilized broken English in their full-page ad in the *New York Herald* to describe the collection and announce the weeklong appearance of the Native employees in the Macy's children's department: "Macy's takes green clay, and turquoise from warbonnet, adds yellow from sun." The ad was accompanied by several photographs, including one with Bilagody in headdress and loincloth with non-Indian children holding his bow and arrow, Bilagody dancing with his hand to his mouth as if he were letting out a war whoop, a teenaged

Indian boy and an Indian woman teaching sign language to three non-Indian girls, and an Indian woman in a buckskin showing non-Indian girls her Indian doll.[62]

One year later Universal looked for Apaches to publicize *Battle at Apache Pass*. Universal employee Archie Herzoff visited the Mescalero reservation to show the film to local Apaches and find likely candidates for the publicity tour. In his letter to Charles Simonelli in the New York office, Herzoff explained that the Apaches he met were not what he expected: "I saw most of the tribe, and unfortunately there were no other young women photographically suitable. . . . Unfortunately, the Apaches as a whole aren't too Indian looking in the accepted sense. They aren't too stalwart physically either. However, appropriately garbed, they will pass muster."[63]

Herzoff located a few Apache men who looked the way the studio expected. Because the men had to wear what Universal considered to be Native clothing at all times, the tribe located costumes for them. Herzoff suggested the tribe never used Indian costumes and had to work fairly hard to even locate some: "The tribe is digging up enough traveling costumes so that four or possibly five of the troupe will look like Indians are supposed to look on arrival."[64] The clothing supplied by the tribe was supplemented with rentals from Western Costume Company in Hollywood.[65] The Apache men were to appear in Indian wardrobe at all times, as defined by the studio. To assure the quality of the men's wardrobe, Universal gave the tour manager permission to use the travel-expense money to repair any damage to their costumes.[66] Universal's New York office also wanted the troupe to carry authentic Apache cultural artifacts with them, but Herzoff mournfully informed them that the Apaches did not create such objects any longer: "In past years they did some basket and bead work but present generation has lost the touch."[67]

When the producers decided they wanted to hire Apache men, they quickly defined for themselves how the Apaches should look, act, and speak. They imagined Apaches to be related to famous Apache men of the nineteenth century and to be articulate in Apache history and culture. They preferred dark-skinned Apaches, but if they had other qualifications, the filmmakers would tolerate the light-skinned actors. In addition, Universal expected women to have petite figures and no children. After making these decisions, producer Archie Herzoff set out to find Apaches who fit his specifications. He visited New Mexico personally to screen the film for the tribal council and "others of importance" in hopes of securing their approval. He planned to look for Cochise's nephews as well as descendants of Geronimo during his visit.[68]

Upon his return to Los Angeles, Herzoff corresponded with the Mescalero Apache reservation superintendent, Lonnie Hardin, to coordinate casting. After returning home, he decided to hire Donald Blake, Emmett Botella, Art Botella, Eustace Fatty, Robert Geronimo, Sam Kenoi, William Magoosh Sr., and Davis Spitty. Kenoi had been a prisoner of war during the 1880s and had relocated to the Mescalero reservation in 1913. Eustace Fatty was born at Fort Sill and also relocated to Mescalero. Magoosh worked for the tribal nation for many years. Donald Blake, Emmett Botella, Art Botella, and Davis Spitty were all born at Mescalero.[69] Herzoff did not hire any Apache women, perhaps because none fulfilled his stringent requirements.

Herzoff desperately wanted to include Robert Geronimo in the tour because he was the only living son of Geronimo. Because he was afraid Robert would not join the team, Herzoff worked diligently to convince him to be part of the publicity troupe. As of March 12, Robert had refused Herzoff's offer of $25 a day and was pressing for $5,000 and nothing less.[70] In defending his pursuit of Robert Geronimo to another Universal employee, Herzoff explained that Robert was not especially "Indian-looking" but had been born on the reservation. He also noted the bonus of Robert being bilingual. He went on to seek the employment of Eugene Chihuahua (son of Chief Chihuahua) at $12 a day, but here he failed. Upon discovering that Geronimo's granddaughter had gained fifty pounds and would need to bring her children on the tour, he promptly dropped his offer.[71] Apache children and Apache women who were not petite were not part of the Universal vision of Indians. Herzoff eventually realized his goal with Robert Geronimo, who conceded to $25 a day.

There was some confusion about how to pay the Apache men, but human resources decided they should be made employees, and Mescalero superintendent Hardin completed their payroll forms.[72] The Apache men were paid $9 a day; Jesse Campbell, their non-Indian manager, earned $14 a day, and Robert received $25 a day. Their traveling expenses were paid for directly by Universal, which spent far more on their travel than their pay: they were transported by bus from Mescalero to Boston for $6,000. They were housed in hotels, two to a room. Only their white manager had his own room. Reservation superintendents completed the necessary employment forms and their travel-expense reports submitted by Campbell.[73] The Apache men were given no latitude. The men were also explicitly told to conduct themselves "well" on tour, a demand they must have satisfied, as there were no complaints about the Apache men.

At each stop the Apache men danced for non-Native audiences. They participated in presentations about Apache history and culture, although Universal often spoke for the men. During the tour Sam Kenoi encountered difficulties and went home early. He was seventy-eight years old, had a wooden leg, and was unable to handle the hectic schedule.[74] The PR department hoped to create a fashion line with Apache influences to promote the film's opening, as they had done with *Comanche Territory*, but this never materialized.[75]

This publicity tour in effect replicated film production. The Apache men received only minimal pay for their work. They were expected to create an idyllic, nineteenth-century past, and when their performance fell short of Universal's expectations, the studio blamed the Apaches. The studio controlled how the Apaches were represented to the non-Native public, and the studio cast them as people of the past, not the present. But these men existed in the present in spite of the studio's attempts to place them in the past; they were not passive victims of the studio. Although the studio held ultimate control, the Apache men alone held the key to the authenticity the studio was seeking, and Robert Geronimo in particular knew that and negotiated for higher wages because of it.

Universal Studios replicated the same public relations move but with the Seminole Nation for the film *Seminole* (1953). The studio turned to a Seminole superintendent for assistance with their search. One of the men they sought was Mike Osceola, a relative of the famous Seminole leader and warrior Osceola, but they never found him.[76] Eventually they secured the employment of eight Seminole men, with Henry Cypress acting as the leader of the troupe (Cypress also worked as an extra and technical advisor on *Distant Drums* [1951]). Cypress, the son of a Baptist minister, was referred to as "a magnificent full-blooded Indian" by Universal. They also hired Jack Osceola, who was another relative of Osceola, as well as Curtis Osceola, who may or may not have been a relative of Osceola. Cypress received $100 a week, and the other Seminoles were paid $10 a day plus expenses. For Seminoles other than Cypress, Universal guaranteed them one month's work and the right to continue the tour after the first month. Jack Coppinger served as the liaison between Universal and the Seminoles. For his work, he was paid a flat sum of $100. Universal secured the same bus company it had used in the past and also paid $6,000 to transport the men around the country, just as it had done for the *Battle at Apache Pass* tour.[77]

The Seminoles toured the country from March 26 to April 4, 1953. Universal organized a handicraft contest, a costume party, and an archery contest. They also produced an Indian war-cry record, which could be ordered from the Thomas Valentino Company.[78] These artifacts of popular culture were staples of publicity departments. The costs of sending the leads on tour would have been prohibitive. Sending (white) leads on tour meant airplane costs, mink coats for women, expensive hotel stays, and additional costs for husbands and wives to travel with the actors. The publicity department knew the cheapest and most effective way of drawing attention to *Seminole* was to employ Indians at minimal rates to perform the culture expected by non-Natives.

Conclusion

Like non-Indians, studios arranged for their Native employees to be painted, wigged, and feathered for the camera, and their Native employees complied with this arrangement. Native employees became part of the non-Indian vision of what constitutes an American Indian. This vision relied heavily on dark skin, dark eyes, buckskin, and long black braids. In the minds of the filmmakers, the key way to communicate Native identity was through the visual use of certain signs. Creating Indian characters relied heavily on material objects. Every step was calculated in cost and representation. Studio employees carefully planned the creation of Indian characters. They went to a great deal of trouble to find the right wigs and makeup, order the correct number and amount, and have them sent to the set, wherever it might be. Studios hired additional makeup artists to paint the bodies of everyone who played Indians. These costs were carefully evaluated. Makeup artists worried about whether they would have enough or too much makeup. Creating Movie Indians—whether those characters were to be created from performers who were Indian or non-Indian—was in no way a simple process. Although these images are steeped in stereotype, their creators worked intentionally on them and hoped their product would fetch a profit.

Studios held steadfastly to their ideas about what Indians should look like. They used their images against Native employees, who almost always came up short in the comparison. When filmmakers asked themselves what made Indians Indian, they confronted cultural paradoxes and produced ironies. Filmmakers confronted the paradox of their own making when they went to sets and met Native people whose hair was cut like theirs, whose skin was often the same color as theirs, and whose clothes were the same as theirs. In one instance the film crew was completely shocked when the Diné suffered from sunburns just like the non-Indians. The studio did not provide sunscreen for them because they assumed Navajo skin would not burn. They expected Indians to be fundamentally and essentially different, yet they discovered people who were not entirely dissimilar from non-Indians.

In response to the complicated picture of midcentury Native people— rather than the Indians of the past they expected—filmmakers produced ironic gestures. They approached Indians with a rigid idea about Indian identity that relied on widely accepted notions of authenticity, and they expected dark-skinned men with long black hair. Actual Indians rarely had the look they sought and did not possess the skills desired by the studios, yet studios continued to hire them. They continued to search for and hire Native people, yet they also held firmly to their belief that Indian identity resides in outward signs. Those Indian signifiers could be easily re-created because they were physical, tangible markers: hair, skin, and eye color.

But filmmakers also explored another avenue of Indian signs: material culture. In the next chapter I explore their attempts to discover and secure material tribal culture from the reservation Indians they employed. Just as the reservation Indians they hired often did not fulfill their fantasy of the right bodies, hair, noses, and wardrobe, the Indians they hired often failed to re-create what they defined as Indian culture. In further solidifying the idea that Indian identity resides in cultural objects, not people, the filmmakers turned to non-Indian technical advisors to re-create supposedly authentic tribal objects.

"Dig Up a Good Indian Historian"

The Search for Authenticity

Underneath all the conflicting images of the Indian one fundamental truth emerges—the white man *knows* that he is an alien and he *knows* that North America is Indian—and he will never let go of the Indian image because he thinks that by some clever manipulation he can achieve an authenticity that cannot ever be his.
—Vine Deloria Jr., "American Fantasy"

While Congress embraced the destruction of tribes through termination policies in the postwar period, filmmakers ruminated over notions of the authentic Indian. They expressed disappointment at what they considered a lack of authentic Indian culture among Indians. Non-Natives had developed notions about Indian traditions in their own minds, then looked to Native employees to validate their imaginings. Film studios fit into this larger pattern, and they too looked for Indians who would re-create the traditions they imagined. Filmmakers never asked Indians to help them see Indians as Indians saw themselves. How Indians viewed themselves and defined their culture was irrelevant to filmmakers, especially if those ideas failed to reinforce their preconceived notions. The most important element when filmmakers were seeking out Indians was difference. They equated difference with authenticity and regarded similarities as alien to authenticity. For filmmakers, Native employees had to present ideas and cultural objects radically different from anything with which white Americans were familiar, yet those ideas had to simulate or build on what white people already believed they knew about Indians. Of course, this process of seeking confirmation for white preconceptions about Indians took place in the films themselves, but here I delve into the film archives to demonstrate how that same process dictated relations between Indians and non-Indians in the production process. The film archives provide ample evidence of studio employees seeking the authentic from American Indians but also instructing American Indians on authenticity. Native film workers participated in this closed loop of cultural knowledge while using the studios for economic gain.

Unable to picture the past exactly the way the studio did, none of these Native employees portrayed the Indian that whites imagined. The way non-Indians imagined Indians took on a life of its own and, without Indian intervention, would have eclipsed any other interpretation of these films. A rather humorous office memorandum from the Fox studio, written during the production of *Broken Arrow* (1950), confirmed the idea that actual Indians could only fulfill non-Indian demands by looking to white definitions of what constituted a Native American. Determined to present authentic Indians, Twentieth Century Fox hired Apaches to fill in the background in various scenes. In addition, the film's director, Delmer Daves, asked these Apaches to create cultural artifacts for use as props. Daves came to look at their work and found they were studying a book instead of working on the project. The studio's public relations department used broken English to depict the Apache men's response and ridiculed the men for being unfamiliar with their own culture when in fact they were unfamiliar with the non-Indian imitation of their culture: "'These things you ask for,' responded one of the two Indians, 'we have never used ourselves at the reservation. First we must learn how to make. That is why we are studying this book.' They proudly showed Daves the volume: *Boy Scout Handicraft Book*."[1]

In a sense, the press release played with what Michelle Raheja calls red-facing in the movies, which had created such powerful images of Indians that even Indians had to study for the roles assigned to them. Here the studio was yet again reveling in the dominant position, a position it occupied only because the studio's idealized, imagined, and authentic Indian is an outgrowth of non-Natives' occupation of Indigenous America. Through their actions, the Apaches suggested that this imagined ideal is a construct rooted in the fetishistic imaginary of the colonial mind. Had the studio been at all concerned with American Indians, it would have allowed the Apaches in this instance to create objects they knew, understood, and used. Instead, the studios embraced simulated acts of Indians playing Hollywood's version of an Indian. The studios intended to make the Apache men sound illiterate and uneducated through the representation of their dialogue, and perhaps this story was not even true. The intent was certainly to blame contemporary Apaches for their lack of cultural knowledge, to claim that knowledge as their own, and in that sense the story is a statement of the impossibility of Indian modernity in the context of an occupied land.

Authenticity, Narrative, and History

Scholars, particularly in the field of anthropology, have worked and reworked the concept of authenticity in reaction to a shift in the field beginning in the late twentieth century. Perhaps this moment began with the significant and targeted scholarship of James Clifford: *The Predicament of Culture* (1988). In that work Clifford critiqued the idea that the search for tradition and authenticity had led anthropologists to ignore distinctiveness among the marginalized groups they studied. Likewise, folklorist Regina Bendix writes in her book *In Search of Authenticity* (1988) that the origins of folklore studies are situated in historical moments of modernity and in the cultural desire to discover group origins and legitimate their existence on the basis of that uncovered authenticity. Two decades later Bendix was viewing the impulse in folklore studies and related fields to be one of recognizing diversity and globalization, as well as sometimes acting as advocates for marginalized people attempting to assert their rights to their own culture.[2]

Filmmakers expected Indians of the present to behave the way they thought Indians of the past behaved. They believed that authentic Indians lived as though the twentieth century had never happened and that they could naturally re-create the nineteenth-century world of their ancestors. They also tended to think of Lakotas and Apaches of the nineteenth century as Indian prototypes. Although this notion had a great deal to do with their vision of the past, their expectations were deeply rooted in a denial of history. History has to do with change, and the filmmakers rejected the idea that Indian people and culture had been changed by their contact with Europeans; the studios defined real Indians as people unchanged by contact with Europeans. When Indians of the present failed to match Hollywood's imagined Indians of the past, the studios exaggerated this point. They referred to the changes in Indian cultures as losses and always blamed Indian people for those losses. They failed entirely to acknowledge they were meeting Native people whose parents the government had sent off to boarding schools, away from their families and tribal nations, in places where they were not allowed to speak their Native languages and were cut off entirely from any tribal cultural activities. These children grew up to start families of their own, and it was those children whom the studios hired for their films. To blame them for their cultural losses was a deeply aggressive move. Some Indians lacked familiarity with their tribe's language and culture specifically because the U.S. government had interfered in the most private aspects of Native people's lives: their families. American Indians themselves may have used the language of loss to describe their changing relationship with their tribal cultures, but they, unlike the studios, would never have used that idea to criticize themselves. The press releases pointing out the Indians' lack of familiarity with white notions of Indian culture were intended to make whites laugh at Indians. Hollywood's publicizing of the situation was an implied insult to Indians, mocking them for their cultural losses, but Hollywood's motives involved making money by pretending to celebrate Indian cultures while ignoring the ways in which the United States was responsible for the erosion of tribal cultures.

The film production teams assumed that twentieth-century Indian cultures were largely an empty shell or mere skeletons of their former selves. In this view, contemporary Indian culture simply represented what once was or what Indians no longer were from the 1940s onward. Any presence of Indian identity or culture was presumed to be a nineteenth-century remnant. In this schema, whites faulted Indians for straying so far from their supposedly nineteenth-century origins.

The desire for authenticity played itself out in complicated ways. Filmmakers looked to reservation Indians to provide authenticity to their films. Although studios sometimes hired Italians and other non-Indians to play Indians in the movies, at other times they found it essential that real Indians have a physical presence, constituting the backdrop to these westerns. But these reservation Indians were sometimes unfamiliar with the series of symbols that constituted the images filmmakers wanted to create. The complications arose because filmmakers wanted Indians to create and demonstrate these symbols, but Indians sometimes did not know how. Filmmakers, then, turned to non-Indians who were well versed in the white version of Indian culture to teach the Indians how to create these symbols. This path resulted in a complicated cultural ventriloquism: whites said who Indians were, and Indians spoke in a voice created by whites for Indians. Yet the Native participants engaged this as a temporary strategy to make quick and easy cash on film sets by selling the asset the studio valued: their Indian identity.

Studios hired technical advisors to teach Indian employees and non-Indians playing Indian characters how to act the way the studios imagined Native people to act. This draws on a larger historical pattern of non-Indian appropriation and theft of Indian culture. Just one example would be hobbyists in Germany who appropriated Indian culture for recreation and cared deeply about the historical accuracy of their Indian clothing, jewelry, and songs. They wanted unequivocal assurance that the original from which they were copying was entirely Indian in origin, in no way influenced by whites. Their copying relied on rigid boundaries between Indian and non-Indian, yet their hobby stood as a testament to cultural borrowing. Engaging in the hobby changed their identities, making it far more than a social pleasure. While they knew they were not Indian, they stood fairly close to the line that divides Indians from non-Indians in claiming profound knowledge and respect. They believed their imitations of Indian culture were extremely accurate and their knowledge of Indian culture quite deep. Like the studios, when they encountered actual Indians who were unfamiliar with certain aspects of their tribal culture, the hobbyists seemed to think the Indians were somehow not Indian for their lack of knowledge. But where the hobbyists held knowledge, Indians held ancestry. By midcentury the hobbyist and film circles were defining authentic Indians as those with a high blood quantum. Yet blood quantum measurements were neither Indigenous nor authentic; they were an invention of the federal government. Nonetheless, ancestry became the objective barrier between Indian and non-Indian, though many Indians and non-Indians continued to take cultural knowledge into account when determining Indian identity.[3] The German hobbyists could be easily dismissed, but this same dynamic holds true when it comes to the tourism industry's engagement with Native people, as well as salvage anthropology. This conundrum created by non-Indians in which Indian identity was reduced to a particular kind of cultural knowledge played out in a similar fashion on film sets.

Truth and Lies

Mimicry was easy when it came to clothing but far more difficult when it involved Native languages. Although *Dances with Wolves* (1990) was unusual because Native characters spoke Lakota, taught to them by a Lakota speaker, filmmakers of the 1940s and 1950s also hired Indian language experts to teach their actors American Indian languages.[4] After the immense labor involved in learning correct pronunciation and memorizing lines in Indigenous languages for these earlier films, actors found their Native-language lines limited to intercultural moments between Indians and non-Indians. Not until *Atanarjuat* (2001) was a Native language used for an entire film. Thus, although it may sometimes appear that Hollywood did not care about authenticity, film archives contain the details of how studios during the post–World War II period conducted research in hopes of presenting accurate and authentic images of Indians.

The studios' research methodologies for obtaining knowledge of historic Indian cultures usually began with standard historical texts from the downtown branch of the Los Angeles Public Library. These sources of information were mainly about treaties and wars. However, the studio researchers were less interested in the legal past of tribes than they were in culture, especially private, spiritual knowledge. For that information, the studios looked to anthropology, often consulting Bureau of Ethnology reports, which were based on Indian interviews and ethnography, which is itself a form of cultural appropriation. For example, the producer and staff of *Broken Arrow* (Twentieth Century Fox, 1950) conducted extensive research on Apache culture.[5] In preproduction for *Colt .45* (1950), Warner Bros. producers requested information about dress, governmental policy, reservation boundaries, treaties, and names of Indian leaders from their research staff, who dutifully acquired extremely long and accurate lists of Lakota treaties.[6] In the end, however, the producers' real concern was creating an authentic Indian look rather than an accurate portrayal of American Indian history. Studios defined American Indian history as the story of conflict between Indians and whites, with a major focus on whites rather than Indians, effectively making Indian cultural authenticity and Indian perspective a moot point.

The producers' devotion to accuracy and authenticity was partial in that they used research to confirm their beliefs and presuppositions. Whatever the original desire for authenticity in regard to Native American history, it mostly fell by the wayside, usually in preproduction. Most filmmakers made some effort to obtain accurate historical data, but when answers failed to materialize quickly or affirm their purposes, they fell back on invention and casually lied about their research. When Warner Bros. was unable to locate a government-issued map of the Klamath Indian Reservation for *Drum Beat* (1954), a producer suggested they create one and simply mark the map with the Department of the Interior's stamp.[7] Similarly, a producer for *The Battle at Apache Pass* (Universal, 1952) was prepared to fabricate an academic article falsely claiming that the Apache Nation had never signed a treaty with the federal government if the researchers discovered information to the contrary.[8] For another Universal film, *Column South* (1953), the producer outlined a plan in which a historian would be told what to say, instead of the historian providing information to the producers: "Dig up a good Indian historian and have him say in a feature interview that the movies have done (and are doing) more to perpuate [*sic*] the historical facts about Indian lore than most history books. Could say that the Indians would be a fading bit of America if it weren't for the picture makers and their research."[9] Just as studios required Native employees to wear costumes and pretend to be presenting a past that never was, the studios handed scripts to scholars and asked them to lie for Hollywood.

Not only did studio executives suggest lies in place of research, at least one lied about the finished product. For its film *Broken Arrow* (1950), Twentieth Century Fox publicized its efforts to obtain authenticity from the White River Apaches it hired: "We wanted to deal with Indians who would not look like cardboard cutouts of redmen. . . . They taught us how to build their wickiups, showed us their devil dances and ceremonials, allowed us to record the music of their native instruments and their chants. Every prop you will see in the picture is authentic; and although their war paint looks exactly like the product of a Hollywood make-up department, it isn't. It's their own."[10] The same employee who wrote this press release also informed the press about the Apaches not owning their own head-dresses, drums, or buckskins. He also wrote the story about the Apache men consulting the Boy Scout handbook to create Indian artifacts. By his own account, Twentieth Century Fox had failed to capture the Indian authenticity it sought, yet here the studio wants U.S. audiences to believe something untrue: that because of Twentieth Century Fox's sensitivity and diligence, they captured authentic Apache culture on film. Thus, one or more of these press releases is a lie.[11]

The desire for authenticity was trumped by lack of patience, time, and visual perspective. In these films, authenticity, when sought after, often only went as far as the audience could see. On one set the filmmakers went to a local museum to borrow Indian pestles, but the Indian extras were given corn flakes to grind with the pestles. The studio's goal was not to create historical accuracy to the fullest extent possible; it was only to create a relatively authentic image.[12] On the set of *Comanche Territory* (Universal, 1950), the prop department borrowed Comanche relics from the Museum of Natural History for display at the film's opening at the Rivoli Theatre, yet they had employed Diné to play Comanches.[13] The search for authenticity was always compromised in some way, either by finances or by relying on the ignorance of the American public about Native people.

When Native employees entered the orbit of the white American search for American Indian authenticity, the studios usually became frustrated. In one fascinating case, the studio turned to a Native expert, but they did not trust his expertise entirely, as they turned to a non-Indian expert as well. After the production of *Broken Arrow*, Fox was concerned with the authenticity of their film's title. They wondered if Indians would agree that the broken arrow meant peace among any Indian tribes, even though they had already decided it did. Twentieth Century Fox's attorney sent several inquiries on the matter to Ambrose Roanhorse, director of the Navajo Arts and Crafts Vocational School. Roanhorse responded briefly that "the Broken Arrow is a symbol of peace used by all Indian Tribes as I have been told by older Indians."[14] But the attorney also wrote to a Mr. Harrington of the Southwest Museum asking about the broken arrow symbol. Harrington felt that "it would have been very plausible for any Indian to have had the idea of breaking an arrow to symbolize peace," but "it was not a custom among any of the tribes." Attached to his letter were seven pages of ethnological references to broken arrows from the annual reports of the Bureau of Ethnology.[15] The studio reached out to a museum expert, the Navajo teacher Roanhorse, and the ethnological reports. The studio stood by its chosen film title. Ironically, the museum turned to Bureau of Ethnology reports, which in turn relied for their validity on information garnered from Indians. Yet those who invoked the Bureau of Ethnology reports and similar documentation thought of the texts as authentic knowledge because they bore the stamp of approval from non-Indian scholars.[16]

Americans enjoyed watching Indians playing Indians, and this partially accounts for what the studios perceived as accurate and authentic. For instance, a previewer chosen by Universal to react to their new film *Taza, Son of Cochise* (Universal, 1954) commented, "I was extremely pleased to find that the picture was filmed with 'REAL,' Indian people."[17] Another offered this compliment: "The Indians looked like real Indians not Hollywood. This is an improvement."[18] Professional film reviewers writing for news outlets also appreciated the presence of Native extras. One reviewer of *Canyon Passage* (Universal, 1946) noted the presence of Indians and offered biographical details provided by the publicity department to add to the sense of authenticity: "The Indians, whose presence adds a touch of menace to the scene, were descendants of the Yakima and Rogue Indians who figured in the famous rebellion of '56. One of them, Nipo Strongheart, is the great-grandnephew of the man responsible for the uprising, and great-grandson of Owhi, the chief of the Yakima Indians at that time."[19]

The studio had provided inaccurate details: Owhi led the Yakamas, but he was not a chief. He participated in the 1855 treaty negotiations, and in 1856 war broke out. Many plateau Indians joined the fighting, and fights between and within tribes eventually ended the war. After the war Owhi was shot and his son, Qualchin, was hanged. Nipo Strongheart was adopted by a Yakama family, and his name was added to the Yakama rolls.[20] But Strongheart was possibly not Yakama in the sense of being born to a Yakama parent. His parents may have both been white. Regardless of these important details, audiences believed Strongheart was a Yakama because he told Hollywood he was, and Hollywood repeated this identification to the public. For that reason audiences viewed his filmic presence as adding something authentic to the film. Historian Andrew Fisher has conducted extensive research on Strongheart and the Yakama Nation. Fisher makes these connections as well, linking the importance of Strongheart's passing as Native, how he was used by the studio, and how he challenged the studios on representations of Native people.[21] Strongheart provided services as a technical advisor on many films, including *Across the Wide Missouri* (MGM, 1951), *Black Gold* (Allied Artists, 1947), *Canyon Passage* (Universal, 1946), and *The Charge at Feather River* (Warner Bros., 1953). A reviewer of *Jim Thorpe, All American* (Warner Bros., 1951) felt the presence of Indian actors Jack Big Head and Suni Warcloud was to "remind the customers that this is a picture about an Indian."[22] In response to *Valley of the Sun* (RKO, 1942), a critic exclaimed, "Hey fellers, Indians! Real, honest-to-gosh redskins on the war path . . . and their presence furnishes authentic flavor to proceedings."[23] The film reviewer at *Variety* also complimented *Valley's* use of Indians, and the *Motion Picture Herald* seemed impressed by the director's use of Native Americans.[24] A reviewer of *Massacre River* (Allied Artists, 1949) noted and appreciated the presence of Native people: "Real Indians take part and speak their own language in parleys with the whites."[25]

Audiences and movie critics thus made it known that they thought the use of real Indians made films more authentic and enjoyable.

Throughout the 1940s and 1950s studios hired Indians whose job was to provide the crew with information about their tribe's culture, history, or language. These were always men, and some of these Native men fulfilled the filmmakers' expectations. Ben American Horse, a cousin of Crazy Horse, and Dewey Beard, who called himself Iron Hail, were two such men. Beard spent his life on the Pine Ridge Reservation and survived the Wounded Knee Massacre of 1890. Yet the studio oddly labeled him a survivor of the Battle of the Little Bighorn instead of Wounded Knee. He was a survivor indeed, but he survived the massacre at Wounded Knee. He gave an extensive interview for *National Geographic* poignantly summarizing the actions at Wounded Knee: "They murdered us."[26] Through his multidecade friendship with the non-Indian painter and technical advisor David Miller, he and American Horse worked for MGM on *The Last Hunt* (1956) and for Universal on *Tomahawk* (1951) and *Battles of Chief Pontiac* (1952). They sang a buffalo-calling song and performed a dance that made it into the final version of *The Last Hunt*.[27] MGM filmed this performance but made no effort to make the song and dance fit into the film's sequencing and failed completely to explain its cultural significance. On another occasion Paramount affirmed that the Lakotas on the set of *The Savage* (1952) had captured the essence of their ancestors. When the men stood in front of the cameras, the filmmakers believed they were not acting but were instead riding back into time, providing a close copy of their nineteenth-century ancestors.[28] Here again we see the notion that any twentieth-century Indian presence is a nineteenth-century remnant. For Paramount and other studios, real Indians had to possess a close connection to nineteenth-century Indians. Although some Indians were presumed to be inauthentic because of their difference from Hollywood's image of Indians, others, such as these Lakota extras, were assumed to be one and the same as the imagined, ideal Indian.

Knowledge functioned as an important piece in the puzzle of Indian authenticity. Many Indians gave the studios cultural information the producers found quite helpful and deemed valid. Warner Bros. hoped to create authentic Seminole culture in *Distant Drums* (1951), and the oldest Seminole at the time, Charlie Cypress, age ninety-four, carved a canoe that was used in the film. He also answered their questions about Seminole history and culture. The studio hired one hundred Seminole extras, rented cypress canoes, and filmed in a Seminole village, all of which was made possible by their Seminole employees.[29] The makers of the film *Distant Drums* believed they were in an ideal situation: they had found a Native man who looked the way they believed a Native man should look, who acted the way they thought a Native man should act, and he was creating cultural artifacts they felt were authentic. What the above examples point to is not that some Indians were authentic Indians. Rather, these Indians shared knowledge that coincidentally fit into the filmmakers' preexisting framework or was so far outside their framework they had no room to judge its accuracy. Nonetheless, this gave Native employees little room for negotiation. Even though Native people had the knowledge and artifacts Hollywood wanted, they did not earn more pay because of it.

Although Indians playing Indians could contribute to authenticity, that alone did not guarantee authenticity from the perspective of the filmmakers. Authenticity operated somewhat separately from the issue of Indians playing Indians. Their use of the term "authentic," in fact, described objects and was primarily a visual understanding. This meant that hiring Indians to play Indians fulfilled only part of studios' and audiences' hopes for authenticity. Authenticity also meant a certain look and feel that could not be captured by putting modern Indians in front of the screen without any additional props. Audiences looked for signs of the authentic, a vague category that could lead in many directions. One direction authenticity never leaned toward, however, was anything modern. Authenticity did not include an Indian woman with a contemporary hairstyle driving a trendy, new car to a drive-in. Focus group members whom the studios paid to preview movies used the term "authentic" many times on their response cards but seemed to think the term was so transparent that the studios would understand immediately what they meant. In regard to *Tomahawk* (Universal, 1951), one previewer replied simply: "Indian costumes and land language [*sic*] were interesting and authentic."[30] A previewer of *Taza, Son of Cochise* enjoyed the "authentic dress, etc.," and another "liked the authenticity of the picture."[31]

For filmgoers, authenticity seemed related to appearances and props but not the story itself. Narrative existed as a separate category in their minds, and many movie fans made known their feelings about the limits of westerns. They clearly articulated a desire for films that would create something entirely new about the story of Indians and whites. Many previewers were tired of traditional westerns altogether. One complained, "I'm sick of Indian pictures, more love pictures."[32] After viewing *Pillars of the Sky* (Universal, 1956), some audience members expressed their boredom with westerns: "Why another Western?" wrote one. "Another Western?" asked another, and a third queried, "Will they ever stop making cowboy and Indian stories with the same old plot?"[33] Some of those who previewed *Tomahawk* (Universal, 1951) wrote, "Sick and tired of cowboy and Indian pictures," and, "Frankly I am sick and tired of Westerns. Good or bad."[34] For some, this desire for new story lines related to capturing a deeper sense of historical reality and veracity. For instance, one previewer of *Taza, Son of Cochise* wrote, "I like the real life portrayal of Indian life!"[35] Yet another asked for "more pictures showing the true Amer. Indian."[36] These previewers challenged the industry to provide films with human drama, as well as American Indian characters shaped with the same respect given to white characters. A previewer of *Column South* (Universal, 1953) wrote, "It was nice to see a movie that showed Indians as humans, not animals for a change."[37] Finally, and perhaps presenting the biggest challenge of all, one previewer demanded something historians and filmmakers struggle with even today. In response to the film *Tomahawk*, a reviewer pointed out, "Still does not show Indians' side of story."[38] Although most previewers simply circled their answers and did not offer any comment in the blank spaces provided, those who took the time to complete the surveys consistently made strong statements, both positive and negative. Filmmakers had creative license and could have written stories from what they thought would have been an Indian perspective, but they normalized the settler colonial viewpoint repeatedly and consistently.

In sorting out what Indians brought to film sets and what they left behind, one thing is clear: filmmakers looked to actual Indians for authenticity and were disappointed in what Indians had to offer. The interest in authenticity for audiences and studios as a plan for filmmaking started with hiring Native people. On some occasions American Indian employees provided filmmakers with information and knowledge that proved helpful and matched the filmmakers' goals. But filmmakers also met modern Indians and constantly expressed disappointment that they were not identical to their nineteenth-century ancestors. When Indian actor John War Eagle required time to learn to ride a horse bareback, Universal expressed dismay, shock, and even ridicule that an American Indian lacked such skills, and studio personnel implied that he was not Indian because of his inability to ride.[39] Even worse in the studios' view were Indians who mimicked Movie Indian culture. Just as the Apaches hired for *Broken Arrow* enlisted outside help in the form of a Boy Scout handbook, the Diné hired for *A Ticket to Tomahawk* (Twentieth Century Fox, 1950) turned to movies for knowledge of the generic Indian dances: "The Navajo Indians, many of them G.I.s[,] swung right into a war dance without any coaching. . . . Director Sale asked them where they learned the dance. . . . The spokesman grinned sheepishly. . . . 'We see many movies,' he said. 'We learn all about Indian dances.'"[40]

As was the case with many studio press releases, this exchange may have been entirely fabricated. The tale presents Diné as fully engaged with movie culture. These Navajo men had perhaps viewed westerns when they were enlisted men in World War II, but living on the reservation in the 1950s would have made it difficult for them to be dedicated movie attendees. In exchange for pay, the Diné gave the studios an Indian dance constructed by the movie industry. The studio was looking for an authentic, archaic past and trying to avoid anything inauthentic, modern, copied, or mass produced. Studios wanted reservation Indians to be part of a past that relied on hand-made objects perceived as truly Indian. Instead of offering archaic Indian knowledge, the Navajo GIs offered information based on their knowledge of movies, not on Navajo culture. Most important, these Navajo men may have possessed the cultural information the filmmakers were seeking and protected the content to keep it private. They may have felt Navajo dances were meant to be danced with other Diné on Navajo land, not in front of cameras for Twentieth Century Fox.[41]

The presence of Native employees and the search for authentic Native culture on film sets often worked against each other and created these convoluted scenarios in which Indians were taught Native American culture according to Hollywood. When Indian extras were unfamiliar with Indian culture as imagined by the film's white producers, filmmakers hired non-Indians and sometimes Indians (from other tribes) to teach Indian extras how to act Indian in the ways expected. This was a form of cultural ventriloquism in which Indians appeared to be speaking and moving, but the filmmakers held the strings and dictated their moves.

Studios arranged virtual clinics on being Indian in the 1950s. Technical advisors set out to teach reservation Indians how to use bows and arrows, bead, ride bareback, and set up tipis. The *Broken Arrow* crew employed a non-Indian, Al Lenan, to teach the Apaches how to use the bow and arrow due to "civilization's inroads on time-honored tribal customs."[42] Diné learned archery from non-Indian Arnie Williams for *Sergeant Rutledge*.[43] White Mountain Apaches were taught how to use the bow and arrow for *Drum Beat* (Warner Bros., 1954).[44] Crows worked in *Warpath* (Paramount, 1951), and they were taught bareback riding, how to set up tipis, and Hollywood's version of a war dance by the non-Indian archery expert Carl Coleman.[45] Lakotas learned how to shoot with bows and arrows for *The Savage* (Paramount, 1952) from a non-Indian archery expert. Universal hired technical advisor Joe Pocaterra on the Alberta set of *Saskatchewan* (1954) to teach Cree men how to throw tomahawks.[46]

Filmmakers' attempts to make Indians move and act like Indians constituted only one aspect of the complicated re-creation of a certain type of Indian culture. Directors and producers also sought to make their movies more Indian with the use of artifacts. When non-Indians taught Native employees how to perform Indian culture or make American Indian objects, studios magnified the irony. Producers of *Mrs. Mike* (United Artists, 1949) decided to employ Geraldine O'Connor, "expert on Indian beadwork[,] to teach the Indians how to bead and check all finished products to be used in the film."[47] The studio could have purchased products from O'Connor, but with O'Connor teaching the Indians to bead, the studio could claim they had tapped into Indian authenticity because the Native employees had, in fact, produced the beaded products. The fact that real Indians stood behind the façade meant, for the studios, that the films themselves were grounded in reality and therefore authentic. This belief that hiring Native employees legitimized all sorts of re-creations also meant that an Indian from one tribe could stand in as an Indian of another tribe. *Comanche Territory* (Universal, 1950) embodied the whole tangled nature of movie-derived realities. The director created an artificial montage that stood in for Oklahoma on a sound stage. He used Arizona as though it were Oklahoma, hired Apaches and Diné to play Comanches, and used a man pretending to be Cherokee to teach Diné and Apaches how to play Comanches.[48]

Language

The search for authenticity did not stop with artifacts and appearances; it extended to language and often led in ridiculous directions. Where the objects of Indian culture could be painstakingly re-created through information garnered from books and other materials, Indian languages could never be so easily reproduced. Language acquisition can only be partially gained through written materials and audio recordings. A person must invest time speaking the language with fluent speakers. Unlike material culture, language requires face time with a Native speaker. Material culture lends itself well to cultural borrowing and mimicry, but language remains a formidable opponent to cultural fluidity.

Just as studios hired technical advisors—some Indian, others not—to teach Indians how to use bows and arrows and how to dress, they also sought advisors to teach actors Indian languages but also to create fake Indian languages. The fake languages were sometimes based loosely on Native languages and at other times were simply gibberish. Fake Indian languages probably emerged from the belief that for white filmgoers, all Indian languages were essentially the same. Native languages show tremendous diversity, but for white audience members they would have sounded equally foreign and meaningless. When using either gibberish or a real Native language, the film characters quickly provided the audience with an English translation. Indian characters also spoke English, but the words were poetic, ungrammatical, or full of anger. Regardless of the language or style of speech used, filmmakers thought Indian characters had to sound different from other characters because they perceived historic Indians' speech as fundamentally different from the way whites spoke. Some filmmakers believed that by making Indian characters sound different, regardless of the means, they were capturing something authentic and true about Indians of the past on film.[49]

Filmmakers seemed to think that in seeking the advice of Indian technical advisors, accurately translating English into various Native languages, and presenting something akin to a Native language, they would successfully remedy the dilemma of inauthenticity. Yet in the cases where Native speakers consulted with studio executives and taught actors a handful of lines, those Native people had no influence over the script. They were teaching non-Indians in lead roles, and they were never offered those lead roles. For most films, producers made no effort to duplicate a Native language. They thought they knew what would be accurate and they usually settled for gibberish, broken English, or poetic, wise speeches. Language may have seemed an especially easy aspect of Indian culture to falsely imitate, but some evidence shows that non-Native speakers could detect obvious false imitations and felt disdain for the ubiquity of inaccurate Indian speech.

From the perspective of filmmakers, gibberish was a perfectly acceptable remedy to the challenge of replicating complex and unfamiliar Native languages. At times studios hired Native speakers but often limited their role to translating small portions of a script and teaching the lines to their actors. In 1947 Boris Karloff memorized lines in Seneca for his part as Guyasuta in *Unconquered*.[50] Warner Bros. claimed its actors spoke Nez Perce in *The Charge at Feather River* (1953).[51] A Pueblo man taught Navajos how to speak Ute on the set of *Red Mountain* (Paramount, 1951).[52] A lead white character in *Ambush* (MGM, 1950) possibly spoke Apache and Navajo, learned from Bob Wilson, Navajo Johnny, and Chief Deerfoot.[53] Ed Lonehill (who played Spotted Hand and can be seen in Victor Masayesva's *Imagining Indians*) taught Lakota to a non-Indian actor for *The Last Hunt* (MGM, 1956). David Miller, who was not Lakota, also provided Lakota language instruction on that film.[54] Jake Herman, artist, athlete, and, later an Oglala tribal council member, taught Susan Cabot and Van Heflin their lines in Lakota for *Tomahawk*.[55] The actors in *Devil's Doorway* (MGM, 1950) memorized some Shoshoni, and actors playing Navajo code talkers memorized some Navajo for the World War II films *Battle Cry* (Warner, 1955) and *Never So Few* (MGM, 1959).[56] Finally, an Apache speaker from Oatman, Arizona, translated a handful of lines into Apache for *Foxfire* (Universal, 1955) and received a small part in the film.

Because the studios made movies primarily for a white audience, they may have taken great liberties even when they claimed actors were speaking a true Native language. In one case, I was able to document that either the studio or the technical advisor lied about a Native language being spoken in a film. According to MGM, Nipo T. Strongheart translated a lullaby and other portions of the *Across the Wide Missouri* (MGM, 1951) script into Blackfeet (with one term in Nez Perce). Strongheart was an adopted Yakama but probably non-Indian by birth. According to Darrell Robes Kipp, founder and language instructor at the Piegan Institute, the characters in *Across the Wide Missouri* do not speak Blackfeet at any point in the film. Yvonne Curley, a Navajo speaker, watched several John Ford films and heard the extras speak Navajo, but this is not surprising because the extras were Navajo and the studio never claimed the extras were speaking a language other than Navajo, although they were playing Indians of other tribes.[57]

Studios and filmmakers assumed their film audiences needed Indian characters to sound different from other characters, but difference could mean almost anything. The most extreme example comes from the 1930s serial *Scouts to the Rescue*. The producers simply ran the film sequence featuring Indian characters backward so that their English dialogue sounded unintelligible. Because the Indians moved very little, the reversal of the film was not detectable.[58] This example demonstrates the lengths to which filmmakers would go to make sure Indians sounded different from white characters. The use of spoken English played in reverse also shows how anything weird could pass as a Native language. Although actual Native languages may have been spoken in some films, technical advisors often admitted to creating fake Indian languages based in gibberish, but the actors memorized fake words for the sake of consistency and, thereby, legitimacy. In the serial *Black Arrow* (Columbia, 1944), a Zuni character speaks in a language that is supposed to be Zuni and is not or is mangled to the point of unrecognizability. Invented Indian languages are used in *The Oregon Trail* (Twentieth Century Fox, 1959), *Comanche Station* (Columbia, 1960), and the comedy *The Sheriff of Fractured Jaw* (Twentieth Century Fox, 1959). Indian characters also speak a fake Lakota in *Buffalo Bill Rides Again* (Screen Guild, 1947).

Few studios publicized their use of gibberish, but viewings of these films reveal that most relied on fake rather than real Native speech. The studio head at Twentieth Century Fox approved the use of gibberish in *Siege at Red River* (1954) and justified the decision by arguing, "There is nothing [the Indians] have to explain."[59] In other words, although many characters in a film speak, some speech contains important information that contributes to the story line, whereas other characters simply appear. Non-Indian characters often translated gibberish into English for other non-Indian characters. Very few Indian characters were bilingual in the movies of the 1940s and 1950s, yet somehow white characters could easily interpret any Indian language. Cochise speaks fake Apache in *Fort Apache* (RKO, 1948), and the officers use an interpreter to convey his message. A white man named Fiske interprets for the "Tomanches" in *The Tall Texan* (Lippert, 1953). In *The Prairie* (Screen Guild, 1947), a white male character interprets for an anonymous Indian and then kills him. Chief Yellowstone, played by Iron Eyes Cody, speaks in gibberish in *Massacre River* (Monogram, 1949), and a white man interprets.[60] In *The Searchers* (Warner Bros., 1956), Chief Scar speaks with Ethan (John Wayne) in what is supposed to be Comanche. A general speaks in fake Seminole to a Seminole soldier in *Naked in the Sun* (Allied Artists, 1957). Although *Canyon Passage* (Universal, 1946) used gibberish, an Indian-hating character translates the gibberish into English.

When not speaking memorized lines in Native languages or speaking gibberish, Indian characters spoke poetic English. Speaking in this way, Indians were cast as wise and stoic. When being wise, Indians were granted poetic license and allowed to use English correctly. In *Indian Agent* (RKO, 1948), Red Fox complains to the agent about the lack of rations the imprisoned Indians are receiving. He tells him, "Their hearts are heavy, and their stomachs are hungry." The chief in *Massacre at Sand Creek* (Columbia,

1956) offers this bit of wisdom to his son: "A horse is like a wife. All men think theirs is the greatest." Still later in the film, the chief, who is supposed to be Cheyenne, borrows a famous statement made by the Nez Perce leader Chief Joseph: "And from where the sun now stands, I shall fight no more forever." In *Captain John Smith and Pocahontas* (United Artists, 1958), Powhatan delivers a brief monologue: "I do not say I can love the whiteskin, but there is no reason why we cannot live together in peace. If the whiteskin would only realize that the earth and all it bears does not belong only to them." In *The Great Sioux Uprising* (Universal, 1953), Red Cloud wisely warns, "Where there is justice, there will be peace." Although the content of these statements spoke to certain truths, the ways in which these characters spoke did not elicit audience identification. Instead, this kind of language continued to push Indians aside, where their words were not taken seriously by non-Indians. Studio executives and movie producers and directors thought poetic Indian speech mirrored historical reality, making this kind of speech, in their minds, authentic.

The majority of Native speech in movies was more often ungrammatical. The dialogue offered by Native characters in the movies stems from the virtual absence of verbs or from improper verb conjugation. From the 1940s and 1950s the earliest example comes from the character Geronimo. In *Valley of the Sun* (RKO, 1942) Geronimo demands that Jim, the Indian agent, be killed for withholding the Apaches' rations. When Johnny, the white hero, informs Geronimo they are brothers because of Johnny's adoption by the Apaches, Geronimo disagrees in the broken English common to Movie Indians:

> GERONIMO: You no my brother. No white man my brother. He
>   [Jim] die.
> JOHNNY: Then start war.
> GERONIMO: Me like war.
> JOHNNY: War is no good for your people.
> COCHISE: Brother speak true.

In *Canadian Pacific* (Twentieth Century Fox, 1949) an Indian apologizes, saying, "I sorry. Me see this not happen again." In *Mrs. Mike* (United

Artists, 1949) Atenou, played by Chief Yowlachie, offers Mrs. Mike his freshly removed tooth, telling her, "Ah, tooth of wisdom. You take. Love charm. Keep love always," and later, "Me good Indian." In *She Wore a Yellow Ribbon* (RKO, 1949) Pony That Walks, played by Chief Big Tree, excitedly greets the soldier played by John Wayne, proclaiming, "I am a Christian. Hallelujah! Old friend me. Long time. . . . Smoke pipe good." In *Pony Express* (Paramount, 1953) Yellow Hand haggles with Buffalo Bill over ponies. The conversation ends with a threat: "You buy or come down on ground. . . . I fight Cody. We wait. We meet." Probably the most famous of broken Movie Indian English is that of Tonto, as played by Mohawk actor Jay Silverheels. In *The Lone Ranger* (Warner Bros., 1956) Tonto proclaims, "Trouble find Tonto even when him not look for it."[61]

In the handful of films depicting modern-day Indians, Indians spoke in standard English. The writers and producers simply wanted to make it easier for audiences to understand the dialogue.[62] However, filmmakers continued to find ways to make these twentieth-century Indians seem different in generically Movie Indian ways. Studios seemed to think that the anomaly of an Indian character speaking standard English had to be explained to audiences. One producer claimed that "long-winded speeches full of metaphors . . . characterize . . . the people."[63] Indians speaking perfect English was the exception to the rule for Hollywood and was typically attributed to a character's unusual cultural background or experience.

In trying to capture a sense of the authentic, *Broken Arrow*'s production crew claimed that Cochise's lines were direct translations from Apache to English. Twentieth Century Fox applauded itself for its cultural sensitivity. In reality, however, a studio writer drafted a script in English, and an Apache speaker translated some lines into Apache. The writer thus created standard English speech that sounded the way the non-Indian crew thought Indians should sound. In the end, this meant a character would be speaking the non-Apache-language lines in correct English but also demonstrating a solid command of the stylized dialogue of Indian characters.

When a young Indian character with light skin enters his first scene in *Broken Lance* (Twentieth Century Fox, 1954), the studio decided he should use "'medicine man' talk" to inform the audience of his Native ancestry.[64]

One Fox executive expressed his concern that the white person playing the Indian female lead in *The Last Wagon* (Twentieth Century Fox, 1956) spoke too well. He recommended an explanation or changing her speech to "an Indian-manner of speaking; OR: there must be an explanation offered as to why she speaks so well. Perhaps we can assume, or even mention, that she was educated in an Indian-American school. But even with this explanation, she should not talk as she did in the test. I had a feeling I was watching a character from a Broadway show."[65] Studios and filmmakers thought they knew how Indians of the past and present spoke. They felt they had no choice other than reducing modern Indian characters' speech to "medicine man talk" or "wise Indian" speech.

Whereas some scripts had modern Indian characters speak wisely to communicate their Indian identity, others featured Indians lashing out at non-Indian characters, especially when the topic of their Indian identity came to the fore. Even though Burt Lancaster as Jim Thorpe in *Jim Thorpe, All American* (Warner Bros., 1951) speaks perfect English, his verbal performances are marked by anger when his Indian identity is introduced at the lowest point of his life. In a scene about halfway through the film, well after Thorpe's Olympic medals have been taken and his son has suddenly died, Thorpe's wife, Margaret, suggests they return to Oklahoma. She dreams of building a home on the allotment he had received as a member of the Sac and Fox Nation. The movie begins with Thorpe's father teaching him that he must leave the confines of Oklahoma to make something of himself, which is precisely the path Thorpe takes for the remainder of the film. As the film shows, "making something of himself" means leaving Oklahoma and his Indian identity behind. When Margaret makes her suggestion, Thorpe is at his lowest point emotionally, feeling trumped by racism and the arbitrary invocation of Olympic rules and regulations. With the mention of Oklahoma and Indian land, Thorpe feels trapped by his Indian identity:

THORPE: They'd all like to see me go back to the reservation, wouldn't they? You'd like to see me go back to the reservation, wouldn't you?

MARGARET: Jim, I didn't say that.

THORPE: Good old Jim Thorpe, back in the blanket where he belongs, sitting in front of a tipi, smoking a corncob pipe. Can't get into any trouble, no money, no firewater.

MARGARET: Jim, please.

THORPE: Stupid, illiterate Indian boy!

MARGARET: Jim, stop!

THORPE: Make plenty of fine handmade moccasins, purses with pretty beads, sell them to tourists at the railway stations! Make lots of wampum for fine squaw!

The films' writers had intentionally "refrained from using the topical gags and funny names that spring so easily to mind" about Indians in movies.[66] But the writers, like their lead character, were trapped in a certain interpretation and representation of Indian identity. In *Buffalo Bill* (Twentieth Century Fox, 1944) the local schoolteacher, Dawn Starlight, speaks perfect English, so Buffalo Bill asks for her help in writing a letter, as he is barely literate. Although she is the literate schoolteacher, the studio head suggested that she occasionally "grope for a word, indicating that she is not completely familiar with the language."[67] Just as the studio could not choose between representing her as literate or semiliterate, they also could not decide whether she wanted to be white or Indian. Starlight clearly wishes she were white: she sneaks into a white character's room to try on her fancy dresses. When caught, Starlight is pleased to hear that she looks beautiful but becomes outraged when her Indian identity is brought up. She screams, "Indian! Indian!" as though she can no longer accept this identification made about her by whites. She abandons her teaching position to join her brother, Yellow Hand, in attacking the U.S. Army.[68] The moment in the white woman's dress marks the turn toward her radicalization as an Indian woman. Being shamed for wearing the dress over her Indian body shifts her mind toward her tribe and their larger needs.[69]

Speaking Native languages sits at one end of the extreme of filmic representations of Indians, while at the other is the silence of many Indian characters who never uttered a word from the film's beginning to its end. English professor Armando José Prats titles his book *Invisible Natives* to reflect this very phenomenon. Movie Indians often simply enter the scene with guns or bows and arrows, hooting but never speaking. In some of these films the viewer never sees Indian characters. Instead, filmmakers used symbols denoting the presence of Indians—flying arrows, white women staring into the camera and screaming in terror, the shadow of a feather, or dead whites with arrows protruding from their bodies—to express the presence of Indians without actually showing Indians. Prats argues that the western both erases and requires American Indian characters. He writes, "The Hollywood Western never produced an Indian antagonist more memorable, or more familiar, than the one whom we never quite see."[70]

Conclusion

In producing films, Hollywood sought to possess, inhabit, and control the Native people who worked for them. They wanted to see their notion of the ideal Indian performed by actual Indians. The studios' efforts, however, produced some disappointment, which arrived from several directions. It came when the studios were unable to erase their own manipulation and control over Indian representations. However, their manipulation was a product of their disappointment in Native employees. American Indians were given no artistic freedom to produce self-representations. Instead, studios gave them narrow parameters within which to work. Filmmakers doomed themselves to disappointment because they wanted Native people to work in their films, but they wanted them to behave naturally—in ways that suited the studios. Studios wanted to avoid teaching Indians how to act Indian because it cost them money, but even more important was that it profoundly undermined their motive for hiring Indians. When Indians did not have special, exclusive Indian knowledge, hiring Indians became less meaningful to filmmakers, and filmmakers found themselves in the contradictory position of teaching Indians how to act the way Indians acted in movies.

Instead of critiquing their imaginings of Native people, studios prepared publicity releases that emphasized the encroachment of modernity upon Native people and thus the inauthenticity of the Indians they hired. Their pieces were meant to be humorous, or at least ironic, because they intended the image of a modern Native person to be funny and incongruous, at the expense of Native people. Studios never allowed Native people to be modern without assigning a negative tone to their place in the modern moment. Hollywood, as it went looking for Native people who matched their definitions of Native people, only reified their imagined Indian over and above their Native employees. But studios never asserted total control over images of Indians. In the final analysis, Native employees who worked in movies held the reins to the cultural capital of Indian culture and identity. Studios needed Native people desperately. Even when Native people failed in their eyes, the studios publicized that dissonance to highlight the presence of Native people in their films.[71]

Although filmmakers had the power to access a variety of resources on Native history and culture, they obstructed their own efforts to harness Indian authenticity by adhering to stereotyped notions of what was and was not Indian. When they hired Indians who held and shared knowledge the studios found valuable, which was extremely rare, the filmmakers held Native power in check by limiting their creative control to minute aspects of the filmmaking process. According to Hollywood's stereotypes, other Indians lacked the knowledge Hollywood wanted but were willing and able to provide them with an ersatz Indian culture. Apaches thus borrowed from the Boy Scouts. Diné copied Indian dances from movies. Filmmakers were looking for something they believed existed but could not locate in actual Indians, and so they turned to nonwhite experts on Indian culture to help Indians with beadwork, archery, and tipis. In the ultimate irony, filmmakers concocted actors' lines consisting of gibberish that meant nothing but connoted generic difference. In the 1940s and 1950s filmmakers guessed that the American public would reject lengthy dialogue in real Native languages or English subtitles, although at least two focus group members asked for such features in their preview comments on *Chief Crazy Horse* (Universal, 1955): "The dialogue should have been in the Indian language with English captions" and "Why not put the dialogue in the individual Indian language[?]."[72] Instead, filmmakers created films they believed the American public would understand with ease, which meant story lines focused on whites and Indians who looked and acted like Indian characters already familiar to movie audiences.

For filmmakers of the 1940s and 1950s, Native American identity had more to do with physical objects than with people. Initially they thought authenticity would be found in Indian people but turned away from them in disappointment. Indian authenticity came to mean certain types of knowledge, activities, and objects. Yet even this meaning proved unsatisfactory, as it created the irony of whites teaching Indians about all things Indian. The blame for this conundrum landed at the doorstep of actual Indians, not whites, when in reality it was U.S. government policies aimed at assimilating American Indians by destroying their culture that created the conundrum, which Hollywood later reinforced. For twentieth-century American Indian culture, the governmental program of boarding school education for American Indian children hindered the transmission of American Indian culture in families more than any other federal policy. Boarding schools drew a firm and sharp line between parents and children, and this policy of separation was written and executed by the federal government. This policy can explain the lack of tribal knowledge in Indians who spoke only English or did not know how to produce objects specific to their tribe. Knowledge and skills relating to horses, tomahawks, and tipis were largely unnecessary for young men working in factory jobs or performing other manual labor. This is not to say that Indian cultures took their last breath in the twentieth century. Indians survived the nineteenth and twentieth centuries, and these are the people who worked in the movies.

Filmmakers seeking "authenticity" focused on locating Indians who exhibited traits Hollywood considered deeply and completely Indian. This search became problematic because Native Americans had changed, and the notion of authenticity, at least implicitly, suggested that somewhere there existed an Indian who had not changed. Most scholars label this thinking ahistorical. The term "traditional" captures a standard similar to authenticity, yet the term can acknowledge change. To say that certain Indians are traditional does not necessarily mean they do not watch television, enjoy baseball, or wear corrective lenses. Traditional can refer to someone who is deeply familiar with their tribal culture and also lives in the world today, as it is, and not in another time or place, as authenticity implies. Native people create space for this kind of identity, but filmmakers refused to create characters based in the kind of identity created by Indians for Indians.

Although authenticity, as the filmmakers used the term, was clearly not captured in their films, the entire concept need not be abandoned in a postmodern purge of all definitions and categories. Some people are Indians and some are not. How to distinguish between the two becomes difficult in many situations, and mid-twentieth-century filmmakers' attempts to answer that question tell us a great deal about what non-Indians attribute to those definitions. For Hollywood, the ideal Indian lived on a reservation, spoke the tribal language, and knew how to create culturally specific objects. Yet even this ideal could have potentially disappointed filmmakers who sought a different knowledge, such as tipis instead of hogans, or who found Native languages cumbersome and unnecessary. Expecting Indians to look and act certain ways took filmmakers straight into the quagmire of identity politics that Indians face today in contexts ranging from college campuses to tribal councils. Today Indians have to somehow determine authenticity among those seeking tribal, cultural, and social membership as a Native person, and sovereignty is what allows tribes to do so.

Filmmakers of the 1940s and 1950s had the option to abandon their notions of authentic Indians and embrace the perspectives of their Native employees, as they were, in all their complexity, with all their variety. This would have required new story lines and breaking out of genre, and perhaps these kinds of films would have been unintelligible to non-Native audiences. Many of those who previewed the films expressed a desire to see American Indians on the screen, but they equated American Indians with the past. Filmmakers captured their vision of America's past, steeped in conflict between whites and Indians, with little attention paid to contemporary Indian people. Although previewers never provided specific details, they seem to have desired positive images of Indians, a term still used today. But "positive" means different things to different people and remains tied to Indian stereotypes that prevent variety in representations of American Indians. Focusing on the creation of positive images also reinforces the plot device of conflict with whites rather than turning toward stories centered on particular tribes, conflict between tribes, or conflict within tribes.

Although the archival evidence shows that filmmakers compromised their goals of capturing the authentic, they at times erased the facts of this arrangement. They pretended they had acquired the real thing with their Native employees, and now these films are remembered for their artificiality and racism. However, the production of these films speaks to the larger phenomenon of the gap between Native people and the beliefs in circulation by non-Natives about Native people. The filmic imitations of Indian culture seem obvious, ill intentioned, and misguided, but the issues filmmakers faced in the mid-twentieth century remain. Filmmakers and other artists continue to struggle with how to represent Indians without turning them into caricatures.

Just as studios assiduously created stark markers between Natives and whites on the screen, they looked for those same rigid markers during production. When film crews were eating, relaxing, and dancing, Indians and whites created all sorts of understandings of one another, yet the studios exaggerated or fabricated any dissimilarity, big or small, that may have put their identities at odds. But they also tried to erase differences by highlighting their commonalities, such as family and friendship, which created a sense of compatibility and similarity. The creation and erasure of difference was a symbiotic relationship. The studios never failed to invoke difference without also denying it. In this way the studios mirrored their filmic narratives of difference, defeat, and submission on the set as they instructed Native people on how to act Native for the camera, castigated them for their appearance and language, and demanded tradition, yet also happily concocted artificiality, blaming it on convenience. For non-Indians, these forms of play tie back in with the anthropological endeavor to locate and possess Native culture. *Play* is a benign word, yet the demands for certain kinds of Native culture, the disdain for Native engagements with modernity, and the assertion that Natives lack culture and have to learn it from non-Indians all serve as the nonviolent complement to films that mock the genocide and violence enacted on Indian people by the nation-state's military and citizens.

Epilogue

Indigeneity is a category of analysis that is distinct from race, ethnicity, and nationality—even as it entails elements of all three of these. However, indigenous peoples' assertions of distinction and cultural difference are often heard as merely essentialist and therefore resembling static identities based on fixed inherent qualities. . . . [O]ne of the tenets of any claim to indigeneity is that indigenous sovereignty—framed as a responsibility more often than a right—is derived from original occupancy, or at least prior occupancy.

—J. Kēhaulani Kauanui, "'A Structure, Not an Event'"

Movies are entertainments, but they are also modes of social production. Like any productive process, movies involve human beings, material objects, and particular social contexts, as well as ideas or cultural tropes. This project, based as it is in historical method, goes beyond the content of films. Films are more than the sum of their plots and characters. The story of American Indians in film is not the text in itself, not the audience response in itself, but production in relation to all of these factors. The conditions of filmmaking constitute film as much as narrative, structure, and character, and this is particularly true when filmmakers, struggling for reality and verisimilitude, recruited Indians to play Indians throughout the 1940s and 1950s. The larger story of the United States, with settler colonialism and genocide at the center, serves as the backdrop for the stories told on the screen about Indians, and with that context, these movies misinterpret and mock the past. Today, Native artists work against past representations to bring something Native-centered to the fore. Pueblo film scholar Beverly R. Singer writes of her intention to "wipe the war paint off the lens" by writing about and creating films that represent "Indians differently." She admits to the tremendous endurance and effort required to bring the "dream to reality."[1]

Movies, especially those of the 1940s and 1950s, that include Indian characters gave the United States a distilled version of American racism toward Native people. In many ways the movies reduced Native people to sound bites, yet the films reflect a tremendous diversity not easily subjected to reductions, let alone simplistic analyses. Here, I speak of the films as a whole, but each deserves analysis in its own right. Additionally, film history has made immense contributions, but even many detailed works neglect the microeconomy of film production. I found few models useful for exploring the working conditions of actors, bits, and extras. I decided that production was critical to this project. That decision was partially due to what I found in studio archives, but it came from a recognition that film consumption satisfies to the degree that the production process is hidden. I therefore wanted to expose the production process at the detailed level of each film while drawing attention to the larger historical processes of settler colonialism to unsettle that easy consumption.

In turning to the production process, I looked beyond the American Indian male and white male actors who played Indian characters in movies. Instead, I have evaluated studio executives, actors, bits, extras, and even the reception of the films by the American public. I defined these categories inclusively to embrace Indians as well as non-Indians, men as well as women. The study could have focused strictly on representation, yet I aimed to look at the movies as a site of work as well as art: representation, narrative, labor, bodily constructions, social relationships, pay, and the intellectual impetus in these productions.

These films situate themselves in the settler colonial version of U.S. history in the most unthoughtful of ways. American society knows itself and understands its origins through history, whether through brutal conquest or heroic civilizing struggle. So-called progressive films such as *Broken Arrow* (Twentieth Century Fox, 1950) tell stories of brutal conquest, and they tell those stories from the perspective of a white male character. In the 1940s and 1950s casting history as a civilizing mission was commonplace, even when complemented by Indians being treated unfairly. The bar for deeming a film considerate of Indians stands too low.

The inequality and systemic racism of the films under study here go beyond the images projected on the screen. The very structure of filmmaking replicated racism toward American Indians, and that racism was manifested in profound differences in pay and job opportunities. In scanning production budgets and contracts, I learned of several Indian male actors who were paid as much as and sometimes more than white bit actors. Additionally, reservation Indians throughout the West were often employed in film productions. They were paid slightly less and sometimes more than Hollywood extras. Inequality played itself in a layered and multidirectional fashion. The archives containing details about the making of these films leave insubstantial and confounding tracks as far as American Indians are concerned, but they overwhelmingly document and substantiate the famous, who were always white. Yakama actor Daniel Simmons (Chief Yowlachie) lacks his own special collection, carefully controlled and monitored by archivists, unlike the Irish American director John Ford, whose collection is housed at the well-endowed Lilly Library at Indiana University. The powerful and even the not-so-powerful performers earned far more than Indian actors and obscenely more than Indian extras. The directors, writers, and producers of these films left behind remembrances of their lives in multiple and complicated contracts with studios and agencies that remain today's powerhouses. In contrast, the evidence of Indian extras in the studio archives is scattered and subtle. As far as film archives are concerned, such evidence can be found only in production budgets, often in anecdotes, and not always by name. When I arrived at studio archives to do research, I was always told there would be nothing in the boxes about Native people. There always was. Why did they not see what I saw?

Indians in movies, as actors, extras, and characters, demonstrate a central function of racism: its adherence to a belief in the fixed, tangible, physical aspects of race, all of which is a fiction taken very seriously by American society, including filmmakers. With Native people, this fiction is used not just to denigrate, not just to deny economic equality and opportunity, but also to destroy tribal sovereignty. The studios embraced their definition of an Indian, then generated hundreds of powerful images based on that definition. Those filmic images seem distorted and slightly ridiculous, at least in hindsight, and they seem to lack foresight or planning. Even though the images stemmed from someone's imagination, the creation of those images showed up on film sets and flexed their imaginative muscle in physical form. Their ideas became a reality in the boxes of wigs, containers of brown makeup, contact-lens cases, rubber noses, and stacks of buckskins. Native actors and extras, just as much as whites, stepped into this mythology and its physical repertoire. Virtually everyone on set came into the orbit of the story of white innocence, white strength, and white victory over Native people and all that story demanded. In places and moments where Indians and non-Indians worked together, each group made strategic decisions about how to negotiate the film narrative of difference and conflict while waiting to film. Native people collected their pay and left.

The non-Indian men who wrote, produced, directed, and distributed these racist movies actually gave thought to their product. They undertook these projects with intellectual effort and aim. They envisioned films that would be authentic. They wanted their movies to contain authentic Indians, landscapes, language, and artifacts. But most of all, they sought profit. In films like *Distant Drums* (Warner Bros., 1951), they thought they had achieved authenticity, but in other cases, such as *Broken Arrow* (Twentieth Century Fox, 1950), they knew they had compromised. The filmmakers' compromises, however, were inevitable because of their intellectual and cultural assumptions about Indians. Whether or not they used Indians in these productions, the filmmakers' social and cultural expectations had to be met. Indian characters had to look and sound different from white characters. The insistence on difference, which stemmed from the desire to create authentic and accurate images, is what resulted in ironic and ridiculous representations of Indians. Racist representations stemmed from the desire for authenticity and accuracy, both of which emerge from settler colonial mentalities.

Why are movies about Indians, and westerns in particular, so mythically loaded? What is it about Indians that so profoundly captures U.S. history and identity? This book has explored these questions by focusing on the idea that films including Indian characters provide a potent historical backdrop, in imagery and in the act of producing film, for the production of Indian and non-Indian identity. The historical backdrop of these films heightens their sense of grandeur and import. Although westerns present us with white men and women trapped in love triangles and settler colonial violence, they also delve into nothing less than the conquest of Native America. By denying American Indian survival both on screen and off, non-Natives explored their fascination with this conquest. Indian presence and survival serve as a critical political fact and a site for intervention in fields of representation, or as Michelle Raheja puts it in *Reservation Reelism*, "On the broader national stage, the erasure of Native Americans, represented as more or less conceding their homelands to European invader-settlers, conjoined with these filmic representations to create a national fantasy wherein European Americans could perform as autochthonous by stepping into territories and roles ceded to them through putative Native absence."[2] In other words, the mythology of Native erasure and absence allows non-Natives to claim the United States as their own, as though it has always been their own, in reality and in film. These filmic representations then support the ongoing theft and occupation of Native lands. Film analysis generates a responsibility to understand, unpack, and challenge these representations for their methods of displacing, erasing, and replacing Native people.

In the mid-twentieth century filmmakers and audiences alike displayed a fascination with the particular historical moment of the Indian wars of the nineteenth century. Wild West shows had fetishized this particular moment in American Indian history as well, but the nineteenth century found its most profound expression in the movies. For that nineteenth-century context, mid-twentieth-century films about Indians set up a limited spectrum of ways Indians were used: as resolutions for white love triangles, temporary friends, and comedic relief or as hopelessly incompatible with the twentieth century. Sadly, this movie lexicon has become foundational to the way non-Indians understand and continue to represent Indians.

Focusing on the materialization of ideology allows one to explore the boundaries between the real and the imagined. The terms "real," "authentic," and "imagined" are immediately perceived as problematic because they presuppose a sense of purity that does not exist. But the texts that tease out this rupture between the real and the imagined thrive on the terms "real" and "imagined." Although film plays with those boundaries, the boundaries remain and are repeatedly called upon as sources of artistic tension and attention. The films themselves pretend to represent a history that is undoubtedly accurate, objective, and factual. Their truth claims make it necessary to tease out the true from the false and to resort to that language.

Nonetheless, these terms provide a language for thinking through the ways Indians have been represented and how Native workers have been drawn into those representations. Reservation and urban Indians worked on these sets and stepped into this crazy circulation of images of Indians. We can watch these movies and spot Native people in the background, and this study has focused on the pre- and postproduction processes to do so. Native workers need not be posed in contradistinction to on-screen images of Indians. But actual Indians do exist on the screen, and their presence in the loop of filmmakers creating filmic images of Indians based on their preconceived images of Indians makes this process more complex, interesting, and meaningful.

The modern reproduction of art differs radically from that of previous eras in its link to the power of modern technology. Movie cameras allowed viewers to see a recorded representation of movement, a copy closer to reality than anything they had experienced before. This copy then influenced non-Indians' beliefs and perceptions about Native people. The vast majority of Americans, having no knowledge of or direct contact with American Indians, used movies to know and understand American Indians and American history. This poses a serious problem when non-Natives apply knowledge derived from movies to the Indians they encounter or to political issues. Even when Indians challenge each idea non-Indians hold about them, non-Indians can leave these interactions with their ideas unchanged.

When those non-Indians happen to be filmmakers, they use their ideas about Indians to create new representations of Indians that tell us nothing new and simply recycle the old. The only way out of this endless cycle in which whites create images of Indians based on their images of Indians is to decolonize and indigenize film by situating American Indians at the center of the creative process. By thinking through the ways Indians spoke and were heard or ignored, we can make the looping of images of Indians producing filmic images of Indians far more complex. One place to start is for Native people to become part of the production of film. If studios could have, they would have presented their films as authentic, transparent representations of the past with actual Indians in the background. But they were unable achieve their goal because actual Indians never lived up to their expectations. Studios aimed to avoid the produced and artificial nature of their creations. When they knew their images were not even an accurate copy of actual Indians, they blamed modern Indians, which ultimately reified the notion of the existence of untainted, premodern Indians.

Non-Natives have been told all sorts of stories to convince them that what they were seeing in these movies had something to do with Native America.[3] In the immediate postwar period the studios persistently told Americans that the production of their films involved Indians, not just in the background but as technical advisors and consultants. Although these aspects of production were acknowledged and distributed to the public, they were entirely controlled by non-Indians. Indian action was the source of these stories, but Indians had nothing to do with the choice of topic, story content, or narrative methods.

What Indian identity comes down to in the movies is a certain look. All movie characters were visually marked, and for Indian characters this was especially true. Their speech, their look, and their names all indicate Indian identity. Movies have pictured Indians for all of us: Indians have dark skin, dark hair, and dark eyes. Indians wear their hair in two long black braids.

Indians speak English, but they never sound like non-Indian characters. When going beyond looks, Indian identity, as defined by the midcentury movies, ventured into the area of culture. Indians were supposed to hold values in contradistinction to white society and the culture of consumerism, but Indians in the movies also engaged in mindless acts of violence meant to foster a belief in white innocence and fragility.

Today the American public continues to see Indians and non-Indians as distinct and materially different, as categories set in opposition to each other. More non-Natives today than ever hold great sympathy for Native people and want to stand against America's genocidal past, yet they seem to communicate their convictions through simplistic ideas about Indians. But what all Indians know to be true is that Indians are different from non-Indians for complicated reasons, the most important of which is their legal relationship to the United States as members of sovereign nations. This knowledge never showed up in movies of the 1940s and 1950s. From my vantage point, even positive images of Indians and images produced by Indians remain tethered to these foundational representations of Native Americans and have to be challenged at their very foundation to truly decolonize and indigenize the film industry.

Some blame the inaccuracies of these films on the inherent artifice of moviemaking. But the problem here stems not from filmic representation or even from the misrepresentation of tribes or particular historical moments. Instead, the problem with these representations is that of difference: How do filmmakers represent difference without rigidity? How can they represent Indian identity as being something important and meaningful without catering to the extremism that makes Indians so different that they cannot even recognize themselves? How do Indians wish to be represented?

Many Americans still assume only whites played American Indians in these films, and that if Indians watched such movies, they would neither enjoy nor endorse them. However, Indians did appear in these films. Moreover, although the issue is not addressed in this book, some Indians like the films, including the Indian characters from the 1940s and 1950s and even *The Searchers*, and some Indians use the same categories as non-Indians to explain why they like them.[4] But others, such as Billy Yellow (Navajo) or Louis Andrade (Luiseño), have little interest in the films. Cecil Meares (Muscogee), however, enjoyed watching the film in which he appeared because it brought back memories of his youth, not because he understood his Indian identity through the film. In fact, his resentment of the films' production team runs through his memories.

At midcentury white Americans retained their ability to go from white to Indian and back to white through makeup and wigs, perhaps borrowing from blackface. In maintaining the blackface impulse, the studios loved to darken the skin of famous white actors for film roles.[5] The tradition of creating Movie Indians through makeup, wigs, and contact lenses continued into the 1960s despite raging debates on equality and the dramatically different representations of African Americans.[6] And even when filmmakers hired Indians to play Indians, they marginalized American Indians through screen time and the lack of an Indian viewpoint.

Films about Indians have long been part of Hollywood, but the conditions of production changed in the 1940s and particularly in the 1950s. In the 1950s the U.S. film industry was fighting for its audience because it was being besieged by the success of television. Filmmakers had to distinguish their product from television, and one of their trademarks was Native workers in their movies. Unlike television, the film industry hired reservation Indians and shot their films on reservations, often in Monument Valley, the ultimate marker of authenticity in westerns. Movies could claim a sense of situatedness in Native space that was outside the reach of television developers and producers. Indians functioned as a powerful device for filmmakers who needed to entice and enrapture U.S. audiences.

Hollywood has served in the supporting role of settler colonialism in the United States. Just as settler colonialism seeks to eliminate and replace the Native, so too has Hollywood. In the 1940s and 1950s studios were hiring Indians to work in their movies when tribal sovereignty was being assaulted as never before and when poverty was striking at the heart of many Indian communities. In the case of the Diné and others, Indian employment in movies represented one element of an emerging new dependency on scarce wage labor, brought on by reservation economies steeped in exploitation by corporations. The possibility of Indians being simultaneously similar to and different from other Americans was left unexplored by studios at midcentury. Thus, in the movies of the midcentury, Indians had to be fundamentally different from non-Indians and separate from non-Indian society, or they had to be "not Indian," that is, assimilated and incorporated. Despite Hollywood's tremendous capital and liberal intentions, it created narratives that either presented Indians as different or, at best, ridiculed notions of difference.

Just as Hollywood held deep ambivalence about American Indians, so too did the federal government. The federal government set up the contradictory policy of designating tribal groups as "domestic dependent nations," reflecting an inability to see Native people as dual citizens. In the mid-twentieth century the U.S. government instituted policies of "termination and relocation," which would remove tribes' status as dependent nations and relocate Indians from reservations to urban locations. They applied this policy to those tribes considered prepared for such a transition—in other words, for those that did not seem different from non-Indians. All Indian tribes were divided into two categories: ready for termination (assimilated) or slotted for termination at a later date (unassimilated). The federal government's midcentury liberalism was rooted in the elimination of difference in hopes of achieving equality. For the federal government, erasing difference was a liberal and progressive plan. Government officials saw their policies as the recognition of Indian ability to transcend difference and embrace conformity. To be American at midcentury, for the federal government at least, meant the negation of all difference. In the movies and in the United States, Indians could not be seen by non-Indians as both different and similar.

Moreover, when it came to how non-Indians thought about Indians, they proved themselves tremendously resistant to change. Midcentury films demonstrate that, despite major political, economic, and social shifts in the twentieth century, non-Natives largely failed to change the way they portrayed Indians in movies. The shifts that took place among tribes have rarely been reflected in film. In the 1940s and 1950s films and film sets were haunted by the nineteenth century. While waiting to film, Indians and whites interacted in ways that were marked with love and hate, and most of the movies were marked by fear. On screen and off, Indians have come to embody all sorts of characteristics: warlike, noble, quiet, strong, dark skinned, dark haired, isolated. The non-Indian world, including nonwhites, remains blissfully unaware of what Indians know about themselves.

Indians know that Indian identity goes beyond the superficial features and stereotypes put out by popular culture. Indians know that Indian identity is bound to family, band, clan, tribe, culture, politics, kinship, tradition, place, and language. On the simplest level, to be an Indian is to be, first and foremost, a member of a tribe, not an ethnic group. To be a member of a tribe is to be at least a member of a family (but also a band or clan), to be with people who cultivate your identity over a lifetime in a multitude of ways.

The racism deployed against Native people in the twentieth century roots itself deeply in the representations from film. When twentieth-century Indians worked off the reservation, moved to Los Angeles, or entered the armed services, they encountered whites entirely unfamiliar with Indian identity as understood by Indians. They knew Indians primarily through movies and perhaps novels or cartoons. Indian men were referred to as "Chief," a term used sarcastically to feign respect and impart dignity. During the midcentury Indians would have encountered ridicule for long hair, accents, or any lack of familiarity with modern technology. The ridicule must have seemed endless on topics like alcoholism, reservation life, and tipis. Indians of the 1960s and 1970s fought back against these stereotypes and the poverty in urban and reservation communities. Indian nationalism received press coverage for dramatic moments such as when activists occupied Alcatraz Island, the Bureau of Indian Affairs, and the town of Wounded Knee and stood before Congress insisting on protections for Native children, introducing new understandings about treaty rights and American Indian survival to the general public. The era of Indian nationalism also showcased amazing Indian actors such as Will Sampson and Chief Dan George, along with Indians writers such as N. Scott Momaday and Leslie Marmon Silko and Indian visual artists Jerome Tiger, George Morrison, and R. C. Gorman. Although Indians had protested, acted, written, and created art prior to that period of growing

Indian nationalism, the national dimension of this late twentieth-century movement created a demand for Indian-controlled representations. But Indian nationalism, with its assertive demands for change, also forced the national culture to allow Indians into areas previously segregated as white-only spaces.[7]

Since 1960, Native people have pushed their way back into the film industry, on their own terms, especially in the documentary genre. Urban Indians who were not actors performed their own stories and created their own monologues in *The Exiles* (1961), telling the story of their relationships with their families, their reservations, and Los Angeles.[8] Anishinaabe literary scholar Gerald Vizenor put out a filmic version of his novel *Harold of Orange* in 1984, giving birth to a visual of his "postindians." Navajo filmmaker Arlene Bowman created *Navajo Talking Picture* (1985) about her own family, all controlled and determined by Bowman.[9] On a global level, when Māoris blocked access to their lands on Bastion Point in Aotearoa (New Zealand), they gave access to the Māori documentarian Merata Mita that others were denied. The result is the twenty-six-minute documentary *Bastion Point: Day 507* (1980).

Dances with Wolves (1990) simply proves the point of my book: it is entirely possible to make a terrible movie even when you employ Native people. Released shortly before the five-hundredth anniversary of Columbus invading America, *Dances with Wolves* was a low point in Native film, yet non-Indians saw it as the filmic highlight of the century. Without consulting Native people, they began slapping themselves on the back for having hired Native people, listened to the Lakota language in the film, and watched Kevin Costner's character befriending Lakotas. Just as they had with *Little Big Man* (1970) and other movies about whites with small roles for Natives, they told themselves they were excellent friends of Indian people and doing a marvelous job at portraying them in film. Two similar films from the early 1990s—*Last of the Mohicans* (1992) and *Thunderheart* (1992)—had the same problems as *Dances*. Then the height of American settler mythology emerged with Disney's *Pocahontas* (1995). These films were not well received by most Indigenous people even though Indigenous actors and extras appeared in these productions.[10] The media saturated the

United States with news and details about these films, and they remain key figures in discourse today about Native Americans in film.

Yet, Native people had taken back space in filmmaking before and after *Dances with Wolves*. Abenaki filmmaker Alanis Obomsawin made dozens of films in Canada, the most famous of which, *Kanehsatake: 270 Years of Resistance* (1993), had the most impact then and now. Like *Bastion Day*, *Kanehsatake* offers the viewer privileged access, through the lens of Obomsawin, to the story of Mohawks protecting their land at Oka in 1990. The images are unparalleled, and many faculty members continue to use this film in the classroom. Hopi filmmaker Victor Masayesva released *Imagining Indians* in 1992, which hilariously unpacked representations of Indians, including *Dances with Wolves*, with sustained focus on an interview with a Lakota extra who worked in the film, in addition to interviews with several other Native actors, some of whom are far less critical of Hollywood.

Today more than ever Indians hold cameras, microphones, pens, and paintbrushes, creating their own stories and images. Yet the problematic blockbusters continue, as do the celebrations and easy access to mediocre films. Clearly, just adding Indians to the film industry in no way guarantees financial success for films, praise by reviewers, distribution by significant companies, or access to the films for audiences. The results are deeply uneven; for example, *Pocahontas* employed Russell Means and Irene Bedard, both Native, yet the film perpetuates the same tropes of sexualized and tragic Native women. In that sense, placing Natives in parts already written by ignorant screenwriters fails to solve the problem.

The point here is that after 1960, both before and after *Dances with Wolves*, films with Natives in the cast had uneven outcomes. Some of the films garnered major media attention and profits while others straggled along with only Native applause and barely entered the cultural discourse. For instance, *Dance Me Outside* (1994) and *Once Were Warriors* (1994) seemed like major departures, and Native people appreciated these films, though they were more important in the Pacific region than in the United States. Then came Spokane/Coeur d'Alene novelist Sherman Alexie, who sold rights to his book *The Lone Ranger and Tonto Fistfight in Heaven* to make *Smoke Signals* (1998), with Cheyenne/Arapaho director Chris Eyre and Native actors such as Adam Beach, Evan Adams, Irene Bedard, Gary Farmer, and Tantoo Cardinal. For a moment this seemed like the antidote to *Dances with Wolves*. Literary scholars crowded around the topic. Joanna Hearne even named her book on Native cinema after the film *Smoke Signals*. The scholarly field deeply appreciated the Native cast, writer, and director, though some felt it was not a challenge to Hollywood whatsoever. Yet for some Native people, it felt like the first time they saw Native actors on the screen and heard Native humor, making it a film to applaud. Non-Native Hollywood congratulated itself for supporting the film and becoming more open to films with an Indian center. The films Hollywood produced in the wake of *Smoke Signals* did not fundamentally challenge the status quo, but they did feature Indian actors, Indian protagonists, and stories about Native people. Among them were *Windtalkers* (2002) and *Flags of Our Fathers* (2006), starring Saulteaux actor Adam Beach, who played the lead in both of those films, and the industry gave modest approval. After *Smoke Signals*, many proclaimed the ground had shifted as a result, but in fact Native people were part of performance and film from the very beginning. I have shown that Native people were present even in the 1940s and 1950s in the film industry. They were in movies and making movies before *Dances with Wolves* and *Smoke Signals*.

A film like *The Return of Navajo Boy* (2000), which began like *Dances with Wolves* with a focus on a white man and his needs, journey, predicaments, and search for answers, turned into a truly Indian movie. This was absolutely not the intention of Jeff Spitz, but as he turned the film over to Lorenzo Begay, he and his Navajo relatives transformed *Return* into a film about exploitation on their reservation by tourists, the film industry, missionaries, and mining. Elsie Cly became the unplanned star of the film, and the best film footage of Native people is Elsie reuniting with her brother John for the first time since white missionaries took him when he was two years old. Other films that have been overlooked in many cases by the media industry but loved by Native audiences are *Powwow Highway* (1989), *Whale Rider* (2002), *Skins* (2002), *Rabbit-Proof Fence* (2002), *Ten Canoes* (2006), and *Charlie's Country* (2013). Despite not receiving much media coverage, they received Native applause.

The success of *Smoke Signals* may have worsened the problem of the media paying no attention to low-budget films with high-quality Native acting or documentaries focused on Native people, which only makes it more difficult to hear about these films, find them, and view them. Netflix, Hulu, and Amazon Prime now sit as the powerhouses in the film and television industry but have taken no notice of nor made a financial commitment to buying the many solid Indian-written, directed, or produced films of the last several decades. Films with Indian directors, writers, or actors, such as *Amá* (2019), *Dawnland* (2018), *Mekko* (2015), *This May Be the Last Time* (2014), *Drunktown's Finest* (2014), *By Blood* (2013), *Frozen River* (2008), *Reel Injun* (2009), and *Atanarjuat* (2001), plus many others, need to be watched, discussed, and publicized, not only because Indians were involved in the production of these films but because they contribute something new and original to the medium of film and to the filmic representation of Indians. Of all of these twenty-first-century films, *Atanarjuat* stands outside the pack and represents a true insider film that is in every way for the people who made and acted in the film. Director Zacharias Kunuk of the village of Igloolik, the last village in Canada to accept television, directed the film and only cast Indigenous people from his village. The story is theirs, and the film is unparalleled. Yet you cannot stream it anywhere online; only the DVD is for sale. Very few of the films mentioned above can be seen online, a format that has almost entirely replaced the DVD mode of film viewing. Films that are not available for streaming today cannot be part of filmic discourse.[11]

The representations these films use to tell stories about Indians push the envelope in that often they are speaking of realities known and understood mostly by Native people. I watched approximately two hundred films made in the 1940s and 1950s and at least one hundred from the decades since, and the most recent films with Native actors, directors, writers, or producers give me tremendous hope for the future of Native film and reaffirm my dissatisfaction with and even despair over midcentury films.

Drunktown's Finest (2014), an excellent film starring Navajo trans actor Carmen Moore, is about a fictional effort to get a spot on the Navajo "Women of the Tribe" calendar. *100 Years* (2016) features the story of the embezzlement of Native America. The total sum of funds stolen from individual Natives never was exactly calculated due to its vastness, but it did result in the largest payout by the federal government in American history. *Dawnland* (2018) looks at the Wabenaki adults who were separated from their families by American social workers. The camera stays focused on their trauma as a truth and reconciliation committee seeks to document their experiences. *Amá (Mother)* (2019) places the camera in front of Jean Whitehorse, a Diné woman who was sterilized without her consent in an Indian Health Services hospital. Why do these films go largely unnoticed? Audra Simpson and others have argued that multiculturalism acts as an extension of settler colonialism by celebrating ethnicity and ethnic differences amid the ongoing territorial dispossession of Indigenous people. This is perhaps why movies that transform Indigeneity into ethnicity gain popularity and profit while those that feature Indigeneity and land claims languish and falter, except among Native people.[12]

On the other hand, easily available from many vendors for streaming are two troubling movies: *The Lone Ranger* (2013) and *Wind River* (2017). *The Lone Ranger* stars Johnny Depp as a Comanche, and the movie is predictable as a buddy movie full of light comedy. *Wind River*, distributed by convicted rapist Harvey Weinstein's company, tells the story of a non-Native FBI agent's emotional journey into the missing and murdered Indigenous women's crisis as she investigates an unsolved murder. We watch her learn of the crisis, a reality about which she possessed no prior knowledge. Her character progresses from ignorant and hardworking to flummoxed and distraught. We, as viewers, are meant to identify with this white female protagonist and leave the film feeling we have shown sympathy for the dead Native woman lying face down in the snow. The film describes "man camps" and jurisdictional issues perpetuating the crisis, and it features a horrifying gang rape scene through a flashback of the dead Native woman.[13]

Non-Indians may sometimes feel that Indians take movies too seriously. When Indians criticize another newly released film, the issue is not movies, which really are not terribly important. When Indians protest and complain, their issue is with the ways movies act as powerful agents, disseminating ideas throughout the country and the world. Indians have to live with those ideas, be reminded of those ideas, and confront the overwhelming amount of inaccurate information in the world about Native people, often on a daily basis. The constant attention given to the same recycled themes and stories suppresses new themes and stories, especially those that try to visualize Indigenous viewpoints. Art holds the power to transform the world through the way we see the world and each other. Native artists are doing this vital work in which they are not only talking back to the film industry but talking to each other.

NOTES

ABBREVIATIONS

CAL, USC	Cinematic Arts Library, University of Southern California
DI, NA	Department of the Interior, National Archives
FHG-HRL	Frances Howard Goldwyn–Hollywood Regional Library
LBML, AFI	Louis B. Mayer Library, American Film Institute
MHL, AMP	Margaret Herrick Library, Academy of Motion Picture Arts and Sciences
OHPA, SMU	Oral History Program Archive, Southern Methodist University
SC-YRL, UCLA	Special Collections, Charles E. Young Research Library, University of California, Los Angeles
URL, UCLA	University Research Library, University of California, Los Angeles

PREFACE

Epigraph: Quoted in Estes, "'There Are No Two Sides to This Story,'" 40.

1. James Scott's *Domination and the Arts of Resistance* informed my reading of our reception as a group of American Indian students looking for our Navajo friend who worked as an extra on the TV show. Scott sees the less powerful as creating "hidden transcripts" that read against and challenge the official transcripts put forth by the powerful.

1. Byrd, *Transit of Empire*, xi.
2. Jesse Wente, interviewed in the documentary *Reel Injun* (2009).
3. Oakes quoted in Blansett, *Journey to Freedom*, 221.
4. Vigil, *Indigenous Intellectuals*; McNenly, *Native Performers*.
5. White, *Roots of Dependency*; Beck, *(Un)Fair Labor?*
6. Raibmon, *Authentic Indians*, 4 (quote), 8, 11, 13.
7. Bauer, *We Were All Like Migrant Workers Here*; Child, *Holding Our World Together*, xxvi.
8. Child, *My Grandfather's Knocking Sticks*, 5.
9. Hosmer, *American Indians in the Marketplace*, xii, 5. See also R. White, *Roots of Dependency*, 320.
10. Purdy, "Tricksters of the Trade."
11. Berkhofer, *White Man's Indian*; Lonetree, *Decolonizing Museums*, 23–24.
12. Bold, *Selling the Wild West*.
13. Edward Curtis's images seem to be everywhere even now, with exhibits still being devoted to his work. You cannot experience a Native art exhibit without a curator throwing in some Curtis, an example being the exhibit at the Palm Springs Art Museum in summer 2019. See Gidley, *Edward S. Curtis*.
14. See Bokovoy, *San Diego World's Fairs*.
15. Jay, "'White Man's Book No Good.'"
16. A. Smith, *Shooting Cowboys and Indians*, 71–99.
17. Griffiths, *Wondrous Difference*, xix; Griffiths, *Shivers down Your Spine*; Griffiths, *Carceral Fantasies*. See also Edwards, *Anthropology and Photography*; Hutchinson, *Indian Craze*; and Parezo and Fowler, *Anthropology Goes to the Fair*.
18. Moses, *Wild West Shows*.
19. Yellow Robe, "Menace of the Wild West Show"; Moses, *Wild West Shows*.
20. Greenblatt, *Marvelous Possessions*; Pratt, *Imperial Eyes*, 3, 4, 7, 9.
21. Goeman, *Mark My Words*, 13; Warrior, *Tribal Secrets*; Vizenor, *Fugitive Poses*; Vizenor, *Manifest Manners*; Weaver, *Red Atlantic*; Womack, *Red on Red*; Byrd, *Transit of Empire*; Schweninger, *Listening to the Land*.
22. Shohat and Stam, *Multiculturalism, Postcoloniality and Transnational Media*, 17.
23. Byrd, *Transit of Empire*, xiii–xiv, xvii, xxiv.
24. For example, Seminoles worked in the 1951 film *Distant Drums*, but film scholar Denise K. Cummings analyzes the film with no mention and perhaps no awareness of their labor in the movie. Cummings, "*Distant Drums*"; Clifford, *Returns*, 5, 7, 42, 211, 315.
25. Graham and Penny, *Performing Indigeneity*.

26. See Meyer and Royer, *Selling the Indian*; and Carstarphen and Sanchez, *American Indians and the Mass Media*.

27. P. Deloria, *Playing Indian*; Huhndorf, *Going Native*, 5, 7, 10, 11, 15; Huhndorf, *Mapping the Americas*; P. Deloria, *Indians in Unexpected Places*; Rosenthal and Black, "Representing Native Peoples." This explosion in the literature on representation and appropriation may have been a reaction to the immense reach of the film *Dances with Wolves* (1990), which ultimately grossed an astonishing $424 million. In fact, random conversations with nonacademics about my book always center on *Dances*.

28. P. Deloria, *Becoming Mary Sully*, 12.

29. Rader, "*Broken Arrow*," 78.

30. Lewis, *Alanis Obomsawin*, 123, 191; Lewis, "*Navajo Talking Picture*."

31. Rosenthal, "Painting Native America in Public," 47.

32. Tahmahkera, *Tribal Television*, xvi, 7, 24, 53, 166.

33. Tahmahkera, "Hakaru Maruumatu Kwitaka?," 100, 101, 103.

34. See Limbrick, *Making Settler Cinemas*. See also Lippard, *Partial Recall*, on photography.

35. Shohat and Stam, *Unthinking Eurocentrism*; Hokowhitu and Devadas, *Fourth Eye*; Limbrick, *Making Settler Cinemas*.

36. Columpar, *Unsettling Sights*, xv.

37. Hilger, *From Savage to Nobleman*; Hilger, *Native Americans in the Movies*. The second book appears to be almost identical to the first except for material added to the filmographies.

38. Bird, *Dressing in Feathers*.

39. Rollins, *Hollywood's Indian*, 2, 3, 7.

40. Jojola, "Absurd Reality II," 12.

41. Fienup-Riordan, *Freeze Frame*, xi.

42. Bataille, *Native American Representations*; Bataille and Silet, "Entertaining Anachronism"; Bataille and Silet, *Images of American Indians on Film*; Bataille and Silet, *Pretend Indians*. See also Friar and Friar, *Only Good Indian*.

43. Prats, *Invisible Natives*.

44. Ginsburg, "Indigenous Media," 96, 102.

45. Ginsburg, "Screen Memories and Entangled Technologies," 82.

46. Cummings, *Visualities*, xiii.

47. The Leuthold works are "Native American Responses to the Western" and *Indigenous Aesthetics*.

48. Rader, *Engaged Resistance*, 1. Rader invokes the work of LeAnne Howe, who relies on many disciplines and genres, as well as personal and tribal identities, to understand Indigenous literature and art. See Howe, "Tribalography."

49. Howe, Markowitz, and Cummings, *Seeing Red*, xvii, 64, 115.

50. Buffalohead and Marubbio, *Native Americans on Film*, 6–7.

51. Marubbio, *Killing the Indian Maiden*.

52. Hallett, *Go West, Young Women!*

53. Rickard, "Sovereignty," 51.

54. Dowell, *Sovereign Screens*, 1, 2, 3, 4, 19.

55. Schweninger, *Imagic Moments*, 1–11.

56. Kilpatrick, *Celluloid Indians*; Raheja, *Reservation Reelism*; Raheja, "Visual Sovereignty," 29, 31.

57. Hearne, *Native Recognition*, 256. Hearne later devoted an entire book to the film *Smoke Signals* and its screenwriter, Sherman Alexie. See Hearne, *"Smoke Signals."* See also Alexander C. Kafka, "'Sokal Squared': Is Huge Publishing Hoax 'Hilarious and Delightful' or an Ugly Example of Dishonesty and Bad Faith?," *Chronicle of Higher Education*, October 3, 2018, https://www.chronicle.com/article/Sokal-Squared-Is-Huge/244714.

58. Frankel, *"The Searchers."* Citing a dissertation from the 1980s to claim that Native people identify with the white heroes of the film, he ignores altogether the literature in Native film studies in his lengthy, successful, and detailed treatment of just one film. I cannot decide which I despise more: Ford's film *The Searchers* or Frankel's book *"The Searchers."*

59. Gubar, *Racechanges*; Lott, *Love and Theft*; Roberts, *Blackface Nation*; Sammond, *Birth of an Industry*; Brundage, *Beyond Blackface*.

60. Caddoo, "Envisioned Communities"; Caddoo, *Envisioning Freedom*; Erigha, *Hollywood Jim Crow*. Neither of the two books cited here addresses Native Americans in film.

61. Berg, *Classical Mexican Cinema*; Berg, *Latino Images in Film*; Noriega, *Chicanos and Film: Representation*; Noriega, *Shot in America*; Noriega, *Visible Nations*; Noriega, *Chicanos and Film: Essays*; Valdivia, *Latina/os and the Media*; Valdivia, *Latina in the Land of Hollywood*; Molina-Guzmán, *Dangerous Curves*; Castañeda, *Soap Operas and Telenovelas in the Digital Age*; Nericcio, *Tex{t}-Mex*.

62. Hamamoto and Liu, *Countervisions*; Feng, *Screening Asian Americans*; Ono and Pham, *Asian Americans and the Media*.

1. "JUST LIKE A SNAKE"

1. Hearne, *Native Recognition*, 258.

2. In the official records for the film, the spelling is Sacajawea rather than Sacagawea, which is now the preferred version.

3. Jafri, "Desire, Settler Colonialism, and the Racialized Cowboy."

4. L. Young, *Fear of the Dark*.

5. Brands, *Devil We Knew*; Chafe and Sitkoff, *History of Our Time*; Polenberg, *War and Society*; Maddox, *United States and World War II*; Adams, *Best War Ever*; Engelhardt, *End of Victory Culture*.

6. Horne, *Fire This Time*, 16, 133.

7. Rogin, *Blackface, White Noise*, 252–53.

8. Cripps, *Slow Fade to Black*, 349, 387, 388, 389.

9. Neale, "Vanishing Americans"; Hearne, "'Ache for Home.'"

10. V. Deloria, "Distinctive Status of Indian Rights."

11. Fixico, *Termination and Relocation*; Olson and Wilson, *Native Americans in the Twentieth Century*; Murray, *Modern Indians*; Holm, "Fighting a White Man's War"; Wilson, *Underground Reservation*, chaps. 8 and 9; Foster, *Being Comanche*, chap. 5; Prucha, *American Indian Treaties*, chap. 15; Fowler, *Arapahoe Politics*, chap. 4; Parman, *Indians and the American West in the Twentieth Century*.

12. Vine Deloria categorizes termination as "a weapon against Indian people." V. Deloria, *Custer Died for Your Sins*, 76.

13. Susman, *Culture as History*, esp. 271–85.

14. Bernstein, *American Indians and World War II*, 86.

15. Rosenthal, *Reimagining Indian Country*, 78. Population figures for urban Indians in the war and postwar periods are problematic. They cannot take into account the movement to and from reservations or other areas where family members lived. They are also inaccurate because of inconsistent definitions of Native American identity, and thus many people who are Native are being counted as non-Native. See Weibel-Orlando, *Indian Country, L.A.*, 1, 13.

16. For a much lengthier filmography of the early silent period, see Hilger, *American Indian in Film*.

17. Bataille and Silet, "Entertaining Anachronism," 37. Miles Orvell calls this movement "a significant reverse current of nostalgia, carrying the individual backward to a simpler time." Orvell, *Real Thing*, 69. Marshall Berman defines modern as antimodern. Berman, *All That Is Solid Melts into Air*, 13–14.

18. Lee Clark Mitchell sees the white hero's function as a blank screen on which audiences could project any desire. Mitchell, *Westerns*, 53–54. Westerns could easily be one of the antimodernist veins T. J. Jackson Lears traces in *No Place of Grace*.

19. Warren Susman connects historical contradictions with the power of instinct: what Americans had repressed surfaced in the 1950s. See Susman, "Did Success Spoil the United States?," 30–31, 33.

20. Leah Dilworth draws attention to desire, fear, and subjectivity. See Dilworth, *Imagining Indians in the Southwest*, 100.

21. See P. Smith, *Everything You Know*, 43–53. Smith also argues that Indian presence in films is largely irrelevant because "they aren't made for an Indian audience, and they were not written by Indians" (38; see also 37–42).

22. Yoggy, "Prime-Time Bonanza!," 160, 165; Lenihan, "Westbound." However, John Lenihan refers in his study to an interview with Delmer Daves in which the film-maker explains that he had not set out to have American Indians represent America's political problems. Lenihan, *Showdown*, 43.

23. Nachbar, "Horses, Harmony, Hope, and Hormones," 27.

24. On Indians as metaphor, see Fienup-Riordan, *Freeze Frame*, 15, 118, 119, 120; P. Smith, *Everything You Know*, 43–53; and Coyne, *Crowded Prairie*, 4–5. Jon Tuska's *American West in Film* excoriates several celebrated directors because their westerns marginalized Indian characters and issues.

25. Lenihan, "Classics and Social Commentary," 40. Later in the article, however, Lenihan contradicts himself by suggesting that some of these films pointed to the drawbacks of civilization and symptomatic racism.

26. Cheney, "Reel Indians."

27. Hearne, *Native Recognition*, 202.

28. Whitfield, *Culture of the Cold War*, 12.

29. L. May, *Recasting America*, 1.

30. Mitchell, *Westerns*; Cawelti, *Six-Gun Mystique*; Etulain, *Western Film*; Brownlow, *War, the West, and the Wilderness*; Slotkin, *Gunfighter Nation*; Tompkins, *West of Everything*; Tuska, *American West in Film*; French, *Cowboy Metaphysics*; R. M. Davis, *Playing Cowboys*; W. Wright, *Six Guns and Society*. Some of these studies offer fairly straightforward analyses, while others allow for complex narratives, arguments, and analyses, such as Richard Slotkin's *Gunfighter Nation* and Will Wright's *Six Guns and Society*. See also Fenin and Everson, *The Western*; and Lenihan, *Showdown*.

31. Many scholars agree that texts about Indians often say more about non-Indians than Indians. For example, see Carr, *Inventing the American Primitive*, 16, 252–53.

32. On the set of *Winchester '73* (Universal, 1950), Jimmy Stewart bet Rock Hudson $25 that he could not convince anyone he was an Indian. In Tucson, Hudson got some trinkets, sat cross-legged on a railroad platform, sold $3 worth of trinkets, and won the bet. See Press Releases, *Winchester '73*, File 11952, Box 424, Universal-International Collection, CAL, USC.

33. *Broken Arrow* is only loosely based on historical events, although it claims to represent the truth. On *The Searchers*, see the work by the Cherokee/Choctaw writer Louis Owens, *Mixedblood Messages*, 106.

34. P. Deloria, *Playing Indian*; P. Deloria, *Indians in Unexpected Places*; A. Smith, *Shooting Cowboys and Indians*; Marubbio, *Killing the Indian Maiden*; Hearne, *Native Recognition*; Hearne, "Smoke Signals."

35. On gendered stereotypes of Indian men and women, see Bird, "Gendered Construction of the American Indian in Popular Media"; and Green, "Pocahontas Perplex."

36. Richard Widmark does much the same in *The Last Wagon* (Twentieth Century Fox, 1956). Both Cochise and Geronimo fought against the U.S. Army. Cochise died after he came to a truce, and Geronimo died at Fort Sill, Oklahoma, as a captive in 1909.

37. Sollors, *Beyond Ethnicity*, 102–3. David Murray claims that Indian leaders were described as monsters to bolster the heroism of military leaders. See Murray, *Forked Tongues*, 69.

38. Jeffords, *Remasculinization of America*, xv, 178; Lenihan, "Classics and Social Commentary," 37, 38.

39. E. May, "Explosive Issues"; E. May, *Homeward Bound*. William Chafe emphasizes the family as backdrop to male wartime bravado in his *Unfinished Journey*, 134.

40. Fred Pfeil argues that male rampage films are steeped in misogyny. See Pfeil, *White Guys*, chap. 1. See also Chauncey, *Gay New York*; and Cohan, *Masked Men*.

41. Bordo, *Twilight Zones*, 168; Scheckel, *Insistence of the Indian*, 151.

42. Murray, *Forked Tongues*, 42.

43. In the production stills, Chris and Johnny stand amid Indians, suddenly united as a couple in the face of their capture. Stills, *Valley of the Sun* Production Files, Core Collection, MHL, AMP.

44. Some of the men were blood brothers, a concept with European origins. See Tuska, *American West in Film*, 243.

45. Buddy Adler asked screenwriter Nunnally Johnson to redo the opening scene of *Flaming Star* to indicate a lack of what he called color lines within the lead's family. I believe he meant that even though the mother was Kiowa and the father was white, Adler wanted Johnson to not write anything into the script for the opening scene that would indicate the mother was Kiowa or even Native. See Buddy Adler to Nunnally Johnson, Memorandum, April 25, 1958, 1–2, *Flaming Star*, Twentieth Century Fox Collection, CAL, USC.

46. On World War II films in general, see Doherty, *Projections of War*.

47. Erenberg and Hirsch, *War in American Culture*, 4.

48. L. May, *Big Tomorrow*.

49. Aleiss, *From Adversaries to Allies*, 110–11.

50. Robert Stam highlights the illogic of race in his "Bakhtin, Polyphony, and Ethnic/Racial Representation," 251.

51. Chief Thundercloud was most likely Mexican American in spite of being accepted by Hollywood studios as an American Indian.

52. Jenkins, *What Made Pistachio Nuts*.

53. The Universal Studios description of Rainwater was as follows: "An Indian who spouts Oxford English and wears Bond Street clothes; who after a brief whirl at movie acting, has returned to his tribe to commercialize every tradition known to the redskins and who makes suckers out of any and all tourists who cross his path." John Joseph, "Production Data from Universal Studios," December 15, 1941, Directory of Advertising and Publicity, *Ride 'Em Cowboy* Production Files, Core Collection, MHL, AMP. Rainwater was played by Douglass Dumbrille, a non-Indian Canadian actor. See Douglass Dumbrille Biography Files, Core Collection, MHL, AMP, which contain no mention of any Native ancestry.

54. The name of the depot may have referred to the actual Gower Gulch, the drugstore hangout for movie cowboys at the corner of Sunset and Gower in Hollywood. See Carey, *Hollywood Posse*, 139–40.

55. In the original script it is very clear that Rainwater and the other Indians selling their wares at the depot only play Indian when the tourists arrive. See "Revised Screenplay," June 9, 1941, *Ride 'Em Cowboy*, File 2140, Box 9, Universal-International Collection, CAL, USC.

56. In the first draft, Willoughby shoots Rainwater when he discovers that his arrows were made in Cleveland. See "Revised Screenplay," June 9, 1941, *Ride 'Em Cowboy*.

57. This scene was extremely brief in the June 9, 1941, screenplay draft and was later expanded in the June 27, 1941, draft. See *Ride 'Em Cowboy*, Files 2139 and 2138, Box 9, Universal-International Collection, CAL, USC.

58. Winokur, *American Laughter*.

59. After days of wigging and dewigging hundreds of men playing Indians on the set of *They Died with Their Boots On* (1941), hairstylist Jean Burt Reilly experienced the same nightmares: "I dreamed of Indians that night, Indians were on top of my bed, they were under my bed, they were scalping me, they were doing war dances around the room." "Jean Burt Reilly, Motion Picture Hair Stylist," interview by Elizabeth I. Dixon, 1962, oral history transcript, 30, Center for Oral History Research, Special Collections, URL, UCLA.

60. In the June 9 draft, Willoughby was going to dress as an Indian and ride out of the rodeo with Moonbeam on his horse with him. In the June 27 draft the script story line made Duke pretend to be Moonbeam. See *Ride 'Em Cowboy*, Files 2140 and 2139, Box 9, Universal-International Collection, CAL, USC.

61. One scholar summarizes the Abbott and Costello comedy *Lost in Alaska* (1952) as simply being a white man's projection of Native Alaskans and also claims that popular culture on the whole has failed to find the humor in American Indian stereotypes. See Fienup-Riordan, *Freeze Frame*, 132, 115, respectively.

62. An identical accident takes place in *Tulsa* (1949).

63. Paul Chaat Smith recommends moving outside prescribed genres. See the chapters "Land of a Thousand Dances" and "The Big Movie" in P. Smith, *Everything You Know*.

64. Vine Deloria writes, "No one could see the connection between the Indians they were reading about and the Indians who lived down the road a piece." V. Deloria, "The Twentieth Century," quoted in Tyler, "Red Men and Hat-Wearers," 157.

65. See, for example, Bannon, *Spanish Borderlands Frontier*, 135–36, 140. See also N. Davis, *Slaves on Screen*; H. White, *Content of the Form*; and Rosenstone, *Visions of the Past*.

66. P. Smith, *Everything You Know*, 99.

2. "INDIANS AGREE TO PERFORM"

1. See P. Deloria, *Playing Indian*; and R. M. Davis, *Playing Cowboys*.

2. Susan G. Davis encountered the same lack of attention in studies of theme parks. See S. Davis, *Spectacular Nature*, 3. Steven J. Ross, in *Working-Class Hollywood*, his thorough study of class and silent film, considers the relationships between those who wanted to censor images of the working class in film and those producing the images. While he steers clear of the specifics of hours and pay, he ably demonstrates the interconnectedness of class, representation, politics, and silent films.

3. Hansen, *Babel and Babylon*, 85. See also Perry and Perry, *History of the Los Angeles Labor Movement*, 318–61. On labor in the film industry, see L. May, "Movie Star Politics"; Prindle, *Politics of Glamour*; Nielsen and Mailes, *Hollywood's Other Blacklist*; and Clark, *Negotiating Hollywood*. On labor conditions in the film industry at the end of the twentieth century, see Gray and Seeber, *Under the Stars*.

4. Not only is this idea unpleasant to some in the present, it was also unpleasant to some Americans in the 1950s. The *Arizona Daily Star* featured a photo of Jimmy Stewart and Shelley Winters with Indian extras. The caption explained that the Indian extras were being "used" in the film. The newspaper received many letters complaining about the word "used." Universal made a statement that it was a word commonly used in the "business" and that the Indians were in fact being paid $10 a day. See Press Releases, *Winchester '73*, File 11952, Box 424, Universal-International Collection, CAL, USC. Most scholars assume that only non-Indians played Indians. For example, "Another glaring Hollywood practice that undermines the credibility of many films is the prevalence of non-Indians in Indian roles . . . the appearance of white actors in Indian roles undermines these films' credibility. Casting whites as Indians limits the ability of Native Americans to benefit economically." Leuthold, "Native American Responses to the Western," 160.

5. Jack Padjan, a cowboy actor, told a story about Blackfeet who were not acting when they attacked whites for a film scene: "Well, by God . . . come time to shoot the battle scene them Injuns all piled on their paint horses. . . . They was breathin'

smoke. When the director called 'action' you never seen so much goddammed action all at once in your life. Them bucks hit the warpath for real, all liquored up and painted and fightin' mad as a young cow on the prod. We men of Custer's command was supposed to stand them off for quite a while according to the script, but the Indians was bent on wipin' us all out fast. Their arrows was the real McCoy and they was firin' 'em at us so thick it looked as if somebody had turned the wind machine into a mile-high stack of cut willows." Quoted in Cary, *Hollywood Posse*, 190–92.

6. One scholar claims that Jay Silverheels was the only Indian in *Broken Arrow*. See Lupis, "Person of the American Indian," 92. Mistakes such as these are common.

7. Unlike Indians, a few black actors did reach the highest levels of earning power in the 1940s and 1950s. See Cripps, *Making Movies Black*, 48.

8. On Indians and Wild West shows, see Moses, *Wild West Shows*; and P. Smith, *Everything You Know*, 46. See also McBride, *Molly Spotted Elk*, 64–71; Thiel, "Omaha Dance"; and Collings and England, *101 Ranch*. The 101 Ranch papers are held in the University of Oklahoma's Western History Collection.

9. Brookings Institution, Institute for Government Research, *Problem of Indian Administration*, 722–23. According to Diana Serra Cary, Artie Ortega and his wife, Mona Darkfeather, were Indian actors in the early silent period. By the 1930s they were working as riding extras. On the set of *Man of Conquest* (1939), Ortega claimed that they were asked to use sign language in the film, and they asked for a wage adjustment to reflect their new speaking parts. When the studio denied their request, they went to the Screen Actors Guild (SAG), which gave them a favorable ruling. According to Ortega, as a result of the ruling they tried "pushin'" for sixteen-fifty a day, if we wear our own native costumes," which they were getting from Cecil B. DeMille on the *Union Pacific* set. See Cary, *Hollywood Posse*, 209.

10. Billy Wilkerson, the Cherokee president of the group, later went on to become the editor of the *Hollywood Reporter*. See *Screenland's First Americans* (Los Angeles: Pioneer Press, 1935), held in Special Collections, FHG-HRL.

11. Ann Little, interview by Robert S. Birchard in "The Western in the 1920s," looseleaf compilation, 1975, 224, 227, 230, in Special Collections, LBML, AFI. See also Brownlow, *War, the West, and the Wilderness*, 253–62.

12. McBride, *Molly Spotted Elk*.

13. Ware, *Cherokee Kid*, 102.

14. Major players in the drama of organized labor in Los Angeles claimed that this was a dilemma manufactured to defeat the strongest union: the Conference of Studio Unions. See "You Don't Choose Your Friends: The Memoirs of Herbert Knott Sorrell," interview by Elizabeth I. Dixon, 1963, Center for Oral History Research, Special Collections, URL, UCLA. See also Dunne, *Hollywood Labor*

Dispute, appendix; Jack Dales, "Pragmatic Leadership: Ronald Reagan as President of the Screen Actors Guild," interview by Mitch Tuchman, 1981, Center for Oral History Research, Special Collections, URL, UCLA; and Hollywood Studio Strike Collection, Special Collections, URL, UCLA.

15. See Perry and Perry, *History of the Los Angeles Labor Movement*, 35, 319, 320.

16. According to the 1968 labor agreement, day players (those "employed by the day, other than an extra, stunt man, professional singer, or airplane pilot") were to be paid $100 a day in 1968, $112 a day from April 1968 to June 1968, and $120 a day from July 1969 on. Any time spent waiting or in the makeup chair was to be time and a half. Freelance players (those "employed for a specific picture in a designated role on a weekly basis") worked at a minimum salary of $350 per week or more up to March 31, 1968, then $392 or more from April 1, 1968, to June 30, 1969, and $420 a week from July 30, 1969 on. They were to receive time and a half on Saturdays and regular time for chair time. There were also provisions for freelance players who earned more than $1,500 per week but less than $25,000 guaranteed for the picture, multiple picture players who received less than $1,500 per week and were guaranteed less than $25,000 for the film, and contract players whose weekly guaranteed salary was $1,500 or less but were not beginners, and beginners. See *Producer–Screen Actors Guild Basic Agreement of 1967* (Los Angeles: Parker & Son, 1968), 35, 49, 102, 103, accessed in Reference Annex, MHL, AMP.

According to the 1971 supplement to that agreement, actors and stunt performers were to be paid $138 minimum per day. By the week, actors were to be paid $483, and stunt performers were to be paid $518 a week. Contract players were to be paid $414 a week in ten nineteen-week contracts. For contracts of twenty weeks or more, they were to be paid $345 a week. Beginner contract players were to earn $186 a week for their first six months and $207 a week for their second six months. See *1971 Supplement to Producers–Screen Actors Guild Codified Basic Agreement of 1967* (Los Angeles: Parker & Son, 1972), 37, in Reference Annex, MHL, AMP.

17. *Producer–Screen Actors Guild Revised Basic Agreement of 1947* (no publishing information), in Folder 8, Box 10, Mary Pickford Collection, MHL, AMP.

18. *Producer–Screen Actors Guild Revised Basic Agreement of 1947*, 3, 4, 7, 8, 9, 10.

19. Almost none of the Indian actors kept their birth names and opted instead for names that sounded Indian to non-Indians. In terms of pay, Yowlachie, for instance, received $750 a week for *Winchester '73* (Universal, 1950), and John War Eagle earned $55 a day as an Indian interpreter. See "Day Player Agreements," *Winchester '73*, March 14, 1950, File 7501, Box 213, Universal-International Collection, CAL, USC.

20. For the film *Seven Cities of Gold* (Twentieth Century Fox, 1955) much the same applies. There is a large list titled "Mexican Cast" with approximately thirty names that appear almost daily on the production reports. These actors may or may not

have played Indians, because on other days gross numbers are listed for extras playing Indians. Jeffrey Hunter played a supporting role as Matuwir and was paid $750 a week. Rita Moreno played the supporting role of Ula and earned $300 per week. For his role as Captain Portola, Anthony Quinn earned "$50,000 for 8 wks., plus 2 free wks." "Cash Sheet," Production Files, *Seven Cities of Gold*, File A-750, Box FX-PF-6, Collection 051, Twentieth Century Fox Film Corp., SC-YRL, UCLA.

I found scant records of discussions between agents and studios about leading roles. This makes it difficult but not impossible to draw conclusions about casting. In *The Last Wagon* (Twentieth Century Fox, 1956), Abel Fernandez was hired to play an Indian at "$300/wk.—1 wk. guar."; Susan Kohner was paid $1,000 a week for her role as Jolie. See Production Files, *The Last Wagon*, Box FX-PF-2, Collection 051, Twentieth Century Fox Film Corp., SC-YRL, UCLA; "Cash Sheet," *The Last Wagon*; and "Screen Actors Guild, Inc. Minimum Free Lance Contract," *The Last Wagon*, April 12, 1956, both in Box FX-LR-1370, Collection 095, Twentieth Century Fox Film Corp., SC-YRL, UCLA. Richard Widmark was paid "$200,000 for 10 wks" to play the hero. Fox hired extras to play Indians, but there is no information given as to their names, their pay, or how they were obtained. There is only one daily production report in which an Abel Fernandez is singled out for his workload for unknown reasons. See "Sequence Shot Index," 21, 33, 34, 43, 44, 45, 46; and "Daily Production Report[s]," for May 2, 22, 23, 1956, all in Production Files, *The Last Wagon*, Box FX-PF-2, Collection 051, Twentieth Century Fox Film Corp., SC-YRL, UCLA.

21. No women fall into this category. Only Beulah Archuletta and Belle Mitchell (*Unconquered, Tumbleweed*) appear to have acted on more than one occasion. I have found little information on either of these women.

22. Two Indian actors offered their services but were turned down as production on *They Died* had already begun. See Bud Leith, c/o U.S. Department of the Interior, Chiloquin, Oregon, to Jack Warner, October 6, 1941; and Monte Blue to Jack L. Warner, July 22, 1941, both in Box 2303 (T-81), Warner Bros. Collection, CAL, USC. Monte Blue was not enrolled as an Oklahoma Cherokee, and neither were his parents. Monte Blue is not listed on the Dawes Roll or the Final Rolls of the Five Civilized Tribes, nor were his parents. Blue's mother's name was Lousetta Springer Blue, born in April 1854. His father was William Jackson Blue, a Civil War veteran. Blue was born on January 11, 1887, in Indianapolis, Indiana, and died on February 18, 1963. He is buried at the Forest Lawn Cemetery in Glendale, California. Monte Blue's first job was in *Birth of a Nation*, followed by *Intolerance* and several years later, *The Squaw Man*. He went on to work in many films from the 1910s through the 1940s.

23. Cal Smith (Mohawk), telephone interview by author, September 2018. Cal Smith is the great-grandson of Jay Silverheels. Silverheels was born on May 26, 1916, on

the Six Nations reservation in Ontario, Canada. His birth name was Harold J. Smith. His father was Alexander George Edwin Smith, and his mother was Mabel Doxtater (Smith). His father was a major in the Canadian army during World War I. Silverheels went to Brantford Collegiate Institute. However, he became a professional lacrosse player and later entered wrestling and boxing. He went to California to join a lacrosse team, which dissolved. He then began acting and became part of the Pasadena Playhouse troupe.

24. Moore with Thompson, *I Was That Masked Man*, 144, 145.

25. Press Releases, *Drums across the River*, File 21403, Box 663, Universal-International Collection, CAL, USC.

26. Press Releases, *Drums across the River*, File 21403, Box 663, Universal-International Collection, CAL, USC.

27. Press Releases, *Column South*, File 13130, Box 447, Universal-International Collection, CAL, USC.

28. Press Release, *Stand at Apache River*, File 13120, Box 447; Production Notes, *Stand at Apache River*, File 3732, Box 468, both in Universal-International Collection, CAL, USC.

29. *TV & Movie Western*, March 1960; Virginia Wright, *Los Angeles Daily News*, August 18, 1947. See also Biography Files, MHL, AMP.

30. *Variety*, July 12, 1967, in Biography Files, MHL, AMP.

31. "Obituary," *Hollywood Reporter*, June 7, 1960; Howard McClay, "Shooting Star," *Los Angeles Daily News*, March 20, 1952; Biography Files, MHL, AMP. He appeared as Young Bird in *Buffalo Bill Rides Again* (Screen Guild, 1947) and as Crazy Dog in *A Ticket to Tomahawk* (Twentieth Century Fox, 1950).

32. He also appeared as Chief Lone Tree in *Laramie Mountains* (Columbia, 1952), Red Bird in *Saginaw Trail* (Columbia, 1953), Red Cloud in *The Great Sioux Uprising* (Universal, 1953), Geronimo in *The Last Outpost* (Paramount, 1951), Black Cloud in *Last of the Comanches* (Columbia, 1953), War Cloud in *The Black Dakotas* (Columbia, 1954), Quanah Parker in *They Rode West* (Columbia, 1954), Sitting Bull in *Tonka* (Buena Vista, 1958), and unnamed parts in *Westward Ho the Wagons* (Buena Vista, 1957) and *The Wild North* (MGM, 1952).

33. Hogan was born in Wanette, Oklahoma. After leaving Roosevelt High School in St. Louis, Missouri, he went to Los Angeles with a football scholarship; he was earmarked for USC but was sent to Pasadena Junior College. He married Jacquelyn Gibson, an interpretive dancer. He was adept in Indian sign language, which he learned from his father. On Hogan, see "Press Release," *Pillars of the Sky*, File 12524, Box 423, Universal-International Collection, CAL, USC.

34. John Lachuk, "Rodd Redwing," *TV & Movie Western*, June 1959, 30; Mary Blume, "Redwing Bites Dust Again, Again, Again," *Los Angeles Times*, May 25, 1968; Hank

Grant, "Coast to Coast," *Hollywood Reporter*, May 21, 1968; "Warner Bros. Press Release," Biography Files, MHL, AMP.

35. One useful source is Cody himself; see Cody, as told to Perry, *Iron Eyes*. I am truly fascinated by the fascination with Cody's ethnicity. The debate continues to be of immense importance to whites and Indians. Angela Aleiss, who wrote a dissertation on Indians in movies at Columbia University, now works as a freelance writer in Los Angeles. In 1996 Aleiss wrote an article for the *Times-Picayune* newspaper in New Orleans announcing that Cody was in fact Italian. Aleiss had tracked down his half sister in a nursing home to get the story. See Angela Aleiss, "Native Son," *New Orleans Times-Picayune*, May 26, 1996, D1. Aleiss's article was later reprinted in *Indian Country Today* after Cody's death in 1999. The *New Times LA* published a piece based on Aleiss's research in 1999 as well. See Ron Russell, "Make-Believe Indian," *New Times LA*, April 8, 1999. Those who argue that Cody was not an Indian rely on genealogical documents. Others fight for Cody's Indian identity by pointing to his birthplace (a reservation) and his good deeds for Indians. Like so many cases of Indian identity, the debates become vicious and the evidence introduced comes from different directions.

36. Cody, as told to Perry, *Iron Eyes*.

37. Biography Files, MHL, AMP. See also Pima County, Arizona, 1900 U.S. Federal Census, District 46, Sheet No. 14, copy emailed to the author by Tressie Nealy of the Oklahoma Historical Society. The 1850 Census was the first to list every member of the household. In the short film *Tonto Plays Himself* (2010), filmmaker Jacob Floyd claims a Muscogee identity and says that he is related to Daniels through his Muscogee father. Floyd, "Negotiating Publicity and Persona."

38. See Solomonsville City, Arizona, 1900 U.S. Federal Census, Sheet No. 10, Oklahoma Historical Society. On similar figures, see D. Smith, *From the Land of Shadows*; and D. Smith, *Chief Buffalo Child Long Lance*.

39. See Debo, *Geronimo*, 39, 90.

40. Howard McClay, "'Bravo' 200th Role for Him," *Los Angeles Daily News*, November 20, 1953, accessed in Biography Files, MHL, AMP.

41. Bill Cappello, "Noble Johnson, Part I," *Classic Images*, January 1992, 42, 43, 63; "Noble Johnson, Part II," *Classic Images*, February 1992, 50, 51; Jim McPherson, "Story of a 'Lost' Actor," *Toronto Sunday Sun*, undated clipping, all in Biography Files, MHL, AMP. The American Film Institute holds the scrapbooks of Henry Hathaway, who directed several westerns starring Randolph Scott, John Wayne, and Gary Cooper, including one for *Ten Gentlemen from West Point*, featuring Noble Johnson as Tecumseh. However, the scrapbook contains no photos of Johnson. See also Gaines, *Fire and Desire*.

42. They may not have been working under union contracts; there was a major strike in Hollywood during production. Higham, *Cecil B. DeMille*, 283.

43. "*Ambush* Production Notes," Core Collection, MHL, AMP. On the other hand, the use of a trained actor may have been the result of producer and writer Dore Schary's involvement in the film's production. In MGM's records, he suggested that the Indians be more personalized and less confined to background roles. See Dore Schary to Armand Deutsch, Interoffice Communication, April 21, 1949, *Ambush*, MGM Collection, CAL, USC.

44. Lenihan, "Westbound," 123.

45. Rogin, *Blackface, White Noise*, 29–30, 220. Rogin also concludes that the blackface tradition continued into the civil rights movement, as Jews spoke for African Americans. He also argues that Jews moved away from blacks in the twentieth century and acquired the dream that African Americans were seeking (see chapter 8 of Rogin's book). I have not drawn on this particular aspect of his argument because I found that the non-Indian actors who played the Indian leads were not of any predominant ethnicity. They came from a variety of ethnic backgrounds, and only a handful were Jewish.

46. For example, Matt Damon, Jason Patric, and Wes Studi appeared in *Geronimo* (1995). Matt Damon went on to achieve star status with *Good Will Hunting* (1997) and many subsequent starring roles. While Jason Patric did not become the successful, high-grossing actor that Damon did, he dated a major star (Sandra Bullock) and was often written up in popular publications. Studi, on the other hand, will probably never have a seat at the Oscars—and certainly not in the first ten rows—simply because neither Indian movies nor Indian actors have ever been given Hollywood's highest honors. In fact, Studi received the Academy Honorary Award at the 2019 Governors Award ceremony, which has become the method for the Academy of Motion Picture Arts and Sciences to give awards to those who are not white males. The Governors Award is not televised and is given months apart from the Oscars. Sex appeal can now include brown skin, yet fame and stardom remain elusive for Indian actors.

It is readily apparent that it is an actor's Indian identity and not a character's Indian identity that determines the potential for movie stardom. John Price noted in 1973 that "most of the important Hollywood stars of the 1940s and 1950s played an Indian role at least once: Douglas Fairbanks, Boris Karloff, Robert Taylor, Yvonne de Carlo, Rhonda Fleming, Paulette Goddard, Jennifer Jones, Loretta Young, and so forth." Price, "Stereotyping of North American Indians," 164.

47. "Press Releases," *Drums across the River*, File 12027, Box 432, Universal-International Collection, CAL, USC.

48. Sollors, *Beyond Ethnicity*, 127. I would argue that American Indians have in fact entered the world of pornography, or at least certain forms of pornography. Indians may or may not be used in pornographic films and magazines, but they were definitely used as sexualized images for advertising in the 1940s and 1950s. Both men's and women's bodies were left exposed when they were playing Indians. The model Jeanne Carmen wore a buckskin bikini, as did actresses Vera Hunt and Alice Talton. Today we see Indian men on the covers of romance novels and scantily clad Indian men and women gracing the canvases of bad art in suburban malls. I discuss this issue in more detail in other chapters.

49. "The white heroes got the billing, and the Indians got the pratfalls." Bataille and Silet, "Entertaining Anachronism," 40.

50. Throughout his career, Jay Silverheels lived at 1445 N. Bronson, an apartment building located across from a studio at the corner of Sunset and Bronson. His apartment was in a building of four apartments in what is now a working-class neighborhood. To my knowledge, Silverheels/Smith died as a renter.

In 1959 Disneyland, Warner Bros., and Universal were outside the city limits of Los Angeles; both Paramount and RKO moved from Melrose and Gower to Melrose and Ridgewood; Twentieth Century Fox was on Pico in west Los Angeles. Columbia was at Sunset and Bronson. See *Richfield Street Guide*. Three years earlier, Columbia had been in that same location. See *Central Section of Los Angeles*. But in 1954 the location was owned by Paramount. See Los Angeles, California, [map], December 1954, scale not given, *Fire Insurance Maps from the Sanborn Map Company Archives: Los Angeles, CA, 1911–1991*, Reel 25, Vol. 9A, Government Publications, URL, UCLA.

51. "Summary of Production Budget," April 26, 1954, *Four Guns to the Border*, File 93, Box 463, Universal-International Collection, CAL, USC.

52. The disparity was not always present. For instance, Rock Hudson was supposed to earn $5,500 for his role as Young Bull in *Winchester '73*, but that figure appears to have been cut to $2,500. Yowlachie earned $750 a week for his role as an Indian. See "Contract Memo"; "Day Player Agreement," March 14, 1950; and "Summary of Production Budget," February 7, 1950, all in *Winchester '73*, File 7501, Box 213, Universal-International Collection, CAL, USC.

53. Based on the films I was able to view, the number of times Indian actors were hired each year is as follows: 1941: 9; 1942: 3; 1943: 5; 1944: 2; 1945: 0; 1946: 4; 1947: 7; 1948: 10; 1949: 11; 1950: 25; 1951: 13; 1952: 12; 1953: 16; 1954: 10; 1955: 6; 1956: 6; 1957: 3; 1958: 4; 1959: 1; 1960: 1.

54. "Contract Memo," November 18, 1955; "Day Player Agreements," December 27, 1955, both in *Walk the Proud Land*, File 5450, Box 175, Universal-International Collection, CAL, USC.

55. "Summary of Production Budget," n.d., *War Arrow*, File 3561, Box 357, Universal-International Collection, CAL, USC.

56. However, non-Native actors typically earned more than Native actors, even for supporting character roles; Boris Karloff earned a surprising amount of money for his rather small role as Guyasuta in *Unconquered* (1947).

57. Non-Indian actors Joseph Vitale and Henry Brandon earned $1,000 and $750 a week respectively. Chief Yowlachie and Iron Eyes Cody earned $450 and $350 a week, respectively. See "Production Budget," File 1, Production Records, *The Paleface*, Paramount Collection, MHL, AMP. Bob Hope earned $135,000 and Jane Russell, $100,000, for their work in *The Paleface*. Not incidentally, that film was the biggest box-office hit of Hope's career, bringing in $4.5 million. Morella, Epstein, and Clark, *Amazing Careers of Bob Hope*, 143.

58. Jay Silverheels was paid $141 a day. The non-Indian actor Antonio Moreno was paid $166 a day, and the non-Indian actor Tony Caruso was paid $125. See "Summary of Production Budget," March 13, 1952, *Saskatchewan*, File 5996, Box 152; "Contract Memos and Final Talent List," File 06809, Box 130; "Production Budget," File 09824, Box 292, all in Universal-International Collection, CAL, USC. Some of the Indian extras were Henry Snaggle Tooth, Buffalo Chip Waters, Harvey Hole-in-the-Ground, and Ruth Bear Bottom, all of which are probably fabricated names that ridicule Indian naming customs. On one occasion, *Saskatchewan* director Raoul Walsh hired some of the tourists who were watching the filming to play Indians; see "Press Releases," *Saskatchewan*, File 13110, Box 447, Universal-International Collection, CAL, USC.

59. "Contract Memos," *Tomahawk*, File 7487, Box 213, Universal-International Collection, CAL, USC.

60. Irene Stewart graduated from the Haskell training school in Kansas in 1926, and she, Grey Eyes, and their eleven-year-old son, Earl Lee, all moved to Burbank, California. "File Production," *Colorado Territory*; Clips, "Indian Can't Speak English," *Omaha World Herald*, November 21, 1948; "Production Notes," 3, *Colorado Territory*, all in File Miscellaneous, Box 685, Warner Bros. Collection, CAL, USC.

61. "Production Notes," *Tomahawk*, File 13182, Box 444, Universal-International Collection, CAL, USC.

62. *Winchester '73*, File 11952, Box 424, Universal-International Collection, CAL, USC.

63. Louella Parsons column, *Los Angeles Examiner*, February 5, 1954, in Production, Clips, File *Battle Cry*, Box 646, Warner Bros. Collection, CAL, USC. The *Los Angeles Times* got Applegarth's tribal affiliation wrong, referring him to as a Papago Indian; see Edwin Schallert, "Moby Dick to Glory in CinemaScope; Judith Evelyn, Kasznar Cast," *Los Angeles Times*, February 19, 1954, in Production, Clips, File *Battle Cry*, Box 646, Warner Bros. Collection, CAL, USC.

64. Robert Collins, "The Two Lives of Jonas Applegarth," *Maclean's Magazine*, November 1, 1954, 16, 17, 54, 55, Production, Clips, File *Battle Cry*, Box 646, Warner Bros. Collection, CAL, USC.

65. Raoul Walsh considered Applegarth's acting work to be a Cinderella story of sorts. Fred Kennedy, "Alberta Indian Scores Another Movie Success," *Calgary Herald*, July 20, 1954, 10, Production, Clips, File *Battle Cry*, Box 646, Warner Bros. Collection, CAL, USC; Myron Laka, "Cree Indian Becomes Film Star Overnight," *Calgary Herald*, March 16, 1954. Applegarth died in a car accident in the 1970s; see Biography Files, MHL, AMP.

66. Whyte, *Organization Man*.

3. "NOT DESIRED FOR PHOTOGRAPHING"

1. Moses, *Wild West Shows*, 250–51.

2. Moses, *Wild West Shows*, 272.

3. "Press Releases," *Taza, Son of Cochise*, File 14708, Box 503, Universal-International Collection, CAL, USC.

4. "Press Releases," *Taza, Son of Cochise*, File 13184, Box 444, Universal-International Collection, CAL, USC.

5. "Press Releases," *Comanche Territory*, File 14290, Box 475, Universal-International Collection, CAL, USC. An article that repeated the press release verbatim appeared in the *New Orleans Picayune News*, September 18, 1949.

6. "Press Releases," *Taza, Son of Cochise*, File 13184, Box 444, Universal-International Collection, CAL, USC.

7. Harry Brand, "20th Century Fox Press Release," September 13, 1946, 1–2, *My Darling Clementine* Production Files, MHL, AMP.

8. Robert Rosenstone distinguishes between certain kinds of filmic historical genres by separating films engaged with historiography from those that are not. See Rosenstone, *Visions of the Past*. On the relationship between heroism and defeat as a moral tale, see Ray, *Certain Tendency*.

9. Robert Yellowtail's sister, Agnes, was married to Warren Bends by parental arrangement. Warren may have been a relative of William Bends. William Bends was the chairperson of the Crow Nation from 1927 to 1934. Robert Yellowtail was chairperson from 1946 to 1954. See Voget, *They Call Me Agnes*, 116–18.

10. John Whiteman was probably Robert Yellowtail's brother-in-law and may have been related to Harry Whiteman. See Voget, *They Call Me Agnes*, 106, 159. See also Bernardis, "Robert Yellowtail," 705.

11. Hoxie, *Parading through History*, 317, 326–43.

12. "Production Notes," 4, File *Drum Beat*; and "Indian Liaison Signed," *Hollywood Reporter*, June 15, 1954, Clips, both in File *Drum Beat*, Box 6516, Warner Bros.

Collection, CAL, USC. MGM may have hired Diné extras for *Escape from Fort Bravo*. They also hired horse trainer Carl Petti (a non-Indian) to play an Indian so he could keep the horses in check during certain scenes. MGM may have also hired other non-Indians to play Indians, as there are pictures of them with William Holden. See *Escape from Fort Bravo*, MGM, Stills Collection, MHL, AMP. Apache actor Charles Stevens appeared to use his own hair, but one of the men hired to play an Indian was painted with an extremely dark base makeup. See *Escape from Fort Bravo*, John Truwe Collection, MHL, AMP.

13. Hoxie, *Parading through History*, 363. This festival was probably the version that excluded self-torture because they would not have allowed religious ceremonies to be photographed. Information on the Sun Dance from Alvin Josephy, personal conversation with author, June 30, 1998, Los Angeles, California; and Bernardis, "Robert Yellowtail," 705.

According to Voget, the last nineteenth-century Crow Sun Dance took place in 1875, and it included piercings and flesh offerings. In 1941 the Crows began practicing the Wind River Shoshone Sun Dance. Several individuals were important in this renewal, including John Truhujo, William Big Day, Robert Yellowtail, and others. One of many motivations in practicing the Sun Dance was to pray for men fighting in the war. See Voget, *Shoshoni-Crow Sun Dance*, 43–44, 78–79, 127, 143, 145, 146, 147–50, 161, 198, 280–81, 284.

14. Contract from Crow Agency, *Buffalo Bill*, Box FX-LR-468, Collection 012, Twentieth Century Fox Film Corp., SC-YRL, UCLA.

15. *Buffalo Bill*, Box FX-ST-35, Collection 012, Twentieth Century Fox Film Corp., SC-YRL, UCLA.

16. Jerry Hoffman, Regal Films, "Production Notes," 7, HO 9-7381, *Mrs. Mike* Production Files, Core Collection, MHL, AMP. Local Mexicans were hired to play Indians in *Sitting Bull* (United Artists, 1954). MGM hired two hundred Indian extras for *The Omaha Trail*, filmed near Sonora, California, but archival information does not indicate their tribal affiliations. See *The Omaha Trail*, MGM, Stills Collection, MHL, AMP.

17. Dane-zaa Nation population statistics: 1911: 380, 1978: 912, 1991: 1,405. Malinowski and Sheets, *Gale Encyclopedia of Native American Tribes*, 65.

18. "Press Releases," *War Arrow*, File 11948, Box 424, Universal-International Collection, CAL, USC. On the *Winchester '73* set, Universal hired stunt performers even though they had already hired Diné who probably would have done the stunts, especially for the extra pay of $100 a fall. See *Winchester '73*, File 11952, Box 424, Universal-International Collection, CAL, USC.

19. According to an anonymous reader's report, Dr. Frank Clarke received his medical degree in 1950 from St. Louis University. He received the Indian Council Fires

Award in Chicago in 1961. Dr. Clarke also attended the Sherman Institute in Riverside, California. He was not, however, one of the men who worked as an extra in *Foxfire*. At the time, he was in the navy. He doubts that there were any Hualapai medical doctors on the set in 1955, as he was one of fewer than ten Indian men with a medical degree in 1950. Dr. Franke Clarke, interview by author, May 24, 2004, Woodlake, California.

20. "Production Notes," 1–2, *Foxfire*, File 106, Box 463, Universal-International Collection, CAL, USC.

21. "Press Releases," *War Arrow*, File 11948, Box 424, Universal-International Collection, CAL, USC.

22. Between the years of 1941 and 1960 Diné appeared as Indian extras in the following films: *Western Union* (Twentieth Century Fox, 1941); *Bugles in the Afternoon* (Warner, 1952); *Buffalo Bill* (Twentieth Century Fox, 1944); *Flaming Feather* (Paramount, 1952); *My Darling Clementine* (Twentieth Century Fox, 1946); *Red Mountain* (Paramount, 1952); *Colorado Territory* (Warner, 1949); *Arrowhead* (Paramount, 1953); *She Wore a Yellow Ribbon* (RKO, 1949); *Column South* (Universal, 1953); *Ambush* (MGM, 1950); *Escape from Fort Bravo* (MGM, 1953); *Rio Grande* (Republic, 1950); *Drum Beat* (Warner, 1954); *Ticket to Tomahawk* (Twentieth Century Fox, 1950); *The Lone Ranger* (Warner, 1956); *Wagonmaster* (RKO, 1950); *The Searchers* (Warner Bros., 1956); *The Battle at Apache Pass* (Universal, 1951); *Fort Dobbs* (Warner, 1958); *The Last Outpost* (Paramount, 1951); *Sergeant Rutledge* (Warner, 1960); and *Only the Valiant* (Warner Bros., 1951).

23. "Production Notes," 5, File *Sergeant Rutledge*, Box 660, Warner Bros. Collection, CAL, USC. On a slightly different note, Jesse Stevens (Apache) spoke at a 1958 meeting in Claremore, Oklahoma, to protest filmic representations of Indians. He stated, "The producers should hire some of us to show them how real Indians act. It's just a farce that . . . one white guy always manages to kill off a bunch of Indians. I was in an Alan Ladd picture once and got bumped off just like (fingersnap) that!" Quoted in Spears, *Hollywood*, 390.

24. On the set of *Saskatchewan* (Universal, 1954), the Cree and Lakota extras were paid $10 extra per fall.

25. "Billy Yellow," interview by Ronald L. Davis, September 13, 1991, Number 484, 9, OHPA, SMU. I am indebted to Ronald Davis for permission to use his oral history material and his scholarship on Hollywood. See R. L. Davis's *Glamour Factory*, *Hollywood Beauty*, and *John Ford*.

26. See "Application for Permission to Take a Motion or a Motion and Sound Picture under Department Order No. 2029 Dated February 26, 1945," 2, Records of the Legal Department, *My Darling Clementine*, Box FX-LR-803, Collection 095,

Twentieth Century Fox Film Corp., SC-YRL, UCLA. Henry Fonda, one of the stars of *Clementine*, had little to say about the film in retrospect other than to defend Ford, Wayne, and himself in regard to their escapades between films. See Fonda, as told to Teichmann, *Fonda*, 171, 174, 176.

27. Harry Brand, Twentieth Century Fox publicity document, September 13, 1946, 1–2, *My Darling Clementine* Production Files, Core Collection, MHL, AMP. Like most press releases, the racist language ridicules the Diné on many levels, with this one continuing in that vein: "Six weeks ago the first big salary pow-wow took place at Kayenta. Prices were set for cattle, for ponies, for the services of Indians, of squaws and even prices for papooses strapped to boards and unstrapped were discussed. The debates lasted weeks."

28. See "Screen Actors Guild permit," Bob Ellsworth to Fox, September 16, 1940, Records of the Legal Department, *Western Union*, Box FX-LR-444, Collection 095, Twentieth Century Fox Film Corp., SC-YRL, UCLA. Universal-International filmed in Kanab, Utah, at least twice and did not employ Indians as extras or as laborers; see File 95829 and File 05828, both in Box 176, Universal-International Collection, CAL, USC.

29. T. C. Wright to Hoyt Bowers, Interoffice Communication, June 4, 1951, *Bugles in the Afternoon*; and Wright to Bowers, Interoffice Communication, June 5, 1951, both in Box 374, Warner Bros. Collection, CAL, USC.

30. Jason J. Joy to William Goetz, June 25, 1943, Records of the Legal Department, *Buffalo Bill*, Box FX-LR-468, Collection 095, Twentieth Century Fox Film Corp., SC-YRL, UCLA.

31. Interoffice Correspondence, June 22, 1943, Records of the Legal Department, *Buffalo Bill*, Box FX-LR-468, Collection 095, Twentieth Century Fox Film Corp., SC-YRL, UCLA.

32. Interoffice Correspondence, June 22, 1943, Records of the Legal Department, *Buffalo Bill*. The assistant commissioner of Indian affairs asked Diné service superintendent James Stewart for photos Fox may have taken of Diné working, but he probably never received them. See William Zimmerman, Assistant Commissioner, to James Stewart, Superintendent, Diné Service, Chicago, Illinois, August 28, 1943, Central Classified File 33023-43-048, Office of Indian Affairs Files, DI, NA.

33. See George Dixon, "Indian Situation Kanab," n.d., 1, 2, 3, Records of the Legal Department, *Buffalo Bill*, Box FX-LR-468, Collection 095, Twentieth Century Fox Film Corp., SC-YRL, UCLA.

34. George Dixon, "Indian Situation Kanab," n.d., 1, 2, 3.

35. See R. C. Moore to Mr. J. M. Stewart, General Superintendent, Diné Service, July 20, 1943, Records of the Legal Department, *Buffalo Bill*, Box FX-LR-468, Collection 095, Twentieth Century Fox Film Corp., SC-YRL, UCLA.

36. James Stewart, General Superintendent, Diné Service, to Office of Indian Affairs, Department of the Interior, Chicago, Illinois, August 3, 1943, Central Classified File 33023-43-048, Office of Indian Affairs Files, DI, NA.

37. Mike Goulding, interview by Ronald L. Davis, September 13, 1991, Number 484, 29, OHPA, SMU.

38. Goulding interview; Limbrick, *Making Settler Cinemas*, 59–98; *Return of Navajo Boy* (2000). On Diné use of the tourism market to sell Diné goods, see Bsumek, *Indian-Made*; and Mullin, *Culture in the Marketplace*.

39. Two Indian actors had offered their services but were turned down, as production had already begun. See Bud Leith, c/o U.S. Department of the Interior, Chiloquin, Oregon, to Jack Warner, October 6, 1941; and Monte Blue to Jack L. Warner, July 22, 1941, both in Box 2303 (T-81), Warner Bros. Collection, CAL, USC.

40. T. C. Wright to Russel Trost, Interoffice Communication, July 7, 1941, Warner Bros. Collection, CAL, USC. The goal of using Indians in the foreground is further validated in "List of Indian Shots to Be Made by Second Unit," September 9, 1941, File *They Died*, Box 2303 (T-81), Warner Bros. Collection, CAL, USC. On pages 1–2 they used the word "Indian," but on page 3 they wrote, "Two real Indians mounted on two mechanical horses."

41. "Agreement with Indians, Fort Yates, No. Dakota," August 2, 1941, File *They Died*, Picture File, Box 2881, Warner Bros. Collection, CAL, USC. The legible names included Francis Flying Cloud (Carlisle graduate), Alvin Elk Nation, Jack Red Bear, Mike Gray Eagle, Raymond Hairy Chin, William Village Center, Frank Shooter, Moses Brave, Joseph Fasthorse Sr., Joshua White Shield, Emmet La Frombaise, and Pemmican. Many of these men were related to famous Lakotas. "Sioux Indians: They Died with Their Boots On," File *They Died*, Box 2303, Warner Bros. Collection, CAL, USC.

42. Frank Mattison to T. C. Wright, Interoffice Communication, August 20, 1941, *They Died*, File 372, Box 1487, Warner Bros. Collection, CAL, USC.

43. Mattison to Wright, Interoffice Communication, August 28, 1941.

44. "Postal Telegraph," September 2, 1941, File *They Died*, Box 2303 (T-81), Warner Bros. Collection, CAL, USC. On September 16, 1941, the day after the Lakota men were involved in an accident (discussed later), the *Los Angeles Times* reported an upcoming Indian ceremony to be held at Sycamore Grove, where Monte Blue and other "film players of Indian descent" would be initiating an unnamed California Indian "into the Pale Face tribe by Governor Wilson."

45. Frank Mattison to T. C. Wright, Interoffice Communication, September 3, 1941, *They Died*, File 372, Box 1487, Warner Bros. Collection, CAL, USC.

46. Frank Mattison to T. C. Wright, Interoffice Communication, September 4, 1941, *They Died*, File 372, Box 1487, Warner Bros. Collection, CAL, USC.

47. Car accidents like this were normally reported in the *Los Angeles Times*. The studio probably made efforts to keep this one a secret. "Dances to Feature Indian Day Fete," *Los Angeles Times*, September 16, 1941, 1.

48. Frank Mattison to T. C. Wright, Interoffice Communication, September 15, 1941, *They Died*, File 372, Box 1487, Warner Bros. Collection, CAL, USC.

49. Frank Mattison to T. C. Wright, Interoffice Communication, September 20, 1941, File *They Died*, Picture File, Box 288, Warner Bros. Collection, CAL, USC.

50. Mattison to Wright, Interoffice Communication, September 15, 1941.

51. On September 23 a Mr. Obringer, an employee of Warner Bros., wrote Arthur Freston of Freston & Files about the possibility of seeking payment of $71.60 from Murray for anesthesia, first aid, one x-ray, and room charges. Obringer to Arthur Freston, September 23, 1941, File *They Died*, Picture File, Box 2881, Warner Bros. Collection, CAL, USC. The Los Angeles Police Department found no records of this accident. The hospital had destroyed all records prior to 1970 unless there was an outstanding issue involved. Freston & Files replied to Obringer that same day. Freston believed that Obringer was effectively lending funds to the Indians by paying their bills and thus had a claim against the Indians, not the car owner. He suggested a "third-handed agreement" between Warner Bros., the Indians, and the car owner's insurance company. Freston & Files to Obringer, September 23, 1941, File *They Died*, Picture File, Box 2881, Warner Bros. Collection, CAL, USC.

52. See Tahmahkera, "'We're Gonna Capture Johnny Depp.'"

53. Lakotas were probably hired for *Across the Wide Missouri* (MGM, 1951) as well. See *Across the Wide Missouri*, MGM, Stills Collection, MHL, AMP.

54. The studio claimed High Eagle was Custer's nephew, but he was not. He was, however, present at the Battle of the Little Bighorn.

55. "Production Notes," *Tomahawk*, File 13182, Box 444, Universal-International Collection, CAL, USC. Two young Lakota men did agree to work as extras: George Looks Twice and Pat La Deaux.

56. *Variety*, February 24, 1954, 18; March 10, 1954, 13; September 1, 1954, 7; September 8, 1954, 5, 18.

57. "Press Releases," *Smoke Signal*, File 17805, Box 580, Universal-International Collection, CAL, USC.

58. "Production Notes," *Tomahawk*, File 13182, Box 444, Universal-International Collection, CAL, USC.

59. Studio records show Conner signed up Indians from a reservation about thirty miles southeast of La Grande, but they do not name the reservation. They may have meant Klamath Indian Reservation.

60. "Production Notes," *Pillars of the Sky*, File 12524, Box 423, Universal-International Collection, CAL, USC.

61. Information on his death is at "Gilbert Edward Conner," Find a Grave, http://www
.findagrave.com/memorial/42698119/gilbert-edward-conner.

62. "Production Notes" and "Campaign Ideas," both in *Pillars of the Sky*, File 12524,
Box 423, Universal-International Collection, CAL, USC.

63. Agnes Yellowtail Deer Nose claims that Donald Deer Nose recruited Indians for
"a couple other pictures at Paramount." Voget, *They Call Me Agnes*, 133. Like other
reservation Indians who worked temporarily in movies, his usual income-earning
activities ranged from farming (on other people's farms), cattle raising, and exca-
vating to janitorial work (128).

64. "Press Releases," *Winchester '73*, File 11952, Box 424, Universal-International Collection, CAL, USC.

65. "Paramount Press Sheets, Releases Season 1950–51," Group A-10, *The Last Outpost*,
Paramount Collection, Special Collections, MHL, AMP.

66. "Production Notes," *Tomahawk*, File 13182, Box 444, Universal-International Collection, CAL, USC.

67. "Press Release," *Crazy Horse*, File 12270, Box 421, Universal-International Collection,
CAL, USC.

68. See Leith, c/o U.S. Department of the Interior, to Warner, October 6, 1941; and
Blue to Jack L. Warner, July 22, 1941.

69. Fishgall, *Pieces of Time*, 209.

70. "Memo from Casey Robinson," May 24, 1949, 2, *Two Flags West*, Twentieth Century
Fox Film Collection, CAL, USC.

71. "Personnel List" and "Daily Production and Progress Reports," R. Walsh File 373,
Distant Drums, Box 1490, Warner Bros. Collection, CAL, USC.

72. "Advance Production Notes," 3, File Production, *Hondo*, Notes, Box 667, Warner
Bros. Collection, CAL, USC; Clippings from *Reporter*, June 22, 1953, *Examiner*,
June 23, 1953, and *Valley Times*, June 23, 1953, all in File Production, *Hondo*, Clips,
Box 667, Warner Bros. Collection, CAL, USC.

73. "Production," File *The Command*, Box 649; and "Well-Represented," *New York
Mirror*, December 27, 1953, Clips, both in Warner Bros. Collection, CAL, USC.

74. Production Files, *Bad Bascomb*, Core Collection, MHL, AMP. *The Wild North* was
filmed in Wyoming and Idaho, and Indian extras appear in the stills. However,
there is no conclusive evidence as to hires or tribal affiliations. See MGM, Stills
Collection, MHL, AMP.

75. *Devil's Doorway*, MGM, Stills Collection, MHL, AMP. MGM also hired veteran actor
John Big Tree for the film.

76. *Across the Wide Missouri*, MGM, Stills Collection, MHL, AMP. Robert Mathews played
the Indian woman's baby in the film. Jack Holt, Ricardo Montalbán, María Elena Mar-
qués, and J. Carrol Naish were non-Indians brought from Hollywood to play Indians.

77. M. Ross, *Stars and Strikes*, 66–68, 70–73.

78. According to CCC, extras were paid between $10 and $17 a day between 1938 and 1946. Specifically, 1938: $10.78; 1939: $10.61; 1940: $11.08; 1941: $11.72; 1942: $11.77; 1943: $12.63; 1944: $12.71; 1945: $13.00; 1946: $17.34.

79. *Motion Picture Production Encyclopedia*, 1944–48 (Hollywood CA: Hollywood Reporter Press, 1949), 605, held in Special Collections, FHG-HRL.

80. "Producer–Screen Actors Guild Basic Minimum Contract of 1937," Screen Actors Guild, 2, Folder 18, Box 10, Mary Pickford Collection, MHL, AMP.

81. "Producer–Screen Actors Guild, Modification Agreement of 1938," Screen Actors Guild, 1, Folder 18, Box 10, Mary Pickford Collection, MHL, AMP.

82. "Producer–Screen Actors Guild Supplemental Agreement of 1941," and "Producer–Screen Actors Guild Supplemental Agreement of 1945," both in Screen Actors Guild, Folder 18, Box 10, Mary Pickford Collection, MHL, AMP.

83. *Producer–Screen Actors Guild Revised Basic Agreement of 1947*, 29.

84. Unlike Indian extras, New York extras wielded tremendous power in the Screen Actors Guild. They had their own supplement to the Basic Agreement of 1947. They had a union shop agreement that applied to a radius of seventy-five air miles with a center in Columbus Circle for films not based in New York. For films outside the seventy-five air miles but within three hundred air miles, SAG scale and working conditions had to be enforced. The producers were not held responsible for locating guild extras or transporting them. See *Producer–Screen Actors Guild Revised Basic Agreement of 1947*, 31.

85. R. White, *Roots of Dependency*, 216, 219.

86. See George Dixon, "Indian Situation Kanab," n.d., 1, 2, 3.

87. "Memorandum of Agreement between James Stewart, General Superintendent, Diné Service, and George Wasson, Assistant Secretary," July 19, 1943, Twentieth Century Fox Film Corporation; Harold Ickes, Secretary of the Interior, "Order No. 1472," April 20, 1940; and Harold Ickes, Secretary of the Interior, "Order No. 1445," February 7, 1940, all in Central Classified File 33023-43-048, Office of Indian Affairs Files, DI, NA.

88. Lewis, "*Navajo Talking Picture*," 22.

89. R. L. Davis, *John Ford*, 95–96, 99–100.

90. "Production, Miscellaneous," "Production Notes," 3, File *Bugles in the Afternoon*, Box 648, Warner Bros. Collection, CAL, USC. *Westward the Women* was shot in Kanab, Utah, but it is unclear whether local Indian extras were hired. See MGM, Stills Collection, MHL, AMP. On Bradley's pay, see Joseph J. Barry to T. C. Wright, Interoffice Communication, May 11, 1951, 2, File *Bugles in the Afternoon*, Box 374, Warner Bros. Collection, CAL, USC. Lee Bradley worked as the interpreter for many films, including *Bugles in the Afternoon* (Warner Bros., 1952), *Taza, Son of Cochise* (Universal, 1954), and *Smoke Signal* (Universal, 1955).

91. See "Application for Permission to Take a Motion or a Motion and Sound Picture under Department Order No. 2029 Dated February 26, 1945," 2, Records of the Legal Department, *My Darling Clementine*, Box FX-LR-803, Collection 095, Twentieth Century Fox Film Corp., SC-YRL, UCLA.

92. See W. F. Fitzgerald to Jason Joy and George Wasson, Interoffice Correspondence, June 11, 1946; Twentieth Century Fox Film Corporation to Mr. Frank Bradley, June 6, 1946; Twentieth Century Fox Film Corporation to Fred Yazzie, June 6, 1946; J. B. Codd to George Wasson, Interoffice Correspondence, June 14, 1946; George Wasson to J. Codd, T. Frazer, Interoffice Correspondence, June 20, 1946; George Wasson to Location Department, Interoffice Correspondence, June 27, 1946; George Wasson to Frank Bradley, June 27, 1946; George Wasson to Fred Yazzie, June 27, 1946, all in Records of the Legal Department, *My Darling Clementine*, Box FX-LR-803, Collection 095, Twentieth Century Fox Film Corp., SC-YRL, UCLA.

93. R. L. Davis, *John Ford*, 271. Frank Bradley Jr. is pictured with Constance Towers in a photo accompanying the article "John Ford's New Utah Film Slated," *Deseret News and Telegram*, April 25, 1960, Production, Clips, File *Sergeant Rutledge*, Box 660, Warner Bros. Collection, CAL, USC. See also "Production Notes," 4–6, File *The Searchers*, Box 660, Warner Bros. Collection, CAL, USC. Ford used Diné workers and Monument Valley as the set in preparing *Two Rode Together* (1961) as well. However, he hired African American actor Woody Strode to play the significant Native role of Stone Calf. Ford also chose Strode to play the Native lead in *Sergeant Rutledge* (Warner, 1960). R. L. Davis, *John Ford*, 305. Ford filmed *Cheyenne Autumn* (Warner, 1964) in Moab, Utah, and employed Diné. Ford's camera assistant Jack Woods reported that the young Diné women were wearing "Capri pants and modern hairdresses," and the roads were paved and had signs alongside them (321–22).

94. "'Searchers' Paying Navajo $35,000," *Hollywood Reporter*, June 6, 1955, Clips, File *The Searchers*, Box 660, Warner Bros. Collection, CAL, USC. In 1960 Ford hired only twenty-seven Diné extras for *Sergeant Rutledge* (1960), and their wage rates are unknown. See "Daily Production and Progress Reports," File *Captain Buffalo* #855, aka *Sergeant Rutledge*, Box 1492, Warner Bros. Collection, CAL, USC.

95. "Press Releases," *Comanche Territory*, File 11825, Box 422, Universal-International Collection, CAL, USC. The location records may not be accurate, however, because Universal press releases claim that the time cards were "dummy cards." Further, some of the Diné that Universal claimed were hired for the film are not listed on the cards. The Diné extra Mary Martin was paid more than the others because she also interpreted, for $11.60 a day.

96. "Production, Miscellaneous," "Production Notes," 3, File *Bugles in the Afternoon*, Box 648, Warner Bros. Collection, CAL, USC. However, Lee Bradley was only

paid $25 a day in 1952, the same rate he was paid in 1939. Joseph J. Barry to T. C. Wright, Interoffice Communication, May 11, 1951, 2, File *Bugles in the Afternoon*, Box 374, Warner Bros. Collection, CAL, USC. Paramount hired hundreds of Diné for *The Last Outpost* (Paramount, 1951), *Flaming Feather* (Paramount, 1952), *Red Mountain* (Paramount, 1951), *Arrowhead* (Paramount, 1953) at unknown wage rates. "Paramount Press Sheets, Releases Season 1950–51," Group A-10, *Warpath*, Paramount Collection, Special Collections, MHL, AMP. Paramount also hired Chief Yowlachie for *Warpath*; see Paramount, Stills Collection, Special Collections, MHL, AMP.

97. Barry to Wright, Interoffice Communication, May 11, 1951.

98. T. C. Wright to Hoyt Bowers, Interoffice Communication, June 4, 1951, June 5, 1951, and June 9, 1951, all in File *Bugles in the Afternoon*, Box 374, Warner Bros. Collection, CAL, USC. The Diné men hired for *Bugles in the Afternoon* were Joe Allen, Kee Allen, Ed Austine, John Billietsosie, Hall Burns, Levi Chief, Carl Coleman, John Crank, Kay Denaltsio, Kid Denaltsio, Pete Graybyer, Little Laughter, Felix Manymiles, Frank Parrish, Henry Parrish, Melvin Parrish, Phillip Parrish, Rodney Parrish, Herbert Russell, Harry Savage, Slim Smith, John Standley, Jack Standley, Kee Standley, John Standley Jr., Joe Whitehorse, and Charley Yellow.

99. "Production Budget," Production Records, *Arrowhead*, Paramount Collection, Special Collections, MHL, AMP. Heston claims the Indians he worked with on *Arrowhead* were Chiricahua Apaches, not Diné. Heston, *In the Arena*, 28.

100. "Contract Memos," *Column South*, File 07144, Box 217; "Production Budget," File 09871, Box 288; "Tentative Cast Costs," File 07463, Box 219; "Summary of Production Budget," March 15, 1952, File 16362, Box 556, all in Universal-International Collection, CAL, USC.

101. "Press Releases," *Taza, Son of Cochise*, File 14708, Box 503, Universal-International Collection, CAL, USC.

102. See Luebben, "Study of Some Off-Reservation Navaho Miners"; and O'Neill, "Navajo Workers and White Man's Ways," 158–59. Warner Bros. hired two hundred Diné extras in Kanab, Utah, for the filming of *The Lone Ranger*. "Production Notes," 4, File *Lone Ranger*, Box 655a, Warner Bros. Collection, CAL, USC; "Movement List," July 25, 1955, File *The Lone Ranger*, Heisler, #410, Box 1490a, Warner Bros. Collection, CAL, USC.

103. R. J. Obringer to C. H. Wilder, "Interoffice Communication," August 6, 1941, File *They Died*, Picture File, Box 2881, Warner Bros. Collection, CAL, USC.

104. "Production Budget," "Check Requisition," August 10, 1954, Production Records, *Far Horizons*, Paramount Collection, MHL, AMP.

105. "Summary of Production Budget, May 2, 1952," and "Summary of Production Budget, June 19, 1954," *Chief Crazy Horse*, File 6031, Box 168, Universal-International

Collection, CAL, USC. An Indian boy named Todd Fast Wolf play Crazy Horse as a boy. "Press Release," *Chief Crazy Horse*, File 12270, Box 421, Universal-International Collection, CAL, USC.

106. "Production Budget," October 21, 1950, File *Red Mountain*, Production Records, File 2, Paramount Collection, MHL, AMP. Iron Eyes Cody was paid $75 for one day of technical advising; Jay Silverheels was paid $2,975 for playing Little Crow; Hal Wallis was paid $60,000 for producing and William Dieterle, $75,000 for directing; Alan Ladd was paid $151,000; extras were paid a total of $10,721.31. "Production Budget," October 21, 1950, File *Red Mountain*, Production Records, File 2; "Authorization for Engagement of Artist," in File *Red Mountain*, Production Records, File 3, October 28, 1950; "Paramount Salary Distribution," File *Red Mountain*, Production Records, File 4; "Detail Production Cost," in File *Red Mountain*, Production Records, File 14, January 23, 1952, all in Paramount Collection, MHL, AMP. For photos of Diné on the set, see Paramount, Stills Collection, MHL, AMP.

107. "Time Cards," *Tomahawk*, Files 5721 and 5722, Box 174; File 7877, Box 239, all in Universal-International Collection, CAL, USC.

108. These ranges are large because in the production reports the word "Indian" might be used several times with many different wage rates indicated. My conclusion is that this is because sometimes these people played chiefs (a role that paid more); sometimes they were women or children (who often were paid less); and still other times when the studio wrote "Indian," they were referring to stunt performers who played Indians. This makes it difficult, but not entirely impossible, to know how much the extras from reservations were paid.

109. Myron Laka, "From Farmer to Star: Indian Hits Jackpot," [*Calgary Herald*], May 8, 1954, 21, 39. See also Hedda Hopper, "Real Type Casting," *Los Angeles Times*, March 2, 1954; "Indian Lands Part in Movie," *Calgary Herald*, February 12, 1954; and Myron Laka, "Cree Indian Becomes Film Star Overnight," *Calgary Herald*, March 16, 1954, all in Production, Clips, File *Battle Cry*, Box 646, Warner Bros. Collection, CAL, USC. That same year Applegarth received a bit role for $350 a week (about $58 a day).

110. "Press Releases," *Saskatchewan*, File 13110, Box 447, Universal-International Collection, CAL, USC. Wages for falling from a horse depended on the type of fall and, sometimes, whether the extra was playing an Indian or a cowboy. Hoot Gibson, a famous cowboy actor, remembers being paid $2.50 when playing an Indian in 1950 and getting $5 for horse falls when playing a cowboy in the 1920s. See the Hoot Gibson interview in "The Western in the 1920s," loose-leaf compilation, 1975, 167, in Special Collections, LBML, AFI. Due to the danger involved, mounted extras received much higher pay when they had to use a device called a "running W" (it caused the horse to fall at an appointed time and the rider to be thrown; the device

had been outlawed by World War II). See Cary, *Hollywood Posse*, 152–53, 190, on horse falls as well as a general history of cowboy extras in Hollywood. Diana Serra Cary herself worked as an extra in the early twentieth century and gives an excellent account of a day's work as a movie extra. See Cary, *Hollywood Posse*, 150–52.

111. There is some confusion in the records as to who actually played the Indians in the background. In other places there are indications that Palouses were hired over the Nez Perce but that the Nez Perce were used to play cavalry troops when there were not enough white extras. See File 12524, Box 423, Universal-International Collection, CAL, USC.

112. "News from Twentieth Century Fox," May 4, 1950, *Two Flags West* Production Files, Core Collection, MHL, AMP.

113. "Production Budget," Production Records, *Unconquered*, Files 1 and 2, Paramount Collection, MHL, AMP. Gary Cooper was paid $300,000, Cecil B. DeMille received $46,000, and Paulette Goddard was paid $91,000. "Production Notes," *Unconquered*, Core Collection, MHL, AMP. Victor Romito was one of the men DeMille hired to play an Indian, but his ethnicity is unclear. See "Off-Camera Stills," *Unconquered*, Cecil B. DeMille Collection, MHL, AMP. An in-house organ referred to this hiring as the "largest army of American Indians to be used in a picture in years." "Army of Indians for *Unconquered*" (newsreel transcript), *Paramount News*, June 3, 1946.

114. "Production Budget," *The Paleface*, Production Records, File 1, Paramount Collection, MHL, AMP.

115. "Production Budget," *Pony Express*, Production Records, Files 1 and 3, Paramount Collection, MHL, AMP. Charlton Heston was paid $25,000. Pat Hogan was paid a total of $1,050 for playing Yellow Hand and was referred to as an "Irish Indian" in a photo caption. See *Pony Express*, Paramount, Stills Collection, MHL, AMP.

116. See *Winchester '73*, File 8210, Box 274; "Press Releases," *Winchester '73*, File 11952, Box 424; "Summary of Production Budget," *Seminole*, File 07581, Box 126; File 06808, Box 130; File 14305, Box 537, all in Universal-International Collection, CAL, USC.

117. Fox secured an agreement with H. B. Jolley of Fort Yuma Indian Agency to use a portion of the Indian school reserve in the production of *The Oregon Trail* (Twentieth Century Fox, 1959). Fox paid $100 for the benefit of using land that had been planted with beans, and the studio paid an outside contractor $700 to build a dike for filming purposes. See Fox Film Corporation to Mr. Justus Jackson, April 17, 1930; and Mr. Justus Jackson to Fox Film Corporation, April 5, 1930, both in Records of the Legal Department, *The Oregon Trail*, Box FX-LR-1009, Collection 095, Twentieth Century Fox Film Corp., SC-YRL, UCLA.

118. "Vital Statistics on 'Two Flags West,'" *Two Flags West*, Production Files, Core Collection, MHL, AMP.

119. "Production Notes," 2–3, File *Fort Dobbs*, Box 652, Warner Bros. Collection, CAL, USC.

120. "Press Release," *Chief Crazy Horse*, File 12270, Box 421, Universal-International Collection, CAL, USC.

121. See "Application for Permission to Take a Motion or a Motion and Sound Picture under Department Order No. 2029," February 26, 1945, 9, Records of the Legal Department, *My Darling Clementine*, Box FX-LR-803, Collection 095, Twentieth Century Fox Film Corp., SC-YRL, UCLA. According to this application, "Any cattle used shall receive $1.00 per day. Cattle to be fed by the Company at a minimum of 20 lbs. of alfalfa hay per day per head. Said cattle to be herded, not corralled, for day or overnight periods. All expenses of herding shall be paid by the Company.... Any water used by the Company from Government owned wells or reservoirs will be paid for at the flat rate of 15 [cents] per 100 gallons.... Where water is being taken from wells with windmills and storage tanks a minimum of 25,000 gallons of water will be maintained in storage tank at all times. Said water is for the purpose of watering livestock not being used by the Company. Said amount of water will be maintained at the expense of the company."

122. J. M. Cooper, Assistant Superintendent, to Mr. W. F. Fitzgerald, Unit Production Manager, June 6, 1946, Records of the Legal Department, *My Darling Clementine*, Box FX-LR-803, Collection 095, Twentieth Century Fox Film Corp., SC-YRL, UCLA.

123. See J. R. Lynn, Acting Superintendent, to Mr. Clarence D. Hutson, Manager, Location Department, September 1, 1948; "Purchase Order," September 1, 1948, Bureau of Indian Affairs, U.S. Department of the Interior; George Wasson to Clarence D. Hutson, Interoffice Correspondence, September 7, 1948; George Wasson, Fox Legal Counsel, to Mr. J. R. Lynn, Acting Superintendent, Diné Service, September 17, 1948, all in Records of the Legal Department, *My Darling Clementine*, Box FX-LR-803, Collection 095, Twentieth Century Fox Film Corp., SC-YRL, UCLA.

124. R. L. Davis, *John Ford*, 190.

125. See "Whitebear Contract," July 7, 1943; and "Takes Horse Contract," July 8, 1943, both in Records of the Legal Department, *Buffalo Bill*, Box FX-LR-468, Collection 095, Twentieth Century Fox Film Corp., SC-YRL, UCLA.

126. George Wasson to Mr. T. R. Frazer, Interoffice Correspondence, June 22, 1943, Records of the Legal Department, *Buffalo Bill*, Box FX-LR-468, Collection 095, Twentieth Century Fox Film Corp., SC YRL, UCLA. There was no explanation given as to who Mr. Maddox was or how Fox found him.

127. "Contract from Crow Agency, Montana, June 17, 1943, to Twentieth Century Fox Film Corporation," 1–4, Records of the Legal Department, *Buffalo Bill*, Box FX-LR-468, Collection 095, Twentieth Century Fox Film Corp., SC-YRL, UCLA.

128. "News from Twentieth Century Fox," May 4, 1950, *Two Flags West* Production Files, Core Collection, MHL, AMP. Zanuck wanted Darnell's character to be "California-Spanish" due to the fact she was "part Indian" and to make her character more interesting. See "Memorandum from Darryl Zanuck to Casey Robinson and Robert Wise," February 25, 1950, 4, *Two Flags West*, Twentieth Century Fox Collection, CAL, USC.

129. "Production Notes," 3, File *Fort Dobbs*, Box 652, Warner Bros. Collection, CAL, USC.

130. Dr. Cecil Meares, interview by author, September 27, 2001, Oklahoma City, Oklahoma.

131. Meares interview.

132. Louis Andrade (Luiseño), interview by author, August 20, 2004, Oxnard, California.

133. "Press Releases," *Comanche Territory*, File 11825, Box 422, Universal-International Collection, CAL, USC.

134. "Press Releases," *Smoke Signal*, File 17805, Box 580, Universal-International Collection, CAL, USC.

135. "Press Releases," *Comanche Territory*, File 11825, Box 422, Universal-International Collection, CAL, USC.

136. "Press Release," *Saskatchewan*, File 13110, Box 447, Universal-International Collection, CAL, USC.

137. "Production Notes," *Tomahawk*, File 13182, Box 444, Universal-International Collection, CAL, USC.

138. *Ambush*, MGM, Stills Collection, MHL, AMP. *The Man from Laramie* (Columbia, 1955) was shot in New Mexico as well. Columbia used Santa Fe as a base but also filmed on Pueblo lands. See Fishgall, *Pieces of Time*, 251.

139. See O'Neill, "Navajo Workers and White Man's Ways."

140. *Comanche Territory*, File 11825, Box 422, Universal-International Collection, CAL, USC.

141. Sidney Skolsky column, *Hollywood Citizen-News*, June 30, 1954, Clips, File *Drum Beat*, Box 6516, Warner Bros. Collection, CAL, USC.

142. "Press Releases," *Comanche Territory*, File 11825, Box 422, Universal-International Collection, CAL, USC.

143. See "The Big Movie," in P. Smith, *Everything You Know*.

4. "MORE THAN SKIN DEEP"

1. Bataille and Silet, "Entertaining Anachronism," 40.

2. "Vital Statistics on *Broken Arrow*, Twentieth Century Fox," 2, *Broken Arrow* Production Files, Core Collection, MHL, AMP.

3. Memmi, *Colonizer and the Colonized*, 151. Earlier he writes, "The colonialist stresses those things which keep him separate, rather than emphasizing that which might contribute to the foundation of a joint community" (137).

Third-grade children interviewed in 1994 agreed that Indians have a certain look: "One male responded, 'they wear paint on their face.' Another female student said, 'they have long hair.' Another student, 'they have tan-like skin.'" Despite the fact that three of the students interviewed identified as American Indian (by raising their hands when asked about their identity), "many students responded that there were no Indians left, that they had all disappeared or died. Other students felt that there were some Indians left though not as many as there use to be. Many thought that their numbers were in the hundreds or thousands." Terronez, "Images of American Indians in Contemporary Popular Film and Television," 34–35.

4. For instance, Ralph Ellison writes, "The role with which they are identified is not, despite its 'blackness,' Negro American (indeed, Negroes are repelled by it); it does not find its popularity among Negroes but among whites; and although it resembles the role of the clown familiar to Negro variety-house audiences, it derives not from the Negro but from the Anglo-Saxon branch of American folklore. In other words, this 'darky entertainer' is white." Ellison, *Collected Essays of Ralph Ellison*, 101. Like Albert Memmi and others, Ellison also sees the power of the image as being so great that it far outweighs the human standing behind it: "The racial identity of the performer was unimportant, the mask was the thing (the 'thing' in more ways than one), and its function was to veil the humanity of Negroes thus reduced to a sign, and to repress the white audience's awareness of its moral identification with its own acts and with the human ambiguities pushed behind the mask" (103).

5. Michael Rogin sees the emphasis on the magic of transformation as "the deepest mystification of all, for it attributes the ability to change identity to individual construction of the self." Rogin, *Blackface, White Noise*, 183.

6. According to Khalil Muhammad, "For white Americans of every ideological stripe—from radical southern racists to northern progressives—African American criminality became one of the most widely accepted bases for justifying prejudicial thinking, discriminatory treatment, and/or acceptance of racial violence as an instrument of public safety." Muhammad, *Condemnation of Blackness*, 4.

7. *Colorado Territory* Stills, Production Files, Core Collection, MHL, AMP.

8. On whiteness and purity in film and the tension between the actor and the roles actors play, see Lott, "Whiteness of Film Noir," 87, 99.

9. "Discouraging Note to Manufacturers of Skin Whitener—Mebbe White Is More Than Skin Deep!," *Los Angeles Tribune*, November 20, 1948, Clips, File Production, *Colorado Territory*, Box 685, Warner Bros. Collection, CAL, USC (emphasis added). Almost the same article appeared in a Boston newspaper: "Jinny Puzzles Film Folk," *Boston Post*, December 6, 1948.

10. "Campaign Ideas" and Lowell Benedict to Sam Israel, March 24, 1952, *The Battle at Apache Pass*, both in File 15937, Box 532, Universal-International Collection, CAL, USC.

11. "Campaign Ideas," *Walk the Proud Land*, File 14359, Box 510, Universal-International Collection, CAL, USC. They also hoped to work the non-Native actor Mara Corday's role in *Raw Edge* (1956) into the article to connect this with the non-Native actor Anne Bancroft's role as Tianay in *Walk the Proud Land*.

12. "Bronx Indian," *Parade*, April 6, 1952, 20, clipping on *The Battle at Apache Pass*, File 15958, Box 539, Universal-International Collection, CAL, USC.

13. See "Stills," *White Feather*, Box FX-ST-2546, Collection 012, Twentieth Century Fox Film Corp., SC-YRL, UCLA.

14. I address only documented uses of makeup for this study. Although I could visually determine the use of makeup in films not mentioned, I have decided to rely on the studio records. This limits my examples to the studios whose records are accessible and favors the 1950s.

15. "Inter-Office Communication from Edward Salven to Mr. Westmore," File Production Records, *Unconquered*, File 2, November 8, 1946, Paramount Collection, MHL, AMP.

16. Stills, File *The Half-Breed*, RKO Collection, MHL, AMP.

17. *The Charge at Feather River*, Stills Collection, Warner Bros. Collection, CAL, USC.

18. *Arrowhead*, Stills Collection; and "Production Budget," *Arrowhead*, Production Records, both in Paramount Collection, MHL, AMP.

19. *Variety*, June 19, 1953, Clips, *Hondo*, File Production, Box 667, Warner Bros. Collection, CAL, USC. Paramount hired stunt performers to play Indians in *Thunder in the Sun* (1959) as well. See "Production Records," *Thunder in the Sun*, File 2, Paramount Collection, MHL, AMP. That same year white actors were "smeared with brown make-up" and "dressed in long brown underwear and skullcaps to which ordinary chicken feathers were attached!" for *Captain John Smith and Pocahontas* (United Artists, 1953). Spears, *Hollywood*, 365–66. Jack Spears has no citation for his claim, but it is possible because some of them can be seen to be wearing tattered chicken feathers. However, there are others wearing feathers in better condition and that at least simulate eagle feathers.

20. Stills, *White Feather*, Box FX-ST-2546, Collection 012, Twentieth Century Fox Film Corp., SC-YRL, UCLA.

21. Stills, *Deerslayer*, Box FX-ST-3531, Collection 012, Twentieth Century Fox Film Corp., SC-YRL, UCLA.

22. In the 1920s, actors and extras were sprayed with a product called "bolomania" to create the darker look. Jim Rush and Edna Miller, interview, March 1, 1972, in "The Western in the 1920s," loose-leaf collection, 1975, 280, Special Collections, LBML, AFI. On makeup and American women, see Peiss, *Hope in a Jar*.

23. Ray Rennahan, interview by Charles Higham, June 1970, 41, 42, 76, in File OH-11, Special Collections, LBML, AFI. It is possible that in the early westerns, women

appearing on the screen had to do their own makeup. See "Interview with Ann Little," 221, in "The Western in the 1920s," Special Collections, LBML, AFI. See also Roth, "Looking at Shirley, the Ultimate Norm."

24. Notes from Sherry Shourds's call from Kanab, Utah, Interoffice Communication, June 9, 1951, File *Bugles in the Afternoon*, Box 374, Warner Bros. Collection, CAL, USC.

25. "Production Notes," 3, File *Bugles in the Afternoon*, Production, Miscellaneous, Box 648, Warner Bros. Collection, CAL, USC.

26. Sherry Shourds from Kanab, phone call, Interoffice Communication, June 6, 1951, June 7, 1951, File *Bugles in the Afternoon*, Box 374, Warner Bros. Collection, CAL, USC.

27. See Stills, *Pony Soldier*, Box FX-ST-4034, Collection 012, Twentieth Century Fox Film Corp., SC-YRL, UCLA. Some of those hired to play Indians for *Pony Soldier* were Anthony Earl Numkena, Adeline de Watt Reynolds, Stuart Randall, Muriel Landers, Frank de Kova, Grady Galloway, Nipo T. Strongheart, Carlow Loya, Anthony Numkena Sr., John War Eagle, Chief Bright Fire, and Richard Thunder-Sky. Nash and Ross, *Motion Picture Guide*, 2428.

28. "Production Notes," *Pillars of the Sky*, File 12524, Box 423, Universal-International Collection, CAL, USC.

29. David Selznick to Charles Glett (Selznick's studio manager) and Argyle Nelson (Selznick's production manager), October 29, 1945, in Behlmer, *Memo from David O. Selznick*, 366.

30. Stills Collection, *Drum Beat*, Warner Bros. Collection, CAL, USC.

31. "Press Releases," *Taza, Son of Cochise*, File 13184, Box 444, Universal-International Collection, CAL, USC. Audience members were critical of the makeup jobs. In their preview comments, some offered criticism such as, "In a lot of scenes the makeup job was awful," or, "Makeup was lousy." One said, "Anything with Rock Hudson I like," but another felt "Hudson makes a lousy Indian." Others lauded the makeup artists' work: "Very fine makeup artist—particularly in the instances of Oona, Taza, and Grey Eagle." Comments quoted in Richard Cahoon to Executives, Interoffice Communication, November 11, 1953, *Taza, Son of Cochise*, File 12931, Box 436, Universal-International Collection, CAL, USC.

32. "Pressbook," *Chief Crazy Horse*, File 12356, Box 414, Universal-International Collection, CAL, USC.

33. *Chief Crazy Horse*, File 12270, Box 421, Universal-International Collection, CAL, USC.

34. "Summary of Production Budget," August 9, 1955, *Pillars of the Sky*, File 9930, Box 303, Universal-International Collection, CAL, USC.

35. "Campaign Ideas" and Benedict to Israel, March 24, 1952, *The Battle at Apache Pass*, both in File 15937, Box 532, Universal-International Collection, CAL, USC.

36. Stills Collection, *The Charge at Feather River*, Warner Bros. Collection, CAL, USC.

37. Stills Collection, *The Far Horizons*, Paramount Collection, MHL, AMP; Stills, *White Feather*, Box FX-ST-2546, Collection 012, Twentieth Century Fox Film Corp., SC-YRL, UCLA; *Broken Arrow*, Box FX-ST-2364, Twentieth Century Fox Film Corp., SC-YRL, UCLA. Universal purchased forty Indian wigs for *Apache Drums*, but it is unknown whether the extras playing Indians were Indian or non-Indian. See "Summary of Production Budget," August 10, 1950, *Apache Drums*, File 8298, Box 207, Universal-International Collection, CAL, USC.

38. "Jean Burt Reilly, Motion Picture Hair Stylist," interview by Elizabeth I. Dixon, 1962, oral history transcript, 30, Center for Oral History Research, Special Collections, URL, UCLA.

39. "Jean Burt Reilly, Motion Picture Hair Stylist," oral history transcript, 30.

40. See "Production Notes," 4, File *They Died*, Box 682, Warner Bros. Collection, CAL, USC.

41. "Jean Burt Reilly, Motion Picture Hair Stylist," oral history transcript, 29–30, 36.

42. See Stills, *Deerslayer*, Box FX-ST-3531, Collection 012, Twentieth Century Fox Film Corp., SC-YRL, UCLA.

43. See Stills, *Pony Soldier*, Box FX-ST-4034, Collection 012, Twentieth Century Fox Film Corp., SC-YRL, UCLA.

44. Stills Collection and "Production Budget," *Arrowhead*, both in Production Records, Paramount Collection, MHL, AMP. Both Indian and non-Indian actors on this film were probably painted and wigged, as there are purchases of many wigs and a large quantity of body makeup listed in the production budget.

45. Jean Burt Reilly described falls in great detail: "Falls come in different sizes. There is the neck-fall, which fits just at the neckline. The person's hair is combed over it, and with the falls underneath, it makes the hair appear longer. There is the half-fall which comes to a halfway point on the back of the head, and that also gives length. And then we have what we call a three-quarter fall. If the player has short hair, high on his head, which then and now many women do have, we can use a three-quarter fall. It comes up to the top of the head, and we then comb their own hair back over it. It looks like they have long hair, as long as need be. We also have what we call a five-eighths fall, which comes over the head almost to the hairline. We only use the hairline over that." "Jean Burt Reilly, Motion Picture Hair Stylist," oral history transcript, 92–93.

46. Stills Collection, *Drum Beat*, Warner Bros. Collection, CAL, USC.

47. "Summary of Production Budget," August 9, 1955, *Pillars of the Sky*, File 9930, Box 303, Universal-International Collection, CAL, USC.

48. "Summary of Production Budget," June 10, 1954, *Chief Crazy Horse*, File 6031, Box 168, Universal-International Collection, CAL, USC.

49. "Press Releases," *Taza, Son of Cochise*, File 13184, Box 444, Universal-International Collection, CAL, USC. The Indian actors Charles Stevens, Chief Thundercloud, and Chief Yowlachie probably also appeared in this film along with Indian extras. See *The Half-Breed*, RKO, Stills Collection, MHL, AMP. On Rush, see Gilbert Kurland to Robert A. Palmer, Interoffice Memo, *Taza, Son of Cochise*, File 14708, Box 503, Universal-International Collection, CAL, USC.

50. "Warner Bros. Studio; Burbank, Calif.," HO 9-1251; and "Production Notes on *Jim Thorpe, All American*," 4, both in Warner Bros. Collection, CAL, USC.

51. "Press Releases," *Drums across the River*, File 12027, Box 432, Universal-International Collection, CAL, USC. See also Cohan, *Masked Men*, 150–51.

52. See Stills, *White Feather*, Box FX-ST-2546, Collection 012, Twentieth Century Fox Film Corp., SC-YRL, UCLA.

53. On the question of Indian body hair, see Chris Spotted Eagle's fascinating short film *Do Indians Shave?* (1972), https://www.youtube.com/watch?v=yBx7mele67g.

54. "Press Releases," *Taza, Son of Cochise*, File 13184, Box 444, Universal-International Collection, CAL, USC. On Rush, see Gilbert Kurland to Robert A. Palmer, Interoffice Memo, *Taza, Son of Cochise*, File 14708, Box 503, Universal-International Collection, CAL, USC.

55. "Press Releases," *Taza, Son of Cochise*, File 13184, Box 444, Universal-International Collection, CAL, USC.

56. "Press Release," *The Stand at Apache River*, File 13120, Box 447, Universal-International Collection, CAL, USC. Likewise, Ralph Moody was fitted with contact lenses the day he left for the Wyoming location of *The Far Horizons* (Paramount, 1955), but it is unclear whether this was to darken his eyes; see "Work Authorization," July 5, 1954, *The Far Horizons*, Production Records, File 2, Paramount Collection, MHL, AMP.

57. "Vital Statistics on *Broken Arrow*, Twentieth Century Fox," 2, *Broken Arrow* Production Files, Core Collection, MHL, AMP. One writer remarked upon how Paget looked extremely Caucasian in the film and moved like a swimsuit model. See Quirk, *James Stewart*, 202.

58. *Broken Arrow*, Box FX-ST-2364, Twentieth Century Fox Film Corp., SC-YRL, UCLA.

59. "'Broken Lance,' Memorandum on Writer's Working Script of 7/9/53, From Zanuck to Sol Siegel and Richard Murphy (D. Z. dictated to Sally Black)," August 21, 1953, 6, *Broken Lance*, Box FX-PRS-694, Produced Scripts, Collection 010, Twentieth Century Fox Film Corp., SC-YRL, UCLA.

60. See Stills, *White Feather*, Box FX-ST-2546, Collection 012, Twentieth Century Fox Film Corp., SC-YRL, UCLA.

61. See Stills, *Seven Cities of Gold*, Box FX-ST-4103, Collection 012, Twentieth Century Fox Film Corp., SC-YRL, UCLA.

62. "Press Releases," *Column South*, File 13130, Box 447; "Press Releases," *Winchester '73*, File 11952, Box 424, both in Universal-International Collection, CAL, USC.

63. See Stills, *Pony Soldier*, Box FX-ST-4034, Collection 012, Twentieth Century Fox Film Corp., SC-YRL, UCLA.

64. *Saskatchewan*, File 06809, Box 130, Universal-International Collection, CAL, USC.

65. Susan Bordo writes, "Moreover, as the body itself is dominantly imagined within the West as belonging to the 'nature' side of a nature/culture duality, the more body one has had, the more uncultured and uncivilized one has been expected to be." Bordo, *Unbearable Weight*, 195.

66. See Bill Cappello, "Noble Johnson, Part II," *Classic Images*, February 1992, 50, in Biography Files, MHL, AMP.

67. "*Broken Lance*, Memorandum on Writer's Working Script of 7/9/53, from Zanuck to Sol Siegel and Richard Murphy (D. Z. dictated to Sally Black)," August 21, 1953, 6.

68. See Stills, Burt Lancaster Biography Files, Core Collection, MHL, AMP. Both biographical sketches prepared by Universal list Lancaster's nationality as "American." "Universal Studios, Burt Lancaster—Biography, April 25, 1946," "Universal-International, Burt Lancaster—Biography, March 15, 1947," 3, both in Biography Files, Core Collection, MHL, AMP. On his English ancestry, see "Paramount Studios, Biography, Burt Lancaster," n.d., Biography Files, Core Collection, MHL, AMP.

69. Lynn Bowers, "Jim Thorpe," *Los Angeles Examiner*, August 31, 1951, in Production Files, Core Collection, MHL, AMP.

70. Leonard M. Cripps to Ellingwood Kay, April 19, 1949, File *Thorpe*, Box 1761, Warner Bros. Collection, CAL, USC.

71. "(Notes on Jim Thorpe Story); copied April 8, 1949; Bright Path by Douglas Morrow," 2, Warner Bros. Collection, CAL, USC.

72. Higham, *Cecil B. DeMille*, 279–80, 283.

73. As western scholar Lee Clark Mitchell writes, "With bodies as developed but with reputations still to be built, Rock Hudson and Jeff Chandler appeared frequently in Westerns as bare-chested braves, allowing the camera to focus on hairless torsoes and muscular arms." Mitchell, *Westerns*, 157.

74. See Stills, *The Deerslayer*, Box FX-ST-3531, Collection 012, Twentieth Century Fox Film Corp., SC-YRL, UCLA.

75. Ray Rennahan, interview by Charles Higham, June 1970, transcript, 187, File OH-11, Special Collections, LBML, AFI.

76. One scholar has claimed that Indian women characters were made to look "more Caucasian-looking" than Indian men in movies. Leuthold, "Native American Responses to the Western," 176. I did not find this to be true.

77. The buckskin worn by Susan Cabot in *Tomahawk* had to be shipped by air mail from Western Costume Company to the South Dakota location to protect the

garment and ensure that it was of high quality. See Frank McFadden to Ben Katz, January 15, 1951, *Tomahawk*, File 12156, Box 431, Universal-International Collection, CAL, USC.

78. Stills Collection, *The Charge at Feather River*, Warner Bros. Collection, CAL, USC.

79. See Behlmer, *Memo from David O. Selznick*; Thomson, *Showman*.

80. Significant westerns featuring women bathing include *Unconquered*, *The Prairie*, *Apache Woman*, *Canyon Passage*, and *Duel in the Sun*. Lee Garmes shot the nude bathing scene in *Duel in the Sun*, and King Vidor claimed a representative of the Production Code Administration visited the set during the shooting of the dance and nude scene to make sure it complied with the so-called Hays Code rules. See "Filming of *Duel in the Sun*: Recollections of Ray Rennahan, Lee Garmes, and King Vidor," transcript of interview by James Ursini, 1969, 17, 23, 25, Center for Oral History Research, Special Collections, URL, UCLA.

81. Geoffrey M. Shurlock to Dore Schary, June 2, 1955, April 5, 1955, *The Last Hunt*, MPA Files, Paramount Collection, MHL, AMP.

82. On images of Indian women in film and Indian actresses, see Leuthold, "Native American Responses to the Western."

83. See Stills, *Flaming Star*, Box FX-ST-2520, Collection 012, Twentieth Century Fox Film Corp., SC-YRL, UCLA.

5. "A BIT THICK"

1. Dr. Cecil Meares, interview by author, September 27, 2001, Oklahoma City, Oklahoma.

2. Rare examples of Indians being considered dark enough for the camera come from *The Paleface* (Paramount, 1948) and *Ambush* (MGM, 1950). A Paramount representative claimed the studio saved $3,200 in makeup charges by using "dark skinned extra players." William Cowitt to R. L. Johnston and Frank Caffey, Interoffice Communication, October 3, 1947, *The Paleface*, File 3, Paramount Collection, MHL, AMP.

   Although Jack Dawn had painted many Indian extras to make them into Movie Indians, for the *Ambush* production MGM hired Navajos, and therefore the "job was simplified by the fact that real Indians in New Mexico were used mostly." This is the only example I found of a film company considering Diné to be dark enough for the camera without makeup. *Ambush*, Production Notes, Core Collection, MHL, AMP. The Apache actor Charles Stevens was hired to play an Indian for this film as well. See *Ambush*, MGM, Stills Collection, MHL, AMP.

   As for the scholar Jacob Floyd, his particular interest is in how Native men used the publicity world to their own advantage, but he also spells out its functions quite carefully. See Floyd, "Negotiating Publicity and Persona."

3. Lester D. Friedman, on the other hand, claims that "this notion that underneath surface differences, Jews, Catholics, and Protestants (and by extension other minority-group members) all think alike permeates [the film *Gentleman's Agreement*]. It also represents the dominant ideology of the commercial movie industry. In fact, even the overt physical characteristics between ethnic minorities are downplayed." Friedman, "Celluloid Palimpsests," 24.

4. This eclipse is similar to the phenomenon of Shamu at SeaWorld. Susan G. Davis found that "the whale is simultaneously a transcendental being and a souvenir. Indeed, it is a question of whether the living animal or the mass image has a greater reality." S. Davis, *Spectacular Nature*, 223.

5. On the idea of blackface as the simultaneous visibility of both absence and presence in a different cultural form, see Lhamon, *Raising Cain*, 136–40.

6. "Press Releases," File 13184, Box 444, Universal-International Collection, CAL, USC.

7. "Requisition for Extra [illegible]," July 3, 1951, File *Bugles in the Afternoon*, Box 374, Warner Bros. Collection, CAL, USC.

8. "Production Budget," July 16, 1957, 18, File *Fort Dobbs* 1444, Box 839, Warner Bros. Collection, CAL, USC. Nick Roddick categorizes filmmaking as resembling a factory system: "In between the distillation from and the release into reality came Burbanking. Warners' studio system was a factory process, and, like any factory system, it processed raw material into product. . . . The process of the studio/factory was thus film production and the representation of reality." Roddick, *New Deal in Entertainment*, 253.

9. Ben Book, "Hollywood Film Shop," April 22, 1951, 1–2, File *Distant Drums*, Production, Wire Stories, Box 651, Warner Bros. Collection, CAL, USC.

10. "Press Releases," *Winchester '73*, File 11952, Box 424, Universal-International Collection, CAL, USC.

11. *Comanche Territory*, File 10607, Box 340; and File 08084, Box 207, both in Universal-International Collection, CAL, USC.

12. Harrison Carrol, "Indian Battle Deadly on Film Sound Stage," *Los Angeles Herald*, August 19, 1950, File *Only the Valiant* #365, Box 1490b, Warner Bros. Collection, CAL, USC.

13. See Hearne, *Native Recognition*, 80–81; Bhabha, *Location of Culture*; Fanon, *Black Skin, White Masks*; Babcock, "Pueblo Cultural Bodies"; Babcock, "First Families"; and Doane, "The Close-Up."

14. James F. Denton, "The Red Man Plays Indian," *Collier's*, March 18, 1944, 19.

15. *Buffalo Bill*, Box FX-ST-35, Collection 012, Twentieth Century Fox Film Corp., SC-YRL, UCLA.

16. Richard White writes, "Americans had to transform conquerors into victims." R. White, "Frederick Jackson Turner and Buffalo Bill," 27.

17. Stills and "Production Budget," Production Records, *Arrowhead*, both in Paramount Collection, MHL, AMP. For example, when Universal hired Diné for *Winchester '73*, there is evidence that the studio rented sixty "Indian" wigs for the production. "Production Budget," February 11, 1950, *Winchester '73*, File 25813, Box 814, Universal-International Collection, CAL, USC.

18. "Production Budget," *Column South*, File 09871, Box 288, Universal-International Collection, CAL, USC.

19. "Production Notes," 4, File *Fort Dobbs*, Box 652, Warner Bros. Collection, CAL, USC. Among the men hired by Warner Bros. were Billy Hasky, Sammy Nochedench, Kee Wilson, John Johnson, Edwin Drye, John Finley, Norman Butler, and Gilbert Yazzi. See Kenneth Cox, Interoffice Communication, File *Fort Dobbs* #1444, Box 839, Warner Bros. Collection, CAL, USC. There are photos of Indian extras on *Fort Dobbs* who appear to be Indian; they may be the men listed here. See *Fort Dobbs* Stills Collection, Warner Bros. Collection, CAL, USC.

20. *Comanche Territory*, File 10607, Box 340; and File 08084, Box 207, both in Universal-International Collection, CAL, USC.

21. "Summary of Production Budget," June 21, 1954, *Smoke Signal*, File 11531, Box 406; and File 17805, Box 580, both in Universal-International Collection, CAL, USC.

22. Harry Brand, "Vital Statistics on Zane Grey's *Western Union*," 3, *Western Union* Production Files, Core Collection, MHL, AMP. John Collier had concerns about the representation of Indians in *Western Union*. According to Twentieth Century Fox, "Washington authorities sent word back that they would be glad to co-operate with studios filming historical stories such as *Western Union* but frowned on blood-and-thunder type where Indian was made scapegoat." "Press Release," *Western Union*, Production Files, Core Collection, MHL, AMP.

23. The possible binary of thin Indian men and muscular white men could be compared with the Victorian binary of indulgent men and thin women. According to Bordo, a bourgeois man, in striving for the appearance of aristocracy, could acquire a wife "who looked like [an aristocrat], a wife whose non-robust beauty and delicate appetite signified her lack of participation in the taxing public sphere." Bordo, *Unbearable Weight*, 117. See also the various chapters in Bordo's *Unbearable Weight*: "Anorexia Nervosa: Psychopathology as the Crystallization of Culture," 139–64, "The Body and the Reproduction of Femininity," 165–84, and "Reading the Slender Body," 185–214.

24. "Press Releases," *Comanche Territory*, File 11825, Box 422, Universal-International Collection, CAL, USC. On another film set, even though meals for the Indian and white actors cost the same, they were tabulated separately. *Saskatchewan*, File 06809, Box 130, Universal-International Collection, CAL, USC.

25. News item by Johnson, *News* (unidentified location), August 4, 1950, clipping in File *Only the Valiant* #365, Box 1490b, Warner Bros. Collection, CAL, USC.

26. *The Battle at Apache Pass*, File 07053, Box 129; and File 11849, Box 399; "Campaign Ideas," *The Battle at Apache Pass*, File 15937, Box 532, all in Universal-International Collection, CAL, USC.

27. "Campaign Ideas," *Pillars of the Sky*, File 12524, Box 423, Universal-International Collection, CAL, USC.

28. See P. Deloria, *Indians in Unexpected Places*, 138, 141, 144, 146.

29. "Warner Bros. Production Notes," 2–3, *Only the Valiant* Production Files, Core Collection, MHL, AMP. This situation was also reported in the *Hollywood Citizen*, September 9, 1950, File *Only the Valiant* #365, Box 1490b, Warner Bros. Collection, CAL, USC. Perhaps ironically, white men at the turn of the century created parallel definitions of masculinity and civilization: "Masculinity was the achievement of a perfect man, just as civilization was the achievement of a perfect race." Bederman, *Manliness and Civilization*, 27.

30. "Press Releases," File 13184, Box 444, Universal-International Collection, CAL, USC.

31. As a result, the studio rented only seven wigs for the production. "Press Release," *Smoke Signal*, File 17805, Box 580; and "Summary of Production Budget," May 24, 1954, File 25059, Box 746, both in Universal-International Collection, CAL, USC.

32. Denton, "Red Man Plays Indian," 19. Bataille and Silet criticize Denton: "Denton's essay reveals a total lack of historical perspective in portraying Indians on the screen as well as echoing the uncritical acceptance of traditional Indian stereotyping." Bataille and Silet, "Entertaining Anachronism," 42.

33. *Buffalo Bill*, Box FX-ST-35, Collection 012, Twentieth Century Fox Film Corp., SC-YRL, UCLA.

34. "Hurry-Up Hairdo Gives Diné the Utes' Look," in "Paramount Press Sheets, Releases Season 1951–52," Group A-11, *Flaming Feather*, Paramount Collection, MHL, AMP. In fact, Utes traditionally wear their hair down with bangs, and the Diné wear their hair up. This Paramount article's author called Lakotas "shaggy-headed" and compared them with Utes, whose hair was "neatly barbered with bangs." In addition to expressing their concern about getting the accurate Ute look, the Navajo men did not want to wear their hair down because it would "propitiate the rain gods," the release stated. In any case, the story demonstrates the ability of the Diné to differentiate themselves from Utes and the studio's inability to do so. On Utes in the twentieth century, see R. Young, *Ute Indians of Colorado in the Twentieth Century*.

The Diné on the set of *Column South* (Universal, 1953) had not previously had access to vaccinations, so because they would be in proximity to Audie Murphy, the studio had the Diné extras vaccinated so as to protect Murphy. The makeup artists had to spend extra time covering the vaccination marks, but it is unclear whether the extras were darkened all over with makeup. See "Press Releases," *Column South*, File 13130, Box 447, Universal-International Collection, CAL, USC. The Diné on the *Winchester '73* set also had their vaccination marks covered with makeup. See *Winchester '73*, File 11952, Box 424, Universal-International Collection, CAL, USC.

35. See "Jean Burt Reilly, Motion Picture Hair Stylist," interview by Elizabeth I. Dixon, 1962, oral history transcript, 96, Center for Oral History Research, Special Collections, URL, UCLA.

36. Robert Collins, "The Two Lives of Jonas Applegarth," *Maclean's Magazine*, November 1, 1954, 54, Production, Clips, File *Battle Cry*, Box 646, Warner Bros. Collection, CAL, USC.

37. "Production Notes," 4, in File *They Died with Their Boots On*, Box 682, CAL, USC.

38. See Stills, *Two Flags West*, Box FX-ST-2373, Collection 012, Twentieth Century Fox Film Corp., SC-YRL, UCLA.

39. *Canadian Pacific* Production Files, 4, Core Collection, MHL, AMP. A further example of applying "war paint" comes from RKO, which inexplicably decided to try and save money by giving artistic freedom to Pueblos on the set of *Valley of the Sun* (1942). While filming in New Mexico, RKO hired Pueblos to play Apaches. Instead of having makeup artists do the work, the Pueblo extras painted each other with geometric designs on their chests and faces for the film. See Stills, *Valley of the Sun* Production Files, RKO Collection, MHL, AMP.

40. "Twentieth Century Fox News," July 10, 1950, *Broken Arrow* Production Notes, Core Collection, MHL, AMP.

41. "Paramount Press Sheets, Releases Season, 1950–51," Group A-10, *Warpath*, Paramount Collection, MHL, AMP. The film's director does not seem to have taken this production too seriously. In a 1970 interview, the interviewer asked, "[Is] *Warpath* of any special interest?" Rennahan answered, "No, that was practically a shoot-up Indian thing; it was a Western picture." Ray Rennahan, interview by Charles Higham, June 1970, transcript, 162, File OH-11, Special Collections, LBML, AFI.

42. "Paramount Press Sheets, Releases Season, 1950–51," Group A-10, *Warpath*, Paramount Collection, MHL, AMP. See also *Warpath*, Stills Collection, MHL, AMP. Donald Deer Nose, Robert Yellowtail, and Bernard Comes Along were among the Crow extras who were painted brown.

43. "Production Notes," 3, File *Jim Thorpe, All American* 745, #8295, Box 1014, Warner Bros. Collection, CAL, USC.

44. *Saskatchewan*, File 06809, Box 130, Universal-International Collection, CAL, USC.

45. "Press Releases," *Saskatchewan*; and Alyce Canfield, "Canada Goes Hollywood," *Movieland*, December 1953, 74, both in File 13110, Box 447, Universal-International Collection, CAL, USC.

46. "Production Notes," 4, File *They Died with Their Boots On*, Box 682, Warner Bros. Collection, CAL, USC.

47. *Warpath*, Stills Collection, MHL, AMP.

48. "Summary of Production Budget," December 4, 1952, *Stand at Apache River*, File 9820, Box 292, Universal-International Collection, CAL, USC.

49. *Seminole*, File 07581, Box 126, Universal-International Collection, CAL, USC. They purchased scalp locks (twelve at $18 each) and Indian wigs (eighty-five at $26 each). "Summary of Production Budget," May 2, 1952, *Chief Crazy Horse*, File 6031, Box 168, Universal-International Collection, CAL, USC.

50. "Daily Minutes," Committee Meeting, July 7, 1953, 2, *Saskatchewan*, File 18237, Box 397, Universal-International Collection, CAL, USC.

51. *Saskatchewan*, File 06809, Box 130, Universal-International Collection, CAL, USC.

52. *Pillars of the Sky*, File 12524, Box 423, Universal-International Collection, CAL, USC; Fred Kennedy, "Alberta Indian Scores Another Movie Success," *Calgary Herald*, July 20, 1954, 10, Warner Bros. Collection, CAL, USC.

53. "Press Releases," File 13110, Box 447, Universal-International Collection, CAL, USC. Wally Waits of the Muskogee Public Library suggested in a brief conversation that it was the duty of the administrative assistant to the BIA area director to locate Indians to appear in *Battle Cry*. Waits also informed me that someone at the Creek Nation remembers that a Creek man whose pen name is Bear Heart appeared in the movie. I have written him through his publisher. Waits was also told that George Proctor of Muskogee and JoAnn Landrum of Mustang, Oklahoma, were in the movie as well.

54. "Paramount Press Sheets, Releases Season 1952–53," Group A-12, *The Savage*, Paramount Collection, MHL, AMP.

55. "Production Notes," 2, File *Jim Thorpe, All American* 745, #8295, Box 1014, Warner Bros. Collection, CAL, USC. These extras were only used for about one week; see "Daily Production and Progress Reports," File *Jim Thorpe, All American* 745, Box 1489, Warner Bros. Collection, CAL, USC.

56. Darryl Zanuck, Memorandum, February 6, 1956, 5–6, Records of the Legal Department, File *The Last Wagon*, Box FX-PRS-575, Collection 095, Twentieth Century Fox Film Corp., SC-YRL, UCLA.

57. See Frank H. Ferguson to Mr. James Ruman, re: "The Last Wagon"—Letter Agreement with Tribal Council, Interoffice Correspondence, Records of the Legal Department, File *The Last Wagon*, Box FX-LR-1370, Collection 095, Twentieth Century Fox Film Corp., SC-YRL, UCLA.

58. The studio also created a tour for *Tomahawk*, but there are no records documenting the tour.

59. Directors and producers may have had control over advertising. At least one producer, David Selznick, objected to the stunts being planned by publicity for *Duel in the Sun* (1947). See David Selznick to Paul McNamara of Vanguard Films, May 2, 1947, in Behlmer, *Memo from David O. Selznick*, 358.

60. "Press Release," April 13, 1950, *Comanche Territory*, File 13995, Box 476, Universal-International Collection, CAL, USC. In a letter from Cliff Cane to David (no surname), Cane asks for eight Indians and an agent. See Cliff Cane to David, April 10, 1950, File 15361, Box 486, Universal-International Collection, CAL, USC.

61. Herman Kass to Charles Simonelli, May 12, 1950, *Comanche Territory*, File 13995, Box 476, Universal-International Collection, CAL, USC. John Horton was in charge of the tour, and he was Simonelli's contact. See Simonelli to John Horton, April 10, 1950, *Comanche Territory*, Box 476, File 13995, Universal-International Collection, CAL, USC.

62. Full-page ad, *New York Herald Tribune*, April 16, 1950, 11.

63. Herzoff to Simonelli, March 12, 1952, *Battle at Apache Pass*, File 15937, Box 532, Universal-International Collection, CAL, USC.

64. Herzoff to Simonelli, February 26, 1952, 2, *Battle at Apache Pass*, File 15937, Box 532, Universal-International Collection, CAL, USC.

65. Herman Kass to Jesse Campbell, March 25, 1952, *Battle at Apache Pass*, File 12074, Box 433, Universal-International Collection, CAL, USC.

66. Herzoff to Marion Pecht, Interoffice Communication, February 28, 1952, *Battle at Apache Pass*, File 12074, Box 433, Universal-International Collection, CAL, USC.

67. Herzoff to David Lipton, Interoffice Communication, February 13, 1952, *Battle at Apache Pass*, File 12074, Box 433, Universal-International Collection, CAL, USC.

68. Herzoff to Marion Pecht, Interoffice Communication, March 24, 1952, *Battle at Apache Pass*, File 12074, Box 433, Universal-International Collection, CAL, USC.

69. Herzoff to Pecht, Interoffice Communication, March 24, 1952.

70. Herzoff to Simonelli, March 12, 1952, *Battle at Apache Pass*, File 12074, Box 433; Herzoff to Marion Pecht, Interoffice Communication, March 18, 1952, *Battle at Apache Pass*, File 15937, Box 532; Herzoff to Simonelli, February 29, 1952, *Battle at Apache Pass*, File 15937, Box 532, all in Universal-International Collection, CAL, USC.

71. Herzoff to Simonelli, February 26, 1952, 1–2, *Battle at Apache Pass*, File 15937, Box 532, Universal-International Collection, CAL, USC.

72. Herzoff to Marion Pecht (NY), Interoffice Communication, March 18, 1952, *Battle at Apache Pass*, File 12074, Box 433, Universal-International Collection, CAL, USC.

73. Archie Herzoff to Jerry Evans, March 25, 1952, *Battle at Apache Pass*; Invoice, Southwestern Greyhound Lines, June 6, 1952, both in File 12074, Box 433, Universal-International Collection, CAL, USC.

74. Like the Standing Rock Lakotas who worked in *Buffalo Bill* (1944), the men had personal difficulties that the studio representatives were unable or unwilling to mediate. When Kenoi and Geronimo had a disagreement, Herzoff felt he and Kass did not need to deal with their contentions. Herzoff assured Hardin that the men would "bend to a conciliatory overture once they are all home again." See Herzoff to Lonnie Hardin, April 11, 1952, *Battle at Apache Pass*, File 12074, Box 433, Universal-International Collection, CAL, USC; Kass to Herzoff, April 10, 1952. Meanwhile, Herzoff assured Kass that Hardin was especially able at handling Indians due to his patience and understanding. In essence, Herzoff and Kass did nothing to ameliorate the situation. See Herzoff to Kass, April 11, 1952, *Battle at Apache Pass*, File 12074, Box 433, Universal-International Collection, CAL, USC.

75. "Campaign Ideas," *Battle at Apache Pass*, File 15937, Box 532, Universal-International Collection, CAL, USC.

76. Archie Herzoff to Charles Simonelli, Interoffice Communication, January 5, 1953, *Seminole*, File 11910, Box 426, Universal-International Collection, CAL, USC.

77. Jerry Evans to P. Gerard, Memorandum, January 20, 1953, *Seminole*, File 11910, Box 426; Charles Simonelli to Archie Herzoff, Memorandum, January 7, 1953, *Seminole*, File 12909, Box 436, both in Universal-International Collection, CAL, USC.

78. "Seminole Indian Tribe Downstate Illinois Itinerary," March 18, 1953; "Press Release"; "Exploitation Bulletin," all in *Seminole*, File 12909, Box 436, Universal-International Collection, CAL, USC.

6. "DIG UP A GOOD INDIAN HISTORIAN"

1. "Press Release," 1950, *Broken Arrow*, Twentieth Century Fox Collection, MHL, AMP.

2. Clifford, *Predicament of Culture*; Bendix, *Culture and Value*; Bendix, *In Search of Authenticity*.

3. P. Deloria, *Playing Indian*.

4. There is tremendous interest in reinvigorating Native languages throughout the United States. See James Brooks, "American Indians Trying to Save Languages from Extinction," *New York Times*, April 9, 1998. See also Prats, "Image of the Other."

5. Fishgall, *Pieces of Time*, 208.

6. Hetta George to Seton I. Miller, Interoffice Communication, August 28, 1947, File *Colt .45* 734, #8290, Box 1011, Warner Bros. Collection, CAL, USC.

7. Carl Milliken to Charles Clarke, Interoffice Communication, May 24, 1954, File *Drum Beat* 394, #8507, Box 1012, Warner Bros. Collection, CAL, USC. MGM compiled 126 pages of research notes for *Westward the Women* (1952), a hefty

amount by contemporary standards. See *Westward the Women*, MGM Collection, CAL, USC.

8. Bob Rains to David A. Lipton, Interoffice Communication, September 20, 1951, *Battle at Apache Pass*, File 15958, Box 539, Universal-International Collection, CAL, USC.

9. "Campaign Ideas," *Column South*, File 22133, Box 669, Universal-International Collection, CAL, USC.

10. Quoted in Philip K. Scheuer, "Indian's [*sic*] Culture Captured in Film: 'Broken Arrow' Stars Jimmy Stewart and Apache Cast in Arizona Epic," *Los Angeles Times*, May 21, 1950. Apache women may have taught Debra Paget to weave, but Paget may have just been pictured in such a way that she appears to be learning how to weave. In any case, the Apache women may have lent their work to the studio as props. See *Broken Arrow*, Box FX-ST-2364, Special Collections, Twentieth Century Fox Film Corp., SC-YRL, UCLA.

11. "Twentieth Century Fox News," *Broken Arrow*, Production Notes, Core Collection, MHL, AMP.

12. "Press Releases," *Column South*, File 13130, Box 447, Universal-International Collection, CAL, USC.

13. Simonelli to David Lipton, Memorandum, March 28, 1950, *Comanche Territory*, File 13995, Box 476, Universal-International Collection, CAL, USC.

14. See Frank Ferguson to Roanhorse, February 18, 1953; Roanhorse to Ferguson, March 17, 1953, both in *Broken Arrow*, Box FX-LR-347, Collection 095, Twentieth Century Fox Film Corp., SC-YRL, UCLA.

15. Harrington quoted/paraphrased in Frances C. Richardson to Frank Ferguson, Interoffice Correspondence, February 17, 1953; "References of Symbolism of Arrows of American Indians," all in *Broken Arrow*, Box FX-LR-347, Collection 095, Twentieth Century Fox Film Corp., SC-YRL, UCLA.

16. P. Deloria, *Playing Indian*.

17. Quoted in Richard Cahoon to Executives, Interoffice Communication, November 11, 1953, 10, 11, *Taza, Son of Cochise*, File 12931, Box 436, Universal-International Collection, CAL, USC.

18. Quoted in Cahoon to Executives, Interoffice Communication, November 11, 1953, 10, 11, *Taza, Son of Cochise*.

19. "Stars Build Cabin for Oregon Film: 160 Residents Play Roles of Forefathers in 'Canyon Passage,'" *Los Angeles Times*, November 11, 1945.

20. Owhi was a chief but not the only chief. Strongheart's great uncle was probably Qualchin. Hoxie, *Encyclopedia of North American Indians*, 703.

21. Fisher, "Tinseltown Tyee"; Fisher, "Speaking for the First Americans"; Fisher, "Indian in the Studio."

22. Tom Coffey, "Lancaster's 'Thorpe' Genuine," *Los Angeles Daily Mirror*, August 30, 1951.

23. "Marshall Turns Tricks with Injuns," *Hollywood Reporter*, January 8, 1942.

24. "Valley of the Sun," *Variety*, January 8, 1942; "Valley of the Sun," *Motion Picture Herald*, January 17, 1942. Although reviewers greatly appreciated the "real" Indians, RKO's local advertisement for the film called it "Indian infested." See ad for the Pantages and Hill Street theaters in Los Angeles, California, in *Los Angeles Daily News*, June 21, 1950.

25. "A Romantic Triangle Played against Pioneer Background," *Los Angeles Times*, April 7, 1949. Indians who were "speaking their own language" in the film had Francis McDonald as the on-set interpreter for *Valley*. See Parish, *RKO Gals*, 445.

26. Burnham, *Song of Dewey Beard*, 78.

27. *The Last Hunt*, MGM, Stills Collection, MHL, AMP. Nearly all of the archival records, when referring to Indian men, gave "Chief" as their first name. I drop "Chief" when referring to them, as it is a derogatory unless the men were actually tribally elected leaders. See also Fisher, "Speaking for the First Americans."

28. "Paramount Press Sheets, Releases Season, 1952–53," Group A-12, *The Savage*, Paramount Collection, MHL, AMP.

29. "Production Notes," 3, 4, File *Distant Drums*, Box 651, Warner Bros. Collection, CAL, USC. Cypress was born in about 1857, so his family, or at least his parents, must have survived the Second Seminole War, which began in 1835 and did not end until 1842. As a result, about 3,612 Seminoles were relocated to Indian Territory, and 350 to 500 remained in Florida, mostly near the Big Cypress Swamp, Lake Okeechobee, and throughout the Everglades. Cypress was born in the midst of the Third Seminole War, which lasted from 1855 to 1858. This last war resulted in an expulsion of another 300 Seminoles from Florida. Other wars involving Seminoles, however, were in Oklahoma, not Florida (e.g., the Green Peach War, 1882–83). In 1911, under Executive Order 1379, three reservations were created in Florida: Brighton, Big Cypress, and Dania. The Florida Seminoles were officially organized in 1957. The Miccosukees decided to organize separately and established their own reservation. See J. Wright, *Creeks and Seminoles*, 281–321. See also Sattler, "Seminole."

30. "Preview Comment Cards," Interoffice Communication, August 31, 1950, 34, 36, in File *Tomahawk*, File 13182, Box 444, Universal-International Collection, CAL, USC.

31. Quoted in Cahoon to Executives, Interoffice Communication, November 11, 1953, 10, 11, *Taza, Son of Cochise*.

32. "Preview Comment Cards," Interoffice Communication, October 26, 1954, 8, *Smoke Signal*, File 22736, Box 689, Universal-International Collection, CAL, USC.

33. "Report on Preview Comments," December 29, 1955, *Pillars of the Sky*, File 15669, Box 549, Universal-International Collection, CAL, USC.

34. "Preview Comment Cards," Interoffice Communication, August 31, 1950, 20, 33, *Tomahawk*.

35. Quoted in Cahoon to Executives, Interoffice Communication, November 11, 1953, 10, 11, *Taza, Son of Cochise*.

36. Quoted in Cahoon to Executives, Interoffice Communication, November 11, 1953, 10, 11, *Taza, Son of Cochise*.

37. Quoted in Cahoon to Executives, Interoffice Communication, November 11, 1953, 10, 11, *Taza, Son of Cochise*. I noticed this attitude in reviewers from many movies; *Taza* is simply an example. Another is *Column South*; see previewer comments for that film in File 13631, Box 455, Universal-International Collection, CAL, USC.

38. "Preview Comment Cards," Interoffice Communication, August 31, 1950, 34, 36, *Tomahawk*, Universal-International Collection, CAL, USC.

39. "Production Notes," *Tomahawk*, File 13182, Box 444, Universal-International Collection, CAL, USC.

40. Quoted in "Vital Statistics," 6, *Ticket to Tomahawk*, Production Files, Core Collection, MHL, AMP.

41. According to Leuthold, the mimicking of Movie Indian culture concerned a Blackfeet man during a showing of *War Party* at the Two Rivers Native Film and Video Festival. The man stated, "In our tribe, we have certain customs now that actually have been transformed by film. . . . We're doing stuff out of film now: face painting, for instance. Youths . . . are painting their faces, not in the traditional way we did that, by clan, by family, by color, but they're doing it out of what they see in the damn movies." The man's name is not given. The film was shown at the Two Rivers Native Film and Video Festival. Leuthold, "Native American Responses to the Western," 163–64.

42. "Press Release," July 10, 1950, *Broken Arrow*, Box FX-LR-347, Collection 095, Twentieth Century Fox Film Corp., SC-YRL, UCLA.

43. Production Notes, 5, File *Sergeant Rutledge*, Box 660, Warner Bros. Collection, CAL, USC.

44. Production Notes, 4, File *Drum Beat*, Box 6516, Warner Bros. Collection, CAL, USC.

45. "Paramount Press Sheets, Releases Season 1950–51," Group A-10, *Warpath*, Paramount Collection, MHL, AMP; *Warpath*, Stills Collection, MHL, AMP.

46. "Press Releases," *The Savage*, File 13110, Box 447, Universal-International Collection, CAL, USC; "Paramount Press Sheets, Releases Season 1952–53," Group A-12, *The Savage*, Paramount Collection, MHL, AMP.

47. Jerry Hoffman, "Production Notes," 3, *Mrs. Mike*, Production Files, Core Collection, MHL, AMP.

48. *Comanche Territory*, File 11825, Box 422, Universal-International Collection, CAL, USC.

49 On one known occasion, a director specifically requested Indians who were "as civilized as possible and with no trace of an accent." He hired three Indian actors and one actor who was not known to be Indian; this fourth person was the one who spoke in the film, even though the director felt he had found the "most 'un-Indian Indians.'" See "Press Releases," *The Senator Was Indiscreet*, File 18160, Box 544, Universal-International Collection, CAL, USC.

50. Higham, *Cecil B. DeMille*, 282.

51. Carl Milliken to John Roth, Interoffice Communication, February 16, 1953, File *The Burning Arrow* (aka *The Charge at Feather River*) 80, #8463, Box 1011a, Warner Bros. Collection, CAL, USC.

52. Paramount went to this trouble because they believed the public no longer accepted Indian grunts. "Paramount Press Sheets, Releases Season, 1951–52," Group A-11, *Red Mountain*; Produced Scripts, *Red Mountain*, File 2, both in Paramount Collection, MHL, AMP. A similarly convoluted situation occurred on the set of *Taza, Son of Cochise*. The Danish-born and German-trained director Douglas Sirk gave instructions in a heavy accent, and Lee Bradley interpreted, giving the instructions in Navajo. The press material also claimed that Bradley hired a comedian, Kay Dinetse (Yellow Man's Grandson), and that on one occasion he made them laugh by suggesting that they beat the soldiers instead of running away during that day's battle scene. "Press Releases," *Taza, Son of Cochise*, File 13184, Box 444, Universal-International Collection, CAL, USC.

53. *Ambush*, MGM, Stills Collection, MHL, AMP.

54. *The Last Hunt*, MGM, Stills Collection, MHL, AMP.

55. Production Notes, *Tomahawk*, File 13182, Box 444, Universal-International Collection, CAL, USC.

56. "*Devil's Doorway*, Indian Dialogue," July 20, 1949, *Devil's Doorway*, MGM Collection, CAL, USC.

57. Darrell Kipp, telephone interview by author, September 15, 2001. See also Kipp, "Images of Native People as Seen through the Eyes of the Blackbird."

58. Price, "Stereotyping of North American Indians in Motion Pictures," 158.

59. Darryl Zanuck to Leonard Goldstein, Interoffice Correspondence, October 6, 1952, 2, *Siege at Red River*, Twentieth Century Fox Collection, MHL, AMP.

60. Jerry Hoffman, Regal Films, "Production Notes," HO 9-7381, 3, *Mrs. Mike*, Production Files, Core Collection, MHL, AMP.

61. Clayton Moore, who played the Lone Ranger, did not think Silverheels had any negative feelings about his dialogue: "Often he was the only Indian in the script to speak with broken English. It might have been embarrassing for him, but he never

said anything about it; he knew he was playing a part." Moore with Thompson, *I Was That Masked Man*, 126–27. There is no record of how Silverheels felt about his dialogue, but he was a founder of the Indian Actors Association, which advocated Indians playing on-screen Indians.

62. Michael Abel to Darryl Zanuck, Interoffice Correspondence, December 14, 1951, 2, *Pony Soldier*, Twentieth Century Fox Collection, CAL, USC.

63. Richard Sokolove to Darryl Zanuck, "Comments," January 14, 1952, 6; and "Conference with Mr. Zanuck," February 1, 1952, 1, both in *Pony Soldier*, Twentieth Century Fox Collection, CAL, USC.

64. "'Broken Lance,' Conference with Mr. Zanuck, December 3, 1953 (on First Draft Continuity of 10/9/53)," 7, *Broken Lance*, Produced Scripts, Box FX-PRS-694, Collection 010, Twentieth Century Fox Film Corp., SC-YRL, UCLA.

65. Buddy Adler to William Hawks, Memorandum, March 30, 1956, 7, *The Last Wagon*, Twentieth Century Fox Collection, CAL, USC.

66. Bob Goldfarb, "Comment on 'Bright Path' [original title of the film]," File *Jim Thorpe*, Box 1761, Warner Bros. Collection, CAL, USC.

67. "'Buffalo Bill,' Conference with Mr. Zanuck (on Final Script of July 12, 1943)," July 14, 1943, 2, *Buffalo Bill*, Produced Scripts, Box FX-PRS-442, Collection 010, Twentieth Century Fox Film Corp., SC-YRL, UCLA.

68. "'Buffalo Bill,' Conference with Mr. Zanuck (on Final Script of July 12, 1943)," July 14, 1943, 2.

69. "'Buffalo Bill,' Conference with Mr. Zanuck (on Final Script of July 12, 1943)," July 14, 1943, 2.

70. Prats, *Invisible Natives*, 23.

71. See, for example, "'Buffalo Bill,' Conference with Mr. Zanuck (on Final Script of July 12, 1943)," July 14, 1943, 2.

72. Quoted in "'Buffalo Bill,' Conference with Mr. Zanuck (on Final Script of July 12, 1943)," July 14, 1943, 2.

EPILOGUE

1. Singer writes, "Wiping the war paint off the lens is an imaginary scenario from the time I found a colossal old movie camera that was used to film those wild Indian battles in the early days of Hollywood. I looked through the dusty lens and saw splattered spots that turned out to be old, crusted face paint, part of the makeup that had been used for phony war paint. I used my t-shirt to wipe off the lens, and that started me thinking about films that showed Indians differently. I wondered if a toxic solvent would clean the lens. The absurdity of the situation brings me to a moment of clarity that reminds me that it is good to dream, but it must be followed by hard work to bring the dream to reality." Singer, *Wiping the War Paint Off the Lens*, 98–99.

2. Raheja, *Reservation Reelism*, 71, 72.

3. Kilpatrick, *Celluloid Indians*.

4. See Shively, "Cowboys and Indians." The film *Powwow Highway* (1989) suggests as much with the character Philbert's constant references to Indian kitsch, such as that seen in the television series *Bonanza*. Dr. Cecil Meares (Muscogee), interview by author, September 27, 2001, Oklahoma City, Oklahoma; Louis Andrade (Luiseño), interview by author, August 20, 2004, Oxnard, California; Billy Yellow, interview by Ronald L. Davis, September 13, 1991, Number 484, 9, OHPA, SMU.

5. Paramount planned an advertising stunt in which movie patrons could step inside a box that would allow them to see themselves as though they were Indian. Above the box a banner asked, "Would you be handsome, or as beautiful as you are, if you had been born a REDSKIN? You can satisfy yourself on this question by placing your face in the aperture of this cabinet!!" "Paramount Press Sheets, Releases from August 1, 1930, to July 31, 1931," Paramount Collection, MHL, AMP.

6. Chuck Connors starred as Geronimo in the film of that name (United Artists, 1962), but he did not wear contact lenses to cover his blue eyes. During the screen test he wore dark lenses, but the producers thought he looked more "menacing" without them. Trevor Howard, for unknown reasons, also displayed his unadorned blue eyes for his role as a Cheyenne in *Windwalker* (Pacific International, 1980). Tuska, *American West in Film*, 256. Despite the continued use of non-Indian actors for Indian roles in the 1960s, both American Indians and the American public voiced their resentment against non-Indians playing Indians and misrepresentations of Indians. Mohawk actor Jay Silverheels formed the Indian Actors Association in the 1960s. The guild was designed to teach Indians how to act and perform tricks on horses. He also formed the Indian Actors Workshop through the Los Angeles Indian Center with the assistance of Iron Eyes Cody and Rodd Redwing (Choctaw). See Chissell, "Indian Actors Workshop." Silverheels was roundly condemned for his film and television work, however. He participated in a number of commercials after *The Lone Ranger* went off the air. In one, Silverheels stuffs his pockets with pizza (much like the Indians in *The Senator Was Indiscreet*). He rebuffed the criticism by claiming that it "promotes and strengthens the image that projects the Indians as being stoic, undemonstrative, incapable of showing emotion and entirely lacking a sense of humor." See Silverheels, "Lo! The Image of the Indian!"

7. Rosenthal, "Painting Native America in Public."

8. Black, "*The Exiles*."

9. The film *Navajo Talking Picture* attempts to expose many issues of concern to Diné in a Diné context but instead successfully shows us the tremendous challenges involved in a Diné woman creating a documentary on the Diné reservation, where

she was not raised and perhaps does not follow Diné expectations. Bowman's documentary work is discussed at length in Lewis, *"Navajo Talking Picture."*

10. See Leuthold, "Native American Responses to the Western."

11. Evans, *Fast Runner.*

12. Simpson, *Mohawk Interruptus.*

13. According to an IMDb.com biography, the *New York Times* reported that Asbille claimed Cherokee heritage but that the tribe said she was never enrolled. The biographical sketch says that prior to her appearance in *Wind River* she used her legal name, Kelsey Asbille Chow, and that her father was born to Chinese immigrants. "Kelsey Asbille Biography," IMDb Mini Biography by ahmetkhozan, https://www.imdb.com/name/nm2080328/bio?ref_=nm_ov_bio_sm.

BIBLIOGRAPHY

ARCHIVAL SOURCES

Cinematic Arts Library, University of Southern California, Los Angeles
D'Arcy McNickle Center for American Indian and Indigenous Studies, Newberry Library, Chicago, Illinois
Department of the Interior, National Archives, Washington D C
Frances Howard Goldwyn–Hollywood Regional Library, Los Angeles, California
Lilly Library, Indiana University–Bloomington
Louis B. Mayer Library, American Film Institute, Los Angeles, California
Margaret Herrick Library, Academy of Motion Picture Arts and Sciences, Beverly Hills, California
Oral History Program Archive, Southern Methodist University, University Park, Texas
Special Collections, Charles E. Young Research Library, University of California, Los Angeles
University Research Library, University of California, Los Angeles

PUBLISHED WORKS

Adams, Michael C. C. *The Best War Ever: America and World War II*. Baltimore M D : Johns Hopkins University Press, 1994.
Aleiss, Angela. "From Adversaries to Allies: The American Indian in Hollywood Films, 1930–1950." PhD diss., Columbia University, 1991.

———. *Making the White Man's Indian: Native Americans and Hollywood Movies.* Westport CT: Praeger, 2005.

Babcock, Barbara. "First Families: Gender, Reproduction and the Mythic Southwest." In *The Great Southwest of the Fred Harvey Company and the Santa Fe Railway,* edited by Barbara Babcock and Marta Weigle, 207–17. Phoenix AZ: Heard Museum, 1996.

———. "Pueblo Cultural Bodies." *Journal of American Folklore* 107, no. 423 (1994): 40–54.

Bannon, John Francis. *The Spanish Borderlands Frontier, 1513–1821.* New York: Holt, Rinehart, and Winston, 1970.

Bataille, Gretchen M., ed. *Native American Representations: First Encounters, Distorted Images, and Literary Appropriations.* Lincoln: University of Nebraska Press, 2001.

Bataille, Gretchen, and Charles L. P. Silet. "The Entertaining Anachronism: Indians in American Film." In *The Kaleidoscopic Lens: How Hollywood Views Ethnic Groups,* edited by Randal M. Miller, 36–53. Englewood NJ: Jerome S. Ozer, 1980.

———, eds. *Images of American Indians on Film: An Annotated Bibliography.* New York: Garland, 1985.

———, eds. *The Pretend Indians: Images of Native Americans in the Movies.* Ames: Iowa State University Press, 1980.

Bauer, William J., Jr. *We Were All Like Migrant Workers Here: Work, Community, and Memory on California's Round Valley Reservation, 1850–1941.* Chapel Hill: University of North Carolina Press, 2009.

Beck, David. *(Un)Fair Labor? American Indians and the 1893 World's Columbian Exposition in Chicago.* Lincoln: University of Nebraska Press, 2019.

Bederman, Gail. *Manliness and Civilization: A Cultural History of Gender and Race in the United States, 1880–1917.* Chicago: University of Chicago Press, 1995.

Behlmer, Rudy, ed. *Memo from Darryl F. Zanuck: The Golden Years at Twentieth Century Fox.* New York: Grove Press, 1993.

———. *Memo from David O. Selznick.* New York: Viking Press, 1972.

Bendix, Regina F. *Culture and Value: Tourism, Heritage and Property.* Bloomington: Indiana University Press, 2018.

———. *In Search of Authenticity: The Formation of Folklore Studies.* Madison: University of Wisconsin Press, 1988.

Berg, Charles Ramirez. *The Classical Mexican Cinema: The Poetics of the Exceptional Golden Age Films.* Austin: University of Texas Press, 2015.

———. *Latino Images in Film: Stereotypes, Subversion, and Resistance.* Austin: University of Texas Press, 2002.

Berkhofer, Robert, Jr. *The White Man's Indian: Images of the American Indian from Columbus to the Present.* New York: Vintage, 1979.

Berman, Marshall. *All That Is Solid Melts into Air: The Experience of Modernity.* New York: Simon and Schuster, 1982.

Bernardis, Tim. "Robert Yellowtail." In *Encyclopedia of North American Indians*, edited by Frederick Hoxie, 705. Boston: Houghton Mifflin, 1996.

Bernstein, Alison R. *American Indians and World War II: Toward a New Era in Indian Affairs*. Norman: University of Oklahoma Press, 1991.

Bhabha, Homi K. *The Location of Culture*. New York: Routledge, 1994.

Bird, S. Elizabeth. *Dressing in Feathers: The Construction of the Indian in American Popular Culture*. New York: Westview Press, 1996.

———. "Gendered Construction of the American Indian in Popular Media." *Journal of Communication* 49, no. 3 (1999): 61–83.

Black, Liza. "*The Exiles*: Native Survivance and Urban Space in Downtown Los Angeles." *American Indian Culture and Research Journal* 42, no. 3 (2018): 155–82.

Blackhawk, Ned. *Violence over the Land: Indians and Empires in the Early American West*. Cambridge MA: Harvard University Press, 2006.

Blansett, Kent. *A Journey to Freedom: Richard Oakes, Alcatraz, and the Red Power Movement*. New Haven CT: Yale University Press, 2018.

Bokovoy, Matthew F. *The San Diego World's Fairs and Southwestern Memory, 1880–1940*. Albuquerque: University of New Mexico Press, 2005.

Bold, Christine. *Selling the Wild West: Popular Western Fiction, 1860–1960*. Bloomington: Indiana University Press, 1987.

Bordo, Susan. *Twilight Zones: The Hidden Life of Cultural Images from Plato to O.J.* Berkeley: University of California Press, 1997.

———. *Unbearable Weight: Feminism, Western Culture, and the Body*. Berkeley: University of California Press, 1993.

Brands, H. W. *The Devil We Knew: Americans and the Cold War*. New York: Oxford University Press, 1993.

Brookings Institution. Institute for Government Research. *The Problem of Indian Administration: Report of a Survey Made at the Request of Honorable Hubert Work, Secretary of the Interior, and Submitted to Him, February 21, 1928. Survey Staff: Lewis Meriam, Ray A. Brown, Henry Roe Cloud, Edward Everett Dale, and Others*. Baltimore MD: Johns Hopkins University Press, 1928.

Brownell Jewell, Richard. "A History of RKO Radio Pictures, Incorporated: 1928–1942." PhD diss., University of Southern California, 1978.

Brownlow, Kevin. *The War, the West, and the Wilderness*. New York: Knopf, 1979.

Brundage, W. Fitzhugh. *Beyond Blackface: African Americans and the Creation of American Popular Culture, 1890–1930*. Chapel Hill: University of North Carolina Press, 2011.

Bsumek, Erika. *Indian-Made: Navajo Culture in the Marketplace, 1868–1940*. Lawrence: University Press of Kansas, 2008.

Buffalohead, Eric L., and M. Elise Marubbio, eds. *Native Americans on Film: Conversations, Teaching, and Theory*. Lexington: University Press of Kentucky, 2013.

Burnham, Philip. *Song of Dewey Beard: Last Survivor of the Little Bighorn*. Lincoln: University of Nebraska Press, 2014.

Buscombe, Edward. *"Injuns!" Native Americans in the Movies*. London: Reaktion Books, 2006.

Byrd, Jodi A. *The Transit of Empire: Indigenous Critiques of Colonialism*. Minneapolis: University of Minnesota Press, 2011.

Caddoo, Cara. "Envisioned Communities: The African Diaspora and Interwar Race Films." In *Converging Identities: Blackness in the Modern African Diaspora*, edited by Julius O. Adekunle and Hettie V. Williams, 61–82. Durham NC: Carolina Academic Press, 2013.

———. *Envisioning Freedom: Cinema and the Building of Modern Black Life*. Cambridge MA: Harvard University Press, 2014.

Carr, Helen. *Inventing the American Primitive: Politics, Gender, and the Representation of Native American Literary Traditions, 1789–1936*. Cork, Ireland: Cork University Press, 1996.

Carstarphen Meta G., and John P. Sanchez. *American Indians and the Mass Media*. Norman: University of Oklahoma Press, 2012.

Cary, Diana Serra. *The Hollywood Posse: The Story of a Gallant Band of Horsemen Who Made Movie History*. Boston: Houghton Mifflin, 1975.

Castañeda, Mari. *Soap Operas and Telenovelas in the Digital Age: Global Industries and New Audiences*. Bern, Switzerland: Peter Lang, 2011.

Cawelti, John G. *The Six-Gun Mystique*. Bowling Green OH: Bowling Green University Press, 1975.

Central Section of Los Angeles [map]. Los Angeles: Automobile Club of Southern California, 1956.

Chafe, William H. *The Unfinished Journey: America since World War II*. New York: Oxford University Press, 1986.

Chafe, William H., and Harvard Sitkoff, eds. *A History of Our Time: Readings on Postwar America*. New York: Oxford University Press, 1983.

Chauncey, George. *Gay New York: Gender, Urban Culture, and the Making of the Gay Male World*. New York: Basic Books, 1994.

Cheney, Christopher Colt. "Reel Indians: Native American Representation in Film, 1950–1970." PhD diss., Southwestern Oklahoma State University, 2008.

Child, Brenda J. *Holding Our World Together: Ojibwe Women and the Survival of Community*. New York: Penguin, 2012.

———. *My Grandfather's Knocking Sticks: Ojibwe Family Life and Labor on the Reservation*. Minneapolis: Minnesota Historical Society Press, 2014.

Chissell, Kid Noble. "Indian Actors Workshop." *Indians Illustrated* 1, no. 5 (1968): 6–8.

Clark, Danae. *Negotiating Hollywood: The Cultural Politics of Actors' Labor*. Minneapolis: University of Minnesota Press, 1995.

Clifford, James. *The Predicament of Culture: Twentieth-Century Ethnography, Literature, and Art*. Cambridge M A: Harvard University Press, 1988.

———. *Returns: Becoming Indigenous in the Twenty-First Century*. Cambridge M A: Harvard University Press, 2013.

Cody, Iron Eyes, as told to Collin Perry. *Iron Eyes: My Life as a Hollywood Indian*. New York: Everest House, 1982.

Cohan, Steven. *Masked Men: Masculinity and the Movies in the Fifties*. Bloomington: Indiana University Press, 1997.

Collings, Ellsworth, and Alma Miller England. *The 101 Ranch*. Norman: University of Oklahoma Press, 1971.

Columpar, Corinn. *Unsettling Sights: The Fourth World on Film*. Carbondale: Southern Illinois University Press, 2010.

Coyne, Michael. *The Crowded Prairie: American National Identity in the Hollywood Western*. London: I. B. Tauris, 1997.

Cripps, Thomas. *Making Movies Black: The Hollywood Message Movie from World War II to the Civil Rights Era*. Oxford: Oxford University Press, 1993.

———. *Slow Fade to Black: The Negro in American Film, 1900–1942*. Oxford: Oxford University Press, 1993.

Cummings, Denise K. *"Distant Drums."* In *Seeing Red: Hollywood's Pixeled Skins*, edited by LeAnne Howe, Harvey Markowitz, and Denise K. Cummings, 185–88. East Lansing: Michigan State University Press, 2013.

———, ed. *Visualities: Perspectives on Contemporary American Indian Film and Art*. East Lansing: Michigan State University Press, 2011.

———, ed. *Visualities 2: More Perspectives on Contemporary American Indian Film and Art*. East Lansing: Michigan State University Press, 2019.

Davis, Natalie Zemon. *Slaves on Screen: Film and Historical Vision*. Cambridge M A: Harvard University Press, 2000.

Davis, Robert Murray. *Playing Cowboys: Low Culture and High Art in the Western*. Norman: University of Oklahoma Press, 1994.

Davis, Ronald L. *The Glamour Factory: Inside Hollywood's Big Studio System*. Dallas T X: Southern Methodist University Press, 1993.

———. *Hollywood Beauty: Linda Darnell and the American Dream*. Norman: University of Oklahoma Press, 1991.

———. *John Ford: Hollywood's Old Master*. Norman: University of Oklahoma Press, 1995.

Davis, Susan G. *Spectacular Nature: Corporate Culture and the Sea World Experience*. Berkeley: University of California Press, 1997.

Debo, Angie. *Geronimo: The Man, His Time, His Place*. Norman: University of Oklahoma Press, 1976.

Deloria, Philip J. *Becoming Mary Sully: Toward an American Indian Abstract*. Seattle: University of Washington Press, 2019.

———. *Indians in Unexpected Places*. Lawrence: University Press of Kansas, 2004.

———. *Playing Indian*. New Haven CT: Yale University Press, 1998.

Deloria, Vine, Jr. "American Fantasy." In *The Pretend Indians: Images of Native Americans in the Movies*, edited by Gretchen M. Bataille and Charles L. P. Silet, ix–xvi. Ames: Iowa State University Press, 1980.

———. *Custer Died for Your Sins: An Indian Manifesto*. London: Macmillan, 1969.

———. "Distinctive Status of Indian Rights." In *The Plains Indian of the Twentieth Century*, edited by Peter Iverson, 237–48. Norman: University of Oklahoma Press, 1985.

Department of Missionary Education/Board of Education of the Northern Baptist Convention, eds. *The Moccasin Trail*. Philadelphia: Judson Press, 1932.

Dilworth, Leah D. *Imagining Indians in the Southwest: Persistent Visions of a Primitive Past*. Washington DC: Smithsonian Institution Press, 1996.

Doane, Mary Ann. "The Close-Up: Scale and Detail in the Cinema." *Differences: A Journal of Social Theory* 14, no. 3 (2003): 89–111.

Doherty, Thomas. *Projections of War: Hollywood, American Culture, and World War II*. New York: Columbia University Press, 1993.

Dowell, Kristen. *Sovereign Screens: Aboriginal Media on the Canadian West Coast*. Lincoln: University of Nebraska Press, 2013.

Dunne, George H. *Hollywood Labor Dispute: A Study in Immorality*. Los Angeles: Conference Publishing, 1949.

Edwards, Elizabeth, ed. *Anthropology and Photography, 1860–1920*. New Haven CT: Yale University Press, 1992.

Ellison, Ralph. *The Collected Essays of Ralph Ellison*. Edited by John F. Callahan. New York: Modern Library, 1995.

Engelhardt, Tom. *The End of Victory Culture: Cold War America and the Disillusioning of a Generation*. New York: Basic Books, 1995.

Erenberg, Lewis A., and Susan E. Hirsch, eds. *The War in American Culture: Society and Consciousness in World War II*. Chicago: University of Chicago Press, 1996.

Erigha, Maryann. *The Hollywood Jim Crow: The Racial Politics of the Movie Industry*. New York: New York University Press, 2019.

Estes, Nick. "'There Are No Two Sides to This Story': An Interview with Elizabeth Cook-Lynn." *Wičazo Ša Review* 31, no. 1 (2016): 27–45.

Etulain, Richard. *Western Film: A Brief History*. Manhattan KS: Sunflower University Press, 1983.

Evans, Michael Robert. *"The Fast Runner": Filming the Legend of Atanarjuat*. Lincoln: University of Nebraska Press, 2010.

Fanon, Frantz. *Black Skin, White Masks*. New York: Grove Press, 1967.

Feng, Peter X., ed. *Screening Asian Americans*. New Brunswick NJ: Rutgers University Press, 2002.

Fenin, George N., and William K. Everson. *The Western: From Silents to Cinerama*. New York: Bonanza, 1962.

Fienup-Riordan, Ann. *Freeze Frame: Alaska Eskimos in the Movies*. Seattle: University of Washington Press, 1995.

Fisher, Andrew H. "The Indian in the Studio: Nipo Strongheart and the Hidden History of Native Creativity in Hollywood." Paper presented at the Western History Association meeting, Las Vegas, Nevada, October 17, 2019.

———. "Speaking for the First Americans: Nipo Strongheart and the Campaign for American Indian Citizenship." *Oregon Historical Society* 114, no. 4 (2013): 441–52.

———. "Tinseltown Tyee: Nipo Strongheart and the Making of *Braveheart*." *American Indian Culture and Research Journal* 42, no. 3 (2018): 93–118.

Fishgall, Gary. *Against Type: The Biography of Burt Lancaster*. New York: Scribner, 1995.

———. *Pieces of Time: The Life of James Stewart*. New York: Scribner, 1997.

Fixico, Donald L. *Termination and Relocation: Federal Indian Policy, 1945–1960*. Albuquerque: University of New Mexico Press, 1986.

Floyd, Jacob. "Negotiating Publicity and Persona: The Work of Native Actors in Studio Hollywood." *American Indian Culture and Research Journal* 42, no. 3 (2018): 119–35.

Fonda, Henry, as told to Howard Teichmann. *Fonda: My Life*. New York: New American Library, 1981.

Foster, Morris W. *Being Comanche: A Social History of an American Indian Community*. Tucson: University of Arizona Press, 1991.

Fowler, Loretta. *Arapahoe Politics: Symbols in Crises of Authority, 1851–1978*. Lincoln: University of Nebraska Press, 1982.

Frankel, Glenn. *"The Searchers": The Making of an American Legend*. New York: Bloomsbury, 2013.

French, Peter A. *Cowboy Metaphysics: Ethics and Death in Westerns*. Lanham MD: Rowman and Littlefield, 1997.

Freud, Sigmund. "Repression." In *The Standard Edition of the Complete Psychological Works of Sigmund Freud*, volume 14, edited by James Strachey, 146–58. London: Hogarth Press, 1957.

Friar, Ralph E., and Natasha A. Friar. *The Only Good Indian: The Hollywood Gospel*. New York: Drama Book Specialists, 1972.

Friedman, Lester D. "Celluloid Palimpsests: An Overview of Ethnicity and the American Film." In *Unspeakable Images: Ethnicity and the American Cinema*, edited by Lester D. Friedman, 11–35. Urbana: University of Illinois Press, 1991.

Gaines, Jane M. *Fire and Desire: Mixed-Race Movies in the Silent Era*. Chicago: University of Chicago Press, 1993.

Gidley, Mike. *Edward S. Curtis and the North American Indian, Incorporated*. Cambridge: Cambridge University Press, 1998.

Ginsburg, Faye. "Indigenous Media: Faustian Contract or Global Village?" *Cultural Anthropology* 6, no. 1 (1991): 92–112.

———. "Screen Memories and Entangled Technologies: Resignifying Indigenous Lives." In *Multiculturalism, Postcoloniality and Transnational Media*, edited by Ella Shohat and Robert Stam, 77–98. New Brunswick NJ: Rutgers University Press, 2003.

Goeman, Mishuana. *Mark My Words: Native Women Mapping Our Nations*. Minneapolis: University of Minnesota Press, 2013.

Graham, Laura A., and H. Glenn Penny, eds. *Performing Indigeneity: Global Histories and Contemporary Experiences*. Lincoln: University of Nebraska Press, 2014.

Gray, Lois S., and Ronald L. Seeber, eds. *Under the Stars: Essays on Labor Relations in Arts and Entertainment*. Ithaca NY: Cornell University Press, 1996.

Green, Rayna. "The Pocahontas Perplex: The Image of Indian Women in American Culture." *Massachusetts Review* 16, no. 4 (1975): 698–714.

Greenblatt, Stephen. *Marvelous Possessions: The Wonder of the New World*. Chicago: University of Chicago Press, 1991.

Griffiths, Alison. *Carceral Fantasies: Cinema and Prisons in Early Twentieth-Century America*. New York: Columbia University Press, 2016.

———. *Shivers down Your Spine: Cinema, Museums, and the Immersive View*. New York: Columbia University Press, 2008.

———. *Wondrous Difference: Cinema, Anthropology, and Turn-of-the-Century Visual Culture*. New York: Columbia University Press, 2002.

Gubar, Susan. *Racechanges: White Skin, Black Face in American Culture*. New York: Oxford University Press, 1997.

Hallett, Hilary. *Go West, Young Women! The Rise of Early Hollywood*. Berkeley: University of California Press, 2013.

Hamamoto, Darrell, and Sandra Liu, eds. *Countervisions: Asian American Film Criticism*. Philadelphia: Temple University Press, 2000.

Hansen, Miriam. *Babel and Babylon: Spectatorship in American Silent Film*. Cambridge MA: Harvard University Press, 1991.

Hearne, Joanna. "The 'Ache for Home' in Anthony Mann's *Devil's Doorway* (1950)." *Film and History: An Interdisciplinary Journal of Film and Television Studies* 33, no. 1 (2003): 18–29.

————. *Native Recognition: Indigenous Cinema and the Western*. Albany: State University of New York Press, 2012.

————. *"Smoke Signals": Native Cinema Rising*. Lincoln: University of Nebraska Press, 2012.

Heston, Charlton. *In the Arena: An Autobiography*. New York: Simon and Schuster, 1995.

Higham, Charles. *Cecil B. DeMille*. New York: Scribner's Sons, 1973.

Hilger, Michael. *The American Indian in Film*. Metuchen NJ: Scarecrow Press, 1986.

————. *From Savage to Nobleman: Images of Native Americans in Film*. Lanham MD: Scarecrow Press, 1995.

————. *Native Americans in the Movies: Portrayals from Silent Films to the Present*. New York: Rowman and Littlefield, 2016.

Hill, Mike, ed. *Whiteness: A Critical Reader*. New York: New York University Press, 1997.

Hokowhitu, Brendan, and Vijay Devadas, eds. *The Fourth Eye: Māori Media in Aotearoa New Zealand*. Minneapolis: University of Minnesota Press, 2013.

Holm, Tom. "Fighting a White Man's War: The Extent and Legacy of American Indian Participation in World War II." In *The Plains Indians of the Twentieth Century*, edited by Peter Iverson, 149–68. Norman: University of Oklahoma Press, 1985.

Horne, Gerald. *Fire This Time: The Watts Uprising and the 1960s*. Charlottesville: University Press of Virginia, 1995.

Hosmer, Brian. *American Indians in the Marketplace: Persistence and Innovation among the Menominees and Metlakatlands, 1870–1920*. Lawrence: University Press of Kansas, 1999.

Howe, LeAnne. *"Smoke Signals."* In *Seeing Red: Hollywood's Pixeled Skins*, edited by LeAnne Howe, Harvey Markowitz, and Denise K. Cummings, 113–15. East Lansing: Michigan State University Press, 2013.

————. "Tribalography: The Power of Native Stories." *Journal of Dramatic Theory and Criticism* 14, no. 1 (1999): 117–25.

Howe, LeAnne, Harvey Markowitz, and Denise K. Cummings, eds. *Seeing Red: Hollywood's Pixeled Skins*. East Lansing: Michigan State University Press, 2013.

Hoxie, Frederick. ed. *Encyclopedia of North American Indians*. Boston: Houghton Mifflin, 1996.

————. *Parading through History: The Making of the Crow Nation in America, 1805–1935*. Cambridge: Cambridge University Press, 1995.

Huhndorf, Shari M. *Going Native: Indians in the American Cultural Imagination*. Ithaca NY: Cornell University Press, 2001.

————. *Mapping the Americas: The Transnational Politics of Contemporary Native Culture*. Ithaca NY: Cornell University Press, 2009.

Hutchinson, Elizabeth. *The Indian Craze: Primitivism, Modernism, and Transculturation in American Art, 1890–1915*. Durham NC: Duke University Press, 2009.

Iverson, Peter, ed. *The Plains Indians of the Twentieth Century*. Norman: University of Oklahoma Press, 1985.

Jafri, Beenash. "Desire, Settler Colonialism, and the Racialized Cowboy." *American Indian Culture and Research Journal* 37, no. 2 (2013): 73–86.

Jay, Gregory E. "'White Man's Book No Good': D. W. Griffith and the American Indian." *Cinema Journal* 39, no. 4 (2000): 3–26.

Jeffords, Susan. *The Remasculinization of America: Gender and the Vietnam War*. Bloomington: Indiana University Press, 1989.

Jenkins, Henry. *What Made Pistachio Nuts: Early Sound Comedy and the Vaudeville Aesthetic*. New York: Columbia University Press, 1992.

Jojola, Ted. "Absurd Reality II: Hollywood Goes to the Indians." In *Hollywood's Indian: The Portrayal of the Native American in Film*, edited by Peter Rollins and John E. O'Connor, 12–26. 2nd ed. Lexington: University Press of Kentucky, 2003.

Kauanui, J. Kēhaulani. "'A Structure, Not an Event': Settler Colonialism and Enduring Indigeneity." *Lateral: Journal of the Cultural Studies Association* 5, no. 1 (2016). https://doi.org/10.25158/L5.1.7.

Kilpatrick, Jacquelyn. *Celluloid Indians: Native Americans and Film*. Lincoln: University of Nebraska Press, 1999.

Kipp, Darrell Robes. "Images of Native People as Seen Through the Eyes of the Blackbird." *Wičazo Ša Review* 16, no. 2 (2001): 29–34.

Lasky, Betty. *RKO: The Biggest Little Major of Them All*. Santa Monica CA: Roundtable, 1989.

Lears, T. J. Jackson. *No Place of Grace: Antimodernism and the Transformation of American Culture, 1880–1920*. New York: Pantheon, 1981.

Lenihan, John. "Classics and Social Commentary: Postwar Westerns, 1946–1960." *Journal of the West* 22, no. 4 (1983): 34–42.

———. *Showdown: Confronting Modern America in the Western Film*. Chicago: University of Illinois Press, 1980.

———. "Westbound: Feature Films and the American West." In *Wanted Dead or Alive: The American West in Popular Culture*, edited by Richard Aquila, 109–34. Urbana: University of Illinois Press, 1996.

Leuthold, Steven. *Indigenous Aesthetics: Native Art, Media, and Identity*. Austin: University of Texas Press, 1998.

———. "Native American Responses to the Western." *American Indian Culture and Research Journal* 19, no. 1 (1995): 153–89.

Lewis, Randolph. *Alanis Obomsawin: The Vision of a Native Filmmaker*. Lincoln: University of Nebraska Press, 2006.

———. *"Navajo Talking Picture": Cinema on Native Ground*. Lincoln: University of Nebraska Press, 2012.

Lhamon, W. T. *Raising Cain: Blackface Performance from Jim Crow to Hip Hop*. Cambridge MA: Harvard University Press, 1998.

Limbrick, Peter. *Making Settler Cinemas: Film and Colonial Encounters in the United States, Australia, and New Zealand*. New York: Palgrave Macmillan, 2010.

Lippard, Lucy, ed. *Partial Recall: With Essays on Photographs of Native North Americans*. New York: New Press, 1992.

Lonetree, Amy. *Decolonizing Museums: Representing Native America in National and Tribal Museums*. Chapel Hill: University of North Carolina Press, 2012.

Lott, Eric. *Love and Theft: Blackface Minstrelsy and the American Working Class*. New York: Oxford University Press, 2013.

———. "The Whiteness of Film Noir." In *Whiteness: A Critical Reader*, edited by Mike Hill, 81–101. New York: New York University Press, 1997.

Luebben, Ralph A. "A Study of Some Off-Reservation Navaho Miners." PhD diss., Cornell University, 1955.

Lupis, Immaculate J. "The Person of the American Indian as Portrayed in American Indian Film and Video from 1894 to 1994." PhD diss., University of San Francisco, 1996.

Lyon, William H. "The Navajo in the American Historical Imagination." *Ethnohistory* 45 (1998): 237–75.

Maddox, Robert James. *The United States and World War II*. Boulder CO: Westview Press, 1992.

Malinowski, Sharon, and Anna Sheets, eds. *The Gale Encyclopedia of Native American Tribes*. Volume 3. Detroit MI: Gale, 1998.

Marubbio, M. Elise. *Killing the Indian Maiden: Images of Native American Women in Film*. Lexington: University Press of Kentucky, 2006.

May, Elaine Tyler. "Explosive Issues: Sex, Women, and the Bomb." In *Recasting America: Culture and Politics in the Age of Cold War*, edited by Lary May, 154–70. Chicago: University of Chicago Press, 1989.

———. *Homeward Bound: American Families in the Cold War Era*. New York: Basic Books, 1990.

May, Lary. *The Big Tomorrow: Hollywood and the Politics of the American Way*. Chicago: University of Chicago Press, 2000.

———. "Movie Star Politics: The Screen Actors' Guild, Cultural Conversion, and the Hollywood Red Scare." In *Recasting America: Culture and Politics in the Age of Cold War*, edited by Lary May, 125–53. Chicago: University of Chicago Press, 1989.

———, ed. *Recasting America: Culture and Politics in the Age of Cold War*. Chicago: University of Chicago Press, 1989.

———. *Screening Out the Past: The Birth of Mass Culture and the Motion Picture Industry*. New York: Oxford University Press, 1980.

McBride, Bunny. *Molly Spotted Elk: A Penobscot in Paris*. Norman: University of Oklahoma Press, 1995.

McNenly, Linda Scarangella. *Native Performers in Wild West Shows: From Buffalo Bill to Euro Disney*. Norman: University of Oklahoma Press, 2012.

Memmi, Albert. *The Colonizer and the Colonized*. London: Earthscan, 1990.

Meyer, Carter Jones, and Diana Royer, eds. *Selling the Indian: Commercializing and Appropriating American Indian Cultures*. Tucson: University of Arizona Press, 2001.

Miller, David Humphreys. *Custer's Fall: The Native American Side of the Story*. 1957. New York: Meridian, 1992.

Miller, Randall M., ed. *The Kaleidoscopic Lens: How Hollywood Views Ethnic Groups*. Englewood NJ: Jerome S. Ozer, 1980.

Miranda, Deborah A. *Bad Indians: A Tribal Memoir*. Berkeley CA: Heyday Books, 2013.

Mitchell, Lee Clark. *Westerns: Making the Man in Fiction and Film*. Chicago: University of Chicago Press, 1998.

Molina-Guzmán, Isabel. *Dangerous Curves: Latina Bodies in the Media*. New York: New York University Press, 2010.

Moore, Clayton, with Frank Thompson. *I Was That Masked Man*. Dallas: Taylor, 1996.

Morella, Joe, Edward Z. Epstein, and Eleanor Clark. *The Amazing Careers of Bob Hope: From Gags to Riches*. New York: Arlington House, 1973.

Moses, L. G. *Wild West Shows and the Images of American Indians, 1883–1933*. Albuquerque: University of New Mexico Press, 1996.

Muhammad, Khalil Gibran. *The Condemnation of Blackness: Race, Crime, and the Making of Modern Urban America*. Cambridge MA: Harvard University Press, 2011.

Mullin, Molly. *Culture in the Marketplace: Gender, Art, and Value in the American Southwest*. Durham NC: Duke University Press, 2001.

Murray, David. *Forked Tongues: Speech, Writing and Representation in North American Indian Texts*. London: Pinter, 1991.

——. *Modern Indians: Native Americans in the Twentieth Century*. Edinburgh, Scotland: Edinburgh University Press, 1982.

Nachbar, Jack. "Horses, Harmony, Hope, and Hormones: Western Movies, 1930–1946." *Journal of the West* 22, no. 4 (1983): 24–33.

Nash, Jay Robert, and Ralph Stanley Ross. *The Motion Picture Guide*. Chicago: Cinebooks, 1986.

Neale, Steve. "Vanishing Americans: Racial and Ethnic Issues in the Interpretation and Context of Post-War 'Pro-Indian' Westerns." In *Back in the Saddle Again: New Essays on the Western*, edited by Roberta Pearson and Edward Buscombe, 8–28. London: British Film Institute, 1998.

Nericcio, William Anthony. *Tex{t}-Mex: Seductive Hallucinations of the "Mexican" in America*. Austin: University of Texas Press, 2007.

Nielsen, Mike, and Gene Mailes. *Hollywood's Other Blacklist: Union Struggles in the Studio System*. London: British Film Institute, 1995.

Noriega, Chon A., ed. *Chicanos and Film: Essays on Chicano Representation and Resistance*. New York: Garland, 1992.

———. *Chicanos and Film: Representation and Resistance*. Minneapolis: University of Minnesota Press, 1992.

———. *Shot in America: Television, the State, and the Rise of Chicano Cinema*. Minneapolis: University of Minnesota Press, 2000.

———, ed. *Visible Nations: Latin American Cinema and Video*. Minneapolis: University of Minnesota Press, 2000.

Olson, James S., and Raymond Wilson. *Native Americans in the Twentieth Century*. Urbana: University of Illinois Press, 1984.

O'Neill, Colleen Marie. "Navajo Workers and White Man's Ways: Negotiating the World of Wage Labor, 1930–1972." PhD diss., Rutgers University, 1997.

Ono, Kent, and Vincent N. Pham. *Asian Americans and the Media*. Cambridge, England: Polity, 2008.

Orvell, Miles. *The Real Thing: Imitation and Authenticity in American Culture, 1880–1940*. Chapel Hill: University of North Carolina Press, 1989.

Owens, Louis. *Mixedblood Messages: Literature, Film, Family, Place*. Norman: University of Oklahoma Press, 1998.

Parezo, Nancy, and Don Fowler. *Anthropology Goes to the Fair: The 1904 Louisiana Purchase Exposition*. Lincoln: University of Nebraska Press, 2007.

Parish, James Robert. *The RKO Gals*. New York: Arlington House, 1974.

Parman, Donald L. *Indians and the American West in the Twentieth Century*. Bloomington: Indiana University Press, 1994.

Peiss, Kathy. *Hope in a Jar: The Making of America's Beauty Culture*. New York: Metropolitan Books, 1998.

Perry, Louis B., and Richard S. Perry. *A History of the Los Angeles Labor Movement, 1911–1941*. Berkeley: University of California Press, 1963.

Pfeil, Fred. *White Guys: Studies in Postmodern Domination and Difference*. New York: Verso, 1995.

Place, J. A. *The Western Films of John Ford*. Secaucus NJ: Citadel Press, 1974.

Polenberg, Richard. *War and Society: The United States, 1941–1945*. Philadelphia: J. B. Lippincott, 1972.

Prats, Armando José. "The Image of the Other and the Other *Dances with Wolves*: The Refigured Indian and the Textual Supplement." *Journal of Film and Video* 50, no. 1 (1998): 3–19.

———. *Invisible Natives: Myth and Identity in the American Western*. Ithaca NY: Cornell University Press, 2002.

Pratt, Mary Louise. *Imperial Eyes: Travel Writing and Transculturation*. New York: Routledge, 1992.

Price, John A. "The Stereotyping of North American Indians in Motion Pictures." *Ethnohistory* 20, no. 2 (1973): 141–58.

Prindle, David F. *The Politics of Glamour: Ideology and Democracy in the Screen Actors Guild*. Madison: University of Wisconsin Press, 1988.

Prins, Harald E. L. "Chief Big Thunder (1827–1906): The Life History of a Penobscot Trickster." *Maine History* 37, no. 2 (1998): 140–58.

Prucha, Francis Paul. *American Indian Treaties: The History of a Political Anomaly*. Berkeley: University of California Press, 1994.

Purdy, John. "Tricksters of the Trade: Reimagining the Filmic Image of Native Americans." In *Native American Representations: First Encounters, Distorted Images, and Literary Appropriations*, edited by Gretchen M. Bataille, 100–118. Lincoln: University of Nebraska Press, 2001.

Quirk, Lawrence J. *James Stewart: Behind the Scenes of a Wonderful Life*. New York: Applause Theatre, 1997.

Rader, Dean. "*Broken Arrow*." In *Seeing Red: Hollywood's Pixeled Skins*, edited by LeAnne Howe, Harvey Markowitz, and Denise K. Cummings, 75–78. East Lansing: Michigan State University Press, 2013.

———. *Engaged Resistance: American Indian Art, Literature, and Film from Alcatraz to the NMAI*. Austin: University of Texas Press, 2011.

Raheja, Michelle H. *Reservation Reelism: Redfacing, Visual Sovereignty, and Representations of Native Americans in Film*. Lincoln: University of Nebraska Press, 2011.

———. "Visual Sovereignty." In *Native Studies Keywords*, edited by Stephanie Nohelani Teves, Andrea Smith, and Michelle Raheja, 25–34. Tucson: University of Arizona Press, 2015.

Raibmon, Paige. *Authentic Indians: Episodes of Encounter from the Late-Nineteenth-Century Northwest*. Durham NC: Duke University Press, 2005.

Ray, Robert. *A Certain Tendency of the Hollywood Cinema, 1930–1980*. Princeton NJ: Princeton University Press, 1985.

Richfield Street Guide: Los Angeles Central Section [map]. Chicago: H. M. Gousha, 1959.

Rickard, Jolene. "Sovereignty: A Line in the Sand." *Aperture* 139 (Summer 1995): 50–59.

Roberts, Brian. *Blackface Nation: Race, Reform, and Identity in American Popular Music, 1812–1925*. Chicago: University of Chicago Press, 2017.

Roddick, Nick. *A New Deal in Entertainment: Warner Brothers in the 1930s*. London: Garden House, 1983.

Rogin, Michael. *Blackface, White Noise: Jewish Immigrants in the Hollywood Melting Pot*. Berkeley: University of California Press, 1996.

Rollins, Peter C., and John E. O'Connor, eds. *Hollywood's Indian: The Portrayal of the Native American in Film.* 2nd ed. Lexington: University Press of Kentucky, 2003. The first edition was published in 1998.

Rosenstone, Robert A. *Visions of the Past: The Challenge of Film to Our Idea of History.* Cambridge MA: Harvard University Press, 1995.

Rosenthal, Nicolas. "Painting Native America in Public: American Indian Artists and the New Deal." *American Indian Culture and Research Journal* 42, no. 3 (2018): 47–70.

——— . *Reimagining Indian Country: Native American Migration and Identity in Twentieth-Century Los Angeles.* Chapel Hill: University of North Carolina Press, 2012.

Rosenthal, Nicolas, and Liza Black, eds. "Representing Native Peoples: Native Narratives of Indigenous History and Culture." Special issue, *American Indian Culture and Research Journal* 42, no. 3 (2018).

Ross, Murray. *Stars and Strikes: Unionization of Hollywood.* New York: Columbia University Press, 1941.

Ross, Steven J. *Working-Class Hollywood: Silent Film and the Shaping of Class in America.* Princeton NJ: Princeton University Press, 1998.

Roth, Lorna. "Looking at Shirley, the Ultimate Norm: Colour Balance, Image Technologies, and Cognitive Equity." *Canadian Journal of Communication* 34, no. 1 (2009) 111–36.

Sammond, Nicholas. *Birth of an Industry: Blackface Minstrelsy and the Rise of American Animation.* Durham NC: Duke University Press, 2015.

Sattler, Richard. "Seminole." In *Encyclopedia of North American Indians,* edited by Frederick E. Hoxie, 576–78. Boston: Houghton Mifflin, 1996.

Scheckel, Susan. *The Insistence of the Indian: Race and Nationalism in Nineteenth-Century American Culture.* Princeton NJ: Princeton University Press, 1998.

Schweninger, Lee. *Imagic Moments: Indigenous North American Film.* Athens: University of Georgia Press, 2013.

——— . *Listening to the Land: Native American Literary Responses to the Landscape.* Athens: University of Georgia Press, 2008.

Scott, James C. *Domination and the Arts of Resistance: Hidden Transcripts.* New Haven CT: Yale University Press, 1990.

Shively, JoEllen. "Cowboys and Indians: Perceptions of Western Films among American Indians and Anglos." *American Sociological Review* 57, no. 6 (1992): 725–34.

Shohat, Ella, and Robert Stam, eds. *Multiculturalism, Postcoloniality and Transnational Media.* New Brunswick NJ: Rutgers University Press, 2003.

——— , eds. *Unthinking Eurocentrism: Multiculturalism and the Media.* London: Routledge, 1994.

Silverheels, Jay. "Lo! The Image of the Indian!" *Indians Illustrated* 1, no. 6 (1968): 8–9.

Simpson, Audra. *Mohawk Interruptus: Political Life across the Borders of Settler States.* Durham NC: Duke University Press, 2014.

Singer, Beverly R. *Wiping the War Paint Off the Lens: Native American Film and Video.* Minneapolis: University of Minnesota Press, 2001.

Slotkin, Richard. *The Fatal Environment: The Myth of the Frontier in the Age of Industrialization, 1800–1890.* Middletown CT: Wesleyan University Press, 1986.

———. *Gunfighter Nation: The Myth of the Frontier in Twentieth-Century America.* New York: HarperPerennial, 1992.

———. *Regeneration through Violence: The Mythology of the American Frontier, 1600–1680.* Middletown CT: Wesleyan University Press, 1973.

Smith, Andrew Brodie. *Shooting Cowboys and Indians: Silent Western Films, American Culture, and the Birth of Hollywood.* Boulder: University of Colorado Press, 2003.

Smith, Donald B. *Chief Buffalo Child Long Lance: The Glorious Imposter.* Toronto ON: Stoddart, 2000.

———. *From the Land of Shadows: The Making of Grey Owl.* New York: Douglas & McIntyre, 1999.

Smith, Henry Nash. *The Virgin Land: The American West as Symbol and Myth.* Cambridge MA: Harvard University Press, 1978.

Smith, Paul Chaat. *Everything You Know about Indians Is Wrong.* Minneapolis: University of Minnesota Press, 2009.

Sollors, Werner. *Beyond Ethnicity: Consent and Descent in American Culture.* New York: Oxford University Press, 1986.

Spears, Jack. *Hollywood: The Golden Era.* London: Thomas Yoseloff, 1971.

Spivak, Gayatri Chakravorty. "Can the Subaltern Speak?" In *Marxism and the Interpretation of Cultures*, edited by Cary Nelson and Lawrence Grossberg, 271–313. London: Macmillan, 1988.

Stam, Robert. "Bakhtin, Polyphony, and Ethnic/Racial Representation." In *Unspeakable Images: Ethnicity and the American Cinema*, edited by Lester D. Friedman, 251–76. Urbana: University of Illinois Press, 1991.

Susman, Warren. "Did Success Spoil the United States? Dual Representations in Postwar America." In *Recasting America: Culture and Politics in the Age of Cold War*, edited by Lary May, 19–37. Chicago: University of Chicago Press, 1989.

Susman, Warren I. *Culture as History: The Transformation of American Society in the Twentieth Century.* New York: Pantheon, 1985.

Tahmahkera, Dustin. "Hakaru Maruumatu Kwitaka? Seeking Representational Jurisdiction in Comanchería Cinema." *Native American and Indigenous Studies* 5, no. 1 (2018): 100–135.

———. *Tribal Television: Viewing Native People in Sitcoms.* Chapel Hill: University of North Carolina Press, 2014.

———. "'We're Gonna Capture Johnny Depp': Making Kin with Cinematic Comanches." *American Indian Culture and Research Journal* 41 (2017): 23–42.

Taussig, Michael. *Mimesis and Alterity: A Particular History of the Senses*. New York: Routledge, 1993.

Terronez, Azul Joaquin. "Images of American Indians in Contemporary Popular Film and Television: Children's Reactions to Indian Stereotypes in Hollywood." Master's thesis, California State University, Los Angeles, 1994.

Teves, Stephanie Nohelani, Andrea Smith, and Michelle H. Raheja, eds. *Native Studies Keywords*. Tucson: University of Arizona Press, 2015.

Thiel, Mark G. "The Omaha Dance in Oglala and Sicangu Sioux History, 1883–1923." *Whispering Wind* 23, no. 5 (1990): 4–17.

Thomson, David. *Showman: The Life of David O. Selznick*. New York: Knopf, 1992.

Tompkins, Jane. *West of Everything: The Inner Life of Westerns*. New York: Oxford University Press, 1993.

Townsend, Melanie, Dana Claxton, and Steve Loft, eds. *Transference, Tradition, Technology: Native New Media Exploring Visual and Digital Culture*. Banff AB: Banff Centre Press, 2006.

Tuska, Jon. *The American West in Film: Critical Approaches to the Western*. Westport CT: Greenwood Press, 1985.

Tyler, Daniel, ed. "Red Men and Hat-Wearers: Viewpoints in Indian History." Paper presented at the Colorado State University Conference on Indian History, August 1974.

Valdivia, Angharad N. *A Latina in the Land of Hollywood and Other Essays on Media Culture*. Tucson: University of Arizona Press, 2000.

———. *Latina/os and the Media*. Cambridge, England: Polity, 2010.

Vigil, Kiara M. *Indigenous Intellectuals: Sovereignty, Citizenship, and the American Imagination, 1880–1930*. New York: Cambridge University Press, 2015.

Vizenor, Gerald. *Fugitive Poses: Native American Indian Scenes of Absence and Presence*. Lincoln: University of Nebraska Press, 1998.

———. *Manifest Manners: Postindian Warriors of Survivance*. Lebanon NH: University Press of New England, 1994.

Voget, Fred W. *The Shoshoni-Crow Sun Dance*. Norman: University of Oklahoma Press, 1984.

———, ed. *They Call Me Agnes: A Crow Narrative Based on the Life of Agnes Yellowtail Deernose*. Norman: University of Oklahoma Press, 1995.

Ware, Amy M. *The Cherokee Kid: Will Rogers, Tribal Identity, and the Making of an American Icon*. Lawrence: University Press of Kansas, 2015.

Warrior, Robert. *Tribal Secrets: Recovering American Indian Intellectual Traditions*. Minneapolis: University of Minnesota Press, 1994.

Weaver, Jace. *The Red Atlantic: American Indigenes and the Making of the Modern World, 1000–1927*. Chapel Hill: University of North Carolina Press, 2017.

Weibel-Orlando, Joan. *Indian Country, L.A.: Maintaining Ethnic Community in Complex Society*. Urbana: University of Illinois Press, 1991.

White, Hayden. *The Content of the Form: Narrative Discourse and Historical Representation*. Baltimore MD: Johns Hopkins University Press, 1987.

White, Richard. "Frederick Jackson Turner and Buffalo Bill." In *The Frontier in American Culture*, edited by James R. Grossman, 7–65. Berkeley: University of California Press, 1994.

——— . *The Roots of Dependency: Subsistence, Environment, and Social Change among the Choctaws, Pawnees, and Navajos*. Lincoln: University of Nebraska Press, 1983.

Whitfield, Stephen J. *The Culture of the Cold War*. Baltimore MD: Johns Hopkins University Press, 1991.

Whyte, William H. *The Organization Man*. New York: Simon and Schuster, 1956.

Wilson, Terry P. *The Underground Reservation: Osage Oil*. Lincoln: University of Nebraska Press, 1985.

Winokur, Mark. *American Laughter: Immigrants, Ethnicity, and 1930s Hollywood Film Comedy*. New York: St. Martin's Press, 1996.

Wolfe, Patrick. "Settler Colonialism and the Elimination of the Native." *Journal of Genocide Research* 8, no. 4 (2006): 387–409.

Womack, Craig. *Red on Red: Native American Literary Separatism*. Minneapolis: University of Minnesota Press, 1999.

Wright, J. Leitch, Jr. *Creeks and Seminoles: The Destruction and Regeneration of the Muscogulge People*. Lincoln: University of Nebraska Press, 1986.

Wright, Will. *Six Guns and Society: A Structural Study of the Western*. Berkeley: University of California Press, 1975.

Yellow Robe, Chauncey. "The Menace of the Wild West Show." *Quarterly Journal of the Society of American Indians* 2 (July–September 1914): 224–25.

Yoggy, Gary A. "Prime-Time Bonanza! The Western on Television." In *Wanted Dead or Alive: The American West in Popular Culture*, edited by Richard Aquila, 160–87. Urbana: University of Illinois Press, 1996.

Young, Lola. *Fear of the Dark: Race, Gender and Sexuality in the Cinema*. New York: Routledge, 1996.

Young, Richard K. *The Ute Indians of Colorado in the Twentieth Century*. Norman: University of Oklahoma Press, 1997.

FILMOGRAPHY

The first part of this filmography lists all of the movies from 1941 to 1960 that were found to include at least one Indian character. Other films with Native characters outside the period of my study are included in a secondary section below.

1941

Badlands of Dakota (Universal)
Hudson's Bay (Twentieth Century Fox)
The Pioneers (Monogram)
They Died with Their Boots On (Warner)
Thunder over the Prairie (Columbia)
Western Union (Twentieth Century Fox)
White Eagle (Columbia)

1942

Lawless Plainsmen (Columbia)
The Omaha Trail (MGM)
Overland Mail (Universal)
Perils of the Royal Mounted (Columbia)
Ride 'Em Cowboy (Universal)

Ten Gentlemen from West Point (Twentieth Century Fox)
Valley of the Sun (RKO)

1943

Apache Trail (MGM)
Daredevils of the West (Republic)
The Deerslayer (Republic)
Frontier Fury (Columbia)
Girl Crazy (MGM)
The Law Rides Again (Monogram)
Wagon Tracks West (Republic)
Wild Horse Stampede (Monogram)

1944

Black Arrow (Columbia)
Buffalo Bill (Twentieth Century Fox)

1945

Dakota (Republic)
The Man from Oklahoma (Republic)
Navajo Kid (PRC)

1946

Bad Bascomb (MGM)
Canyon Passage (Universal)
Duel in the Sun (Selznick)
My Darling Clementine (Twentieth Century Fox)
The Phantom Rider (Republic)
Romance of the West (PRC)
The Scarlet Horseman (Universal)
Stagecoach to Denver (Republic)
Under Nevada Skies (Republic)

1947

Along the Oregon Trail (Republic)
Black Gold (Allied Artists)
Bowery Buckaroos (Monogram)
Buffalo Bill Rides Again (Screen Guild)
Dangerous Venture (United Artists)

Last of the Redmen (Columbia)
The Last Round-Up (Columbia)
Marshal of Cripple Creek (Republic)
Oregon Trail Scouts (Republic)
The Prairie (Screen Guild)
Rustlers of Devil's Canyon (Republic)
The Senator Was Indiscreet (Universal)
Spoilers of the North (Republic)
Unconquered (Paramount)

1948

Blazing across the Pecos (Columbia)
The Dude Goes West (Allied Artists)
Fort Apache (RKO)
Fury at Furnace Creek (Twentieth Century Fox)
Indian Agent (RKO)
The Paleface (Paramount)
Rachel and the Stranger (RKO)
Red River (United Artists)
Tap Roots (Universal)

1949

Apache Chief (Lippert)
Arctic Manhunt (Universal)
Canadian Pacific (Twentieth Century Fox)
Colorado Territory (Warner)
The Cowboy and the Indians (Columbia)
The Dalton Gang (Lippert)
Daughter of the West (Film Classics)
Ghost of Zorro (Republic)
Gun Runner (Monogram)
Laramie (Columbia)
Ma and Pa Kettle (Universal)
Massacre River (Allied Artists)
Mrs. Mike (United Artists)
Ranger of Cherokee Strip (Republic)
Roll, Thunder, Roll (Eagle-Lion)
Sands of Iwo Jima (Republic)
She Wore a Yellow Ribbon (RKO)

Stallion Canyon (Astor)
Tale of the Navajos (MGM)
Tulsa (Eagle-Lion)

1950

Ambush (MGM)
Annie Get Your Gun (MGM)
Broken Arrow (Twentieth Century Fox)
The Cariboo Trail (Twentieth Century Fox)
Cherokee Uprising (Monogram)
Cody of the Pony Express (Columbia)
Colt .45 (Warner Bros.)
Comanche Territory (Universal)
Davy Crockett, Indian Scout (United Artists)
Devil's Doorway (MGM)
Eagle and the Hawk (Paramount)
I Killed Geronimo (Eagle-Lion)
Indian Territory (Columbia)
The Iroquois Trail (United Artists)
North of the Great Divide (Republic)
Raiders of Tomahawk Creek (Columbia)
Rio Grande (Republic)
Rocky Mountain (Warner Bros.)
A Ticket to Tomahawk (Twentieth Century Fox)
Train to Tombstone (Lippert)
The Traveling Saleswoman (Columbia)
Two Flags West (Twentieth Century Fox)
Wagonmaster (RKO)
Winchester '73 (Universal)
Young Daniel Boone (Monogram)

1951

Across the Wide Missouri (MGM)
Apache Drums (Universal)
Cavalry Scout (Monogram)
Distant Drums (Warner Bros.)
Fort Defiance (United Artists)
Jim Thorpe, All American (Warner Bros.)
The Last Outpost (Paramount)

Little Big Horn (Lippert)
New Mexico (United Artists)
Oh! Susanna (Republic)
Only the Valiant (Warner)
Red Mountain (Paramount)
Roar of the Iron Horse (Columbia)
Santa Fe (Columbia)
Slaughter Trail (RKO)
Snake River Desperadoes (Columbia)
Tomahawk (Universal)
Warpath (Paramount)
Westward the Women (MGM)
When the Redskins Rode (Columbia)

1952

Apache Country (Columbia)
Apache War Smoke (MGM)
The Battle at Apache Pass (Universal)
The Battles of Chief Pontiac (Realart)
Bend of the River (Universal)
The Big Sky (RKO)
Brave Warrior (Columbia)
Buffalo Bill in Tomahawk Territory (United Artists)
Bugles in the Afternoon (Warner Bros.)
Desert Pursuit (Monogram)
Flaming Feather (Paramount)
Fort Osage (Monogram)
The Half-Breed (RKO)
Hiawatha (Allied Artists)
Indian Uprising (Columbia)
Laramie Mountains (Columbia)
Navajo (Lippert)
The Pathfinder (Columbia)
Pony Soldier (Twentieth Century Fox)
Red Snow (Columbia)
The Savage (Paramount)
Son of Geronimo (Columbia)
Son of Paleface (Paramount)
The Story of Will Rogers (Warner Bros.)

Wagons West (Monogram)
The Wild North (MGM)

1953

Ambush at Tomahawk Gap (Columbia)
Arrowhead (Paramount)
Captain John Smith and Pocahontas (United Artists)
The Charge at Feather River (Warner Bros.)
Column South (Universal)
Conquest of Cochise (Columbia)
Escape from Fort Bravo (MGM)
Fort Ti (Columbia)
Fort Vengeance (Allied Artists)
The Great Sioux Uprising (Universal)
Hondo (Warner Bros.)
Jack McCall, Desperado (Columbia)
Last of the Comanches (Columbia)
The Nebraskan (Columbia)
Old Overland Trail (Republic)
Peter Pan (RKO)
Pony Express (Paramount)
Saginaw Trail (Columbia)
Seminole (Universal)
Shane (Paramount)
The Stand at Apache River (Universal)
The Tall Texan (Lippert)
Tumbleweed (Universal)
War Arrow (Universal)
War Paint (United Artists)

1954

Apache (United Artists)
Arrow in the Dust (Allied Artists)
Battle of Rogue River (Columbia)
The Black Dakotas (Columbia)
Broken Lance (Twentieth Century Fox)
Cattle Queen of Montana (RKO)
The Command (Warner Bros.)
Drum Beat (Warner Bros.)

Drums across the River (Universal)
Four Guns to the Border (Universal)
Garden of Evil (Twentieth Century Fox)
Man with the Steel Whip (Republic)
Massacre Canyon (Columbia)
Masterson of Kansas (Columbia)
Overland Pacific (United Artists)
River of No Return (Twentieth Century Fox)
Rose Marie (MGM)
Saskatchewan (Universal)
The Siege at Red River (Twentieth Century Fox)
Sitting Bull (United Artists)
Southwest Passage (United Artists)
Taza, Son of Cochise (Universal)
They Rode West (Columbia)
The Yellow Tomahawk (United Artists)

1955

Apache Ambush (Columbia)
Apache Woman (American)
Battle Cry (Warner)
Chief Crazy Horse (Universal)
Davy Crockett, King of the Wild Frontier (Buena Vista)
The Far Horizons (Paramount)
Fort Yuma (United Artists)
Foxfire (Universal)
The Gun That Won the West (Columbia)
The Indian Fighter (United Artists)
Kiss of Fire (Universal)
The Last Frontier (Columbia)
The Man from Laramie (Columbia)
Many Rivers to Cross (MGM)
Santa Fe Passage (Republic)
Seminole Uprising (Columbia)
Seven Cities of Gold (Twentieth Century Fox)
Shotgun (Allied Artists)
Smoke Signal (Universal)
Strange Lady in Town (Warner Bros.)
The Tall Men (Twentieth Century Fox)

To Hell and Back (Universal)
The Vanishing American (Republic)
White Feather (Twentieth Century Fox)
Yellowneck (Republic)

1956

Around the World in 80 Days (United Artists)
Blazing the Overland Trail (Columbia)
Comanche (United Artists)
Dakota Incident (Republic)
Daniel Boone, Trailblazer (Republic)
Ghost Town (United Artists)
The Last Hunt (MGM)
The Last Wagon (Twentieth Century Fox)
The Lone Ranger (Warner Bros.)
Massacre (Twentieth Century Fox)
Massacre at Sand Creek (Columbia)
Mohawk (Twentieth Century Fox)
Perils of the Wilderness (Columbia)
Pillars of the Sky (Universal)
Quincannon, Frontier Scout (United Artists)
Reprisal! (Columbia)
The Searchers (Warner Bros.)
Secret of Treasure Mountain (Columbia)
Seventh Cavalry (Columbia)
Walk the Proud Land (Universal)
Westward Ho the Wagons! (Buena Vista)
The White Squaw (Columbia)
The Wild Dakotas (Associated Film Releasing)
Yaqui Drums (Allied Artists)

1957

Apache Warrior (Twentieth Century Fox)
Copper Sky (Twentieth Century Fox)
The Deerslayer (Twentieth Century Fox)
Dragoon Wells Massacre (Allied Artists)
Escape from Red Rock (Twentieth Century Fox)
The Guns of Fort Petticoat (Columbia)
The Halliday Brand (United Artists)

Naked in the Sun (Allied Artists)
The Oklahoman (Allied Artists)
Oregon Passage (Allied Artists)
Pawnee (Republic)
Quantez (Universal)
Revolt at Fort Laramie (United Artists)
Ride Out for Revenge (United Artists)
Run of the Arrow (Universal)
Tomahawk Trail (United Artists)
Trooper Hawk (United Artists)
War Drums (United Artists)

1958

Ambush at Cimarron Pass (Twentieth Century Fox)
Apache Territory (Columbia)
Blood Arrow (Twentieth Century Fox)
Bullwhip (Allied Artists)
Cowboy (Columbia)
Fort Bowie (United Artists)
Fort Dobbs (Warner Bros.)
Fort Massacre (United Artists)
Gun Fever (United Artists)
Gunman's Walk (Columbia)
The Law and Jake Wade (MGM)
The Light in the Forest (Buena Vista)
The Lone Ranger and the Lost City of Gold (United Artists)
The Sheriff of Fractured Jaw (Twentieth Century Fox)
Tonka (Buena Vista)

1959

Escort West (United Artists)
The FBI Story (Warner Bros.)
Last Train from Gun Hill (Paramount)
Never So Few (MGM)
The Oregon Trail (Twentieth Century Fox)
Thunder in the Sun (Paramount)
The Wonderful Country (United Artists)
Yellowstone Kelly (Warner Bros.)

1960

All the Young Men (Columbia)
Comanche Station (Columbia)
Flaming Star (Twentieth Century Fox)
For the Love of Mike (Twentieth Century Fox)
Oklahoma Territory (United Artists)
Savage Innocents (Paramount)
Sergeant Rutledge (Warner Bros.)
The Unforgiven (United Artists)
Walk Tall (Twentieth Century Fox)

OTHER FILMS WITH NATIVE CHARACTERS

1914

In the Land of War Canoes

1961

Exiles (Kent Mackenzie)

1979

Images of Indians (TV series, parts 1, 2, 3, 4, 5) (PBS)

1980

Bastion Point: Day 507 (Pohlmann)

1984

Harold of Orange (Film in the Cities)

1985

The Emerald Forest (Embassy Pictures)
Hopi: Songs of the Fourth World (New Day Films)
Navajo Talking Picture (Bowman)

1986

Ikwe (National Film Board of Canada)
Mistress Madeleine (National Film Board of Canada)
Places Not Our Own (National Film Board of Canada)
The Wake (National Film Board of Canada)

1988
War Party (Helmdale Film)

1989
Powwow Highway (Warner Bros.)

1990
Dances with Wolves (Orion Pictures)
Spring of Discontent (WKOW)

1991
Black Robe (Samuel Goldwyn Company)

1992
Columbus Didn't Discover Us (Turning Tide)
Imagining Indians (Masayesva)
Last of the Mohicans (Twentieth Century Fox)
Thunderheart (TriStar)

1993
Kanehsatake: 270 Years of Resistance (National Film Board of Canada)
Transitions: Death of a Mother Tongue (Kipp & Fisher)

1994
Dance Me Outside (Apex)
Once Were Warriors (Fine Line Features)

1995
The Keetoowahs Come Home (PBS)
Pocahontas (Walt Disney Pictures)

1998
Naturally Native (Red-Horse Native Productions)
Preserving Our Past (Ben Baker)
Smoke Signals (Miramax)

1999
Lighting the Seventh Fire (Osawa)

2000

The Return of Navajo Boy (Spitz & Klain)

2001

Atanarjuat (Odeon Films)

2002

The Business of Fancydancing (Outrider Pictures)
Rabbit-Proof Fence (Rumbalara Films)
Skins (First Look Pictures)
Whale Rider (Newmarket Films)
Windtalkers (MGM)

2006

Flags of Our Fathers (Warner Bros.)
Ten Canoes (Palance Films)

2007

Four Sheets to the Wind (Dirt Road Productions)
Miss Navajo (Independent Films)

2008

Barking Water (Indion Entertainment)
Frozen River (Sony Pictures)

2009

Reel Injun (Domino Film)

2010

Tonto Plays Himself (Jacob Floyd)

2013

By Blood (Outcast Films)
Charlie's Country (Rolf de Heer)
Hot Water (Regroup Films)
Kind Hearted Woman (PBS)
The Lone Ranger (Walt Disney Studios)
Rhymes for Young Ghouls (Seville Pictures)

2014

Drunktown's Finest (Indion Entertainment)
This May Be the Last Time (Sundance Channel)

2015

Embrace of the Serpent (Diaphana Films)
Mekko (Sterlin Harjo)
The Revenant (Twentieth Century Fox)

2016

100 Years (Fire in the Belly Productions)

2017

Wind River (Acacia)

2018

Birds of Passage (Snowglobe)
Dawnland (Upstander Films)
Merata: How Mum Decolonized the Screen (Arama Pictures)

2019

Amá (Dartmouth Films)
Basketball or Nothing (Netflix)
The Body Remembers When the World Broke Open (levelFILM)
Etched in Bone (Ronin Films)
L'eau Est La Vie Camp: From Standing Rock to the Swamp (Mutual Aid Media)

INDEX

actors. *See* Indian actors; non-Indian
actors; white actors
advertising, 166, 250n48, 278n59, 285n5
African Americans: as actors, 30, 32, 40, 41,
83, 260n93; progress in treatment of,
32, 33; representation of, 32, 39–41, 225;
and school integration issue, 41; and
segregation issue, 32, 39–40, 53, 57, 91, 92
American Indian labor, 4, 5, 6, 92, 121
American Indians. *See* Indians; Native
people
Annie Get Your Gun, 52, 58
Apaches: about, 36, 49; and cultural
artifacts, 190–91; as extras, 97, 119,
181, 183–85; and identity issue, 82;
skin darkening for, 176; studios' view
of, 192; and *Valley of the Sun*, 50–52;
wage rates for, 184–85. *See also* White
Mountain Apaches
"apartment house Indians," 77–78
Applegarth, Jonas, 91, 179–80
Arrowhead, 53, 153, 167

Asian Americans, 33, 39, 45
Atanarjuat, 8, 27, 194, 231
authenticity: about Indian identity, 162–
63, 187–88; conclusion about, 213–16;
in films, 161–64, 187–88; and history,
191–94; and Hollywood, 212–16; and
Indian culture, 189–90; and language,
204–12; look and feel about, 200;
search for, 203; studios' devotion to,
195–96, 199–202

bare chests, 86, 148, 153
Bastion Point: Day 507, 228, 229
The Battle at Apache Pass, 140, 144, 170,
183, 195
Bilagody, Wesley, 182–83
Birth of a Nation, 32, 82, 246n22
bit parts, 74, 76, 83, 85, 91–92
black braided wigs. *See* braided wigs
blackface, 32, 41, 138, 140, 225, 249n45
Blackfeet Nation, 74, 78, 206, 243n5,
282n41

patterns, 76, 113; of reservation Indians, 100–101, 106–7, 114, 119–20, 225
ethnic fraud, 81–82
eye color, 76, 148–49, 187

fake hair and noses, 9, 144, 145, 146, 150
fake languages, 204–5
The Far Horizons, 37, 38
federal government, 39, 42–45, 194, 195, 226, 232
film archives, 6, 190, 194, 219
film crews, 94, 102, 109, 129, 187, 216
filmmaking, 10, 17, 94–95, 202, 229, 273n8
film production, 126, 185, 192, 196, 216, 218
film reviewers, 197, 198, 201, 229, 281n24, 282n37
films: and advertising, 166, 250n48, 278n59, 285n5; authenticity issues in, 161–64, 187–88; as a corporate project, 11–12; historical backdrop of, 221; inaccuracies in, 103–4; with Indian directors, 231; Indian presence in, 36, 47; interracial friendships in, 53–57; and labor, 1–15; low-budget, 89, 161, 231; made after World War II, 47–48; makeup issues in, 138–44; narratives in, 12, 50, 52, 156, 216; with Native characters, 3, 27, 53, 87, 208; Native extras in, 6, 103, 170, 178; and nostalgia, 46; previewers' comments about, 201–2; and production process, 12–13, 66, 98, 190, 218; and profitability issue, 156–57; protest about, 232–33; racism in, 3, 8, 15, 31–32, 94, 218–20; and "real," "authentic," and "imagined" terms, 222; redfacing in, 17; and settler colonialism, 36–37; sexual objectification in, 154, 155; and shifts among tribes, 226–27; silent, xiv, 16, 231, 243n2; as social production, 217–18; and success of television, 225; uneven outcome of,

229–30; use of gibberish in, 103, 203–7, 213; and wage economies, 122; white narcissism in, 13, 47, 52–53, 65
film studies, 25–33, 36, 113, 238n58
film work and workers, 11, 93–94, 104–5, 120, 127–33
Flaming Star, 155, 241n45
folklore studies, 191
forced assimilation, 39, 42, 43, 99, 100
Ford, John, 122–23
Fort Apache, 103, 207
Fourth Cinema, 24, 25
fur trade, 55, 56

gibberish, use of, 103, 203–7, 213
glass ceiling, 84–91
Governors Award, 249n46
greasepaint makeup, 141, 142, 176
Green Grass, Running Water (King), 150, 151
Grey Eyes, 90, 118, 130, 251n60

hair: black, 133, 156, 162, 180, 187; blonde, 138, 141; brushing of, 171–72; fake, 144, 145, 146; long, 147, 167, 179, 181, 227, 266n3; of non-Indian actors, 144, 148, 167; short, 58, 141, 163, 167, 180, 269n45; synthetic, 144, 146; thick, 148, 171
hair falls, 146, 147, 179
hairlace wigs, 145, 146, 167
hairstyle issues, 153, 166, 174, 200
Herzoff, Archie, 183, 184
Heston, Charlton, 85, 153, 263n115
heterosexuality, 49, 51
Hogan, Pat, 74, 78–79, 263n115
Hollywood: A-list and B-list status in, 85–86; and authenticity issue, 212–16; ethnic fraud in, 81–82; and hierarchy issue, 84–92; makeup issues in, 138–44; pay issues in, 88–90; racial identity beliefs in, 137; and stereotypes, 28; version of Indian history of, 96. *See also* films; studios

Hudson, Rock, 9–10, 88–89, 150, 156, 240n32, 250n52
Hudson's Bay, 53–57
Hunter, Jeffrey, 149, 152

identity issue. *See* Indian identity; Native identity
Imagining Indians, 7, 8
imperialism, 21, 22, 111
Indian actors: about, 10, 11, 13, 47, 68; bit parts for, 74, 76, 83, 85, 91–92; desexualization of, 86–87; early, 71–74; and glass ceiling, 84–91; hiring of, 74–75, 83–84, 106–7, 116–17; and identity issue, 71, 87, 136–37; and introduction of Technicolor, 76; labor of, 71; and lead roles, 75, 83, 85, 180, 205, 246n20; name change by, 245n19; nonsexual roles for, 87; and on-screen romantic liaisons, 86–87; and organized labor, 72, 73; value of, 163
Indian Actors' Workshop, 75, 285n6
Indian characters: about, 3, 8; buckskins worn by, 169; comedies with, 62; costumes for, 180–86; desexualization of, 86; fake noses for, 150; and historical backdrop, 221; and images of Indians, 156; and Indian identity, 210–11; love triangles involving, 49; makeup for, 165; modern, 63–66; movies with, 132, 136–37; muscular body required for, 168, 179; and Native influence, 10–11; and Native languages, 206; physical markers of, 136–37; planning creation of, 186–87; poetic and standard English spoken by, 207–9; as powerless victims, 121; as symbols, 169–70; teaching about how to play, 193–94; in westerns, 48; and white man's Indian, 12, 85; and white protagonist, 135–36. *See also* Native characters
Indian costumes, 153, 169, 180, 200

Indian culture: about, 18, 42, 43, 44; authentic, 189–90; and boarding schools, 214; and cultural artifacts, 4, 67, 183, 186, 190–91, 200; and cultural loss, 192; and oppression, 167; re-creation of, 203–4; research methodologies about, 194–95; and reservation Indians, 193; studios' view of, 192–93; and white characters, 51. *See also* Native culture
Indian extras: about, 10, 12, 14; body painting of, 272n2; and body weight issues, 167–69, 179; buckskins and beads for, 154; costumes for, 180–86; definition of, 120; hiring of, 106–7; lifestyle of, 89; makeup of, 143, 177; reservation Indians as, 70, 90, 101, 129–30; stunt performance by, 121; and unions, 108; in *Valley of the Sun*, 52; value of, 163; and wage issues, 88–90, 121, 123–25, 131–32, 262n110; wigs for, 178. *See also* Native extras
Indian identity: about, xii–xiii, xiv, xv, 7, 27; and Apaches, 82; and authenticity issue, 162–63, 187–88; bound to family and clan, 227; certain look for, 171, 223–24; and comedies, 58; and imitation of Indians, 53; of Indian actors, 71, 87, 136–37; and Indian characters, 210–11; and Indian nose, 150; and movie stardom issue, 249n46; pay issues related to, 88; representing, 224–25; and skin darkening, 174, 176; unfamiliarity with, 227; way to communicate, 186–87. *See also* Native identity
Indian look: about, xiii–xiv, xv, 8–9, 13; consistent, 108–9; conventional, 109; eye color for, 148–49; and Indian identity, 171, 223–24; influence over, 121; makeup for, 6–7, 11–12, 137–38; in the movies, 76; stereotype of, 136
Indian nationalism, 227, 228
Indian New Deal, 42, 43

stunt performers, 121, 141, 245n16, 253n18, 262n108, 267n19

Sun Dance ceremonies, 96–98, 125, 126, 253n13

synthetic hair. *See* wigs

talent agency, 75, 118

Taza, Son of Cochise, 49, 84, 164, 171, 201

technical advisors, 79, 186, 193, 198–99, 203–6, 262n106

termination policy, 39–48, 226

Tewas, 119, 125, 126, 175

They Died with Their Boots On, 75, 119, 144, 178, 242n59

Tomahawk, 114–16, 118, 199, 200, 206

tribal cultures, 188, 192–94, 214

tribal groups, 165, 226

tribal identities, xii–xv, 28, 81, 237n48

tribal lands, 1, 41, 66

tribal languages, 17, 39, 215

tribal sovereignty, 2, 4, 39, 44–45, 220, 225

Tribal Television, 23, 24

Twentieth Century Fox, 96–98, 107–9, 122, 125, 175, 195–96

typecasting issue, 138, 147

Umatilla reservation, 117, 170

Unconquered, 52, 83

union pay scales, 73, 100

unions, 14, 88, 108, 249n42

United Artists, 82, 98

Universal Studios, 99, 118, 168, 172, 181–82, 242n53

uranium mining, 110, 111

urban Indians, 92, 94, 222, 228, 239n15

urbanization and termination policy, 39–48

Utes, 124, 173–74, 275n34

vaccinations, 276n34

Valley of the Sun, 48–53, 198, 208, 276n39

vanishing Indian, 6, 36, 38–39, 64, 98–99, 149

violence: about, 14, 17, 24; colonial-related, 116, 221; and love triangles, 48, 49; and Native people, 1–2, 36, 54, 84, 92

wage economies, 46, 122, 131

wage labor, 5, 126, 225

wage rates: for Apache men, 184–85; for cattle use, 105, 125, 255n27, 264n121; for Diné, 122–23; for falling from a horse, 262n110; generalization about, 124; for Indian extras, 121, 123–25, 131–32, 262n110; and Indian identity, 88; for Lakotas, 124; for reservation Indians, 121; for white actors, 88–90

Warner Bros., 111–14, 119, 123–25, 138, 140–46

war paint, 136, 175–78, 196, 218, 276n39, 284n1

Wayne, John, 110–11

weft wigs, 145, 146

westerns: about, 2–3; analysis of, 27, 28; and comedies, 58; criticism of, 31, 32; and Diné extras, 101–2; filming of, 111; Indian characters in, 48; and interracial friendships, 54; love triangles in, 48–53; Native women in, 49

white actors: about, 49; body type of, 151–53, 274n23; and hair protection issues, 147–48; makeup of, 138–44; monopoly by, 132; and pay issues, 88–90. *See also* non-Indian actors

white characters, 36, 50–53, 62–63

White Mountain Apaches, 97, 119, 176, 181, 196, 203

white narcissism, 13, 47, 52–53, 65

White River Apaches. *See* White Mountain Apaches

whites: ethical and unethical, 49–50, 54; and interracial friendships, 40, 48–49,

53–58, 66, 85, 113; and representation of Indians, 76–77, 85; sexuality of, 51, 86, 87, 154; unfamiliarity of, with Indian identity, 227

white settlers. *See* settlers

white women, 29, 51, 85–87, 90, 155, 212

wigs: about, 7, 12, 15; for actors, 144–48, 178; braided, 141, 144–46, 166–67, 174, 178; hairlace, 145, 146, 167; skullcap, 145, 146, 167; weft, 145, 146. *See also* hair

Wild West shows, 4, 17, 71–72, 77, 93, 221

Winchester '73, 9

Wind River, 232, 286n13

Wiping the War Paint Off the Lens (Singer), 27

world's fairs, 5, 16

World War II, 3, 27, 40, 43, 47–48, 57

Wounded Knee massacre, 16, 18, 199, 227

Yellow, Billy, 104–5, 129, 225

CPSIA information can be obtained
at www.ICGtesting.com
Printed in the USA
LVHW110957181022
730956LV00002B/117